D0081788

PUERTO RICO:
A COLONIAL EXPERIMENT

The Twentieth Century Fund is an independent research foundation which undertakes policy studies of economic, political, and social institutions and issues. The Fund was founded in 1919 and endowed by Edward A. Filene.

Board of Trustees of the Twentieth Century Fund

Morris B. Abram
Peter A.A. Berle, Chairman
Jonathan B. Bingham
José A. Cabranes
Hodding Carter III
Brewster C. Denny
Daniel J. Evans
Charles V. Hamilton
Patricia Roberts Harris
August Heckscher
Matina S. Horner
James A. Leach

Georges-Henri Martin
Lawrence K. Miller, Emeritus
P. Michael Pitfield
Don K. Price, Emeritus
Richard Ravitch
James Rowe, Emeritus
Arthur M. Schlesinger, Jr.
Harvey I. Sloane, M.D.
James Tobin
David B. Truman
Shirley Williams

M.J. Rossant, Director

PUERTO RICO:
A COLONIAL EXPERIMENT

RAYMOND CARR

WITHDRAWN

A Twentieth Century Fund Study

NEW YORK UNIVERSITY PRESS
NEW YORK & LONDON

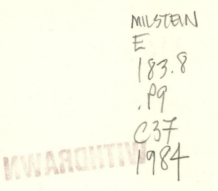

MILSTEIN
E
183.8
.P9
C37
1984
WITHDRAWN

Copyright © 1984 by the Twentieth Century Fund, Inc.
All rights reserved
Manufactured in the United States of America

Library of Congress Cataloging in Publication Data

Carr, Raymond.
Puerto Rico: A colonial experiment.

"A Twentieth Century Fund study."
Bibliography: p.
Includes index.
1. United States—Relations—Puerto Rico. 2. Puerto
Rico—Relations—United States. 3. Puerto Rico—
Politics and government—1952-   . I. Twentieth
Century Fund. II. Title.
E183.8.P9C37 1984   303.4'8273'07295   83-23786
ISBN 0-8147-1389-0 (alk. paper)

Clothbound editions of New York University Press books are Smyth-
sewn and printed on permanent and acid-free paper.

c 10 9 8 7 6 5 4 3 2

Book design by Ken Venezio

CONTENTS

FOREWORD

Relations between the United States and Puerto Rico have been troubled ever since Puerto Rico was acquired by the United States in the aftermath of the Spanish-American War. There are many good reasons, ranging from the clash of cultures to their economic disparities, but the basic difficulty has been the relationship itself, which Puerto Ricans tend to see as one between the ruler and the ruled. Despite the strides that have been made in recent years, the dispute over Puerto Rico's alleged colonial status took on international dimensions as Puerto Ricans tried to involve the United Nations in the status question.

The Twentieth Century Fund has long sought a study of the Puerto Rican – American relationship. Our interest stemmed not only from our program of policy studies on countries of the Caribbean region but also from our special relationship to Puerto Rico. Luis Muñoz Marín, the most enduring and gifted of Puerto Rico's political leaders and the formulator of its Commonwealth status, was, for a time, a Fund Trustee. What is more, three Fund Trustees served on the joint executive-legislative commission (1964 – 66) that examined the status of Puerto Rico.

The major problem in mounting a Puerto Rican study had been the difficulty of finding a scholar, whether Puerto Rican or American, who had not already made up his mind about what the relationship ought to be. The Puerto Rican scholars,

I must add, are even more committed to specific points of view than Americans, perhaps because nothing is more important to them than the U.S. relationship with Puerto Rico.

Our solution, arrived at after careful deliberation, was to interest an English scholar, one who could handle the peculiar history of the Puerto Rican – U.S. relationship with dispassion and sensitivity, in the project. In Raymond Carr, a historian noted for his work on Spain, now Warden of St. Antony's College, and formerly professor of Latin American studies at Oxford, we found the ideal choice for the assignment. Despite his administrative and professional duties, Mr. Carr was intrigued by the idea of a Puerto Rico – U.S. study and took it on with the gusto and energy of a junior scholar. He immersed himself in research, and then, with his wife, spent a summer in Puerto Rico, where he listened to the views of a wide variety of people and gained an insight into the Puerto Rican quest for a separate identity. He then spent time in Washington and in some of the Puerto Rican centers in the United States.

His analysis of the relationship and his ideas for improving it make, I think, a major contribution. Mr. Carr's book can be read as a discrete analysis of the intricate ties that bind mainland and island. But it is far more than that. It is a remarkably rich and understanding examination of the problems inherent in living with, and in loosening, the bonds between a superstate and a quasi-colonial possession. The debate over the political status of Puerto Rico is one that is likely to continue for the rest of this century and beyond, but the wise counsel of a concerned outsider, if listened to by both sides, could make a significant difference.

The Fund is indebted to Raymond Carr for what clearly has been a labor of love. In his analysis, he spares no one, not even Muñoz. He himself makes clear that his views are his own, not those of the Fund, and his exercise of his independence shows no favor to any faction or country. But at the same time, he never loses sight of the human qualities that seem more to divide Puerto Ricans from one another than to unite Puerto Ricans and Americans.

On behalf of the Trustees and staff of the Fund, I salute his effort.

M.J. ROSSANT, DIRECTOR
THE TWENTIETH CENTURY FUND

PREFACE

"In Puerto Rico," Dean Acheson told his French colleagues in 1952, "we had the problem of moving from a colonial relationship to something else." What that "something else" now represents and how it has come about is the theme of this book.

Political development — or the lack of it — must be judged against dramatic changes in the economy. Puerto Rico, a Caribbean island some hundred miles long and thirty miles or so wide, has no significant natural resource base; its capital lies in its people. In 1930, the characteristic representative of those people was the *jíbaro* — the subsistence farmer of the interior, whose mean existence shocked the occasional visitor from the mainland. Now only 5 percent of the work force gains its living from the land, and American tourists, if they leave the tourist trap of Old San Juan, are shocked by the living conditions of *jíbaros* who have poured in from the countryside to seek a livelihood in the cities. In 1930, tourists in search of local color were encouraged by the Puerto Rican government to visit Bayamón, across the bay from San Juan. There they would find "horsemen ambling easily along mounted on wiry little native horses" and "lumbering carts drawn by patient oxen guided by *jíbaros* with long poles" in a sleepy provincial town where the inhabitants were engaged in bargaining "delightfully yet shrewdly in Spanish" in a multiplicity of small stores. But the oxen and horsemen have been driven out by automobiles and the stores bankrupted by supermarkets. Now the tourists' first

impressions, arriving in Puerto Rico by air, are the long traffic
jams along the highways of San Juan and the skyscrapers of
the banks along the "golden mile" of Hato Rey.

Rapid industrialization, which has resulted from American
investment in manufacturing and which has dotted the island
with factories, has brought, together with a rise in living standards, all the social problems that afflict the urban industrialized
societies of the West, from drug addiction to substandard
housing and pollution. These are exaggerated because Puerto
Rico is locked into the economy of the mainland yet remains
the poorest regional economy of the United States. It is impregnated with the expectations of the consumer society of the
metropolitan mainland, but its fragile economy, with a level of
unemployment three times that of the mainland, cannot satisfy
those expectations.

That Puerto Ricans still bargain shrewdly in Spanish shows
that economic integration with America has not brought cultural assimilation; for many Puerto Ricans assimilation goes
no deeper than a growing acceptance of the values of a consumer society supported by easy credit, or addiction to baseball
and basketball as national sports. I have paid particular attention to the continued existence of a separate cultural identity,
however confused, provincial, and ambiguous it may be, and
however threatened in a small society tied to the greatest power
in the Western world.

Part I describes the colonial period and the evolution of
Puerto Rico's present relationship with the United States.
While Puerto Ricans—or at least the political elite of the island
—are only too familiar with the history of that evolution, it is
less well known to the American public. "Ignorance about
Puerto Rico here on the mainland," its present governor has
declared, "can only be described as massive."

Those who are most concerned with contemporary issues

can proceed to the later sections, each of which attacks a particular aspect of a now troubled relationship.

The last chapter treats events and issues between the election campaign of 1980 and mid-1982. It is in part concerned with the behavior of party politicians in Puerto Rico, and in part with the way that these politicians and the establishment in general perceived the impact of changes in national policies under the Reagan administration upon the well-being of the island. Since party politics are fluid and since the policies of the Reagan administration have yet to take their final form, this chapter should be taken as an illustration of attitudes during an uneasy period in the relationship between the United States and Puerto Rico.

ACKNOWLEDGMENTS

I owe a great debt to Murray Rossant and the staff of the Twentieth Century Fund. Without seeking in any way to change my views, they have devoted great care to my work and eased its progress by their kindness.

I also owe a debt to friends and colleagues in Puerto Rico and the United States. They submitted with courtesy to persistent inquiries. It would be a breach of friendship were I, in all cases, to identify them or attribute to them statements made in confidence.

It would nevertheless be churlish not to acknowledge my debt to Judge José Cabranes for his suggestions and his meticulous reading of my manuscript. While the intelligence of his insights has illuminated almost every aspect of my book, he bears no responsibility for, nor would he share, the views I have expressed.

MAIN POLITICAL PARTIES

PPD *Partido Popular Democrático* (Popular Democratic Party or *populares*). Favoring Commonwealth status, the party was founded in 1938 by Luis Muñoz Marín, under whose leadership it held control of Puerto Rico for nearly three decades. Now, headed by Rafael Hernández Colón, the party supports increased autonomy as set forth by the doctrine entitled "The New Thesis."

PDP *Partido del Pueblo* (Peoples Party). Founded by Roberto Sánchez Vilella, who broke from the PPD in 1968, the party also favors Commonwealth. The split weakened the PPD in the 1968 election, allowing the opposition pro-statehood party to enter the governor's office for the first time.

PNP *Partido Nuevo Progresista* (New Progressive Party). The statehood party founded in 1967 by Luis Ferré, who broke off from the long established *Partido Estadista Republicano* (PER) founded by José Celso Barbosa, to participate in the 1967 plebiscite. Ferré was elected the party's first governor in 1968. Present party leader is also the current governor, Carlos Romero Barceló.

PIP *Partido Independentista Puertorriqueño* (Puerto Rican Independence Party). Favoring an independent, social democratic republic, the party was created by *populares* sympathetic to independence after their expulsion from the PPD by Muñoz Marín in 1946. Present leader is Rubén Berríos Martínez.

PSP   *Partido Socialista Puertorriqueño* (Puerto Rican Socialist Party). Supporting a "Cuban" solution for an independent republic, the party was established in 1972, the heir of the older *Movimiento pro Independencia*. Present leader is Juan Mari Bras.

Partido Nacionalista (Nationalist Party). Founded in 1922 to promote the independence of Puerto Rico, turned, under the leadership of Pedro Albizu Campos after the electoral disaster in 1932, to armed struggle for republic.

Partido Socialista (Socialist Party). Founded in 1915 by Santiago Iglesias, the party was the electoral ally of the statehood Republicans in the 1920s; dissolved in 1952.

MAIN EVENTS

1897 Spain grants Charter of Autonomy, giving Puerto Rico home rule.

1898 American troops land in Guánica, Puerto Rico. Treaty of Paris cedes Puerto Rico to the United States.

1898-1900 Rule of the "Tsars" — the U.S. American military governors.

1900 Foraker Act provides Puerto Rico with a civilian government made up of a governor and an upper chamber, the Executive Council, appointed by the President of the United States, and a lower chamber, the House of Delegates, popularly elected.

1904 The Unionist Party of Puerto Rico (UPR) is founded. Supporting greater self-government, under the leadership of Luis Muñoz Rivera the party defeats José Celso Barbosa's pro-American Republican party and dominates political life until the 1930s.

1909 Luis Muñoz Rivera forces a constitutional crisis to expose the shortcomings of the Foraker Act.

1917 Jones Act grants Puerto Ricans U.S. citizenship and a popularly elected Senate.

1922 The Nationalist party for a free and independent republic is founded. (After electoral disaster of 1932, it turns to armed struggle under Albizu Campos.)

1924-29   The UPR and a sector of the Republican party or the *Alianza* (Alliance) to fight the electoral alliance of "pure Republicans" and Socialist Coalition in 1932.

1931   Antonio Barceló leaves the *Alianza* to found the Liberal party committed to independence. Defeated by the Republican and Socialist Coalition in 1932.

1936   Assassination of Colonel Riggs; in response, Tydings bill put forth offering independence in a referendum.

1937   Luis Muñoz Marín expelled from the Liberal party of Antonio Barceló.

1938   The *Partido Popular Democrático* (PPD) is founded by Luis Muñoz Marín.

1944   Overwhelming victory of PPD in elections of November.

1946   The *Partido Independentista Puertorriqueño* (PIP) is formed.

1947   Elective Governor Act allows Puerto Ricans to elect their governor. Luis Muñoz Marín elected governor in 1948.

1947   Operation Bootstrap gets under way. Economic growth continues till 1970s, encouraged by the Development Corporation, Fomento.

1950   Public Law 600 sets in motion the process by which Puerto Rico can establish a new constitution. The constitutional connection with the United States established by the Federal Relations Act.

1950   Nationalist uprising in Puerto Rico.

1952   Installation, after a plebiscite, of Estado Libre Aso-
            ciado (ELA), known as Commonwealth.

1953   Commonwealth of Puerto Rico accepted by the United
            Nations as a self-governing territory.

1954   Nationalist gunning of U.S. House of Representatives,
            which resulted in the wounding of five congressmen.

1959   Failure of Fernós-Murray bill to improve Common-
            wealth.

1960   U.N. General Assembly Resolution 1514 (XV) sets up
            Decolonization Committee giving the *independentistas*
            a forum in which to raise the issue of Puerto Rico's
            "colonial" status.

1964-66   Joint executive-legislative commission to examine all as-
            pects of Puerto Rico's status.

1964   Luis Muñoz Marín retires; Roberto Sánchez Vilella
            elected as PPD governor.

1967   Plebiscite on Commonwealth (60 percent of those vot-
            ing endorse Commonwealth).

1968   Roberto Sánchez Vilella leaves PPD to form *Partido del
            Pueblo*.

1968   Luis Ferré of the *Partido Nuevo Progresista* (PNP) elected
            governor.

1972   Rafael Hernández Colón of PPD elected governor.

1973   The Ad Hoc Advisory Committee to study the further development of the relationship between the Commonwealth and the United States fails to establish a new compact.

1976   President Ford endorses statehood. Carlos Romero Barceló of PNP elected governor.

1978   PPD and *Partido Socialista Puertorriqueño* (PSP) cooperate on Decolonization Committee.

1980   Carlos Romero Barceló reelected governor by a narrow majority. PPD gains control of the legislature.

1981   U.N. Decolonization Committee recommends that the case of Puerto Rico be put on the Agenda of the General Assembly as a "separate item." Move successfully opposed by the U.S. delegation.

1982   Romero Barceló and Hernán Padilla in competition for leadership of the PNP.

INTRODUCTION

Puerto Rico is a pessimistic, bitter and tragic country.
                                        LUIS RAFAEL SÁNCHEZ

I care not if we have a right to make them miserable, have we not an interest to make them happy.
            EDMUND BURKE ON THE AMERICAN COLONIES

All is not well in the colony that the United States acquired in 1898 and that was transformed into the Commonwealth of Puerto Rico in 1952.

At Christmas and the New Year, Puerto Rican newspaper columnists, like their counterparts elsewhere, are wont to reflect on the happenings of the passing year. In the early 1980s, from the women's pages to the political columns, their tone was one of somber pessimism. There was mass unemployment; one out of every three Puerto Ricans was without a steady job, and their plight would be made more painful in the coming years by cuts in federal welfare payments. Politicians, locked in vindictive, internecine feuds, had reduced to impotence a legislature in which, a year after an election, the courts still had to decide which party held a majority. The revival of the traditional "family union," much advocated by the campaigning candidates in the 1980 elections, had not been the consequence of moral renewal but imposed by street crime, which forced families to stay at home in the evenings. Hunger strikers were stationed outside the gates of the university; police patrolled within them. Gloomy predictions of economic recession and zero growth for 1982 were buttressed by a decline in every statistical indicator of well-being. The only record held by Puerto Rico, one columnist concluded, was for prison murders per capita. Even in sports, 1981 had been a bad year: the Puerto Rican basketball team was defeated by the Panamanians whom it had trained; Wilfredo Gómez, the boxer and a national hero, was knocked out by a Mexican.

Such pessimism can be seen as a characteristic Puerto Rican exaggeration of the general malaise of the West in recession, as another symptom of the Puerto Ricans' disease: their insistence on the unique importance of their problems perversely ignored by the world in general and by the United States in particular. Recession falls with particular severity on an island that has the poorest regional economy of the United States, an open, export economy liable to be buffeted by the harsh winds of the international market and further punished by the policies that President Ronald Reagan has proposed to improve the lot of Puerto Rico's Caribbean neighbors.

The problems of economic development, of recovering the buoyant levels of growth that were the achievement of the Commonwealth in the 1950s and 1960s, are central. What distinguishes Puerto Rico is that few, if any, Puerto Rican politicians can see those problems as other than inextricably bound up with the problem of status: that is, the nature of the island's constitutional relationship with the United States, which, in 1898, replaced the Spanish crown as the sovereign power in Puerto Rico. Political parties, in Puerto Rico, are defined in terms of the status positions they support, not in terms of their social or economic programs, which derive from their positions on status. Each party maintains that the status sought by its rivals will entail economic ruin in the short or the long run. This is not to argue that the choice of status is necessarily made on economic grounds; merely that economic problems are never seen, as perhaps they should be, as independent of status choices that may be based on noneconomic considerations: dignity and an escape from a colonial relationship with the United States; the preservation of a separate cultural identity; even the maintenance of Puerto Rican representation in the Olympic Games.

It is the status issue that divides the claustrophobic political world of Puerto Rico into three discrete spheres of discourse, each supported by its particular myths, its peculiar vision of the past, and its specific recommendations for the future. The obsessive and Byzantine discussions of status may lead to the assumption that it provides a harmless occupation for academics and a race of legally minded politicians. But for Puerto Ricans the status issue involves not merely a conception of their own identity or a vision of their history; it is seen to govern their prospects of employment, their income levels, and their living standards. While the power to modify the status of Puerto Rico lies with the Congress of the United States, for most congressmen the status of Puerto Rico, when they think of it at all, is a remote and marginal concern that raises awkward constitutional issues. For the inhabitants of the politically introverted small island community, the issue is of supreme importance.

The present status of Puerto Rico is described in English as "Commonwealth," an unhappy version of the Spanish Estado Libre Asociado de Puerto Rico (ELA), which, literally translated, is Free Associated State of Puerto Rico. This phrase more accurately than Commonwealth describes Puerto Rico's relationship with the United States, created in 1952 by Luis Muñoz Marín as leader of the Popular Democratic Party (PPD), or Populares, as it is known. The defense of that constitutional settlement, ratified by a plebiscite in 1952, remains the raison d'être of the PPD. Puerto Rico is a "state" that, on the basic principle of the consent of the governed, freely chose to be associated with, but not form part of, the United States — a territory with powers of local self-government resembling, but constitutionally quite distinct from, those of a state of the Union.

Commonwealth status, according to the PPD, is based on a bilateral compact between Congress and the "people of Puerto Rico." Riddled with legal ambiguities from its inception, the PPD and Muñoz Marín sought to clarify and expand the powers enjoyed under Commonwealth status; but as the sphere of federal legislation expanded, those powers were eroded. It is the aim of the PPD to reverse this process and to enlarge the autonomy of Puerto Rico without severing the bonds of citizenship (granted in 1917) and without the abandonment of those economic and fiscal advantages—exemption from federal taxes combined with free access to the mainland market — that came after the American occupation and are still enjoyed under Commonwealth status. These peculiar concessions, the PPD argues, have made possible the investment that has fueled the economic growth of a poor economy.

The PPD's main political rival — the New Progressive Party (PNP) — rejects Commonwealth status as concealing a quasi-colonial relationship. It argues that Puerto Rico is still subject to federal laws passed by a Congress in which it is represented only by a voteless resident commissioner in the House of Representatives, and to the executive orders of a president whom it has not elected. Citizenship implies full membership in the

Union. "When we were given citizenship," Carlos Romero Barceló, the present statehood governor, argues, "there was also a moral commitment to give us statehood." The PNP contends that only statehood can bring to Puerto Ricans the liberties and dignity, together with the political leverage on Capitol Hill, enjoyed by their fellow American citizens. That Puerto Ricans do not speak the official language of the Union is no insuperable barrier to statehood, according to the PNP. A Spanish-speaking state can be accommodated in the Union within, as the Republican program of 1976 put it, "the concept of a multicultural society." As for economic considerations, the PNP maintains that the burden of federal taxation, which statehood will bring, can be lightened by a transitional period; the special advantages that Commonwealth offers to potential investors will be outweighed by the long-term political security conferred by statehood.

To the *independentista* parties, the Puerto Rican Independence Party (PIP) and the Puerto Rican Socialist Party (PSP), which advocate an independent republic as the only appropriate status for a people with all the cultural attributes of nationhood, Commonwealth represents camouflaged colonialism and statehood outright imperialist annexation. They hold that the "Commonwealth model" for economic growth has made Puerto Rico a helpless, dependent economy of the United States; it has brought to Puerto Rico, in an exaggerated form, all the problems — from drug addiction and abortion to an unjust distribution of income — of the metropolitan society.

No party in Puerto Rico, therefore, accepts the *existing* Commonwealth status as an appropriate and permanent solution of the island's relationship with the United States; both the *independentistas* and the statehooders see it as outright colonialism or, in the phrase of Romero Barceló, as containing "vestiges of colonialism." The PPD sees the creation of Commonwealth as ending "colonialism" but as an imperfect final solution. According to the PPD, Commonwealth is in need of what is known as "culmination," a process initiated on the morrow of its establishment but that has, so far, been a fruitless quest.

It is the economic consequences of the three classical status options that are now at the center of the status debate, given a new urgency and edge by the economic recession that has prevailed since the late 1970s. For the PPD, the economic concessions that accompany Commonwealth status are a condition of continued growth. For the statehooders, the existing integration of Puerto Rico into the U.S. economy demands political integration as the only course to ensure federal transfers and a secure investment climate. For the *independentistas,* only independence can free the island from the degrading dependence on the United States that blights Puerto Rico's economic future.

If recession — the construction industry, an important barometer of economic activity, reached its peak in 1973 and declined thereafter — has sharpened the debate, its terms have been dramatically shifted by new developments. They are: the advance of the PNP (the statehood party) and the end of the electoral and political monopoly that the PPD (supporters of Commonwealth) had enjoyed since the 1940s; the salience of Puerto Rico as an issue in the United Nations; the poverty programs of successive administrations in the 1960s that, by immensely increasing the size of federal funds available to Puerto Rico, made access to Washington the essential tool for a governor who must extract what he can for a poor island; finally, sudden realization in 1981 that a change in the political philosophy and policies of the mainland administration could mean a substantial reduction of the federal transfers — particularly food stamps — on which, and on the steady increase of which, the island had come to depend.

The advance of the statehood party (it won the gubernatorial election of 1968 by a narrow majority, that of 1976 by a more convincing majority, and that of 1980 by a razor-thin majority) inevitably called into question the *continued* support for Commonwealth. General elections are not necessarily plebiscites on status, but they measure the erosion of the support that Commonwealth once enjoyed.

It is against this weakening of support for Commonwealth and the rise of the statehood vote that we must set recent developments in the United Nations. Since 1953, the United States has denied that the United Nations has any jurisdiction over Puerto Rico. It bases its position on the combination of two propositions, not easily reconcilable. First, it accepts the General Assembly's removal, in 1953, of Puerto Rico from the list of dependent territories under its jurisdiction, since Puerto Rico ceased to be a dependent territory once Puerto Ricans freely accepted Commonwealth status in the plebiscite of the previous year — a position supported by the PPD. Second, the United States maintains that because Puerto Ricans are American citizens, their status is a domestic concern outside the jurisdiction of the United Nations, a view shared by the PNP. Neither of the major Puerto Rican political parties, therefore, officially attended the hearings of the Committee of Twenty-Four (the Decolonization Committee) where the Cuban delegation pressed for the immediate "decolonization" of Puerto Rico. Given that this demand was supported only by the two small *independentista* parties — the "bourgeois" PIP and the Socialist PSP — the United States was not seriously troubled by the annual onslaught on American colonialism in Puerto Rico mounted by the Cubans in the Decolonization Committee.

In 1978, the United States delegation suffered a severe shock. In testimony to the Decolonization Committee it became clear

that *no* party in Puerto Rico supported the *existing* Commonwealth status. That the PSP and the PIP, supported by Cuba
and its allies, demanded immediate independence was no surprise. But for the first time both Governor Romero of the
PNP, a supporter of statehood, and his predecessor, Rafael
Hernández Colón of the PPD, a supporter of Commonwealth,
appeared before the committee in New York. Though he denied the jurisdiction of the United Nations, Romero talked of
"vestiges of colonialism" in Puerto Rico, while Hernández
Colón accused the United States of breach of faith in refusing
to "culminate" Commonwealth by failing to bestow greater
autonomy to the Puerto Ricans. In 1980, the Decolonization
Committee recommended that consideration of Puerto Rico
be put on the agenda of the General Assembly in the expectation that, for the first time since 1953, the whole question of
Puerto Rico's status would be reopened in a forum where
anticolonial sentiment was strong. The United States delegation, by diligent lobbying, managed to keep Puerto Rico off
the agenda in 1981 and 1982.

At the same time that status was under discussion in New
York, the relationship between Puerto Rico and the United
States came under strain in Washington. The policies of the
Reagan administration, designed to foster economic recovery
on the mainland, seemed to Puerto Ricans to threaten economic calamity on the island. Without prior consultation with
Puerto Rico, the food stamp program, which supports 67 percent of the Puerto Rican population, was converted into a
block grant and cut back; the federally funded training program
established by the Comprehensive Employment and Training
Act (CETA), which provided 20,000 jobs on an island cursed
with chronic structural unemployment, was ended. Then came
Reagan's proposed Caribbean Basin Initiative, designed to
resist the spread of Cuban influence by extending to other

Caribbean countries some of the economic and fiscal privileges enjoyed by Puerto Rico. It was only *after* the decisions had been made in light of the economic philosophy of the administration and the interests of its foreign policy, and only *after* the Puerto Ricans had prophesied economic and social catastrophe, that the White House set up a task force to examine the implications for Puerto Rico. The power of the task force to influence policy has yet to be demonstrated.

Colonialism is an emotive term, Commonwealth a singularly elusive one. Is the Commonwealth of Puerto Rico something analogous to the Commonwealth of Massachusetts or Virginia or does it resemble a member state of the British Commonwealth?

It resembles a state in that, while its elected representatives have a measure of control over its domestic concerns, many important issues are settled by federal laws; it differs from a state in that it has no representatives in the body — the U.S. Congress — that makes those laws. The relationship between Puerto Rico and the United States has never become, as Henry Stimson once argued it should, "analogous to the present relation of England to her overseas self-governing territories"; the British Commonwealth is a loose association of sovereign states — thus, for example, the Irish Republic, then a member of the Commonwealth, did not declare war in 1939. This option would not have been open to the Commonwealth of Puerto Rico. Unlike citizens of the self-governing dominions, but like the British citizens of the colonies who were involved in a war declared by a Parliament in which they were not represented, the American citizens of Puerto Rico have been automatically involved in wars declared by presidents and Congresses in whose election they played no part. If the term *Commonwealth* is meant to imply any resemblance to a member state of the Commonwealth, it is delusory, hiding a colonial relationship in which the metropolitan power legislates for the colony and controls its defense and foreign policies.

Puerto Rico is not administered as was a British colony; it deals directly with U.S. government agencies, whereas the demands of the British colonies were channeled through a single paternalistic colonial office. The essential difference, which makes for a unique relationship between Puerto Rico and the United States, is the element of consent enshrined in the phrase "in the nature of a compact," used to describe Commonwealth as the relationship with the United States when it was freely chosen by the Puerto Ricans in 1952. There was no such element of consent in British colonialism, nor was Britain as generous to her colonies as the United States has been in aiding Puerto Rico's economy. Critics of Commonwealth would argue that colonialism by consent is colonialism nevertheless, and that generosity reinforces and consolidates dependence.

The United States is confronted with the moral dilemma that confronted Britain as a colonial power. The liberal tradition of both countries demands that government be based on the consent of the governed *and* their participation in the choice of their governors. Commonwealth may satisfy the demand for consent; it may endow Puerto Ricans with considerable powers of local self-government through their elected representatives. But in vital concerns — from the declaration of war to the level of wages set by the federal laws — Puerto Ricans are governed by those in whose election they play no part. This does not mean that Commonwealth may not prove to be the best of all possible worlds for the Puerto Ricans and that political inertia, a strong force in human history, may not lead the Puerto Ricans to remain as they are out of fear for an uncertain future under statehood or independence.

The official position of the United States, reaffirmed by joint resolution of Congress in 1979, is quite clear. Since 1953, the United States has maintained that the Puerto Rican people chose Commonwealth status by democratic processes and that Puerto Rico is free to change that status by the same processes. At least for the near future, the position is a statement of intent on which Congress will not be required to act. The deep sense of frustration that haunts Puerto Rico is self-induced. Congress will not act as long as the democratic process in Puerto Rico gives no clear indication of the status Puerto Ricans wish to enjoy. In the last election (1980), statehooders and supporters of Commonwealth were divided by the slimmest of margins as the upward surge of the statehood vote flattened out. During the 1980 campaign, Governor Romero promised a plebiscite to decide the "destiny of Puerto Rico" should he win. Elected by only 3,000 votes, he abandoned his promise.

The inertia of Congress is frequently considered a deliberate plot to keep Puerto Rico in colonial bondage. It is not. Without what President Reagan called "a clear signal" from Puerto Rico, the easiest policy to follow is to do nothing. The lead from "the Puerto Rican people" so frequently mentioned by all sides in the United Nations was never given. When the Southern governors, meeting in Puerto Rico in 1982 under Romero's chairmanship, were questioned on this issue by the local press, their answers revealed two clear attitudes. Puerto Rican affairs were not uppermost in their minds — for example, Governor James B. Hunt, Jr., of North Carolina confessed he had "not given the matter a lot of thought" — and they felt that in order for any request for statehood to succeed it must represent a clear and decisive majority decision.

"Divide and rule" was the classic device for the maintenance of colonial rule. The United States does not need to foster it. The Puerto Ricans divide themselves. Decolonization is a painless process only when the political elite of a colony are united in demanding it and are agreed on the form it should take.

It is nevertheless evident that the United States has failed to conceive a systematic policy toward Puerto Rico beyond a wait-and-see attitude presented as respect for self-determination. For instance, U.S. economic policies have, over the years, veered from the benign neglect of laissez-faire to paternalism and back again to faith in the market. Nor has it developed an adequate institutional structure to deal with Puerto Rico's problems. A responsibility of the White House since the Kennedy administration, some presidents — John F. Kennedy and Jimmy Carter, for example — showed an erratic concern; others have evinced little interest in Puerto Rican affairs. Individual congressmen and senators — Senators J. Bennett Johnston, Henry M. Jackson, and Daniel P. Moynihan are among them — have shown a friendly interest in Puerto Rico. Personal connections have been established between island politicians and Washington. But men are mortal, politicians impermanent, and friendships do not always endure. There is no colonial office, and it is doubtful whether there should be one; but occasional attention from the White House is a poor substitute for permanent concern. The fundamental political weakness of Puerto Rico is that it is not a constituency. This is the strongest argument for statehood. No congressman and no senator could be blamed for jettisoning his interest in Puerto Rico should it prejudice his own constituents. For the vast majority of politicians, the island is a remote concern that fits uncomfortably into the American constitutional system and costs their constituents, the American taxpayers, a great deal of money.

If the acquisition of Puerto Rico was an outcome of what Arthur Schlesinger, Jr., has called, in a different context, the "politics of inadvertence," its subsequent governance is a monument to what has been called the policy of "selective inattention." The easy assumption of the bureaucrats who dealt with the affairs of the new colony in its early years that it would somehow become "American" and the equally easy assumption that a political remedy proposed in 1952 — Commonwealth — could persist in a different world have both proved to be illusory. The end result has been the creation of a small society whose political class is obsessively concerned with Puerto Rico's relationship with a vast metropolitan society that, understandably, is unwilling to devote much attention to the affairs of three million of its Spanish-speaking citizens.

These two societies, bound together since 1898, do not fully understand each other. Their political styles are distinct — the notions of compromise and consensus that are so important in the American political system are absent in Puerto Rico. Some Puerto Ricans, however, pride themselves in their 100 percent Americanism. And there are observers in Washington who point to the low percentage of votes for independence as a measure of the weakness of any form of nationalist sentiment. Yet, scratch a Puerto Rican, as the saying goes, and you will discover an *independentista* under the skin. It is the strength of this latent sentiment that will determine the political destiny of Puerto Rico. Is the feeling of identity once called "puertoricanism," fostered by language and a culture that historically has no roots in the Anglo-Saxon world, to be dismissed as mere provincialism destined to be eroded by the advance of the American way of life? Or will it persist to make statehood inconceivable and an expansion of autonomy, even independence itself, the only way out of the colonial closet?

The barrier to understanding is, therefore, not merely congressional indifference or the dictates of administrative convenience. The barriers are psychological and cultural, and these barriers, as I shall argue, are encapsulated in both the Puerto Rican and the American stereotypes. Statehooders and their

American allies see no insuperable problem in absorbing politically what has become a regional economy of the United
States, a society already impregnated with American values,
into a multicultural nation. Their opponents wish to retain the
distinct culture of Puerto Rico and to control the levers of an
independent economy, whether by "enlarged" Commonwealth
or outright independence.

Part I

COLONIAL TIES

I.

FROM SPANISH COLONY TO AMERICAN POSSESSION

That Spanish is the language of everyday speech in Puerto Rico is a legacy of four hundred years of Spanish rule. A poor island of illiterate subsistence farmers and modest sugar, tobacco, and coffee planters, Puerto Rico served as a Spanish outpost, guarding the sea lanes of the Caribbean, as the massive fortifications of San Juan testify to this day. It was long sustained by imperial transfers from Mexico — the eighteenth-century equivalent of current U.S. federal transfers to the island — but with Spain's loss of Mexico and other continental possessions, Puerto Rico ceased to be of strategic importance. Puerto Rico became, like Cuba and the Philippines, a relic of the first great European colonial empire. But Cuba, because of its rich sugar plantations, still was considered the "Pearl of the Antilles."

The Spanish colonial governors of Puerto Rico, who, like their American successors, were often appointed as a reward for political services at home, alternated between paternalism and brutal repression. Under their rule, as the island developed a modest export economy, there emerged a realization of separate interests and a sense of insular identity. With them developed attitudes to the imperial power that were to persist, in one form or another, even after the Congress of the United States replaced the Spanish parliament, the Cortes, as the depository of sovereignty over the island.

As in all late colonial societies, the well-to-do in Puerto Rico were divided between those whose interests and inclinations bound them to the metropolitan power and the preservation of the status quo, and those who sought to change the colonial system in order to accommodate local interests.

Merchants and bureaucrats, largely of peninsular Spanish stock, throve on the existing connection with the metropolis. The merchants had profited from the protected market, which favored trade with Spain; the bureaucrats manned the colonial administration. They were the *incondicionales* — the conservative supporters of Spanish rule, just as the employees of the American corporations and federal employees support the American connection. Small-town professionals and a handful of intellectuals apart, the island liberals were recruited from among the Creole landowners, no friends of the merchants who advanced loans for working capital at exorbitant rates. The liberals wanted free trade and some form of home rule under Spanish sovereignty that would satisfy their local political ambitions and their sense of forming a community apart. In 1887 they founded the Autonomist party to press their claims for "the greatest possible decentralization within national [Spanish] unity." The Autonomists established a political tradition and a program which lives today in the Popular Democratic Party (PPD) and in the Commonwealth it created. Luis Muñoz Marín, the PPD's founder, was the son of the journalist and politician Luis Muñoz Rivera (1886 – 1916), a leading member of the Autonomist party. Muñoz's memoirs make clear his affection for and his political debt to the father whose mantle he inherited.

But the Autonomist party was torn by bitter, internal divisions — divisions that, according to one American observer, rested less on a difference of program than on petty personal rivalries, exhibitions of "unseemly partisan strife" in an island "wracked and torn by political animosities."[1] One faction was headed by Dr. José Celso Barbosa (1857 – 1921), a black who had received his medical training in the United States. A republican by conviction, he was persuaded that only the Spanish Republican party would grant autonomy but in the Cortes, following the monarchical restoration of 1874, the Republican party in Spain was an impotent minority. Barbosa's rival, Muñoz Rivera, saw that autonomy could only come from a governing party in Madrid. Just as his son, Muñoz Marín, was to cultivate political friends and allies in Washington by forming an alliance with the Democratic party, so Muñoz Rivera lobbied in Madrid and supported fusion with the Spanish Liberal party — hence, the political party he would form was called the Fusionists. Given the artificial rotation of parties that was the essential mechanism of Spanish parliamentarianism, his Liberal allies would, sooner or later, come to power.

Spain granted the Antilles home rule in 1897 with the Charter of Autonomy. Home rule came less as a result of Muñoz Rivera's negotiations or as a triumphant conclusion to the persistent pressure of the liberal Autonomists than as part of a package deal in a last-minute bid to save Cuba for Spain. In Cuba, the Spanish army was engaged in a savage guerrilla war against separatist rebels. The Spanish government realized that it could not hope to defeat the separatist rebellion if the United States intervened, and by mid-1897 it was clear that pressure for U.S. armed intervention in support of the Cuban rebels was mounting in Congress and might overwhelm the caution of President McKinley. The only escape was to grant Cuba a generous measure of self-government by a Charter of Autonomy that would satisfy Cuban opinion, isolate the separatist rebels, and remove all grounds for intervention by the United States. The charter was hastily passed by royal decree, its preamble referring to the "agonizing pressure of circumstances" that made it necessary; that is, the urgent need to satisfy Cuban demands. But since the Spanish Antilles was considered as a whole, the autonomy granted to Cuba was extended to Puerto Rico. Autonomy came to Puerto Rico on Cuba's coattails.[2]

The charter did not save Cuba for Spain or stave off the landing of American troops on Puerto Rico, but its generous terms gratified the Puerto Rican Autonomists, as it conceded more than they had demanded. Puerto Rican deputies sat in the Spanish Cortes; the governor was appointed by Spain, and he appointed the insular cabinet. The insular parliament of a fifteen-member Senate — half appointed by the governor, half elected — and an elected Lower Chamber was empowered to legislate on local matters, to regulate tariffs, and, with the approval of the Cortes, to negotiate commercial treaties. Spanish sovereignty was preserved by a clause that gave the Spanish ministry power to veto local laws.

There is no way of telling how the new parliamentary constitution would have worked out in practice. Muñoz Rivera's Fusionist party won an overwhelming victory in the elections of March 1898, and according to the conventions of a parliamentary system, he became prime minister and minister of the interior in the insular government. The new assembly was summoned on July 17, 1898, only to dissolve when American troops landed on July 25. "Our autonomous Constitution," wrote the historian Cayetano Coll y Toste, "is abolished and the people of Puerto Rico changed into a political ward at the mercy of the American Congress."

The charter became the center of a controversy that shows no signs of abatement. Critics of the American presence in Puerto Rico contrast the meanness of American legislators with the generosity of Spain. The island, they argue, enjoyed more freedom under the Spanish charter than it was ever to enjoy under its new master; Puerto Ricans were never to sit and vote in Congress or to be granted power to regulate tariffs. Under the charter, Muñoz Rivera told the Reverend Henry Carroll, who was sent by McKinley to report on conditions in the new acquisition, that the governor had become a constitutional monarch responsible to the Puerto Rican legislature. The Nationalist leader Pedro Albizu Campos went so far as to maintain that the 1897 charter created an independent political entity whose rights could not be bartered away to the Americans by the Treaty of Paris.

It is a perilous enterprise to draw parallels between Spanish rule — for most of its duration rigidly authoritarian — and Puerto Rico's experiences under American colonial administrators and with local representatives of American corporations. Yet the arguments of those who advocate the American connection echo those of the pro-Spanish *incondicionales*. "Is there anyone," questioned a Spanish patriot in 1824, "who wants independence? Are there parricides who incite loyal and fortunate Puerto Ricans to change the happy state they enjoy? Do they want Puerto Ricans to change their flourishing situation for the social dissolution, disorder, robbery, arson, and hunger that afflict our Hispanic brothers in other provinces?"[3] Those who harbored such sentiments, it was suggested, should emigrate. An American patriot of the New Progressive Party (PNP) today might make the same arguments with Nicaragua or Cuba in mind, his convictions strengthened by Cuban exiles' reports of the tyranny of Castro, just as Venezuelan exiles in the 1820s painted to the Puerto Ricans the terrible consequences of independence in their own country.

By the Treaty of Paris in 1898 the Congress of the United States succeeded the Spanish crown as sovereign in Puerto Rico; according to Article 9 of the Treaty, "The civil rights and political conditions of the territories here ceded to the United States will be determined by Congress." An impoverished and neglected colony of Spain became the impoverished colony of the United States as the by-product of a war in which the main issue was Cuba. The manner in which sovereignty over the island was acquired has continued to color the relationship between Puerto Rico and the United States.

In the Treaty of Paris, the cession of Puerto Rico was negotiated as compensation for the expenses of a war that most Americans regarded less as an essay in imperialism than as a humanitarian crusade to liberate the Cuban people vilely oppressed by Spain. The paradox of the Spanish-American War was that the United States acquired not Cuba—long the object of expansionist dreams and where American investment was significant—but Puerto Rico, an island the existence of which few Americans were aware. Puerto Rico, Muñoz Marín was to claim, became an American colony "by accident," as the result of an "error" committed by the United States in the Spanish-American War.[4]

McKinley had tried by every diplomatic device abroad and every political ruse at home to avoid coming to the aid of the Cuban separatists, who had revolted against Spain in 1895.[5] But as the "dirty" colonial guerrilla war dragged on, it became a source of continued embarrassment to the administration: American-owned sugar plantations in Cuba were devastated, American citizens arrested. Humanitarians were outraged by press reports of atrocities committed by the Spanish and pressed for intervention.

McKinley was driven to declare war on Spain to keep his party united and to satisfy the quest for power in a competitive international system, which, clad as it was in the vestments of higher purpose, was dismissed as a peculiar brand of American Protestant hypocrisy.* A "people's war" was forced on the administration from below; Admiral Dewey's victory in Manila Bay, when the Spanish fleet defending the Philippines was blown out of the water, released a flood tide of national self-confidence that led Wilfred Scawen Blunt, who had seen British imperialism at work in Egypt, to prophesy that the "Yankees, as the coming race of the world, would be worse even than ourselves."[6]

Unfortunately, denunciations of American imperialism, useful as they may be for polemical purposes, fail to answer the specific question, Why did the United States invade and *retain* Puerto Rico? Puerto Rican historians are prone to see the conquest as the "culmination of a long process."[7] But American diplomacy had focused on Cuba following the outbreak of the separatist revolt, and Puerto Rico is scarcely mentioned in the diplomatic exchanges of the period or in the debates of either the Spanish Cortes or of the United States Congress; when Puerto Rico is mentioned it is considered as a natural appendage to the Cuban question. "One year ago," wrote the Amer-

*Explanations of imperialism include absentmindedness; "indeed, the United States displayed much of the facility of the mother country for acquiring an empire in a fit of absentmindedness," quoted in R.E. Osgood, *Ideals and Self-Interest in America's Foreign Relations* (Chicago: University of Chicago Press, 1953), p. 42; the influence of Social Darwinism; a search for markets as a reaction to the "physical shock" of domestic recession; pressure from the sugar barons; the influence of the yellow press, etc. In fact, almost any thesis can be supported by a judicious selection of sources. See J.A. Field, Jr., "American Imperialism: The Worst Chapter in Almost Any Book," *American Historical Review* 83, no. 3 (June 1978): 644–83.

ican consul general, "we never dreamed of owning Puerto Rico. In the Providence of God she is ours today."

To Puerto Rican historians of *independentista* inclinations and to revisionist historians in the United States, it is a professional imperative to prove that Puerto Rico fell victim to American "imperialism" as that word is understood by modern protagonists of the anticolonial struggle. In a sense their quest is otiose. Puerto Rico was a victim of "imperialism" as that term was understood at the turn of the century. The United States was acting as other great powers had acted. "The sooner this country realizes that it is a power among the nations of the world and wants colonial possessions, the better," argued Senator Foraker, who was to draft the first Organic Act governing the relations between the United States and its new possession.[8]

To American anti-imperialists (radicals at the time) the conquest and retention of Puerto Rico and the Philippines transformed the United States, hitherto occupied in the legitimate pursuit of continental expansion and the incorporation of the West, into an imperial democracy, a colonial power that had betrayed the principles on which the Union was founded. To their revisionist successors today, the acquisition of the "war booty" of 1898 was the first step in a process that was to find expression in military intervention and dollar diplomacy in the Caribbean and that was to end in Vietnam.[9]

Marxist historians see the economic interests of American capitalism, threatened by the contraction of the home market, as the *primum mobile* of conquest. This motive, though, was marginal in regard to Puerto Rico, where American direct investment was overshadowed by that of the European powers. Sugar production — and Puerto Rico provided only a minute fraction of American imports compared to Cuba — was in dire straits and had attracted little American investment,[10] while coffee, which had replaced sugar as the island's main export crop, was threatened by a glut on the world market and had little appeal for American capitalists. Unlike Cuba, where the safety of the very considerable American direct investments in sugar *centrales* encouraged intervention, economic interest in Puerto Rico was a *result* of a successful war, not its cause.

This is not to deny that Puerto Rico, once acquired, was exploited. To Foraker, the retention of Puerto Rico was "a matter of simple business policy." The first carpetbaggers arrived two weeks after the American troops landed, but American banks did not commit their money in Puerto Rico until the Foraker Act of 1900 guaranteed their profits.[11] Massive investment in sugar estates was, after 1900, to transform the economy of Puerto Rico and to start it on a path that would lead to its incorporation as a regional economy of the United States.

It was not capitalists in search of a market who pressed for the conquest of Puerto Rico but expansionists in search of a navy: a West Indian naval base, Theodore Roosevelt argued, would bring a "proper navy." Within a month of the Cuban war breaking out, Senator Lodge wrote to Colonel Roosevelt, then serving with his Rough Riders in Cuba, "Puerto Rico is not forgotten and we mean to have it." Roosevelt himself wrote that he wanted no truce with Spain unless Cuba was independent and "Puerto Rico ours." By June, Secretary of State Day told Senator Lodge, "There is no question about Puerto Rico, everyone is agreed on that"; its annexation was a matter of course.[12] To the expansionists, Puerto Rico had become a desirable object *before* 1898. In the age of imperialism, any great power geographically situated as was the United States would have regarded the Caribbean as a legitimate sphere of influence, an area of inescapable strategic concern — concern intensified by proposals to construct an Isthmian canal. "Our people are now in an expansive mood and there is a deep and strong

American sentiment that would rejoice to see the British flag, as well as the Spanish flag, out of the West Indies."[13] The Caribbean, to this brand of imperialism, should become an American lake. Captain Alfred Thayer Mahan, the intellectual mentor of the expansionists, had always argued that without a coaling station in the West Indies the Panama Canal would be useless. Surely Mahan's teachings applied to Puerto Rico — a thousand miles from Galveston and from Panama. "It is imperative," he argued, "to take possession, when it can righteously be done, of such maritime positions as contribute to secure command."[14] The war with Spain supplied the necessary righteousness. "Territory," McKinley was to argue, "sometimes comes to us in a just cause."

It was not McKinley's set purpose to annex Puerto Rico; as a side effect of the war in Cuba, General Nelson Miles landed on the island. As in the Philippines, once American troops were there and once the expansionists sensed public opinion behind them, annexation became accepted as the easiest solution to the situation. McKinley, on a speaking tour of the West, sensed the swell of enthusiasm released by Dewey's triumph in Manila and gave in to the expansionists' strategic ambitions in Puerto Rico. Congressman John Wesley Gaines, a fierce critic of the new imperialism, argued that military adventurism had brought the conquest of the Philippines and Puerto Rico and that military adventures entailed colonialism. "We are in and cannot get out."[15] It was as simple as that.

All late – nineteenth-century imperial expansion was impelled, not by one single determinant, but by a bundle of motives, from a mission to convert the heathen overseas to the satisfaction of crude jingoism at home, from the strategists' search for coaling stations and safe harbors to the merchants' search for markets. In the case of Puerto Rico it was the expansionists who forced the pace, both in the narrow and immediate sense that the occupation of Puerto Rico was considered by Miles an essential step in the conquest of Cuba and in the larger sense that the expansionists wanted a permanent base in the Caribbean.

The forward policies of the expansionists left McKinley, who had denounced territorial acquisition in a war for the liberation of Cuba as "criminal aggression," with no alternative but to give in to the expansionists' demands and satisfy the jingoes of his own party. On June 4, he sent a telegram to Miles, stationed in Tampa, asking how long he would need to organize an expedition to "take and retain Puerto Rico," a step that his secretary of state had already told the expansionists was "a matter of course." The American commissioners, sent to Paris to negotiate the final peace treaty with Spain, were instructed to demand Puerto Rico; the demand was given a decent appearance by claiming the island as an indemnity for the expenses of the "just war" that had liberated Cuba.

The naval expansionists were as much concerned with keeping other nations out of the Caribbean as with getting in themselves. To Mahan, the Monroe Doctrine applied to the Caribbean rather than to Latin America as a whole, and the expansionists were unduly exercised by German ambitions to acquire a coaling station in the West Indies. Imperialism was often presented as the need to acquire territory out of fear that others might jump the gun. The British advanced their frontiers in northern India, not because of the intrinsic value, as possessions, of barren mountains inhabited by warlike tribes, but because London followed the dogmas of the "forward" school, which held that unless these areas were controlled by Britain they would fall into the Russian orbit or degenerate into contagious anarchy.[16] Once Puerto Rico and the Philippines were occupied militarily by the United States, this negative imperialism operated to deny any settlement that would allow self-government for the new acquisitions. It was argued that once released from Spanish control — and Spain's feeble power had at least kept other nations at bay—a small, impoverished nation like Puerto Rico under a race of *mestizo* politicians would lapse into anarchy and fall prey to the ambitious grasp of hostile powers. Once "in," it was impossible to "get out."

Strategic considerations brought Puerto Rico under the American flag and kept it there. Roosevelt Roads, the naval base in Puerto Rico, is considered essential to the defense of the West. The island must remain American lest an independent Puerto Rico, through some social or political catastrophe, fall into the Cuban-Soviet orbit. But as the British have discovered in the Falkland Islands, colonies acquired for strategic purposes entail moral obligations and political commitments. These can be both expensive and embarrassing.

In a nineteen-day war, with only three American soldiers killed, General Miles' Puerto Rican campaign was a "picnic." As the Spanish military commanders had repeatedly warned, there was no resistance to be expected from the civil population.[17] The Americans established their hold in the south — always the most disaffected region. On July 25, American troops landed at the port of Guánica to find the town deserted except for an old Negro. Ponce, the largest town in the south, gave the American troops a rousing welcome with bands and a parade of the fire brigade. "Bombarded with cigars and bananas," troops and American war correspondents were overwhelmed by the "hospitality" of the natives.[18] Before any resistance could be mounted in the rest of the island, the war came to an end, when Spain, defeated in Cuba, signed an armistice on August 12, 1898.

The warmth of the Puerto Rican embrace — which corre- spondents claimed came from all classes — has embarrassed

Puerto Rican patriots and is one of the roots of the stereotype of the "docile Puerto Rican." "You can get away with anything in Puerto Rico" was the verdict of a Spanish colonial minister. It now seemed that Puerto Ricans could change overnight from Spanish patriots into enthusiastic potential citizens of the United States. Up to the arrival of the Americans, Autonomists and *incondicionales* had outdone each other in declarations of loyalty to Spain, in denunciations of the Cuban rebels and of the United States' propensity to go to war to rescue these traitors from defeat.

The feeling of desertion by an impotent Spain and craven subservience to the new conquerors are not sufficient explanations for a sudden outburst of "Americanism" evident in the rash of new schools offering "English in seven easy lessons." There was neither love for the old master nor determination among a significant sector of the population to mount a separatist revolt against Spain. Under Spanish rule, the movement for national independence was weak, the monopoly of a few dedicated enthusiasts and conspirators. The separatist revolt of 1868, the *Grito de Lares,* which is still celebrated annually and remains to Nationalists the proof of the existence of a national consciousness, was a local rising led by Creoles ruined by the commercial practice of Spanish merchants. The rebels hoped to gain support from popular resentment of new taxes, but the four hundred or so ill-armed, ill-trained enthusiasts were easily suppressed.*[19]

All attempts to organize a separatist revolt with Cuban aid during the war of 1895 – 98 fizzled out. To organize a Cuban-

*The conspirators of Lares invented both the national flag and the national song, "La Borinqueña." The Borinquen Indians were the original inhabitants of Puerto Rico, who were killed off by disease and the Spanish settlers. The anthem is one of the first evidences of Nationalists seeking a historical tradition in the primitive tribes of Puerto Rico.

type guerrilla war was a difficult enterprise in a small island where rebels can be easily hunted down. A minor rising at Yauco in the southwest — always hostile to San Juan with its Spanish bureaucrats and merchants—was snuffed out without difficulty. The Puerto Rican politicians wanted autonomy rather than independence and were convinced that, as Muñoz Rivera told an advocate of independence, the Puerto Rican masses were lacking in "civic education" and would not fight for independence. Barbosa was even more discouraging. "In all the country it would be difficult to find ten men who have sufficient valor to sacrifice themselves for the ideal [i.e., independence] you propose."[20] Whereas the Charter of Autonomy was dismissed as a farce by the Cuban rebels, who fought for nothing short of independence, it satisfied the Puerto Rican politicians.

It was precisely because they sensed the weakness of the separatist movement in Puerto Rico itself that a section of the Puerto Rican exiles in New York, who were collaborating with the Cuban rebels, appealed to the United States to invade Puerto Rico; some even supported the annexing of Puerto Rico as a territory of the United States as the only way to escape "slavery" under Spain. They provided interpreters for the invaders.

There was, therefore, except in the hearts of a handful of conspirators, no "ideal" to resist the new conquerors, alien in language and behavior. While the majority of Puerto Rican politicians, satisfied with the charter of 1897, had no particular desire to be separated from Spain and even less to risk support for an uprising that would end in disaster, they had no reason to fear the United States. It must be remembered that, at the time, the majority of Latin American writers admired Anglo-Saxon virtues. While they might have feared its nascent imperialism, Latin American liberals were enthusiastic admirers of American institutions.

It was in expectation of obtaining the benefits of these institutions that the Puerto Rican political elite accepted American rule. Muñoz Rivera, their leader, told McKinley's envoy, the Reverend Henry Carroll, that statehood was "the highest aspiration of the natives of the country."[21] "The anti-imperialists," an imperialist could maintain, were "deprived of their plea by the evident willingness of the inhabitants to enjoy the benefits of American rule."[22]

While the vast majority of Puerto Ricans accepted the Americans, either from apathy or a vague notion that change would be for the better, the political elite, in an atmosphere of optimism, believed that they would soon be endowed by their conquerors with republican freedoms greater than those enjoyed under the last-minute concession of home rule by the decadent Spanish monarchy. Miles, the military governor, in a proclamation that is still quoted by every Puerto Rican who chafes under the "colonial" status of his country, seemed to promise the rapid grant of American liberties:

July 28, 1898. To the inhabitants of Puerto Rico: In the prosecution of the war against the Kingdom of Spain by the people of the United States, in the cause of liberty, justice, and humanity, its military forces have come to occupy the Island of Porto Rico.... They bring you the fostering arm of a nation of free people, whose greatest power is in its justice and humanity to all those living within its folds.

The chief object of the American military forces will be to overthrow the armed authority of Spain and to give to the people of your beautiful island the largest measure of liberty consistent with this military occupation.... [We have] come to bring protection, not only to yourselves but to your property, to promote your prosperity and bestow upon you the immunities and blessings of the liberal institutions of our government....

Prime Minister Muñoz Rivera and José de Diego, minister of justice, had asked the Spanish governor for arms to resist the American invasion. They dropped the idea when they read Miles's proclamation, since "that magnificent speech" offered "the blessings and liberties of the American Constitution."[23]

A closer examination of American actions would have revealed Miles's proclamation to be a weapon in psychological warfare, not a pledge that bound Congress. Both in the armistice negotiations (August 1898) and in the hard bargaining that followed in Paris, it was evident that the United States meant to keep Puerto Rico subject to the sovereign will of Congress. According to Elihu Root, who, as Secretary of War, was responsible for governance of the new possession, "as between the ceded islands and the United States, the former are subject to the complete sovereignty of the latter."[24] The new subjects were not consulted. "Do we need their consent," asked McKinley about the new acquisitions, "to perform a great act for humanity?" Clearly, the United States was acting like any other colonial power. In international law, Puerto Rico was acquired by right of conquest, as legitimately ceded by a defeated nation.

The first experience of U.S. rule in Puerto Rico was a harsh though paternalistic military government: the rule of "Czars and Sultans." Military governors unceremoniously dismissed the ministry of Muñoz Rivera in February 1899, censored the press, and proceeded to legislate on education, the legal system, and municipal government as irresponsible but well-intentioned proconsuls. Their assumption was that American institutions were superior to those they found in place and that the island could only benefit from putting "the conscience of the American people" into Puerto Rico. Many of the military reforms were an improvement,[25] but there began a process of disillusionment with the United States that was to endure. It was to find voice in the hearings in Washington when Congress, after a two-year delay, addressed itself in 1900 to the task of settling the civil status and future government of Puerto Rico.

José Henna, the disillusioned advocate of American intervention to escape Spanish rule, recalled Miles's pledge to the House Committe on Interior and Insular Affairs:

> We must not forget how the American army was received. The houses were opened to them; the people said: "We are glad to have you here, you are our redeemers." But instead of that...the occupation has been a perfect failure. We have suffered everything. No liberty, no rights, absolutely no protection, not even the right to travel. We can not travel today because we can not get passports. We are Mr. Nobody from Nowhere. We have no political status, no civil rights. That can not go on very long.[26]

The hearings in Washington disclosed that the Puerto Ricans wanted two things: free trade, that is, inclusion within the tariff walls of the United States, so that Puerto Rican exports — above all its sugar — might enter the continental United States free of duty; and the prospect of eventual statehood via the rapid grant of citizenship and territorial status. Under the American Constitution, the grant of territorial status was the first step toward statehood. On its acquisition by the United States, a new territory was granted limited powers of self-government subject to the sovereignty of the federal government. Once prepared economically, politically, and culturally for statehood, a territory was admitted to the Union by Congress. Territorial status, therefore, was thought to contain a promise of statehood, of the dignity of American citizenship.

Admission to the Union as a territory became the demand of Puerto Ricans who testified before the congressional committees. This would give the islanders time to learn American ways and prepare for statehood as mature citizens. To give them less, the Senate Committee on the Pacific Islands and

Puerto Rico was told, would be to ask "a people with 400 years of civilization in back of them to go to conditions below those freely granted the Zuñi Indians and the lower and more barbaric inhabitants of the Southwest Territories."[27] Free trade — that is, inclusion within the American tariff system — was an absolute necessity for this poor agricultural economy. After its cession to the United States, Puerto Rico was cut off from its former markets in Spain and Cuba by the Spanish tariff and yet prevented, by tariffs protecting the American producer, from selling profitably to the new metropolitan power.

To help Congress and the president in reaching a decision on the future government of the island, three missions had been sent to Puerto Rico. That led by Henry Carroll, a Methodist minister, believed the Puerto Ricans capable of self-government. "They will learn the art of government in the only possible way — by having its responsibilities laid upon them."[28] Rather than listen to the Reverend Carroll, Congress listened to General George W. Davis, the island's military governor in 1899, and, like Root, an admirer of the British colonial system and of the government of Trinidad in particular. The cultural shock of encountering a poverty-stricken population, two-thirds of whom were illiterate with living standards inconceivable outside the Negro South, threw up in the general's mind the prejudices that were to harden into stereotypes that were to be exhibited time after time in the coming years. "The general unfitness of the great mass of the people for self-government," he reported, left them at the mercy of a "selfish oligarcy" (i.e., the Autonomist Liberals) bred in Latin traditions incompatible with democratic practices.[29]

In bitter, acrimonious sessions on the floor of the House and the Senate, most Democrats cried out against an imperialism that denied those brought under the American flag the political rights enshrined in the Constitution; most Republicans maintained that the Constitution did not "follow the flag" and therefore did not apply to what they were prepared to treat as a colony, a mere possession whose inhabitants must be denied the privileges of American citizenship and remain subject to the will of Congress.

The issue of free trade was closely connected with the constitutional issue. If Puerto Ricans became citizens of a *territory* of the United States there was no constitutional power to discriminate against them by a tariff: Puerto Rico must be treated on an equal footing with all other territories and states. Hence the imposition of a tariff was, as it were, a mark of noncitizenship, a corollary of the denial of territorial status. The Republicans in the Senate and the House were both imperialists and protectionists. To the Democrats, the imposition of a modest tariff (15 percent of the U.S. rates) was a triumph for imperialism, a denial of the principles on which the Union was founded, and a cowardly concession to the interests of American beet sugar and tobacco growers.

Just as the acquisition of Puerto Rico had been a consequence of the war in Cuba, so the decision of Congress on the civil status of its new subjects was considered not only in the light of the rights of Puerto Ricans but on the ground that what was decided on Puerto Rico would apply to the Philippines, likewise acquired in the war against Spain.[30] "I understand," declared Representative Williams, "that the administration does not care a fig for Puerto Rico":[31] it was concerned by the perils of setting a precedent for the Philippines.

Many congressmen considered that the "peaceful and friendly" — and, according to the census figures, largely white — Puerto Ricans might make acceptable American citizens, but that the same could not be said of the unruly, barbarous Filipinos who were "physical weaklings of low stature with black skin, closely curling hair, flat noses, thick lips and large clumsy feet... mongrels of the East... with harem habits."[32]

Senator Foraker, who was to be responsible for the act that would settle the new status of Puerto Rico, believed the islanders were not fit for true self-government; but he fought for citizenship, since he believed that this would not give "those people any rights that the American people do not want them to have."[33] He came to realize, however, that if they were made citizens then they would be compelled to pay federal taxes. A poor island, burdened by federal taxes, would be unable, in addition, to levy taxation for local purposes. This would mean that the United States would be forced to practice "paternalism to the extent of feeding them from day to day out of our Public Treasury." It is one of the ironies of Puerto Rican history that this brand of paternalism was precisely what Congress, albeit to the dismay of some congressmen, was practicing by the 1980s.

The result of the congressional debate was the Foraker Act of 1900, which was Congress's first essay in drafting the so-called Organic Acts that were to govern the status of Puerto Rico. Puerto Rico became a new constitutional animal, an "unincorporated territory" subject to the absolute will of Congress, a colonial status that was recognized by the Insular Cases in the Supreme Court.[34] The American Constitution did not apply to Puerto Rico. Puerto Ricans could claim only certain "fundamental liberties" deduced from the provisions of the Constitution that limited the powers of Congress. While Puerto Ricans were denied American citizenship, Puerto Rico was not considered a nation in international law. The Puerto Rican became, as a Democrat remarked, "a man without a country. Can any man conceive of a more tyrannical form of government?"[35]

That government, under the Foraker Act, was to consist of a governor and an Executive Council appointed by the president of the United States, who also appointed all of the justices of the island Supreme Court. The Executive Council functioned as the upper chamber of the legislature, the lower chamber, the House of Delegates, being composed of thirty-five members elected by Puerto Ricans. Since all legislation had to be passed by both chambers and since the governor possessed the right of veto, no legislation that ran counter to the wishes of the Executive Council, dominated by Americans, could pass.

The Foraker Act, Muñoz Rivera wrote in an open letter to McKinley, was unworthy of the United States and without a shadow of democratic principle. Under "Spanish despotism," Puerto Ricans sent deputies to the Cortes; they were now without representation in Congress, which ruled Puerto Rico and whose laws, unless locally inapplicable, applied to the island. The Foraker Act broke every principle in the U.S. Constitution by failing to separate the executive and legislative branches. The "anodyne autonomy" granted was nullified by the "Chamber of Lead" — the Executive Council dominated by presidential appointees.[36] It was, *La Correspondencia* argued (December 5, 1903), "most un-American."

This was not the view of those congressmen and soldiers who had concerned themselves with Puerto Rico. For Davis, the Foraker Act was a "just and necessary step toward ultimate self-rule in Puerto Rico."[37] J.H. Hollander, the presidentially appointed auditor in the Executive Council and who controlled the finances of the island government, like Foraker himself, thought the settlement "generous."[38]

This "generosity" lay not in the political but in the economic settlement. Puerto Rico paid no federal taxes; since Puerto Rico sent no senators or representatives to Congress, this was a concession that could not be avoided without the accusation of taxation without representation. In 1901, the customs duty on Puerto Rican goods entering the United States was removed; dependent for the export of its products, free of duty, to the mainland, the island became a regional economy of the United States. Thus, by 1901 the Foraker Act had set the essential framework of the U.S. connection. The political framework might be enlarged in the direction of home rule in an endeavor to remove the stigma of colonialism; the economic bond would work against any final severance of permanent political union with the metropolitan power.

In these early years, given exemption from federal taxes and free access to the continental market, there first appeared an argument that was to have a long history. The economic advantage of permanent union with the United States made tolerable a political settlement that left the Puerto Rican, "Mr. Nobody from Nowhere," imprisoned in a constitutional limbo as an unincorporated territory. "We are and we are not an integral part of the United States. We are and we are not a foreign country. We are and we are not citizens of the United States.... The Constitution covers us and does not cover us... it applies to us and does not apply to us."[39] These ambiguities were to haunt Puerto Rico's relationship with its new master; they are still unresolved.

The constitutional settlement that set the framework of U.S. – Puerto Rican relations had been made by a Republican Congress and a conservative Supreme Court, despite the Democrats' contention that the Constitution extended to Puerto Rico *ex proprio vigore* and that the acquisition of colonies was unconstitutional. The Republican point of view was that the United States could acquire colonies as could any other great power in a world of competing imperialisms; as Justice White argued in *Downes v. Bidwell*, the key case in the Supreme Court establishing Puerto Rico's status as an unincorporated territory, the United States could not be left "helpless in the family of nations." Representative Richardson's observations on Hawaii were quoted in the debate on the Foraker Act: "Nations have always acted and should govern themselves at all times upon principles entirely different from those which actuate individuals.... In looking at the question of any foreign territory the only question that should enter into consideration by us is one question: Is it best for the United States? The weal or woe, the misery or happiness, the poverty or prosperity of the foreigner or those to be annexed is not involved."[40]

The supreme paradox of the war of 1898, waged ostensibly against Spanish colonialism, was that its end result was the creation of an American colony of indeterminate status, thrusting Puerto Rico into what Justice Harlan, dissenting from the majority in *Downes v. Bidwell*, described as a "disembodied shade." In 1980 his judgment was to be quoted by Representative Dellums in a bill promoting Puerto Rican independence, an indication of the long shadow that the debates on the Foraker Act were to cast over Puerto Rican history. Yet one cannot avoid the conclusion that the Foraker Act was, in some sense, a political accident, just as Muñoz had once remarked that the acquisition of Puerto Rico was itself an accident, the product of an aggresive imperialism that was itself short-lived. The Foraker Act was imposed by a Republican Congress. Opinion in the country, as reflected in the press, was overwhelmingly for generous treatment and for free trade. President McKinley and Elihu Root, seriously concerned with the acute depression which Root believed might foster "sedition," both supported free trade as, in McKinley's words, a simple duty. Democrats denounced the proposed settlement as a "colonial policy inconsistent with Republican institutions." It was the Republican leadership in the Senate that imposed the colonialism implicit in the temporary imposition of a tariff; it was a conservative Supreme Court, appointed largely by Republican presidents, that gave constitutional sanction to imperialism, placing, as Justice Brown was to argue, the liberties of Puerto Ricans in the hands of U.S. citizens as electors of Congress.[41] Once in place, political inertia ensured for years to come the persistence of the colonial pattern set in 1900.

The imperial democracy was unprepared for imperial responsibility in its new acquisitions. This was not surprising. Great
imperial powers, coming into possession of large territories,
perforce create colonial offices and ministries to administer
them, making a virtue of necessity. Since — apart from the
Philippines — the new colonies were, by world standards, insignificant, they were given only occasional bursts of concentrated attention. Nowhere is this more evident than in the
arrangements for administering Puerto Rico once the military
governors were replaced by American politicians. Theodore
Roosevelt, Jr., son of President Theodore Roosevelt and one
of the best presidential appointments as governor of Puerto
Rico, lamented the absence of a colonial tradition, of a reservoir
of trained colonial administrators: "We had no colonial service
and we did not develop one. Most of the men who filled
executive positions in Puerto Rico went there from the United
States with no previous experience whatsoever, speaking not a
word of Spanish. Most of them had no conception either of
Spanish culture or temperament. Most of them never learned
to speak Spanish fluently, and many of them never spoke
it at all."[42]

Until 1934, Puerto Rico was administered from the War
Department; transfer to the Department of Interior resulted
in no improvement. "No one in the [Puerto Rican] section,"
the department's director reported in 1941, "knows Spanish or
has ever visited Puerto Rico for more than a few days on a
holiday trip."[43] When relations with the United States were at
their worst, in the 1930s, Harold Ickes, who as Secretary of
the Interior was responsible for the governance of Puerto Rico,
made a slighting remark about the Puerto Rican legislature as
controlled by the sugar interests when visiting the island. The
pro-American president of the Senate, Rafael Martínez Nadal,
reacted with the outraged sensibility of a colonial: "There is

something of demi-gods about them. They fly in to a place, stay for half an hour and then tell us how to solve all our problems."[44]

The best of the governors were sound administrators with no particular interest in the island. They did their jobs and left. But it was the American members of the Executive Council, not the governors, who ruled Puerto Rico. The auditor general, not the governor, controlled the budget; by the 1930s, he had a staff of 120, compared with the governor's meager six. Neither the governor nor the appointed American officials had much rapport with local politicians. The language barrier was real in the years before a generation of Puerto Rican leaders who could speak English emerged in the 1930s; the members of the Executive Council and the governors took their information from, and reflected the attitudes of, American residents on the island. The federal district judges, according to Wilson's Secretary of War, regarded their main mission to be the defense of U.S. residents, agitating "whatever underlying basis of race prejudice there might be."[45] "He is a man of sound business sense," wrote Taft of one of his appointees, "a graduate of Yale, and I believe would get along as well as any Yankee could get on in Puerto Rico. He doesn't know the language, but I presume that ultimately he would pick up some." Theodore Roosevelt, Jr., described his first treasurer, a party hack, as "a scallawag of the first order who professed great loyalty to the United States and did not speak a word of Spanish." British colonial officers were expected at least to master the tongue of the natives they administered. Not so the rulers of Puerto Rico. (The exception was Governor Beverly, a Texan, who served from 1932 – 33. Governor Roosevelt, to his credit, did attempt to learn Spanish.)

All but the most enlightened of the hundred or so Americans who administered the colony as occasional visitors between

1900 and 1940, and on whose reports Congress and the administration based their vision of the needs of Puerto Rico, came to the island convinced that the Puerto Ricans were incapable of governing themselves. This prejudice was converted into an axiom by their experiences in dealing with local politicians. "Strong home control with considerable deference to local opinion" was the most that Puerto Ricans could expect.[46] After all, this treatment was more generous than that afforded any colonial government in the Antilles. Though there were dissentient voices echoing the protests of the Democratic anti-imperialists,[47] there was self-satisfaction with colonial rule, reflected in a spate of books and articles. The Foraker Act, argued William Hunt of Montana, Governor from 1901 to 1904, "has brought liberty, self-government and prosperity to a million people." By 1904, the Republican program voiced official satisfaction: "We have organized the government of Puerto Rico and its people now enjoy peace, freedom, order and prosperity."[48]

Here lay the fundamental misconception. The United States was confronted by a self-confident political elite that had already grasped the local levers of power, not by a race of Latin illiterates. They could not regard American rule as bestowing "liberty and self-government," or the settlement of 1900, in Hunt's words, as "liberal in its extension of political autonomy."[49] Most Puerto Rican politicians initially advocated statehood, many of them misconceiving the powers of a state in what they called "a Republic of Republics." It was the denial of the hope of statehood that turned them into "malcontents." Without the promise of statehood it appeared that, far from being granted liberty, they had been robbed of liberties they had already won; the island already enjoyed, under the Charter of 1897, an autonomy that Muñoz Rivera had argued (wrongly) brought a measure of home rule more extensive than that enjoyed by Canada. Without the Charter, Muñoz Rivera might well have regarded the Foraker Act as a liberating measure.

It was not that Congress set out to punish or exploit Puerto Rico. On the contrary, it could pride itself on the results of American rule. Every governor presented impressive statistics of hospital and road building, of educational progress. All seemed to be going well enough. American policymakers could therefore avoid making any *fundamental* decision on Puerto Rico. They did not perceive any need to decide whether Puerto Rico should ultimately participate as a state, or whether its dependency should be permanent and, if so, what form that dependency should take. As Governor Roosevelt complained, a parochially minded nation that was unwilling to conceive "a consistent long-range colonial policy" fell into a policy of drift, of which the often unstated premises were a faith in the processes of assimilation and the conviction that Puerto Ricans were not as yet capable of democratic self-rule on the American pattern. Sooner or later Puerto Ricans would become Americans capable of behaving as responsible citizens. Until this process of assimilation was completed, even a liberal statesman like Woodrow Wilson sincerely believed that Puerto Ricans should be treated as political minors, as wards of the United States.

The ward, however, weak and poor as it was, had to be treated as part of the United States. Not only would it be given relief from temporary disasters, such as hurricanes, but it also must be given the same medicine as that administered to the mainland. The economic philosophies that worked on the mainland were expected to work in Puerto Rico. In the early years, the local legislature proposed setting the devastated island economy on the road to recovery through a program of agricultural credit. The proposal was rejected by the auditor general, a presidential nominee, on the grounds that, having failed in the United States, such a policy could not succeed in Puerto Rico. Again, the economic philosophies of the United States dictated that the sugar companies be allowed to expand their activities in Puerto Rico whatever the social and human costs. Laissez-faire capitalism had brought prosperity to the mainland; ergo, it must work on a poverty-stricken island. The result was economic catastrophe in the 1930s.

It is true that in the early 1900s, few colonial powers regarded the possession of colonies — Lloyd George called the British West Indies an "imperial slum" — as imposing a duty to aid them in an effort to climb out of poverty. The notion of aid belongs to an age when the assumption that liberal economics were a universal recipe for prosperity no longer obtained. What distinguishes American colonialism is that Congress refused to acknowledge it possessed a colony: Puerto Rico was an "unincorporated territory," a term that did not fit easily into the vocabulary of classic colonialism.

It is understandable that American policymakers did not make a fundamental decision on the future of their colony in 1900 or in the years immediately after 1900. Nor was the Americans' judgment that Puerto Rico's political elite was not fitted to shoulder the responsibility of guiding an illiterate electorate along the paths of democratic self-government merely an irrational racial prejudice, even if racial prejudice and a sense of inborn Anglo-Saxon superiority undoubtedly existed. Evidence to reinforce prejudice was very soon at hand.

In the elections of November 1900, mob rule prevailed in San Juan. Muñoz Rivera, who realized that redistricting maneuvers by his Republican enemies would rob him of his chances of victory in the election, issued instructions to his followers to abstain from voting. This brought to Puerto Rico the Latin American and Spanish practice of *retraimiento* — the boycotting of an election by a party (in Spain, usually the parties of the extreme right and left) that had no hopes of winning through the ballot box. To Americans it was tantamount to rejecting the democratic process when it did not yield the desired result.

Muñoz Rivera's action made a deep and lasting impression on Americans: "the excitable nature and the uncompromising temperament of Latin Americans," wrote one American observer, "make it difficult for them to learn the lesson of government by majority rule."[50] "Liberty is a habit" not easily learned by "tropical peoples,"[51] commented another. While Americans may have been right in believing that without their political tutelage Puerto Rico might soon have lapsed into those alternations between pseudo-democracy and outright dictatorship that plagued other Latin American nations, seventeen years later Senator Vardaman of Mississippi could state: "They [the Puerto Ricans] will never in a thousand years understand the genius of our government." This was tantamount to condemning Puerto Rico to colonial rule in perpetuity.

Apart from the fact that peoples only learn the arts of self-government by exercising self-government, even if they make a hash of it and bring their countries to the edge of ruin in the process, it is a lesson of colonial history that wherever there is a colonial elite convinced of its capacity to rule, as was that of Puerto Rico, a colonial government is, in the long run, unsustainable. Within a few years of the conquest, the same American observer who so summarily dismissed the Puerto Rican *políticos* as irresponsible demagogues found "the great majority of the people of Porto Rico either dissatisfied with the American Government or openly hostile to it."[52] It was in these conditions that the continued delay in making a fundamental decision about the governance of Puerto Rico became a perpetual grievance. "The United States," complained the essayist-historian Tomás Blanco in 1935, "has neither wished to admit frankly that it intends to keep us as an exploited colony, generation after generation, nor has it ever thought to incorporate us fully as of right in the [American] Federation, nor has it given the people, methodically and intentionally, opportunities to seek its own road to the future."[53] Puerto Rico was left in suspense in the limbo of an unincorporated territory.

What America offered Puerto Rico in the years after 1900 was subjection to an intense process of Americanization without the promise of political dignity. The nature of the offering was understood only by the local *políticos*, not by "the one hundred thousand men who can neither read nor write and who know no more about self-government than the ex-slave did at the close of the Civil War,"[54] i.e., assimilation without incorporation, without the promise of statehood or the prospect of self-government.

2.

COLONIAL CONFLICTS

By the end of World War II, it became evident that the "temporary" settlement of the Foraker Act of 1900 — augmented in 1917 by a second Organic Act that granted Puerto Ricans American citizenship — had not provided a satisfactory civil government for Puerto Rico. To Muñoz Marín, architect of the Commonwealth of 1952, the Foraker Act set up a colonial constitution that was ungenerous and, as his father had insisted it would be, unworkable. To the United States, possession of what Puerto Ricans considered a colony accorded ill with the American liberal tradition and with U.S. efforts to encourage other powers to grant independence to their overseas territories.

It is curious, in retrospect, that Congress did not cast its mind back to America's own colonial experience, when governors appointed by English kings clashed with local assemblies. The Foraker Act set up an Upper Chamber, the Executive Council, where American councillors appointed, like the governor, by the president of the United States held the whip hand over the Puerto Rican councillors. As a result of this arrangement, the clash in Puerto Rico occurred not only with the governor but between the House of Delegates, elected by the

Puerto Ricans, and the Upper Chamber. This arrangement denied effective legislative powers to the House of Delegates while leaving the local politicians in the House with a "voice" to plague every governor. Criticism of the United States became a permanent weapon in the armory of Puerto Rican politicians; as in all colonies, the exploitation of grievance provided the means to create and hold together a loyal clientele for electoral purposes. But however genuine the grievances, the metropolitan power typically reacts by labeling those who exploit them as troublemakers whose factious conduct is a constant proof that they lack "responsibility." To grant a greater degree of self-government to those who lack this essential ingredient for its exercise is to court disaster. Such is the vicious circle of colonialism.

This vicious circle soon operated in the new legislature set up by the Foraker Act, where the two main competing parties were led by the rivals who had split the old Autonomist party: Luis Muñoz Rivera and Dr. José Celso Barbosa.

Though Barbosa was a black, his Republican party included poor whites from the coast; his political trajectory, as he himself claimed, was "diaphanous" in its consistency. He had always stressed equality within Spanish sovereignty; he now claimed equality as an American subject. He sought collective American citizenship for Puerto Ricans as a precondition for the ultimate acceptance by Congress of Puerto Rico as a state of the Union. Statehood and citizenship were, to Barbosa, not the demands of a subservient people, but an assertion of dignity. The necessary revision of the Foraker Act to accommodate dignity would be the reward of loyal cooperation with American-appointed governors.

It was therefore left to Muñoz Rivera to voice the disillusionment of the Puerto Rican elite with the constitutional settlement of the Foraker Act, which robbed the native ruling class of the powers that they were to enjoy under the Charter of 1897 — particularly their local supremacy in municipal government. In 1904, Muñoz Rivera became the leader of the Unionist Party of Puerto Rico (UPR). The UPR was formed to represent the interests of what was called "the Puerto Rican family," injured by the rapid advance of the American sugar corporations, the collapse of coffee prices, and the devaluation of the local currency — all of which, perceived as consequences of American rule, added to the discontents of the established political elite.

At first, Muñoz Rivera also supported statehood, which would convert Puerto Rico into "another California or Nebraska." If this status was refused by Congress, then, since outright independence was an impractical ideal, "rather than accept the status of manumitted slaves," he argued, "we prefer to develop under the autonomous system of Canada" — that is, the home rule solution that had been the program of the Autonomist party.

The home rule that Muñoz Rivera came to accept as "the practical solution" — once it was clear that Congress would grant neither independence nor statehood — was rejected by the radical wing of his party. In 1912, Rosendo Matienzo Cintrón, who since 1906 had been waging a campaign against the invasion of the island's economic life by American capitalism and the destruction of its cultural traditions by galloping Americanization, broke with the UPR, of which he had been a main architect, and became an advocate of independence.[1] For José de Diego, the orator and poet who was to become a prophet of the modern independence movement, "to think in terms of an ambiguous intermediate formula, without the end of statehood in view, would be to introduce into the U.S. Constitution an exotic element contrary to its spirit. There remain, therefore, two solutions: Puerto Rico, State of the Union; Puerto Rico,

Independent State." According to these advocates of independence, home rule did not merely fail to satisfy the old cry for the dignity of equality, it lacked political logic; it could not be accommodated within the Constitution of the United States and would break down in the long run. This criticism brought against Muñoz Rivera's "Canadian" solution would also be brought against the version of home rule—the Commonwealth—that was the creation of his son, Luis Muñoz Marín. Just as Muñoz Marín, once he had renounced the "error of his youth"—independence—for Commonwealth status, was always troubled by the residual advocates of independence in his party, so his father attempted to keep his radical wing satisfied by calculated ambiguities. At one time independence, home rule, and statehood were included in the UPR program. These ambiguities were not the product of intellectual confusion. They were part of the sterile game of colonial politics.

By victory over Barbosa in the elections of 1904, the UPR began a domination of island politics that was to last for twenty-eight years. Barbosa's loyalty to the new rulers, his acceptance of the Foraker Act in the hope that loyal cooperation would open the gates to statehood, had proved electorally disastrous. The lesson was not lost on Muñoz Rivera. A representative of what General Davis had dismissed as a selfish oligarchy, commanding a party that a perceptive American observer saw as the vehicle of "the larger property-holding interests" against Barbosa's "popular party," became, by his advocacy of the claims of the "Puerto Rican family" and his constant criticisms of American rule—the most revered politician in Puerto Rico.[2] To Muñoz, the Foraker Act was totally unacceptable. The more of a nuisance he became to American governors and the Executive Council, the more popular he became in Puerto Rico.

In 1909, Muñoz Rivera used his "voice" in the House of Delegates to force the constitutional crisis implicit in the Foraker Act. The House of Delegates presented three laws, which the Executive Council, acting as the Upper Chamber, rejected. In retaliation, the Lower Chamber rejected the appropriations in the budget presented by the Executive Council. This was a proof to President Taft that Puerto Rican politicians were obstructive and factious, indulging in an exhibition of political spite ill-befitting "the favored daughter of the United States." "The present development is only an indication," he told Congress on May 10, 1909, "that we have gone somewhat too fast in the extension of political power to them for their own good." After debate, in which once more anti-imperialists faced imperialists, the Foraker Act was amended by Congress: it was decided that if the budget had not been passed, the previous year's budget would run for the coming fiscal year. This amendment effectively robbed the Lower Chamber of financial control, its only effective weapon in a bicameral parliamentary system. The tactics of "factious" opposition had been counterproductive. Far from groaning under "an unbearable state of tyranny," as the Unionists maintained, Puerto Ricans, concluded Representative Marlin Edgar Olmsted, had been given "a joy ride" for nine years.

Muñoz Rivera's pressure for greater self-government — complicated by the growth of the independence wing of the Unionist party after the bitter disillusionments of the 1909 crisis — made no progress until the election of Woodrow Wilson as president in 1912. In his first message to Congress, the new president, representing the liberal Democratic tradition, pleaded for more justice for Puerto Rico.[3] Thus was established a necessary political condition for any satisfaction of Puerto Rican demands that was to endure: a president ready to use the influence of the executive branch in Congress in support of Puerto Rican claims. Various bills that proposed, among other things, granting American citizenship, had been buried by a combination of congressional indifference and procedural delays. Now, the change in the political climate that Muñoz Rivera had so long hoped for, there at last seemed to be an opportunity to press for home rule on the "Canadian" model which he had advocated since 1900. His struggle with what he called "the terrible distrust" of Congress, with the factions in his own party in Puerto Rico where de Diego had come out for independence, with the hesitations and backslidings of the president himself and the caution of the Bureau of Insular Affairs, was long and bitter, undermining his health and driving him to bitter despair. The outcome was the Jones Act of 1917. It granted U.S. citizenship and a modest extension of Puerto Rico's powers of self-government.

The Jones Act represented the maximum concession that could be extracted from a Congress reluctant to give much time to the problems of Puerto Rico: the "supreme gift" of citizenship was the fruit of congressional weariness as much as of democratic conviction. Outright racial prejudice was still expressed by Southern racists: "I really had rather that [Puerto Ricans] would not become citizens of the United States. I think that we have enough of that element in the body politic already to increase the nation with mongrelization."[4] However, since *white* Americans had invested in Puerto Rico, the island had to be kept; and "if kept against the will" of the inhabitants, they must be made citizens and irrevocably tied to the United States. Only a handful of Puerto Ricans were ready to face the prospect of remaining citizens of Puerto Rico or, as the United States chose to officially baptize the island, Porto Rico; citizens, that is, of no state since Puerto Rico as such had no international existence. That was the bleak choice left them by the Jones Act.

Muñoz Rivera, worn out by his battles in Washington, died

in November 1916 before the Jones Act came into operation. He accepted it without enthusiasm as a base from which to fight for greater self-government, viewing it as a "field of experiment" for stable self-government which, if successful, might lead America to become the "greatest of great powers" by conceding independence. As it stood, the Jones Act was "meager and conservative."[5] Pragmatism and his desire to get those concessions on offer led him to accept it. He had only to listen to the congressional debates to realize that citizenship in American eyes meant permanent association with the United States. It could not lead to independence. "If you accept and receive citizenship under the American flag," warned Representative Clarence Benjamin Miller, much concerned with Puerto Rico as a strategic base to protect the Panama Canal, "you will take it for yourselves and your children's children for all time."[6] "*Our people*," the House Committe on Interior and Insular Affairs reported, "have already decided that Porto Rico is forever to remain part of the United States." The benefits of civil liberty American citizenship could bring. Independence never.[7]

Nor did citizenship bring participation: it was "passive citizenship" that denied Puerto Ricans representation in Congress. The only representative of Puerto Rico in the body that passed laws that governed important aspects of Puerto Rican life was a resident commissioner in the House of Representatives, elected by Puerto Ricans but without a vote in Congress. "Give us statehood," Muñoz Rivera had insisted, "and your glorious citizenship will be welcome to us and our children." Without statehood the children remained second-class citizens, while the concessions of the Jones Act fell far short of the "Canadian" solution that might have made such an inferior citizenship tolerable. What the Jones Act made clear once more was that the domestic constitution of Puerto Rico represented, not the will of Puerto Ricans, but the will of Congress.

It is a frequent assertion in Puerto Rico that the citizenship granted in the Jones Act, far from being a generous concession, was merely a device to make Puerto Ricans liable to service in the United States Army when the nation was at war. While it is true that the prospect of war helped to convince the president that Puerto Rico's grievances must be satisfied, in its crude form this assertion is unjust both to President Wilson and those Democrats who supported a liberal solution. Wilson may not have been "the first decolonizer"; his liberalism was always tempered by an austere conception of self-discipline as a pre-requisite for democratic self-government, a sophisticated version of the white man's burden.[8] But he had long believed that the Puerto Ricans, in spite of their shortcomings, deserved something better than the Foraker Act.

The coming of the "supreme gift" of citizenship is a classic example of "too little too late," a policy that had long been proved counterproductive in Britain's handling of the Irish question. Granted in 1900 it would have been welcomed by the local politicians.[9] Granted in 1917 without consulting the Puerto Ricans as to whether they wanted it or not (though the majority, as opposed to their political leaders, probably welcomed it), it came after repeated demands for home rule and seventeen years of acrimonious colonial politics.

The two central concessions of the Jones Act that governed relations between the United States and Puerto Rico until 1952 were the *collective* grant of citizenship to Puerto Ricans and the replacement of the Executive Council by a Senate elected in toto by universal manhood suffrage. It was this latter extension of autonomy that had been the main concern of Muñoz Rivera, since it removed the veto of an upper house dominated by presidential appointees. It gave the local legislature more powers than those enjoyed by any Antillean colony. Laws passed by the new legislature were, however, subject to a preliminary veto by a governor still appointed by the president of the United States and a final veto in the hands of the president himself. (Congress preserved its own sovereignty by maintaining a veto on laws passed by the Puerto Rican legislature; it never exercised this right because, given the presidential veto, it never had occasion to do so.)

Rather than providing a satisfactory government for Puerto Rico, as Congress hoped, the concessions of the Jones Act sharpened colonial tensions. If the dangers of a clash between the Executive Council acting as an Upper Chamber and the House of Delegates receded, a popularly elected House of Delegates and Senate now faced a governor and senior officials appointed by the president of the United States and working under the conservative instructions of a section of the War Department, the Bureau of Insular Affairs, presided over by a general.

The bureau and successive governors found the complexities of Puerto Rican domestic politics profoundly irritating. The tone of the relationship in the 1920s was set by President Harding's appointee as governor, E. Montgomery Reily of Kansas City, whose qualification was that he had contributed $11,000 to the president's campaign fund. He soon came up against obstruction in the chambers. The combination of the Unionists' mild anti-Americanism with their scramble for jobs —though it paled beside his own appointment of carpetbaggers from his native state — was beyond his comprehension. He dismissed Antonio R. Barceló, leader of the majority Unionist party after Muñoz Rivera's death, as a "crook"; the resident commissioner as a "professional double crosser"; and island politicians in general as "unsteady" with a lamentable propensity for living with "negro women." Even the local Republicans, who hoped their display of loyal Americanism would compensate for electoral failure in Puerto Rico and provide them with jobs, were glad to see him go.

Reily's successor, Horace M. Towner, who had been the ranking Republican member of the Jones Committee of 1917, a supporter of citizenship, and chairman of the Interior and Insular Affairs Committe of the House, was one of the few governors (1923 – 29) who made a serious attempt to understand Puerto Rican aspirations: he believed that Puerto Rico must become a state and in the interim be granted generous measures of self-government. Unlike Reily, he tried to work with the majority party, the *Alianza*. Formed in 1923, it was an unprincipled coalition of Barceló's Unionists and a dissident sector of the Republican party. Cooperation was by no means an easy undertaking, as Barceló's technique for retaining his hold on local opinion was to attack the governor and the United States. As for the Republicans, they regarded the appointment of Unionists to any job as an insult to their Americanism and black ingratitude to supporters of the president's Republican party. Towner's reward was abuse by the Republicans as a degenerate weakling and a tool of Barceló. They circulated rumors in Washington about the governor's bad health and that his administration was causing "starvation."

It was Towner, in spite of his wishes to cooperate with the elected majority on the island, who was to strike a cruel blow against any idea that the Puerto Rican legislature enjoyed even modest control over local affairs. In 1925, the legislature passed a bill setting up an industrial school in San Juan; it was vetoed on financial grounds by Towner, and the gubernatorial veto was upheld by President Calvin Coolidge. Coolidge had no sympathy for the Unionist demand, presented in a joint resolution of the legislature and conveyed to the president by Colonel Lindbergh, for "justice and self-determination." Like Taft before him, Coolidge believed that, far from meriting more self-government, the Puerto Ricans already possessed more self-government than was good for them. He told them where they stood in language that caused great offense in the island.

Throughout the 1920s, Puerto Rico had been a nuisance; by 1930 it had become a problem. What had always been a precarious economy, ravaged in 1929 by a hurricane that almost destroyed the coffee industry, became, with the world depression, a disaster area, the "poorhouse of the Caribbean."

It was Governor Theodore Roosevelt, Jr. (1929 – 32) — not the local politicians, whom he found "comic or irritating" — who saw the real problem: poverty. He discovered on the island "farm after farm where lean underfed women and sickly men repeated again and again the same story — little food and no opportunity to get more." It was an American organization — the Brookings Institution — that in 1930 published a report which for the first time set out in some detail the appalling living conditions of American citizens in Puerto Rico, 60 percent of whom were living six to a room. Yet nothing effective could be done for this underdeveloped region within the framework of benign neglect born of a faith in the market economy. Roosevelt's paternalism — his wife publicized Puerto Rican needlework in New York, and he himself encouraged tourism by inviting tourists to his official residence — was a gesture, not an economic policy. Moreover, neither Republican presidents nor Congress shared his concern.

After years of presidential indifference, the election of Franklin D. Roosevelt seemed to open up new prospects. Roosevelt himself showed a serious, if intermittent, interest in the island. His wife's concern was deeper. Visiting the island in 1934, she was appalled by what she saw in the slums of San Juan; her interest was maintained by her friendship with the Bournes, who administered the New Deal Agency in Puerto Rico. She invited to tea in the White House the young Luis Muñoz Marín, son of the old Unionist leader who had spent the 1920s in New York and was rapidly becoming a rival to Barceló who had dissolved the *Alianza* and in 1932 formed the Liberal party committed to independence. Largely through his wife, President Roosevelt was better informed about Puerto Rican conditions than any of his predecessors. Above all, the whole philosophy of the New Deal, with its emphasis on federal aid to the poor combined with the president's bold flair for social experiments — whether they worked or not — seemed to offer hope for a poverty-stricken island.

Roosevelt's first appointment, pushed on him by Jim Farley —his campaign manager and Democratic national chairman— was a glaring example of the consequences of the politics of patronage as applied to Puerto Rico. Governor Robert H. Gore (1933 – 34) was a gum-chewing tycoon with the manners of an insurance salesman who confessed that he did not even know the geographical location of the colony he was to govern. His ambition was to create a local Democratic party by a judicious handout of jobs.[10] His candidate for the board of directors of the university was a Socialist, at that time allied with the Republicans, who had left school at fourteen and was the author of an article called "The Mission of the Dog in Human Destiny." Determined to clear Liberals out of the university, Gore abolished their posts, including that of publicity director held by Muñoz Marín's wife, Muña Lee. "The university has no more use for a publicity director," he replied to his critics, "than I do for a poodle dog."

Gore's disastrous governorship highlights the peculiar nature of Puerto Rico's colonial system and the perversions of parliamentary rule that it fostered. Gore could argue that he was acting correctly in trying to rule via the Coalition, an ill-assorted electoral combination of Socialists (a Labor party), and Republicans—who represented what were called "the better elements of society." The Coalition was the majority party in the Puerto Rican legislature after 1932. The Liberals argued that the governor must be above politics in the sense that he must protect the rights of the minority by giving them jobs, without which no party in Puerto Rico could be held together. While the Coalition was the ally of the Republican party in the United States Congress, Muñoz Marín, on his frequent visits to Washington, had direct access to Roosevelt. Scarcely surprisingly, the politicians of the Coalition bitterly resented what to them appeared Muñoz Marín's backstairs intrigues in Washington against the local majority party. The Liberals did everything in their power to blacken Gore's reputation — a well-used technique of disgruntled island *políticos*. They regarded it as a patriotic duty to reduce the extensive powers the governor enjoyed in theory to impotence in practice. "Nowhere in the civilized world," wrote Tugwell, who became governor in 1941, "is there an executive with so little power." Gore came to the conclusion that Puerto Rican politics were a dirty game played with the distribution of jobs; his own experience in Florida should have told him that the game was not a special sport of Puerto Ricans.

It was Muñoz Marín, with his close contacts with New Dealers and journalists in Washington, who first saw that the New Deal could offer "a new panorama for Puerto Rico" if he could bring pressure to extend its benefits to his countrymen.[11] He hoped that the Costigan-Jones Sugar Act could be used to buy out the sugar corporations and restructure at least a sector of the sugar industry by splitting up the great sugar *latifundia* and redistributing their holdings to Puerto Rican farmers. This was the basis of the Chardón plan, so called after the Puerto Rican, Cornell-trained agronomist and chancellor of the university who was responsible for it.

Nothing illustrates more clearly the contradictions of colonialism than the fate of the Chardón plan and the New Deal in Puerto Rico. Congress, hostile to the New Deal, was indifferent to the concerns of an island inhabited by "foreigners for whom we are always being asked to do something without any return." Congressional hostility to the New Deal found allies in the Puerto Rican legislature. The Coalition's distrust of New Dealers was matched only by the right of the Republican party in Congress. The president's "creeping socialism," argued Luis Ferré, later to become the New Progressive Party (PNP) governor, threatened to turn Puerto Ricans into guinea pigs for anticapitalist experiments; food doles, the president of the local Chamber of Commerce declared, would undermine the Puerto Ricans' "love of work and self-reliance." Gore shared the views of his political allies in Puerto Rico. In order to keep radicals within his new Liberal party, Barceló had veered toward independence in 1932 and, as the chief of the Bureau of Insular Affairs observed, when not allowed to have his own way over jobs, became "a bitter critic of the United States' policies in Puerto Rico."[12] The combination of Coalition obstructionism and Barceló's politicking turned Puerto Rico into "a barrel of snakes for which no one could do much." By 1940, Secretary of the Interior Harold Ickes had given up the struggle to do "something for the masses…screened away from him by machinating *políticos*."[13] Nor was this all. The sugar companies' lawyers challenged the Chardón plans at every stage. Congressional hostility, bureaucratic battles, and Treasury parsimony brought the New Deal to a halt in Puerto Rico even before it had petered out on the mainland. The final blow was delivered by Dr. Gruening, appointed by Roosevelt as director of the new Division of Territories and Insular Possessions, which was transferred from the War Office to the Department of the Interior under Secretary Ickes. Given the hostility of the Coalition, the New Deal agencies in Puerto Rico had fallen into the hands of the Liberal supporters of the New Deal. Gruening, who was a friend of Muñoz Marín and had published his poetry, decided the time had come to clear Liberals — the only Puerto Rican politicians with any enthusiasm for the New Deal — out of the agencies. Chardón, the architect of the sugar plan, infuriated by the obstruction of lawyers acting under Gruening's instructions, resigned.

It is scarcely surprising that the New Deal did not tackle the structural problems of Puerto Rico's underdeveloped economy, since it was never intended radically to reform the society of the mainland.[14] The New Deal illustrates a classic dilemma of the relationship between Puerto Rico and the United States: a policy conceived to deal with the domestic economic problems of America — a highly industrialized continental state plagued by depression — could not cure a feeble island economy confronting the problems of a banana republic. Undoubtedly the two New Deal agencies, the Puerto Rican Emergency Relief Organization and its successor the Puerto Rican Reconstruction Organization, staved off complete disaster by providing food doles and employment in public works. But the $1 million a month pumped into the island was dismissed by Muñoz Marín as an extension of "palliatives based on charity." Governor Rexford G. Tugwell, who arrived in 1941, found the island still "sunk in hopeless poverty."

Far from easing tensions, the New Deal corresponded with the most troubled years in Puerto Rico's relationship with the United States. Never had the forces for independence seemed so potent. Barceló's Liberals, now committed to independence, though without a majority, were the most powerful single party in the island. Even the loyal Republicans, as their leader claimed, chafed under "the dullest incomprehension regarding our position [i.e., statehood] on the part of successive administrations in Washington." Earl Hanson, one of the few continental Americans with sympathy for an understanding of

Puerto Rico, found the atmosphere "tense and hateful." Puerto Rico, he reported, "must blow up before too long." "Public order," Muñoz Marín warned President Roosevelt in December 1934, "hangs today by a thread." The most serious threat came from the emergence of a militant Nationalist movement.

The Nationalist party, dedicated to the immediate independence of Puerto Rico, was founded in 1922; in 1930, its leader, Pedro Albizu Campos, injected what had been a near moribund party with a fresh militancy. After the dismal failure of the party in the 1932 elections — it won a mere 5,257 votes — Albizu denounced elections as "a periodical farce" and declared his total hostility to what he castigated as a colonial regime. In October 1936, three Nationalist demonstrators were shot by the police with what Albizu chose to regard as "the deliberate purpose of murdering the national representatives of Puerto Rico."[15] For every Nationalist killed, he threatened, a continental American would die. In February 1936, Colonel Riggs, chief of the police, was murdered by Nationalist gunmen.

The Washington response to these growing tensions was a bill put forward by Senator Tydings, a close friend of Riggs, granting Puerto Rico independence if it was requested in a plebiscite. Tydings had come to the conclusion that "the American system is not functioning properly in Puerto Rico."[16] Ickes seems to have thought that a plebiscite would clear the air and have a "quietening effect" on island politics. Instead, the bill split the Liberal party and alarmed the Coalition. Barceló came around to accepting it, but Muñoz Marín regarded it as a cheap trick, as an "imperialist reaction." The economic provisions, which would reduce Puerto Rico's freedom from U.S. tariffs by 25 percent annually, threatened economic ruin to an island already tied to the mainland market. The Tydings bill, Muñoz Marín wrote in a long memorandum to Ickes on January 5,

1937, was a piece of "political chicanery in extreme bad taste" designed to get a mandate for the existing colonial status "under the threat of literal starvation."[17]

The Tydings bill came as a cold splash of realism. It had the salutary effect of making Puerto Rican politicians, bred in the rhetoric of independence, contemplate its actual consequences. It was clear that independence on the terms of the *independentistas'* congressional ally, Vito Marcantonio of New York — independence with no tariff barriers and free immigration to the mainland — would never be accepted by Congress.

Muñoz Marín was a supporter of independence; but independence under the conditions offered in the Tydings bill could only be accepted by those who chose national freedom whatever the economic costs. Though Muñoz Marín made a powerful plea for independence in his memorandum to Ickes, though he still maintained that ending Puerto Rico's colonial status was "the supreme issue," he was beginning to realize that economic recovery was more important than an *immediate* solution of the status question and that independence must not be a "cruel dogma" standing in the way of fruitful cooperation with an administration ready to help Puerto Rico out of poverty. But the hopes that Muñoz Marín held for support from the president and American liberals petered out in the aftermath of the Riggs assassination: well-intentioned Americans could not forgive Muñoz Marín for his failure to condemn the Nationalists.

Governor Blanton Winship (1934 – 39), another unhappy choice by Roosevelt, appeared to Puerto Ricans to be a military autocrat, worse than the "Czars and Sultans" of 1898 – 1900; at least they had not shot down demonstrators in the main streets of Ponce as the police did on Palm Sunday, 1937, killing seventeen of Albizu's militant followers, bitterly resentful of the imprisonment of their leader on a charge of seeking to overthrow the federal government in Puerto Rico. As Ickes acknowledged, the island was in the grip of the "vicious round" of Nationalist violence, met by the counterviolence of Winship and the head of the new Division of Territories, Dr. Gruening, who had come to the conclusion that "the mailed fist," as Ickes reported, "is the proper policy in dealing with these subject peoples." Nor had the established politicians sloughed off their reputation, in American eyes, for factiousness: politics was the island's "greatest industry."[18] The 1930s represented to Tugwell "the twilight of confused colonialism; the occupiers were defeated by their own bungling and by the everlasting self-interest and intimate knowledge of the occupied. The shell of authority was empty." This was the vicious circle of Puerto Rican politics. The refusal of Congress to address Puerto Rican problems, its negative response to all appeals to improve on the constitutional settlement of 1917, encouraged Puerto Rican politicians to indulge in the petty politics of a colonial opposition. Their "factiousness" then became an excuse for doing nothing. All went back to what Muñoz was later to call the normality of "colonial confusion."[19]

Thus, the years between the Jones Act and the coming of World War II were largely wasted years. A private letter in bad taste from an American doctor stationed in Puerto Rico, boasting that his cure for the population problem was to kill off Puerto Ricans, was published as proof that genocide was official policy. Schoolmasters who arrived from the United States with the best of intentions gave up the struggle to educate sullen classes. "If Americans are going to wait for signs of affection and appreciation," wrote one of them, "before they handle the problem of Puerto Rico, the solution will be forever postponed."[20]

The first attempt to advance beyond relief to a restructuring of the economy as a cure for poverty came in the last phase of classic colonialism, between 1941 and 1948. These years were dominated by the political personality of Luis Muñoz Marín, as president and PPD majority leader of the Senate. His achievements would have been impossible without the cooperation of Rexford G. Tugwell, governor of Puerto Rico from 1941 to 1946. Tugwell was an economist, a New Dealer who had been a member of President Roosevelt's Brain Trust. He claimed that during his governorship he had presided over a "peaceful revolution.... transforming a backward polity and economy into a leading one."[21] The core of this revolution was Tugwell's faith in public corporations and state-financed industry; autonomous planning boards, under democratic control, would avoid the straitjacket of "doctrinaire socialism" and the chaos engendered by laissez-faire capitalism. Applied to Puerto Rico, his ideas would inject new life into the ailing economy of the island. The government would set up industries that would use native skills and raw materials. The money would be provided by the windfall profits of the war. Without whiskey, Americans were drinking rum: the excise on rum duties were remitted to the island government.

Nor was it only money and employment, created by the construction of an enlarged naval base and an airfield, that the war boom brought to Puerto Rico. As in 1917, the island's strategic importance to the Navy caused policy-makers in Washington to listen to Tugwell's pleas that something must be done to cure Puerto Rican discontents by new policies. The choice was economic aid or "suppressing an angry people" in the midst of a war fought for the survival of democracy and in which some 60,000 Puerto Ricans were serving in the U.S. armed forces.

For his "revolution," Tugwell needed and gained what no previous governor had obtained — the cooperation, for constructive purposes, of an island politician who commanded a majority in the legislature: Muñoz Marín.

As a result of his quarrel with Barceló over the Tydings bill, Muñoz Marín was expelled from the Liberal party. He founded his own party, the PPD, in 1938. In the 1940 election, though the PPD obtained only 214,857 votes against the Coalition's 222,423, an arrangement with a dissident group gave Muñoz Marín a narrow working majority and the presidency of the Senate.[22] Muñoz Marín was no longer the agent of the Puerto Rican opposition in Washington, scheming against the governor and majority party in Puerto Rico. The contentious period of Puerto Rican politics seemed to have given way to a new era of constructive politics.

Tugwell could then set about strengthening the governor's power as the only instrument for reform, fighting the American members of the Executive Council who sought to tie him down with red tape. He loosened the legislature's control over the budget, a control that had paralyzed constructive policies. Muñoz Marín and Tugwell encouraged a whole new generation of competent and dedicated public servants and administrators, without whom the subsequent development of Puerto Rico is inconceivable: Teodoro Moscoso, a Michigan pharmacy graduate, was put in charge of the industrialization program; Enrique de Toro, at twenty-five, was named head of the finance division of the Planning Board; Jaime Benítez became chancellor of the university; Rafael Picó, a geographer from Clark University, was made head of the Planning Board; and Roberto Sánchez Vilella, an engineer from Ohio State, municipalized San Juan's bus services. The average age of the new team was thirty-one and they had all, with few exceptions, been educated in stateside universities.

Thus, in those years a new pattern was set that was to persist into the 1960s. Tugwell's "peaceful revolution" was a revolution from above, guided by a strengthened executive power and administered by trained civil servants, most of them familiar with the then-current reformist trends in American public administration. As far as Muñoz Marín's need for control of political patronage allowed, merit and professionalism replaced a system in which government posts were considered favors to be distributed for services rendered to political parties.

It was this team that put into practice Tugwell's ideas about autonomous public corporations as motors of economic progress under the overall direction of Picó's Planning Board. Altogether, fourteen public corporations were established between 1941 and 1946, including the Development Corporation, later popularly known as Fomento. The Development Corporation was to promote investment by Puerto Rican residents "to avoid the evils of absentee ownership"; the government, through the Development Corporation, undertook to run cement, glass, paper, pottery, and shoe factories. The Agricultural Corporation began to put into practice the agrarian radicalism which had won the PPD the votes of the *jíbaros*; it set about redistributing the land of the large absentee sugar corporations to small cane-growers' cooperatives.

The prospects of these enterprises — faultily conceived as they may have been and beyond the managerial capacity of their Puerto Rican employees as they proved to be — were not improved by the persistence of what Tugwell called "the twilight of a confused colonialism." The contradictions of colonialism surfaced in the opposition to what the governor's opponents castigated as a dangerous experiment in state socialism. "Red Rex" Tugwell's policies were challenged in Congress, where he became the bête noire of Republicans like Taft. In collusion with Muñoz Marín, as president of the Senate, and with "the disgraceful complicity of the Legislative Assembly," which could pass forty "revolutionary" bills in a session, "Red

Rex" was seeking, his opponents maintained, to "establish a corporate state of a Fascist type, ruled by a single party." He was, Taft believed, a pro-Russian "in favor of the redistribution of wealth and the totalitarian state."

The troubled spirits in Congress could count on the cooperation of the governor's political enemies in Puerto Rico. They fed congressmen and senators with allegations that Tugwell was engaged in building an unconstitutional "supergovernment," that his "unorthodox" program had as its "principal aim the intensification of the class struggle," that the creation of the Water Resources Authority to replace municipal undertakings that supplied undrinkable water was "the start of tyranny in Puerto Rico." The Bell Committee of Congress, Tugwell claimed, "nearly destroyed all that Muñoz Marín and I had built."[23]

It was the suspicious hostility of Congress that destroyed any hopes of granting greater freedom to Puerto Rico. In 1943, a presidential committee recommended that Puerto Ricans elect their own governor — a demand that Tugwell endorsed — and that any alteration in the constitutional status of Puerto Rico must have the consent of the people of Puerto Rico. This was the first appearance of the doctrine of the compact that would be, for Muñoz Marín, the constitutional basis of Commonwealth status.[24] These recommendations were regarded as attempts to clip the powers of Congress and ran into stiff opposition. The vicious circle of colonial politics in Puerto Rico had made the years between the Jones Act and 1944 years of waste. The refusal of Congress to address Puerto Rican problems, its negative response to all appeals to improve on the constitutional settlement of 1917, encouraged Puerto Rican politicians to play the petty politics of colonial opposition and to indulge in what Tugwell himself called the "colonial whine."

That most congressmen turned a deaf ear to the colonial

whine, even when it represented genuine grievance, is not surprising. Puerto Rico was a voteless territory with no constituents to cultivate; the standard excuse for inaction, often used in the controversies over the application of the New Deal to the island, was that since Puerto Ricans paid no federal taxes they were not deserving of federal largess, a view shared by the Treasury bureaucrats. Few congressmen knew much about island conditions or had visited it in the days before the tourist boom and Muñoz Marín's careful cultivation of his Washington friends.

There was a more legitimate excuse for inaction before 1940. What was one to make of a democracy where politicians made unprincipled electoral alliances and proceeded to win elections by the wholesale buying of votes with money supplied by the sugar interests? Whom did these *políticos* represent? What, indeed, did they want? The election of 1936, for example, was so complicated and confused that, with the best will in the world, it was difficult to discern its significance.[25] To add to the puzzlement, Puerto Rican politicians came to Washington to advocate solutions to the status problem that were mutually incompatible, presenting them in a rhetoric that seemed foreign to American ears.

The ambiguities of these conflicting attitudes served to confuse — as they still confuse — Americans. Those taking any interest in the island were puzzled. The Puerto Rican politicians they met in Washington or San Juan greeted them with what a distinguished Puerto Rican calls "the customary tug of the forelock." Yet behind their backs these same politicians denounced them as imperialists. This came to them, as it came to Tugwell on his arrival, as an unwelcome revelation. "I was," he wrote, "taken by surprise to find that Puerto Ricans felt themselves badly treated by the United States — I didn't know any imperialists."[26]

This reveals what was a deeper reason for hesitations, for the inaction of indifference, for "the parochialism" of which Theodore Roosevelt complained. What was Puerto Rico? Was it, as an unincorporated territory, a "part" of the United States? Or was it a colony, as Jamaica or Trinidad were colonies, and as such in some way incompatible with the anticolonial tradition still alive in a country that had once itself been a colony? For uneasy consciences, confronted with a complicated issue, the natural escape was to do nothing—a policy encouraged by the endless delays and procedural complications of Congress itself. The only alternative was that adopted by Tydings. Puerto Rico was a trouble spot where loyal Americans were shot by fanatics, and which, moreover, did not fit easily into the American system. Why not, by granting independence, get rid of it once and for all? But by 1939, this was impossible: the Navy had discovered that Puerto Rico was an indispensable base in the Caribbean.

If the preconditions of the politics of indifference did not vanish, they were weakened with the ascendancy of Muñoz Marín and the PPD. During the years when the governors, the local legislature, Congress, and the bureaucrats combined to frustrate the New Deal in Puerto Rico, it is scarcely surprising that its application yielded such disappointing results, or that the demands of Puerto Rico for a greater degree of self-government went unanswered. Congress could still do its best to stymie the experiments of Tugwell and Muñoz Marín, consoling itself that the "respectable" politicians in Puerto Rico were the bitter opponents of Muñoz, who had been victorious by the slimmest of electoral margins in 1940 and who relied on the parliamentary support of a minority group to survive. With the crushing victory of the PPD in 1944, these arguments could not hold. Puerto Rico was then represented by a politician with a vision that rose above the "factiousness" and local ambitions of his predecessors, and a party that had fought and won the cleanest election in Puerto Rican history. Like his father, Muñoz Rivera, Muñoz Marín would use the "voice" that represented the wishes of the majority of his fellow island-ers to force Puerto Rico into the attention of Congress and the American people in general. Moreover, he had an advantage his father, struggling with a foreign language in a foreign and strange capital, never possessed: friends in Washington.

With these advantages, Muñoz Marín confronted a formi-dable task: to overcome the psychological legacy of the wasted years between the Jones Act of 1917 and his own accession to power. If tragedy is too strong a word, the essential difficulty that dogs and overhangs the relationship between Puerto Rico and the United States is the barrier created by a difference of perception on both sides. Conditioned by their history, Puerto Ricans have become a nation of paranoiacs to whom the United States is the oppressor, albeit that oppression is recognized as the consequence of indifference rather than of design. Yet at the same time, something of the early enthusiasm for the Amer-ican way of life, for the "Republic of Republics," remains in some form or another in most Puerto Ricans. It burns at its brightest in the hearts of the statehooders; it smolders in the minds of all but the most resolute *independentistas*.

3.

INTERNAL DECOLONIZATION: 1948–80

When President Franklin D. Roosevelt died in 1945, Puerto Rico was still governed by the framework set up by the Organic Act of 1917. Congressional hostility to Governor Tugwell, combined with the strategic importance of Puerto Rico to the United States Navy, blocked attempts at enlarging self-government for Puerto Rico. However, the end of a war fought for the survival of democracy and the breeze that was the precursor of the gale of decolonization opened up new prospects. President Truman acted in the spirit of the charter of the United Nations when he declared that Puerto Ricans should be allowed to settle their own future.

The obvious first step on the road to self-government would be to allow the Puerto Rican voters to elect their own chief executive — the governor — rather than have the governor appointed by the president of the United States. Proposals for an elective governor had been before Congress for a decade, but reluctance to face up to the problems of Puerto Rico had always delayed action. Now these proposals were opposed by Senator Robert A. Taft. Only by persuading Senator Dennis Chavez to pronounce the fatal word "over" on a bill for Army reform supported by Taft did Resident Commissioner Antonio Fernós Isern persuade Taft to withdraw his objections in order to get the Elective Governor Act rushed through Congress at midnight on the last day of the session of the House in July.[1] The bill was signed by Truman on August 5, 1947. The Elective Governor Act was to remain the most important transfer of power, as opposed to any modification of the formal relationship with the United States, ever granted to Puerto Rico by Congress.

Muñoz Marín's influence had been based on his position as president of the Puerto Rican Senate. In 1949, he became the first elected governor. Undisputed leader of a party — the *populares* (PPD) — with an overwhelming majority in both houses of the legislature, his power in Puerto Rico became almost absolute. That power was institutionalized by the reforms recommended in 1949 by a commission chaired by James H. Rowe, Jr., a Washington attorney. The reforms created a hierarchical administrative structure in Puerto Rico, centralizing authority in the hands of the chief executive.[2] It proved easier for American public administration experts to implant what they considered to be a model structure in Puerto Rico than on the mainland itself.

While new attitudes to colonialism and the firm grasp of Muñoz Marín over the political life of Puerto Rico favored Truman's desire that Puerto Ricans settle their own future, that future was to be determined in large measure by a dramatic shift in the economic policies of the Puerto Rican government itself. The "socialist" experiments of the war years had failed to cure rural unemployment. If Puerto Rico was to climb out of poverty and massive unemployment, it had to industrialize, and industrialize rapidly.

The investment needed for such a crash program could only come from *private* American investors. The Aid to Industry Program of 1945 was the first step: private "absentee" capital, which the earlier "socialist" program had sought to drive out, was now to be attracted by the building and leasing of factories on favorable terms to businesses that were prepared to come to Puerto Rico. But the measure that would revolutionize the Puerto Rican economy came in 1947: the Industrial Incentives Act. This act granted a ten-year exemption from local taxes to firms establishing businesses on the island. This local tax exemption combined with the fact that such firms had other advantages: they would not be required to pay federal corporate taxes, and they would benefit from hiring labor at wages well below stateside wages. These were strong inducements — and a well-organized publicity campaign brought them home to prospective investors.

Thus, a pattern was established that would last to the present day: forced industrial development, promoted by government agencies, that would lock the Puerto Rican economy into that of the American mainland; for it was the United States that supplied the private capital and the free market for Puerto Rican products, which, since 1902, have been exempt from U.S. tariff duties. To *independentistas*, this pattern was to convert a "classical" colony, dependent on the agricultural exports of a plantation system, into an "industrial" colony, dependent on foreign investment and cheap native labor. To Muñoz Marín, it presented a puzzle in political engineering. How could Puerto Rico loosen its "colonial" ties with the United States and achieve a greater degree of self-government *without* severing the economic ties that had become the condition of growth?

The new economic policy — popularly termed Operation Bootstrap — was a spectacular success: "a century of economic development in a single decade" was *The Economist*'s verdict in 1957. Between 1947 and 1959, the gross national product (GNP) doubled in Puerto Rico, and in 1958 Puerto Rico's per capita income was the highest in Latin America. It was this impressive growth that led Muñoz Marín, always concerned with the economic consequences of "naked" independence, to abandon his conviction that independence was the *only* dignified escape from what he called "the spiritually corrupting atmosphere of a colony." Some constitutional arrangement that would allow Puerto Rico greater autonomy than it enjoyed under the Organic Acts (the Foraker Act and the Jones Act of 1917) and yet permit the permanent association with the United States that had become an economic necessity might provide the only practical exit from the colonial closet. In 1936, Muñoz Marín had rejected any expansion of autonomy as "fraudulent"; it would be liberty "on a long chain," leaving Puerto Rico still at the mercy of Congress. By 1948, he had convinced himself and the majority of his party that autonomy embodied in a novel political formula — the Estado Libre Asociado (ELA), literally translated as Free Associated State, but known as Commonwealth — could solve the puzzle. Commonwealth would reconcile the democratic rights of the people of Puerto Rico with the economic necessities of continued association with the United States.

After the overwhelming victory of the PPD in the elections of 1948, Muñoz Marín embarked on the political process that would lead to the establishment of the Commonwealth in 1952. Resident Commissioner Fernós Isern in Washington had already established the groundwork for what he termed an "intermediate solution." His *point de départ* was that Puerto Rico did not have a constitution as the democratic act of a sovereign people. The core of his proposal was: "To found the political regime of Puerto Rico, not on the Organic Act granted by Congress but on a constitution adopted by the people of Puerto Rico; and economic and political relations on an organic bilateral pact that consecrates a principle [i.e., democratic self-determination] and continues a reality already in existence [i.e., permanent political and economic union with the United States]."

Such a "third way" was presented as the only practical escape from colonial status. Neither statehood nor independence — apart from their supposedly disastrous economic consequences — would be bestowed by Congress, since neither could muster the overwhelming vote on the island that alone would overcome congressional reluctance. "If we seek statehood," Muñoz Marín said, "we die waiting for Congress, and if we adopt independence we die from starvation — in any case we die."[3] He viewed the "third way," therefore, as the only possible course to reconcile the demand for democracy with the inescapable fact that Congress was the sovereign power. Muñoz Marín argued that Puerto Rican democracy must come within the American system in permanent association with the United States.[4] This implied establishing, in Muñoz Marín's words, a status that was not less than that of a federated state but simply "different." As a compromise between the sovereignty of Congress and the self-determination that was the "moral basis of liberty," this new animal was, from the outset, difficult to define in terms of the constitutional law of the United States.

The road to Commonwealth was opened by Public Law 600, approved by Congress on July 3, 1950. Public Law 600 separated the issue of a domestic constitution for Puerto Rico from that of the constitutional relationship of Puerto Rico to the United States. Public Law 600 was to be ratified by a plebiscite in Puerto Rico, after which an island Constituent Assembly would draw up a constitution to be submitted to Congress for approval. The constitution would then, if necessary, be amended by Congress, and finally it would be submitted to a referendum in Puerto Rico. Puerto Rico's relationship with the United States would be embodied in a new statute — the Federal Relations Act — that would replace the Organic Acts of 1900 and 1917. Since Public Law 600 had to be accepted by a plebiscite in Puerto Rico, this act of self-determination, it was held, would give democratic validity to the association with the United States as set out in the Federal Relations Act — a validity that was indispensable in the decolonizing climate of the postwar years and that the United States was busily encouraging in other imperial powers such as Great Britain.

Representative Vito Marcantonio of New York, the ally of the Puerto Rican independence movement, dismissed the procedures set up by Public Law 600 as a fraudulent reassertion of the status quo, a bogus sanctification of an unaltered colonial relationship. This, he argued, was apparent in the language of the House Committee report: "This bill under consideration would not change Puerto Rico's fundamental political social and economic relationships with the United States.... "[5] Nevertheless, Fernós Isern and Muñoz Marín, though the language they used in Washington sought to conceal it, believed that the whole basis of the relationship would change; if the Puerto Rican people endorsed Public Law 600 in a plebiscite, then they had freely and democratically accepted association with the United States. What had been a relationship dictated by a congressional law would be transformed into a relationship "in the nature of a compact" (the more precise legal term "contract" was avoided) between the Puerto Rican people and Congress — a compact, they were to argue, that could not be altered without the consent of each of the contracting parties. The bill passed in both houses of Congress after a two-hour debate;

neither senators nor representatives explored the meaning of the phrase "in the nature of a compact."

Public Law 600 was submitted to referendum in Puerto Rico on August 30, 1950. The *independentistas* of the Puerto Rican Independence Party (PIP) boycotted the referendum. The Nationalists unleashed in Puerto Rico an abortive protest, an uprising in which twenty-seven people were killed, and on November 2, terrorists, one of them with a note from Albizu Campos in his pocket, attempted to assassinate President Truman at Blair House. Of the island's 777,675 registered voters, 65.08 percent voted, and of these 76.5 percent voted yes. As *independentistas* pointed out, the referendum received support from only 49.76 percent of the registered voters, most of whom probably voted for Muñoz Marín rather than for the new constitutional arrangements as such. Given the abstention of the PIP, the Constituent Assembly came to consist of seventy members of the PPD, fifteen Republicans and seven Socialists. The Constituent Assembly could not consider the "options" of statehood or independence, which were foreclosed when the people of Puerto Rico accepted Public Law 600. Its concern was the *domestic* constitution of Puerto Rico. It drew up a thoroughly democratic constitution based on universal suffrage and the division of powers.

One feature of that constitution deserves special attention. It sought to avoid the legislative paralysis that can afflict Congress by the creation of a strong executive. Given that Muñoz Marín enjoyed a safe majority in both houses, he would preside over "the strongest executive in the American constitutional system." Muñoz Marín enjoyed the power of a British prime minister in that he could turn government bills into law through the use of an obedient majority, but he was untrammeled by the British doctrine of the collective responsibility of the cabinet. Muñoz never consulted his cabinet collectively but dealt individually with the secretaries of departments. It was this concentration of power that gave him the instrument to transform the society of Puerto Rico.[6]

When the Puerto Rican draft constitution was submitted to Congress, it became clear that the sovereign will of the Puerto Rican people *at this stage* was still subject to congressional review. A bill of rights was included in the draft: it established the right to work, free education, and various benefits for the unemployed and pregnant women. Congress insisted that these rights be modified. To defend congressional powers, Senator Olin D. Johnston, a Democrat from South Carolina, wished to insert a clause that the Puerto Rican constitution could not be changed without the consent of Congress. Senator Johnston seems to have shared the views of Representative John T. Wood, an Idaho Republican, that "they [the Puerto Ricans] are setting up a people's democracy which is foreign to our idea of a representative government"; to Johnston, Puerto Rico was a "gigantic incubator of people who do not understand American traditions or ideals but who are glad to qualify for American residence or American charity."[7] Johnston's amendment would have undermined the whole concept of a compact.

In a rare outburst of rage, Muñoz Marín cabled from Puerto Rico that, rather than accept the amendments, he was prepared to reject the new arrangements. The amendment was dropped and in its place a clause inserted that no amendment of the Puerto Rican constitution could be incompatible with Public Law 600, the Federal Relations Act, those dispositions of the United States Constitution applicable to Puerto Rico, or the terms of the congressional act approving the constitution of Puerto Rico. This saved appearances and, for the time being, the constitutional doctrines of the PPD. The congressional amendments to the constitution were submitted to a referendum in Puerto Rico, and the Commonwealth was formally established on July 25, 1952 — the anniversary of the day on which American troops had landed in Puerto Rico.

To Muñoz Marín the new relationship, symbolized in the flag that he hoisted over the old Spanish fortress and in the "national" anthem of Puerto Rico, signified the end of colonialism. To President Truman "the people of the United States and the people of Puerto Rico are entering into a new relationship that will serve as an inspiration to all who love freedom and hate tyranny. We are giving new substance to man's hope for a world with liberty and equality under law. Those who truly love freedom know that the right relationship between a government and its people is one based on mutual consent and esteem." Puerto Rico had ceased to be a colony, the United Nations was told in 1953; it had, through "informed and democratic processes," freely associated itself with the United States.[8] Public Law 600 had done the trick, as the *New York Times* had put it, of scotching Communist charges of "Yankee imperialism." The whole enterprise that had started with Public Law 600 was a brilliant performance in psychopolitics conducted by a master politician. This was revealed in the term Free Associated State. Statehooders had the word "state" and the new Commonwealth was inaugurated on the day American troops landed to bring "liberty" to an oppressed colony. Since one of Muñoz's main problems was to neutralize the *independentistas* in his own party, they were granted the old separatist flag and their "anthem" — "*La Borinqueña*." Just as autonomists could find comfort in the word "Associated," so the *independentistas* could point to the word "free." World opinion in general and most Puerto Ricans, about to enter a period of unparallelled prosperity, accepted Commonwealth as a magnificent political invention, solving Muñoz's puzzle of reconciling Puerto Rican democracy with a continued economic association with the United States.

From the outset, critics charged that the new constitution of the Free Associated State added very litle in the way of self-determination for the Puerto Rican people.[9] Muñoz Marín's political opponents — the Republican statehooders and the *independentistas* — rejected ELA as a "farce," an elaborate camouflage of an unchanged colonial situation, an exercise in constitutional cosmetics designed to deceive international opinion and confuse Puerto Ricans.

The self-congratulatory rhetoric of the PPD and Truman concealed ambiguities in Puerto Rico's relationship with the United States that have not been resolved — ambiguities revealed in the choice of "Commonwealth" as the English translation. The term "free state" was too exotic to be absorbed into the terminology of the U.S. Constitution, in which the word "state" has a precise meaning. The Commonwealth of Puerto Rico did not resemble the Commonwealth of Massachusetts, nor was it remotely similar to the Commonwealth of Australia, a sovereign state with its own army and diplomatic corps. To argue that Puerto Rico had become another Canada — a model that had appealed to Autonomists since the 1890s — was clearly absurd.

Muñoz Marín himself employed ambiguous and contradictory language. While he assured Congress that the new status meant no more than that the law had caught up with existing practices and that it was "a much shorter step" than the Elective Governor Act of 1947 had been, he also spoke of a "new kind of state . . . equal but different from statehood . . . sovereignty within sovereignty." When a journalist quoted the encyclopedia definition of sovereignty, he lost his temper. "What I define as a political leader, what the political leadership in Puerto Rico defines as sovereignty, that is for the Puerto Rican people what sovereignty is."[10]

Conscious of the reluctance of some in Congress to accept

the notion of "compact" as implying the more precise legal
term "contract," of the limitations that congressional control
still imposed on the actions of the Puerto Rican legislature,
and of the impact of federal laws on all aspects of Puerto Rican
life, Muñoz Marín would devote the rest of his political career
to rid the notion of "compact" of all ambiguities.[11] He sought
to expand Puerto Rico's control over its own destiny, freeing
it from federal controls by a process that came to be called
"perfection" or "culmination" of ELA. By 1954, a group of
PPD intellectuals and party members was working, in secret,
on plans to expand autonomy beyond the limits set in 1952. By
1959, Carl J. Friedrich of Harvard, who had praised Puerto
Rico's "middle road to freedom" as a new, flexible, and "dynamic" experiment in federalism, had, like Muñoz himself,
come to the view that Puerto Rico's political status should be
radically altered. According to Friedrich, federal laws, enforced
by federal agencies, "affect the life of every Puerto Rican every
day of his life. The fact that all these activities are carried
forward by officials appointed without the consent of Puerto
Rico, that the policies which they express are adopted without
the consent of Puerto Rico, indicates *the severe limits within
which autonomy is at present defined* [emphasis added]."[12] It
would become increasingly evident that Muñoz had ratified a
system that, over time, would permit the imposition of massive
federal controls merely as a function of the expansion of national legislation to cover new fields.

In 1959, to end what Muñoz called the "eternal bickering"
over the status question and to expand the "severe limits" of
the autonomy bestowed in 1952, Fernós Isern and Senator
James E. Murray proposed a bill that attempted to clarify the
legal and constitutional basis of Commonwealth and to secure
an extension of its existing powers.[13] Their aim was to turn the
vague phrase "in the nature of a compact" into a true contract

between two sovereign bodies: the Puerto Rican people — whose demands were put forward in a joint resolution of the island legislature — and the Congress of the United States. The phrases "dynamic" and "flexible," so often used by the propagandists of ELA to praise their creation, would be given substance by their bill, which would increase Puerto Rico's autonomy by giving Puerto Rico some power over its tariffs, shipping rates, minimum wages, and so on. Relations between Puerto Rico and the United States would be governed by the "Articles of Permanent Association of the People of Puerto Rico with the United States," and most important, amendment of the relationship between the United States and Puerto Rico would have to be submitted to a referendum in Puerto Rico. If the Fernós-Murray bill had been approved, it would have made clear Congress' intention in passing Public Law 600 — an intention that congressional debates had left tantalizingly vague and imprecise. The Commonwealth would be based on a bilateral compact that could not be altered unilaterally by Congress. No one would be able to maintain that Puerto Rico was still an unincorporated territory subject to Congress, and that the processes set in motion by Public Law 600 had been a meaningless exercise in political prestidigitation.

The Fernós-Murray bill ran into opposition in Congress and from Muñoz Marín's political enemies in Puerto Rico as well as, understandably perhaps, from federal employees on the island, who saw their jobs jeopardized by the proposal that Puerto Rico gradually take over federal functions. The Department of the Interior objected to what seemed to be an attempt to "foreclose any future consideration of the status question," to "freeze" the status issue to the exclusive benefit of the PPD. Congressmen visiting Puerto Rico became aware of local opposition to the bill, in particular a pro-statehood groundswell. Given this opposition, Muñoz Marín dropped the Fernós-Murray bill. This was the first sign of a lack of resolution in the PPD leadership at a time when its electoral position in Puerto Rico was unchallenged.

With a sympathetic president in the White House — Kennedy admired Muñoz, consulted him on Latin American affairs and in 1963 awarded him the Presidential Medal of Freedom — Muñoz and Fernós Isern renewed their attack to settle the status question once and for all by means of a plebiscite that would allow Puerto Ricans to choose between the three options of statehood, independence, and a *perfected* Commonwealth. A democratic choice between the three options answered the objection that, in accepting ELA in the 1952 referendum, Puerto Ricans had not been allowed to express their preferences as between ELA, independence, and statehood; they had been asked only to endorse one solution—that of Commonwealth, proposed by the PPD. Congress, having perfected Commonwealth, would agree to accept whatever status gained the support of the majority of Puerto Ricans in the plebiscite.

In order for Muñoz Marín to succeed in securing a plebiscite to "end" the status debate—which had come to obsess Puerto Rican politics as never before—it was necessary for him, given the intransigent opposition of the *independentistas*, to win over the statehood Republicans of *Partido Estadista Republicano* (PER) for a joint approach to Congress. This he secured in the Pact of Trujillo Alto, so called after his house outside San Juan where the agreement was made.

The statehooders of the PER soon realized that they had handed to Muñoz Marín an instrument to convert ELA into a *permanent* solution. A plebiscite in which the power and patronage of the PPD and the prestige of Muñoz Marín could ensure victory for ELA would mean the final defeat of statehood. Muñoz Marín hedged on the issue of "permanence,"[14] but the PER leaders had no doubts. They broke the Pact of Trujillo Alto and lobbied against Muñoz Marín in Washington. They sensed the ebb of the PPD tide. A cartoon presented the ship of the PPD sinking with its Captain Muñoz, ELA inscribed on his cap, swimming in desperation to a raft called "plebiscite." All the while, the *independentistas* stuck to their position that Congress must, by what was called "the transfer of power," grant Puerto Rico sovereign independence *before* any plebiscite could express the free and democratic choice of Puerto Ricans.

The whole episode was a painful experience for Muñoz Marín and Fernós Isern; it demonstrated the weakness of "perfection" as a political strategy. Muñoz Marín himself recognized that Congress would be bound only "morally" to accept the results of the plebiscite. He soon encountered congressional objections to the constitutionality of the new compact: "He's talking seventeenth century metaphysics"; the compact was "vague."[15] The *San Juan Star* expressed the opinion that Muñoz Marín's interpretation of the compact would be unacceptable to Congress: "For the past ten years a painful correspondence has been going on between Puerto Rico and Congress in which neither has understood a word the other was saying." "Even Kennedy," recalled Governor Sánchez Vilella, "did not know what we were after."[16] In the congressional hearings, the statehooders and the *independentistas* revealed to the administration that the plans for a new compact would not be accepted by a significant sector of island opinion. The bill (H.R. 5945), unsupported by the administration, was scrapped.

Instead of a plebiscite, which would include the option of a *perfected* Commonwealth, Muñoz Marín settled for a commission that would investigate the three alternative statuses. This was the United States–Puerto Rico Commission on the Status of Puerto Rico. Muñoz Marín had once more surrendered to the opposition. Fernós Isern was deeply depressed, left, as he was, with the "huge task" of beginning all over again.[17]

Under the chairmanship of James E. Rowe, Jr., already familiar with Puerto Rico's problems from his chairmanship of the committee on governmental reform of 1949, the task of the commission, which worked from June 1964 until August 1966, was to investigate not only the political aspects of the status question, but the economic and cultural consequences of each of the status options: Commonwealth, statehood, and independence.[18] It made the most exhaustive study of Puerto Rico ever undertaken, and its hearings and the supporting papers are a mine that historians and analysts have exploited ever since. The doubts the commission were to clarify were set out by Representative Leo W. O'Brien of New York. He clearly stated in the House Subcommittee on Insular Affairs:

No one, in or out of Congress, or in or out of Puerto Rico, knows exactly what the Commonwealth of Puerto Rico is. There are many opinions, some of them very firm and loud. I have been Chairman of the Subcommittee on Territorial and Insular Affairs for 9 years and I have spent many hours, here and in Puerto Rico, seeking an answer to these questions: What is Puerto Rico? What is its ultimate destiny?

Some have told us that what we did here in 1950 was meaningless rhetoric and statutory double-talk. They insist that Puerto Rico is still, in fact, a colony, a possession, and that the self-government that we granted illusionary [sic] and subject to instant cancellation at the whim of Congress. Others argue that when we created the first and only Commonwealth under the American flag we entered into an irrevocable compact from which there could be no withdrawal and that we actually fitted a sovereign nation into the American mosaic.

Somewhere, the overwhelming majority of the Puerto Rican people believe that the future of that island lies in permanent association with the United States. But the differences in their approach are sharp and unsettling. One group proposes that the answer lies in a perfected Commonwealth.... Another group, equally fervid and patriotic, insists that the Commonwealth is not and cannot be a permanent union, and that such union lies only in ultimate statehood.[19]

Not least because the *independentista* representative, Gilberto Concepción de Gracia, left the commission, it reached a unanimous recommendation, holding that *all three* options — statehood, independence, and Commonwealth — were equally dignified and valid solutions among which it was up to the Puerto Rican people to choose. The implementation of this decision would require the mutual accord and full cooperation of the United States, but the commission saw no legal or constitutional barriers to the grant of statehood, independence, or enhanced Commonwealth status. It pointed to the difficult economic consequences of a sudden change of status to statehood or independence, and the necessity of a transition period, in the case of independence, of at least fifteen years. Apart from abolishing the tax holidays, which the Commonwealth witnesses insisted were the essential instruments of continued prosperity, statehood would entail payment of substantial federal taxes that would more than outweigh the federal payments Puerto Rico would receive. The Bureau for the Budget calculated that statehood would "cost" Puerto Rico $188 million every year.

Both the United States and Puerto Rico, the Commission held, were equally concerned about the continued economic growth of the island, a mutual interest best satisfied over the following two decades by Commonwealth. This did not exclude the option of statehood or independence when a sufficient level of economic well-being was reached. In what proved to be a singularly optimistic forecast, the commission predicted that level would be reached in 1980. The commission reached this conclusion to ensure that statehooders would sign the report and thus make it unanimous. It turned out to be a hopelessly optimistic prediction.

It would be helpful, the commission concluded, to have "an expression of opinion" in a plebiscite as to whether Puerto Rico wished to maintain the Commonwealth, which could be improved, or to change to statehood or independence. Once the Puerto Rican people had decided on their future status, a series of ad hoc committees would be set up by the president of the United States and the governor of Puerto Rico. If the Puerto Ricans chose independence or statehood, then the ad hoc committees would work out the appropriate transitional measures; if they chose Commonwealth, then the ad hoc committees would recommend measures for its development—the "perfection" of Commonwealth.

How did the conclusions of the commission appear to the proponents of each of the three options?

Muñoz Marín immediately pressed for the plebiscite. Victory would give Commonwealth a final democratic legitimacy. "Perfection," however, would be left to a future agreement between Congress and Puerto Rico. This left the radical wing of the PPD, for whom the Free Associated State must be expanded to something little short of independence, dissatisfied. As the radical wing saw it, the plebiscite rejected the sovereignty of the Puerto Rican people and implied the acceptance of unperfected Commonwealth "with all its imperfections and its unquestionable political inferiority."[20]

The statehooders of the PER split on the issue: on the one hand, Miguel Angel García Mendez, a gifted, old-fashioned orator and veteran leader of the PER, rejected the commission report on the grounds that "perfected" status was still a hypothetical option since its terms had not been agreed upon by Congress. This would have made holding the plebiscite impossible had it not been for Luis Ferré, who, heading the rival faction of the PER statehooders, challenged García Mendez and signed the report accepting the plebiscite:

Notwithstanding...that the Commission failed to accept our proposition that Commonwealth status be clearly defined before submitting the various formulas to a plebiscite...we pledge to work, in good faith, to achieve the "expression of will" by the citizens of Puerto Rico, which the Commission recommends, and we promise to continue to seek the clear majority for Statehood which the Commission believes is the "most important requirement" for its achievement. The words and spirit of the Commission report will be a major asset to us in our efforts.[21]

After a bitter struggle with García Mendez and the old leadership, Ferré formed his United Statehooders and prepared to participate in the plebiscite. To García Mendez, Ferré's cooperation with Muñoz Marín's Machiavellian plans for a plebiscite would "kill statehood" by installing Commonwealth as a permanent status.

The *independentistas* rejected a plebiscite out of hand. From their point of view, there could be no true exercise of self-determination without a transfer of power. Algeria had voted for France as long as France could exercise the "moral violence" of its presence.[22] They argued that the plebiscite would be manipulated by a government committed to one solution (Commonwealth) on an island militarily occupied by the colonial power, whose agencies of oppression—the Federal Bureau of Investigation (FBI) and the Central Intelligence Agency (CIA)—were active. Plebiscites, Concepción de Gracia, leader of the Puerto Rican Independence Party, added for good measure, were the instruments of dictators: Napoleon, Hitler, and Somoza.

The plebiscite was held in July 1967. A vote for Commonwealth would mean "reaffirmation" of Puerto Rico as an autonomous community permanently associated with the United States and would imply authorization to *develop* Commonwealth to a maximum of self-government compatible with common citizenship, common defense, a common market, and common coinage. A vote for statehood or independence would mean authorization to approach Congress for the legislation necessary to bring them into being.

So the people of Puerto Rico were confronted with voting for three uncertainties. *Perfected* Commonwealth, statehood, and independence *all* depended on action by Congress at some future date. Still, a majority vote for Commonwealth would satisfy the charge that in 1952 Puerto Ricans were not given a choice among three options but merely asked to endorse one. A majority vote would, in Muñoz Marín's view, at least give unquestioned democratic legitimacy to Commonwealth as it stood.

It was Muñoz Marín, no longer governor after 1964, who bore the burden of the PPD campaign to rally the faithful with the magic of his name and to convince them that only ELA guaranteed the economic well-being of every citizen. Statehood and independence would both bring back the misery of the 1930s. He exhausted himself in a series of meetings reminiscent of his first great campaign of 1938 – 40 that created his party. Yet the result was disappointing and, it could be argued by the opponents of ELA, inconclusive. Abstention ran at 33.7 percent. The vote therefore did not constitute a majority of the Puerto Rican people, although 60.4 percent of those who did vote backed ELA. Even more alarming was the success of

Ferré's United Statehooders, with 40 percent of the vote. It became evident, for the first time, that the electoral strength of the statehooders lay in the urban vote. The United Statehooders won in nine urban districts. In an industrializing society with massive migration to the towns this was an ominous sign, for Muñoz Marín, of future voting patterns.

After the ELA victory in the plebiscite, Resident Commissioner Jaime Benítez was to argue, Commonwealth status was no halfway house to statehood or independence: "It stands upon its own basic strength of democratic self-determination."[23] He was repeating Muñoz Marín's own view: "In 1967 the people voted for Commonwealth as a permanent status, not as a transitory status to another against which the people voted."[24] But this conception of Commonwealth as a *permanent* status was novel and alarming to Muñoz Marín's opponents both within and outside his own party; it turned what they were willing to accept as a means to some other end into an end in itself.

The American press, while it recognized that ELA for the moment satisfied the Puerto Rican people, nevertheless argued that statehood might well be their ultimate choice. Muñoz Marín's claim that Puerto Ricans were "now free of the heavy burden of debate on political status" had a hollow ring.

If the plebiscite of 1967 was at best a relative success for the PPD and Commonwealth, the election of 1968 was a disaster. Ferré's United Statehooders, transformed into a political party — the New Progressive Party (PNP) — won the governorship and a slim majority in the lower house, although the PPD still controlled the Senate. Whereas for nearly two decades the elected government of Puerto Rico had supported one status — Commonwealth — for the first time since 1904, a party resolutely committed to statehood was in power in Puerto Rico. Status had become the football of party politics.

Unlike García Mendez, the leader he had overthrown, Ferré saw the achievement of statehood as a gradual process that could take place within the constitutional framework of the Commonwealth. The first step was to set up an ad hoc committee, as recommended by the commission, to consider the possibility of giving Puerto Ricans a vote in presidential elections.[25] To Muñoz Marín, this step ran counter to the whole spirit of the plebiscite: since the Commonwealth had won the plebiscite, the ad hoc committee could only be legitimately used, he argued, to perfect it. To seek greater participation via a presidential vote *before* perfecting Commonwealth was a "false priority" and would block any move toward greater autonomy. The ad hoc committee appointed by Ferré duly recommended Puerto Rican participation in the presidential vote, but before he could take it to Congress, the recommendation was defeated in a Senate Ferré did not control.

The election of 1972, by returning the PPD to power, once more reversed the status preference of the government in Puerto Rico. The PPD was now under the leadership of a representative of the younger generation of the party:[26] Rafael Hernández Colón, a good-looking, American-educated, and prosperous lawyer, who was an expert in constitutional issues. The younger generation's view of the future of Commonwealth differed from that of Muñoz Marín, for whom the perfected Commonwealth represented a permanent solution. The younger generation talked of "free association" rather than permanent union. This was more than a semantic subtlety: free association would establish beyond all doubt the right of a sovereign people to change the terms of its "compact" with the United States. At the historic meeting at Aguas Buenas in November 1970 — at which Muñoz Marín was not present — the PPD committed itself to free association and called for a Constituent Assembly to define the terms of that association, which they then anticipated presenting to Congress. Whether Congress would accept what was a self-denying ordinance and a radical revision of its relationship with Puerto Rico was, from the outset, debatable.[27] That the party delegates at Aguas Buenas were willing to beat the drum of anti-Americanism is evident from their demand that the United States Navy clear out of the island of Culebra.

But once in power after the election of 1972, the PPD leadership abandoned the strategy of the Constituent Assembly and the language of free association as too radical for the party's conservative hard core, always cautious of "tinkering" with Commonwealth status for fear of raising doubts as to its legitimacy. Instead the new PPD governor, Hernández Colón, used the machinery of an ad hoc committee, as recommended by the Status Commission, to consider modification of Puerto Rico's status. The ad hoc committee, set up in September 1973, on which representatives of the three major Puerto Rican political parties would sit, was to draft a new "compact of association" with the United States. This was to be done without imperiling the basic features of Commonwealth and its democratic legitimacy. The ad hoc committee was to examine "how the *existing* legal status can be improved *within its own terms*" [emphasis added] — that is, keeping a common market, a common coinage, a common defense, and common citizenship.[28]

The committee's hearings immediately revealed the discontent of the statehooders. The committee did not properly represent the PNP. "This has proved to be their [the PPD's] style in every political action. Imposition by absolute power is their standing operating procedure." Keeping the word "state" in Free Associated State was "a neat trick" that turned Puerto Ricans into "spongers" who did not pay federal taxes but who were bailed out by "an unaware Congress." "There is no dignity in being beggars; allow us to acquire dignity," that is, by paying federal taxes as a state. The concessions demanded by the PPD represented their "chauvinism," their hidden intent to turn a Free Associated State into a constitutional animal indistinguishable from independence. "Yankee go home is an essential part of the bill."[29]

Carlos Gallisá, member of the Central Committee of the Puerto Rican Socialist Party, who gave his testimony in Spanish, put forward the standard view of the radical *independentistas*. The proposed new compact was "a monumental lie" to deceive international opinion in the United Nations by presenting a "colonial relationship" as accepted by "the free and sovereign will" of the Puerto Rican people. "A slave cannot consent to a compact with a master." As an "oppressed people" — oppressed, that is, by the presence of the United States on the island — the "arithmetic of elections" could not represent the will of the Puerto Ricans. Denied democratic self-determination, "any means" was legitimate, including "armed struggle" led by those who "affirm the nationality of Puerto Ricans." This was the classic argument of the Nationalists, brought up to date and clothed in the rhetoric of the national liberation movements of the Third World. It expressed the concept that an enlightened minority embodying the suppressed general will of the nation — now called freedom fighters in a liberation army—could force it to be free. Resident Commissioner Jaime Benítez argued against Gallisá, pouncing on independence "by shootings.... I don't see how wanton killing and wounding innocent people can be called patriotism."[30]

The proposals of the ad hoc committee went to the House on December 17, 1975, as House Resolution 11200. They were presented as a fulfilment of the terms of the 1967 plebiscite, which had recognized the function of ad hoc committees to perfect Commonwealth. The suggested "new compact" aimed to "consolidate and improve" the relationship between the United States and "the people of Puerto Rico, a cultural community of Hispanic language and tradition." The United States would continue to be responsible for international relations and defense, but Puerto Rico could make educational, cultural, sporting, commercial, and technical agreements with other countries consistent with the interests of the United States and as agreed to by the president and the governor. The common market and the customs and excise rebates would remain, but in consultation with the United States, Puerto Rico could levy its own tariffs and the island would enjoy observer status on international trade negotiations. It also would have powers to control immigration and regulate its own wage levels. Hitherto unrepresented in the United States Senate, it would be represented in both Houses. Federal laws would apply only if it was specifically stated that they referred to Puerto Rico. The governor could object to any law that adversely affected the island and Congress would then determine whether the law was essential to the interests of the United States.

Nothing came of the committee's recommendations.[31] Congress delayed, and in November 1976 the elections were won by Governor Romero Barceló and the PNP statehooders. In December, President Ford, who acted as if the proposals of the ad hoc committee simply did not exist, unexpectedly declared his preference for statehood. He presented a statehood bill to Congress, but it died away as previous bills had done. Perfected Commonwealth and the "new compact" of association sank below the political horizon. For José Cabranes, administrator of the Office of the Commonwealth of Puerto Rico in Washington, who resigned in 1975, the ad hoc committee's recommendations represented "the last chance" for Commonwealth: if nothing came of them then Puerto Rico "will drift along in a state of limbo." Commonwealth, as it stood, was an "imperfect political system and virtually all Puerto Ricans are unhappy with it...too subtle, too baroque to be understood."[32]

How, then, could Puerto Rico escape from "the state of limbo"? How could the status logjam be loosened? A group of young Puerto Rican intellectuals, who defined themselves as a cabal of liberals and were popularly known as the Puerto Rican Mafia, set about the task under the Carter administration. They included Franklin Delano López, Americans for Democratic Action organizer on the island; José Cabranes (until he became a federal judge in 1979); J.M. García Passalacqua, a prolific political journalist who prided himself on his Washington connections and his "inside" knowledge; Miriam Cruz, placed by López in the White House; and Maurice Ferré, mayor of Miami. Cabranes and Ferré were mainland-based Puerto Ricans. Representing different opinions, the members of the cabal acted independently, sharing only what can be called an "anticolonial" attitude and a belief that Puerto Ricans should take an active role in determining their own fate.

Their aim was to open what were called "alternative futures" for Puerto Rico, to end what they regarded as a commitment by the United States to a solution that had gone stale: Commonwealth status. Their tactic was to break the alliance between the mainland Democratic party and the island supporters of Commonwealth, an alliance of thirty years' standing created by Muñoz Marín and Felisia Gautier, long PPD mayor of San Juan who, as an active campaigner for New York Democrats, was a power of sorts in the national party. Though the alliance was informal, Puerto Rico had been a Democratic fief.[33]

What this alliance meant in practice, the proponents of "alternative futures" argued, was that Muñoz Marín and the PPD had become "interpreters and implementers of the decisions regarding Puerto Rico made by the federal bureaucracy," the faceless men who, by supporting devices like the two ad hoc committees, had indulged in "typical bureaucratic maneuvers to maintain the status quo." That status quo was "colonialism by consent"; Commonwealth was nothing "but a territorial status."[34] The strategy of the proponents of "alternative futures" was to break the stranglehold of these "low echelon officials of a colonial bureaucracy" by entering *national* party politics, to seek "organic" ties with the national parties and commit them to "alternative futures" for Puerto Rico.

The new strategy was made possible by an alteration in the rules of the Democratic party. In 1974, Puerto Rico, with twenty-two votes, became the twenty-sixth largest "state" at the Democratic convention. Now statehooders, by deserting their traditional connection with the national Republican party and participating in the Democratic primaries, could challenge the hold that the PPD had established over the Democratic party on the island and that had committed the mainland Democrats to the defense of Commonwealth status. This maneuver was the work of Franklin Delano López. The island ADA chapter, which he had set up, wrote to all presidential candidates. Only one replied: Jimmy Carter. While the *pure* Republicans of the PNP remained loyal to the national Republican party, those in the ADA endorsed Carter as the Democratic candidate and he received nine delegates. The PPD backed the losing Democratic candidate, Senator Henry Jackson, Chairman of the Interior Committee of the Senate and known for his interest in Puerto Rico.[35] It had done everything it could to sabotage the efforts of the Young Turks of the ADA, including getting their meetings banned in Mayagüez—a PPD stronghold — on the ground that they contravened the fire regulations.

With President Carter's victory, "alternative futures"— proposed by the group that had supported his candidacy and that had joined his Hispanic campaign staff—received the attention of the White House.[36] On July 25, 1978, the anniversary of the landing of U.S. troops in Puerto Rico and of the establishment of Commonwealth, Carter issued a proclamation: statehood, Commonwealth, and independence were all legitimate options if chosen by the Puerto Rican people. He stated, "I will support and urge Congress to support whatever decision the people of Puerto Rico reach." In part, this was an attempt to take the sting out of the annual attack on the United States as a colonial power in the August meeting of the Committee of Twenty-four — the Decolonization Committee — in the United Nations.

Carter's proclamation was a watered-down version of a draft by José Cabranes, which was rejected by the White House domestic staff on the grounds that reinforcement of the idea of political change (however neutral in appearance), by triggering off a plebiscite in Puerto Rico before the 1980 general election, would confront "Carter with a policy choice on something [Stuart] Eizenstat [the president's domestic affairs aide] regarded as problematical." In its final and anodyne form, it was little more than a restatement of President Eisenhower's pledge of 1953 — with the inclusion of statehood. Anodyne as it was, it was greeted as a triumph by the cabal, some of whose members were much concerned with enlarging their public images in Puerto Rico by playing the old game of exaggerating their influence in Washington and by distributing press releases and photographs of themselves on "important" missions. The statehooders regarded the presidential proclamation as an endorsement of statehood; the cabal trumpeted it as a "deliberate end" to the paralysis induced by support for the status quo, a public endorsement of "alternative futures." The Democrats had deserted Commonwealth; the old alliance forged by Muñoz Marín in the 1940s was allegedly dissolved.

The aim of the Puerto Rican Mafia was, in the words of one of them, "to give the statehooders a chance," and if statehooders faltered, to give other options their chances. The chance of the statehooders would come with the 1980 election. It disappeared overnight. Romero Barceló's majority was too thin for him to press for a plebiscite on status that would lead Puerto Rico to its "destiny." All he had accomplished was to back the wrong presidential candidate (President Carter), leaving the American connection in the hands of the loyal PNP Republicans—Luis Ferré, the former governor and elder statesman of the party, and Mayor Hernán Padilla of San Juan, who was to become his rival for the leadership of the PNP. Both voted for George Bush in the primaries and subsequently supported Ronald Reagan, though — and it is another of the paradoxes of Puerto Rico's anomalous status — they could not vote for him.

The "alternative futures" policy collapsed; the status quo endured. Yet something remained. Puerto Ricans had voted in the primaries in the thousands. The Puerto Rican presidential primaries came early in the race and, for a *limited time*, made Puerto Rican concerns of importance to presidential hopefuls, who were forced to brush up on a few words of Spanish. In the text of one candidate's speech, Spanish words were spelled out phonetically. In most cases, the gist of their speeches was translated into Spanish by a Puerto Rican. The mainland Republican party came out loud and clear in favor of statehood. "Statehood Now" had been Bush's campaign slogan. When still a candidate, Reagan endorsed statehood in a strongly worded article in the *Wall Street Journal* (February 11, 1980) as an end to Puerto Rico's "historically unnatural status."

If statehooders failed to find their Great Chance in 1980, Muñoz Marín's Grand Design to establish Commonwealth as a bilateral compact beyond all constitutional doubt had similarly withered away. Muñoz Marín had attempted to get the best of both worlds, retaining the economic advantages of union and enlarging the boundaries of self-government beyond those of a state of the Union to touch the frontiers of independence. The legal ambiguities remained, capitalized on by the opponents of the PPD. Under some federal programs, Puerto Rico is treated as a state; under others, it is either excluded or treated as a special case with an imposed ceiling that does not apply to states.[37] Sometimes Puerto Rico enjoys federal handouts on equal terms with states of the Union; sometimes its allocations are cut, proving, to the indignation of statehooders, that Puerto Ricans do not enjoy equal treatment as American citizens but suffer discrimination as inhabitants of a colony. Something had happened in 1952, but what in precise legal terms that something was remained undefined. "The factual change [initiated by Public Law 600] was of sufficient substance that it brought with it permanent legal consequences," the United States – Puerto Rico Commission on the Status of Puerto Rico reported. "The record," it added, "does not make clear the precise consequences."

Nor has the exact nature of these "permanent legal consequences" been spelled out by court decisions, the method by which "precision" in constitutional issues is achieved in the American system. Up to 1952, the courts treated Puerto Rico as an unincorporated territory, as defined by the so-called insular cases in the early years after 1898.

After the establishment of Commonwealth in 1952, the precedents set up by the insular cases were abandoned in most court decisions. But what constitutional doctrine had replaced the legal limbo of an "unincorporated territory?" The courts were faced with the problem of considering the "legal consequences" of Commonwealth status and the constitutional implications of the "compact." Their answers were neither consistent nor clear.[38] Was Puerto Rico some new form of unincorporated territory, where "territory" was "the constitutional word for an area which is part of the United States and which is not a state?"[39] Was it, as the Supreme Court decided in 1976, a political unit sui generis occupying "a relationship to the United States that has no parallel in our history?"[40] If it was manifestly not a state of the Union, had it become "a State within the common and accepted meaning of the word?" This court decision was viewed by the PPD as a triumph for the doctrine of compact (i.e., that Puerto Rico was bound to the United States by a bilateral contract that could not be altered without mutual consent), a claim that statehooders dismissed as legal nonsense, since Puerto Rico was clearly not an independent "state."

More recent cases have not clarified the issue. In 1980, the U.S. Supreme Court ruled (in *Harris v. Rosario*, concerning equal treatment in the case of welfare benefits) that Puerto Rico was a "territory belonging to the United States and [Congress] may treat Puerto Rico differently from the states as long as there is a rational basis for its actions." Governor Romero Barceló criticized the ruling as proving that Puerto Rico suffers from what he calls "geographical discrimination" under ELA. Commonwealth supporters found their rejoinder in a recent decision of the United States Court of Appeals for the First Circuit. "It is fair to assume," the court ruled in a case involving the application of a clause of the Sherman Antitrust Law to Puerto Rico, "that the framers of the Sherman Act, had they been aware of the Federal Relations Act and the subsequent constitutional developments, would have intended that Puerto Rico be treated as a 'state' under the Act, once Commonwealth status was achieved." Hernández Colón of the PPD immediately claimed that this decision proved that Puerto Rico was no longer a colony, that the setting up of the Commonwealth in 1952 had decisive, recognizable, legal consequences. Romero Barceló found this interpretation unacceptable. According to Romero, the decision did not "canonize Commonwealth status," it merely reflected the shilly-shallying of the federal courts where Puerto Rico was concerned, exposing the confusion surrounding Commonwealth status: "Sometimes we are a state, at others a territory."[41]

The zeal with which Puerto Rican political parties seek succor in court decisions, and the games of legal battledore and shuttlecock between the two major parties, may seem to have little practical significance to nonplayers. In the end, it is not the courts that will determine the political status of Puerto Rico. As the reluctance of the U.S. Supreme Court to come to grips with the issue of Puerto Rico illustrates, that is a political decision to be made by the people of Puerto Rico and Congress. Even if the doctrine of compact as a mutually binding bilateral contract lacks legal endorsement, as some would argue, is it not evident that respect for international opinion would prevent the United States from altering unilaterally the basic terms of the compact against the wishes of the Puerto Rican people? The United States' arguments in the United Nations since 1953, the explicit declarations of presidents, and the Joint Resolution of Congress in 1979 would all be exposed as shallow deceptions. Both President Ford and President Reagan may believe that statehood is the proper and logical status for Puerto Rico. But neither independence nor statehood can be imposed on Puerto Rico, whatever the powers of Congress may be in strict constitutional law. Republican William Lemke of North Dakota, in a speech much quoted by *independentistas*, asserted the absolute powers of Congress to alter Commonwealth: "You know, of course, that if the people of Puerto Rico should go crazy, Congress would be able to legislate another time."[42] The Puerto Ricans would have to be very crazy before Congress took upon itself to alter unilaterally the "compact" made in 1952. To do so would be, in the words of the Court of Appeal to the First Circuit, "to impute to the Congress the perpetration of a monumental hoax."[43]

Like many pragmatic solutions, Commonwealth status has one advantage: as its defenders pointed out to the ad hoc committee, it makes for political stability by being "emotionally acceptable to both factions. If separatists faced assimilationists the whole situation would blow up." Certainly both statehooders and *independentistas* would deny that they are emotionally satisfied by Commonwealth, but each would be even more powerfully emotionally dissatisfied with the triumph of the "logical" solution of the other. The PSP has argued that the triumph of annexation (i.e., statehood) will polarize politics and produce a state of the Union in which a substantial number of its citizens—the *independentistas* and the radical autonomists of the PPD — would reject the constitution as such and seek to overthrow it. While Governor Romero Barceló has threatened that if statehood is denied by Congress he would support independence, it is hard to believe that the hard core of his party would abandon their Americanism for an independent republic. Those in Washington who press for statehood, or who flirt with the idea of independence as conveniently ridding the United States both of a financial liability and charges of "colonialism," tend to forget that when solutions that are attractive because they are "clear" and "logical" are politically impossible, messy solutions may be all that are left. Rather than engaging in floating "alternatives," it might be well to work with what is available to solve what remains Puerto Rico's biggest problem: poverty.

While there may be something to be said for the "flexibility" that is a consequence of the leeway left by legal ambiguities,

this can scarcely be advanced by the supporters of Commonwealth as a virtue. There is no doubt but that the glamor has
worn off Commonwealth, once hailed as an "imaginative" form
of federalism that respects "national diversity" within a unique
relationship with the United States. Its acceptability as a political status was reinforced by its success in presiding over, if not
of promoting, a new prosperity after the dismal Depression
years; with the signs that its economic performance was falling
off, its political attractions fell away as well.

Yet it is easy to forget the early attractions of Commonwealth. In 1954, a British observer could write, "The majority
of thinking Puerto Ricans seem to be today more or less content
with their present status while at any rate a large majority of
thinking British West Indians are not."[44] Now the position is
reversed and Commonwealth may be likened to a palimpsest.
The message inscribed in 1952 is fading, to reveal beneath it an
older inscription: statehood or independence.

Part II

THE PUERTO RICAN PARTIES AND STATUS

4.

PARTY DOCTRINE AND STATUS

Since 1953, it has been the public policy of the United States to support and defend Commonwealth as the legitimate, democratic choice of the Puerto Rican people. But the United States also has accepted the freedom of Puerto Ricans to modify that status *and* reject it in favor of either independence or complete integration as a state of the Union, provided that is the will of the Puerto Rican people. That will is encapsulated in and expressed through Puerto Rico's political parties, each of which champions a status option. If we put aside (and it is a substantial reservation) whether Congress will accept without question that the "will" of the Puerto Rican people, once expressed by them, should govern its own legislative powers, then the status of Puerto Rico should be "settled" once one of the parties obtains a substantial majority both in a general election and in a subsequent status plebiscite. The assumptions here are, first, that one party is capable of winning such a majority and, second, that victory in a general election would entail victory in a status referendum.

Although in the past, Puerto Rican political parties have

been classified as "ideologically weak" and flexible — even ambiguous — in their differing attitudes to the status issue,[1] today
they are defined by their conceptions of what is the appropriate,
profitable, dignified, and *permanent* relationship of the island
to the United States, that is, by their stands on status. The
Popular Democratic Party (PPD) favors the amendment of
Commonwealth by a process now called "culmination," which
will enlarge the autonomy Puerto Rico presently enjoys. The
New Progressive Party (PNP), successor to the old Statehood
Republican Party, is committed to statehood. Both Puerto
Rico's major political parties, therefore, favor Puerto Rico's
continued association with the United States, either as a state
of the Union or, in the case of the PPD, through free association. The two independence parties — the Puerto Rican Independence Party (PIP) and the Puerto Rican Socialist Party
(PSP) — reject this association as condemning Puerto Rico to
a perpetual colonial status; while both favor independence,
they do so through different mechanisms and on different
conditions. But the independence parties have not succeeded
in making any lasting impression on the electorate — they are
unrepresented in the legislature elected in 1980 — and Puerto
Rico has a de facto two-party political system.

Party politics in Puerto Rico are conditioned by the fact that
both of the major political parties are committed to maintaining ties with the United States, yet advocate mutually exclusive
solutions as to the form that connection should take. It is this
that distinguishes Puerto Rican politics from European politics, where parties divide on a right-left spectrum, and from
the politics of accommodation of interest groups as practiced
in the United States. Both major parties are centrist parties
competing for the votes of an electorate in which labor and
other special interests are only feebly represented by organized
interest groups. Accommodation between parties is impossible

as long as they are defined in terms of mutually exclusive legal and constitutional dogmas, that is, their stands on the status issue. Both sense that the status obsession of the political elite may not be shared by the electorate, though it would be an ill-informed voter who did not realize that his vote implied a choice of status option.

Party identification in Puerto Rico, historically stronger than that in the United States, is now weakening, as it is on the mainland; though the parties themselves are better organized than in the past, a more sophisticated electorate no longer blindly follows its *prohombres*, its great men. Floating voters and cross-voting now have a significant effect on election results. In the 1980 election 154,000 out of an electorate of 1.6 million split their votes; the percentages of unaffiliated votes have risen from 2 percent in 1968 to 11 percent in 1980. These floating voters are attracted less by the status preference of the two major parties than by the economic performance of the party in office and the promises of the opposition to improve that performance. Thus, in the 1976 election, the PPD was punished for the recession and for its austerity program, rather than for its defense of culminated Commonwealth. While status was not an issue, victory went to a statehood party. Then the PNP failed in 1980, less because it advocated statehood than because a series of political scandals discredited a government that had failed to stage an economic recovery.

It is the second of the preliminary assumptions mentioned earlier that is questionable: that victory in a general election would entail victory in a referendum. It is possible, for example, to imagine a repeat of the events culminating in the electoral choice of 1976: a disastrous performance by a PPD government might hand the PNP an electoral triumph. But it is by no means clear that statehood would triumph in a subsequent referendum. A recent poll has revealed that many PNP voters are indifferent to the status issue. Voters may, moreover, be influenced by local issues; it has been argued that mayors have become major political figures, assuming the stature formerly enjoyed by only national Puerto Rican leaders.[2]

Until 1968, Muñoz Marín controlled the political life of Puerto Rico, and elections were merely formal ratifications of his leadership and the PPD monopoly of power. But in the elections of 1972, 1976, and, less conclusively, in 1980, the party in power has been rejected by the electorate, as critics of Puerto Rico's democratic credentials in the United Nations — mostly members of one-party states — are annually reminded by the U.S. delegation. Elections are now long and hard-fought contests between the major parties, whose flags flutter on poles in gardens and on roofs, their number scrutinized by journalists in the hope that these visual indications of party affiliation will provide evidence for predicting election results.

It might be thought that Puerto Rican elections are comparable to state elections in the United States, but this is not the case in terms of the intensity of political feeling. To Puerto Ricans, the election of the governor of Puerto Rico has the same significance as does a presidential election to their fellow citizens on the mainland. This indicates something more than a compensation for the fact that Puerto Ricans cannot participate in national elections to vote for their president. It reflects a fundamental feature of the political psychology of Puerto Rico, which can be sensed in every conversation but which cannot be precisely demonstrated — the feeling that Puerto Rico is uniquely important. As outside observers are wont to complain, "Puerto Ricans think Puerto Rico is the center of the world," a world that somehow does not necessarily form part of the United States.

One feature of Puerto Rican party politics deserves emphasis. This is the feuding within each political party, which is often intense and always highly personalized; rivals are subject to criticisms of their political conduct and personal habits as fierce as those which distinguish the campaigns of mutual calumny that the parties mount against each other. Perhaps such dissension should be dismissed as a ritualistic performance for an audience that, for all its condemnation of political buffoonery, regards politics as a spectacle, with journalists serving as its theater critics. Party infighting should not, however, conceal that, by American standards, Puerto Rican parties are now — as oppposed to earlier years — disciplined. Voting in the legislature is usually strictly on party lines.

Just as the government itself is centralized, so are the political parties. Since 1957, their campaigns have been largely financed by government subsidies,[3] thus strengthening the hold of the party leaders who control these funds. This weakens the hold interest groups might acquire by making contributions to party funds, a mechanism that was used by the sugar interests to retain control of party politics until 1940. In many respects Puerto Rican political parties more resemble British than American parties, except that in Puerto Rico the political parties tend to come to life only for registration and during elections, and the party faithful are rewarded by jobs in the administration and government agencies should their party triumph. Governor Rexford G. Tugwell found Muñoz Marín "greedy for jobs." So are his successors.

The following three chapters examine the historical roots of the Puerto Rican parties and pay particular attention to the independence parties, whose existence, while marginal in electoral terms, determines the peculiar nature of the Puerto Rican political system. By examining their social support, these chapters will endeavor to explain the changing fortunes and explore the future prospects of the various political parties.

5.

THE PPD AND COMMONWEALTH

The PPD — the Popular Democratic Party, or *Populares* as it is known — was founded in 1938 by Luis Muñoz Marín. Its history until 1964, when Muñoz ceased to be its leader, has been considered a reflection of the evolution of Muñoz's own changing social, economic, and political ideas. The general trend of this evolution is clear, though the precise timing of shifts and the reasons for such shifts are subjects of obsessive concern for Puerto Ricans. The final resting place is clear enough: "perfected," or "culminated," Commonwealth as a permanent form of union with the United States.

Emphasis on the personal evolution of Muñoz Marín underestimates the contribution of his collaborators, particularly that of Antonio Fernós Isern, who, as resident commissioner in Washington, cajoled Congress into legislation that gave birth to Commonwealth. It also overestimates the originality of Muñoz as the sole begetter of *Estado Libre Asociado* or Free Associated State (ELA). A free associated state, apparently based on the Irish Free State constitution, was on the program of the Unionist party in the 1920s.[1] Luis Muñoz Marín not only inherited the prestige and literary talents of his father, Muñoz Rivera — both were poets[2] — he also inherited his policies: Muñoz Rivera's ideal of "Canadian" autonomy was transformed into Muñoz Marín's ideal of Commonwealth.

Like his father, Muñoz Marín saw that the key to the door that would open up the prospects for greater self-government for Puerto Rico was in Washington. There was no possibility of forcing the lock: Washington must be persuaded and convinced. Here lay Muñoz's great contribution to the establishment of Commonwealth. He was not so much an original thinker as a great persuader; his unmatched powers of expression in both English and Spanish were complemented by the force of his towering personality, reflected even in his stature and revealing facial expressions.

From the days of his acquaintanceship with the Roosevelts, Muñoz Marín exploited every contact in Washington. He was treated with respect in congressional hearings, and even received standing ovations on occasions. It was part of his political technique to present himself in Puerto Rico as the only intermediary who could talk to presidents and congressmen.[3] He once boasted that no other man could match him in extracting federal largess from a reluctant Congress — a claim that became the stock-in-trade of every prominent Puerto Rican politician.

Like all who favor home rule, Muñoz walked a tightrope. In Puerto Rico, he resolutely defended island interests; in Washington, though, he presented himself as a pragmatist (his father's favorite expression), ready to trim his sails to congressional winds to get what he could at any given moment. It was a difficult exercise in political seamanship. His failure to condemn outright the assassination, by Nationalists, of Colonel Riggs in 1936 — for fear of losing political support in Puerto Rico — made him persona non grata with Secretary of the

Interior Ickes.[4] At times, Muñoz despaired of Washington and what he called its "intolerable" betrayals and delays. In 1962, he was accused of making cowardly concessions for fear of losing his leverage on Capitol Hill, while he himself felt let down by his friends in the Kennedy administration who failed to bring pressure on Congress.

Muñoz Marín's first position was clear: he was an *independentista*. But he was not an *independentista* in the traditional mold, one for whom independence was a dogma, an end in itself. To Muñoz, independence was a political instrument to be used to destroy the evil economic consequences of a colonial regime that had dragged Puerto Rico into hopeless poverty. He had no time either for the rhetoric of José de Diego, orator of the independence movement, or for what he called the "petty politics" of the island *políticos*. Indifferent to the condition of the poor—who constituted the electorate to which they were, in theory, responsible but whose votes they could buy for a pair of shoes—these island politicians operated in a self-created vacuum. It was Muñoz's social concern that drove him, as a young man in New York, to desert the party his father had founded and to join the Socialist party of Santiago Iglesias, creating a political scandal. It is typical of the man that he was less concerned with socialist theory than with what he called its moral and aesthetic elements, that is, its concern for the underdog. For him, independence must never become, as he put it, a "cruel dogma" standing in the way of social justice.

By 1936, Muñoz Marín had left the Socialists to become a member of Barceló's Liberal party, the successor to his father's Unionist party, which had come around to supporting independence. But Barceló's acceptance of the "suicidal" independence offered by the Tydings bill forced Muñoz out of the Liberal party — after an attempt to capture it. In 1938, he founded his own party, the PPD, taking with him the young radicals who were resolute *independentistas*.

The electoral campaign of the PPD in 1940 and the previous

two years' campaign for the registration of the new party have become legendary, a model exercise in the political mobilization of a semiliterate electorate on a shoestring budget (fifty dollars a week). Muñoz's tour of the island in an old car, talking directly, he claimed, to half a million people, set the pattern for all subsequent elections. The PPD declared that status was not an issue. (The "People's Catechism," published by the PPD before the election for popular distribution, made it clear, however, that the party favored independence over statehood, largely because statehood would entail liability to federal taxation.) The problem, the PPD claimed, was poverty. The solution was an agrarian reform directed against Muñoz's old enemies: the four sugar companies that monopolized and underexploited the best land in Puerto Rico, draining to the metropolitan mainland the products of native labor. The emblem of the party became the *jibaros'* straw hat, the *pava*. To the PPD, the *jibaro,* the subsistence farmer of the inland regions who was a loyal PPD voter, became the symbol of Puerto Rican identity. A vast monument on the motorway from San Juan to Ponce commemorates the *jibaro* — portrayed, as is not without interest, as a pure Nordic type. Muñoz Marín, rarely a tedious conversationalist, sometimes wearied his court with his eulogies of the *jibaro*'s virtues.

The great achievement of Muñoz was to expand participation in political life beyond the "upper crust";[5] his campaign of 1940, based on a promise to fulfill a populist program, broke the power of the old elitist parties, which had been based on patronage and the massive purchase of votes. His hold over the Puerto Rican electorate, which lasted until his death, was established, not by a party machine — that came later — but by that direct contact which is characteristic of political leadership in some Latin American and Caribbean societies. Identification with "the people" gave Muñoz emotional strength. "I am one of them — way deep down in my body — down through my very bones." Such identification with the ruled can act as a self-justifying mechanism for the ruler, legitimizing, for example, the rejection of dissidents and their views. It also confronts the leader's party with the problem, to use Weberian jargon, of institutionalizing his charisma.

The PPD's parliamentary majority in 1940, though precarious, allowed it to begin to carry out its campaign promises. In the elections of 1944 and 1948, it achieved the massive majorities that gave Muñoz — first as leader of the Senate and after 1949 as governor — complete control of Puerto Rican politics. With few exceptions, every subsequent political leader has sought, by imitating his political style, to recapture his hold on "the people." Personalism, as practiced by Muñoz, cannot be resuscitated; nevertheless, gubernatorial candidates are condemned to the exhausting ritual of electoral "caravans" that visit every district in an extended exercise in "pressing the flesh" on an island where every elector expects a sight of his leader.

Why did Muñoz desert independence? Later he was to claim that he had discovered, on his campaign tours, that the Puerto Rican *jíbaro* and the population in general entertained vague fears that independence was a dangerous option. While the intellectuals of the independence movement concerned themselves with the abstract notion of the *patria*, Muñoz framed his efforts on the concept of the *pueblo*, that highly charged Spanish word that translates as "people" but that covers everything from a village to an entire nation. The *pueblo* (*la gran masa del pueblo*) did not want independence, and forcing it on them, he argued, would mean that "we will never obtain the support of the *pueblo*." In other words, to support independence was to court electoral disaster.[6]

Muñoz's conviction that the granting of independence to Puerto Rico would have calamitous effects was reinforced by points brought out during the debate on the granting of independence to the Philippines: as an independent republic, Puerto Rico would pay U.S. customs duties as a foreign nation, losing privileged, duty-free access for its products to the huge stateside market. The full suicidal economic consequences of independence had been analyzed in a study prepared by economist Ben Dorfman for the United States Tariff Commission.[7] It was not that independence was impossible for the United States, "but it is for us." The realization that independence must be sacrificed was traumatic; after a long conversation with Dorfman, Muñoz sat down and cried.[8]

Freedom to govern oneself must not come at the expense of destroying freedom from hunger. Muñoz argued that "the political relationship between the United States and Puerto Rico is highly undesirable. Not so the economic relationship. The political situation must be changed without destroying the economic conditions which are absolutely necessary for the survival of the people and whatever political status that is established — for no political status can survive if its basis is destroyed."[9] The "realistic" solution demanded that Puerto Rico go outside "the known classical forms" of independence or statehood; "this new road" Muñoz first called "the Associated People of Puerto Rico."

Many of the PPD militants were *independentista* in sympathy. Muñoz now had to carry them with him in his drift away from independence. In Washington in 1943, he insisted on the need to end Puerto Rico's colonial status through the granting of "some form of full internal self-government"[10] short of independence. This alarmed the *independentistas* both within and outside the PPD, who set up the *Congreso pro Independencia* (August 1943) to keep Muñoz on course and, if necessary, to capture the leadership of the party. Muñoz sensed the threat. In February 1945, the Central Committee of the party, strengthened by the presence of the prestigious Council of Founders, declared membership of the so-called *Congreso pro Independencia* incompatible with membership of the PPD. At Barranquitas, where his father was buried, after an epic ten-hour debate, Muñoz persuaded his party that since independence was, for the foreseeable future, an economic impossibility it should adopt what came to be called Commonwealth as a *transitory* solution.

Muñoz presented Commonwealth status as "a new road to old objectives." The *independentista* wing of his party saw it as leaving the old road altogether. Once Muñoz rejected independence, the party suffered desertions—the die-hard *independentistas* left to join the newly formed Puerto Rican Independence Party (PIP) — and expulsions, a process that was euphemistically termed "putting oneself outside the party." Muñoz, as boss of what had become a highly centralized party, used his control of the party machinery ruthlessly, even vindictively, against those whose *independentista* sympathies threatened party unity and his own leadership. At the meeting at Barranquitas, Vicente Géigel Polanco, one of the brains behind the PPD, had struck out against Muñoz's "defeatism," defending independence against "confused" solutions; but like many others, he swallowed his objections to remain in the party for the time being.

When, as Attorney General, Géigel took over as governor during Muñoz's visit to Washington in March 1950, an associate of Albizu Campos, the Nationalist leader, pressed Géigel to use his temporary powers to declare an independent republic. The compromising conversation was allegedly reported by Muñoz's chauffeur; although Géigel immediately supported Muñoz's "creative endeavors," he was sacked unceremoniously. Géigel retired to New York as a journalist, where his career was broken by Muñoz, whom he had accused of "lying" over the true import of Public Law 600. Having "placed himself automatically outside the party," he joined the PIP and wrote a series of frontal attacks on Muñoz and Commonwealth, later collected in his book, *The Farce of the Free Associated State*. To Géigel, Muñoz had made a base surrender in 1952 and had consistently misled the Puerto Rican people; in order to hoodwink international opinion, Muñoz presented the Commonwealth as granting Puerto Rico democratic freedoms when it was merely a continuation of the "asphyxiating colonial system."[11] Those who thought like Géigel left the PPD, especially as the hopes of "culminating" Commonwealth in the direction of greater political independence grew dim.[12]

Nor did the dangers to Muñoz's hold on the PPD come only from those who had joined the party in the belief that it was committed to independence. The older grandees of the party[13] thought Muñoz's plans for "culmination" suggested that the creator of the Commonwealth had lost faith in his creation: to talk of "perfecting" Commonwealth implied that it was imperfect as it stood. "We have got to stop Muñoz."[14]

For the younger spirits of the party, the problem was not to stop Muñoz but to push him along the road to perfection that had been abandoned, it seemed to them, too easily in 1959. By 1964, the exhaustion of a party that had held power for a quarter of a century was evident in a revolt of the ambitious young against the old guard of the party leadership. (The victory of the PPD in 1960 had been an expression of political inertia, helped by the establishment of a Christian Democratic party (the PAC), whose attacks on the secularist policies of the PPD rekindled a spark of the old enthusiasm.) In 1940, Muñoz had incarnated "the noble ambitions of youth"; now the "torch" must be carried by the generation born in the 1940s,[15] representatives of a population whose average age was eighteen. The young PPD members, organized in the so-called Group of 22 — of which the most prolific publicist was Juan M. García

Passalacqua — saw in Ortega y Gasset's theory of generational change the philosophic justification for an attempt to take over the party under the banner of renovation and democratization. This generational split was apparent in all political parties, but it was of particular significance in the PPD. It brought the beginnings of a new style: while PPD electoral propaganda had gloried in past achievements, the young entry emphasized the social and economic problems of the future.

Muñoz clearly was aware of the danger of fossilization. On May 17, 1964, he allowed the Young Turks associated with the Group of 22 to express their views to the party leadership. They were determined both to force the party out of the political doldrums and to make it abandon its passive acceptance of Commonwealth as set up in 1952 as a final solution — at that time the best that Puerto Rico could extract from Congress. Commonwealth, they argued, must be turned into something approaching independence; the constitutional relationship with the United States must be based on a free association that would give substance to the phrase "in the nature of a compact."

The PPD was about to experience its severest crisis. Only Muñoz had been able to keep its radical wing (the political heirs of the *independentista* faction) and the old guard in joint harness. The underlying tensions surfaced when Muñoz announced his decision not to run as the PPD candidate for governor in 1964. His decision appalled the faithful and the old guard; the Group of 22 supported it "for the good of the party." What followed showed that, in spite of his undoubted democratic convictions, Muñoz did not believe his party fit for democracy. The PPD party candidate for governor in 1964 was not democratically nominated: Muñoz simply imposed a relatively unknown administrator, the engineer Roberto Sánchez

Vilella, on a party assembly at Mayagüez. After shouting for Muñoz, the party members chanted, under instruction, for Sánchez Vilella: "That's him, that's him, that's him."

The governorship of Roberto Sánchez Vilella (1964–68) saw the disintegration of the PPD. On the surface, in an island where the minutiae of political life provide an inexhaustible fund of rumor for journalists, this prolonged crisis appeared the consequence of the collapse of personal understanding between Sánchez Vilella as governor and Muñoz as senator and de facto *caudillo* of the party he had created.

It would be absurd to argue that Muñoz acted merely out of personal spite, unable to tolerate that a man of whom it was prophesied that he would become "a puppet of Muñoz" and who had worked his way up as Muñoz's trusted aide should now take first place. (That Muñoz had originally no intention of remaining the leader of Puerto Rico is shown by the fact that he took a long trip abroad after the election.) Muñoz was only too aware that it was his own personality that held the party together; he came to believe that what he regarded as the enthusiastic bungling of his chosen successor was destroying the party he had created and paralyzing the processes of government dependent, as they were, on the support of a strong and unified party. Sánchez Vilella, a man of profound democratic convictions, sympathized with the renovationist ideas of the young, even if he came to suspect their ambitions and their penchant for intrigue. But their obvious thirst for power, as much as what they termed their "liberalism," alarmed the old guard of the party.

In the Senate, the old guard, alarmed by Sánchez Vilella's modest cabinet changes, was in a position to thwart the governor's reformist plans, which were accepted in the House of Representatives. The Senate leader, Luis Negrón López, the PPD *cacique* of western Puerto Rico, became the leader of an opposition that enjoyed the approval of Muñoz and which mauled the governor's project for university reform,[16] attacking his projects for a tax on speculative gains in land deals and for agrarian reform. This obstructionism represented the resistance of the old guard to the policies of the young liberals and to their evident determination to control the party. While Muñoz sympathized with the liberalism of the younger party members, he could not bring himself to discard those party faithfuls whom the liberals regarded as little better than party hacks. A group of Negrón's followers — the *jíbaros de Negrón* — began to tout his qualifications as the PPD candidate for the 1968 gubernatorial election.

Sánchez Vilella weakened his position when he divorced his wife to marry Jeanette Ramos, the eminently attractive daughter of the party's labor leader, Ernesto Ramos Antonini, a mulatto and long-time speaker of the House. After vicious attacks — not devoid of racial overtones — and the desertion of former supporters, including his handpicked Secretary of Justice Hernández Colón, Sánchez Vilella announced that he would not stand for reelection as governor in 1968.

Muñoz, recovering his mastery of the party, addressed the legislature as if he were still governor of Puerto Rico, declaring that Puerto Rico "must be governed from the Senate" and setting before it *his* program. Sánchez Vilella was outraged: he, not Muñoz, was the elected governor.

The breach between the two men, complicated no doubt by personal factors, was widening.[17] Muñoz made public his determination to break Sánchez in the name of party unity — as he had broken Géigel Polanco — by snubbing the governor at a banquet. Sánchez reversed his decision not to run in the 1968 election and announced that he would stand as PPD candidate for governor.

Without the support of Muñoz, and with the old guard

reneged against him, Sánchez Vilella had no hope of gaining the gubernatorial nomination. At the party convention he was shouted down and the old guard triumphed. Negrón López was nominated, a choice that Muñoz regretted; but having vetoed Sánchez Vilella, even he could not veto a second candidate.

Sánchez Vilella then made a decision that temporarily drove him out of political life. He formed his own party, the *Partido del Pueblo*.[18] Its slogan, "Let the people decide," represented Sánchez Vilella's democratic convictions; he viewed the PPD as a party that once had been the party of the poor and was now the party of the new rich. Sánchez Vilella gained 87,832 votes — a surprisingly large percentage — not least because Negrón López was a colorless candidate, the machine politician of a tired party.

The *Partido del Pueblo* took away enough votes from the PPD to ensure the election of Luis Ferré of the PNP as governor. Ferré could not believe his luck and was only persuaded by his son at the last moment to leave his home in Ponce to celebrate his victory in San Juan.

The victory of the PNP in 1968 put the *Populares* (PPD) on the defensive. The PPD regained power in 1972 only to lose it again in 1976; winning the legislature in 1980, it lost the governorship. The shock of defeat in 1968 made the party more strongly committed than ever to the twin concepts of free association and the "culmination" of Commonwealth through substantially increased autonomy. It hoped to achieve these aims through the services of an ad hoc committee that was to present a "culminated" Commonwealth and a new compact of association to Congress. The committee was a disastrous failure.

After his defeat as PPD candidate for governor in 1976, Hernández Colón, who had replaced Sánchez Vilella as leader of the party, retired for a period of reflection: the fruit of his labors was the "New Thesis." Commonwealth, the New Thesis argues, had shown its "dynamism" in promoting economic growth; politically it had not merely been static but regressive. The steady expansion of federal powers and federal legislation had left Puerto Rico with less, not more, autonomy than it possessed in 1952. This process of erosion had to be reversed.

In the New Thesis the extension of autonomy is seen as the PPD's historic mission, and autonomy itself viewed as the true Puerto Rican political tradition, legitimized by the survival of a unique Puerto Rican "personality" and revealed in its "culture." It is considered the duty of the PPD to protect against Puerto Rico's hybridization under statehood.

The New Thesis called for a "historic initiative," "a new strategy." Yet it was the old program of the PPD, first set out in the Fernós-Murray bill of 1959, brought up to date by the ad hoc committee of 1973 and now radicalized and supported by arguments that make it read more like a treatise in political science than a party program. Its fundamental demand is that Puerto Rico be allowed to solve its economic and social problems and return to prosperity through a greater degree of *autosuficiencia* (self-sufficiency) and a progressive reduction of dependence on the mainland. To achieve this, Commonwealth must possess the necessary instruments. To encourage import substitution in agriculture, it must have the powers to protect home products from competition by levying its own tariffs. Labor relations, wage rates, and exploitation of mineral resources must be removed from federal control; the Commonwealth must be allowed to make trade arrangements with other countries, provided they do not injure the interests of the United States.

A sound economy is the foundation of a sound society; a society that is free from degrading political dependence and has control of its own destiny will be free of the "confusion and disorientation" in which Puerto Ricans live. Since the advantages of the Commonwealth connection would be maintained — a common market and federal transfers to the island (converted in the case of food stamps into a block grant that will enable the Commonwealth government to use federal largess as it wishes) — it might seem that the New Thesis claims the political advantages of quasi-independence without paying the economic costs. This is the constant accusation of statehooders who have always sought to label the PPD as containing elements who are *independentistas* under the skin. Former PNP Governor Luis Ferré told a House Ways and Means Subcommittee that the PPD representatives "would have you believe that the only course to follow... is to give Puerto Rico more privileges resulting in a degree of autonomy unknown under the American system. Their proposals in the area are identical to the notions advanced by the Puerto Rican Independence party."[19] Governor Romero's testimony included the statement "The PPD is asking for Puerto Rico to get the rights of a republic while at the same time making demands as if it were a state." The same reproach was later hammered home by Senator Nogueras, the PNP expert on labor: a joint resolution of the Puerto Rican legislature by which the PPD majority in March 1982 sought to use the Caribbean Basin Initiative as a lever to demand enlarged autonomy "illustrates the ambivalence of the PPD in that on the one hand they ask for the powers of a republic and on the other the benefits of a state."[20] The New Thesis does indeed present, in a polite form, many of the economic demands of the PIP[21] while its insistence on the "perturbation" evident in the urban sprawl and drug addiction seems to echo *independentista* condemnations of a society destroyed by Americanization.

The mere fact that it once again proved necessary to restate the case for autonomy lays bare the essential failure of the PPD. Despite twenty years of effort, it had made no substantial progress in obtaining from Congress the increase in autonomy that it repeatedly demanded. The generality of the "new proposals" conceals that they will entail negotiation on *specific* issues with Congress and that they may not easily be achieved, as the New Thesis asserts, "without prejudice to the United States."

Senator Baker views the New Thesis as a bundle of demands that will be "the first step towards eventual separation from our nation" and that will not be welcomed by Congress. Its tariff proposals have been dismissed as not warranting "serious consideration."[22] Many senators and congressmen — not least Senators Baker and Bush, who are close to the pro-statehood New Progressive Party (PNP) leaders — are well aware that the island statehooders are bitter opponents of "culminating Commonwealth" as a process that might, if successful, make statehood less attractive.

What, then, is the strategy that will allow the PPD to accomplish its historic mission? Is it to bring increasing pressure on Washington in spite of senatorial warnings that the New Thesis makes demands that Congress may well find unacceptable? Or is it not better to leave things alone for fear that expression of discontent with Commonwealth as it exists *now* can only encourage those who wish that it did not exist at all? The conservative members of the party harbor the same doubts about the New Thesis that Muñoz's zeal for perfection had aroused in the 1960s. Teodoro Moscoso, representative of the wing of the party that wants to "let things alone," once related to Muñoz Henry Wallace's experience as a seed dealer. Wallace had distributed new seeds on trial to farmers: all but one farmer had splendid results. Wallace visited this farmer, and found him pulling up the plants by the roots to see why they had not grown and prospered. Muñoz was not amused.

The division within the PPD persists. "Radical autonomists"

who favor a plea for an overall increase in autonomy in one operation stand in opposition to those who will not go beyond what is known as the "salami approach" — a series of ad hoc adjustments, made as the need arises, which will leave the existing political structure essentially as it is. These two strategies preserve a division that has haunted the party since its foundation: the old gap between, on the one hand, a radical wing of former *independentistas,* for whom the Commonwealth of 1952 did not represent a permanent solution but merely a step on the road to quasi-independence, and, on the other hand, conservatives for whom tinkering with Commonwealth is seen as a dangerous operation. Even Muñoz, with his dominant political personality, could not bridge this gap, though he succeeded in concealing it. That gap is now evident in the resistance of the conservative grandees of the party to the "radical autonomists" of *Pro Estado Libre Asociado* (PROELA) — the ginger group within the PPD that presses for increased autonomy. PROELA, an acronym for *Pro Estado Libre Asociado,* was organized and flourished when the PPD was out of power (1976 – 80).

It is not so much the objectives as the tactics of those who wish to push for increased autonomy that alarm PPD stalwarts as they give political ammunition to the party's enemies. For example, Hernández Colón, the leader of a respectable bourgeois party, was prepared, in 1978, to enter into what his opponents call an "infamous coalition" with the revolutionary Socialist Mari Bras, leader of the Puerto Rican Socialist Party (PSP), in order to press for free association in the United Nations. Severo Colberg, an aging and crusty survivor of the 1960s generational revolt in the PPD and now Speaker of the House of Representatives, has proposed the creation of an alliance of all "progressive autonomists," an appeal supported by Mari Bras as a new version of the "anti-annexationist front" formed to defeat the statehooders in the 1980 elections.[23] The "progressive autonomists" seek to attract to their alliance

Puerto Rican Independence Party (PIP) sympathizers, who are weary with the dismal electoral performance of their own party.

Severo Colberg's ideas were set out in an interview with the PSP paper, *Claridad,* in March 1981. The PPD was "sluggish"; the *Populares* had preached autonomy for forty years "but didn't kick and scream to get it even when the party had friends in the White House." Now pressure must be brought to bear, through the action of a "common front" of all the anti-statehood forces, to force a conflict with Washington and achieve greater autonomy. Demands were to include rights over the seabed for two hundred miles, full powers over wages and labor, and Colberg's favorite notion — separate Puerto Rican representation in the Olympic Games, a demand dear to the hearts of the *independentistas* who have captured the local Olympic Committee and whose hopes for representation at the Moscow games, disappointed by President Carter's boycott, have been the subject of a fine film. After a transfer of powers, Colberg called for a constituent assembly to draw up a new constitution and a revised version of the Federal Relations Act that would be presented to Congress, not from a suppliant seeking favors — Puerto Rico's traditional posture in Washington — but from one sovereign power to another. The new relationship would be based on a treaty which can be terminated, and not, as in the old Commonwealth concept, on a "compact."

The gap between the radical autonomists and the conservatives within the PPD is now open and public. In the autumn of 1982, it was revealed in a bitter polemic between supporters and opponents of the party's participation in Democratic presidential primaries. Hernández Colón both wishes to capture the island Democratic organization, now controlled by Romero and the PNP and, by participating in the primaries, to help place the party's close political ally and favorite son, Senator

Edward Kennedy, in the White House. "A Kennedy victory is assured," he argues, and Kennedy will support the New Thesis and enlarged autonomy. [Since this was written, Senator Kennedy has announced he will not stand in 1984. What the effects of this decision are on the PPD attitude to primaries is not clear.] To the radical autonomists, participation in the Democratic primaries means tightening the ties with the United States — "statehood bit by bit" — when their aim is to loosen those ties. Entering national partisan politics in order to achieve "leverage" in Washington will accomplish nothing and will, Colberg argues, represent a step on the road to assimilation. Those who support participation claim Colberg is "a cowardly *independentista* hiding behind autonomy."[24] Muñoz's widow views participation as deserting the heritage of her husband, who she claims asserted "the less Puerto Rico gets entangled with the partisan politics of the United States the better."[25]

The controversy over participation in the primaries reveals that the PPD cannot unite on what the appropriate relationship with the United States should be: the conflict between "cowardly *independentistas*" and "convert colonialists" remains unresolved. Driven by feuds, clouded in ambiguities,[26] discredited by a series of public scandals over abuse of control over jobs and allowances rewarding relatives and political friends, the party of Muñoz shows an extraordinary capacity for self-destruction. The struggle between the factions for the vice-presidency of the party was so bitter that the only way to restore a minimum of harmony was to abolish the post altogether. The struggle, as always, was fully reported in the press in the autumn of 1982.

The present disarray of the PPD and its decline from the hegemony it once enjoyed is seen by many as the result of the withdrawal from political life of its creator and master: Don

Luis Muñoz Marín. But to believe this would be to fall into the personalist heresy that views Puerto Rican parties as the creation of a succession of political grandees: once each vanished from the scene, the party he had created fell into warring factions to be regrouped by a new leader. While there might be some truth to this theory in the era before the emergence of a more sophisticated electorate, the reasons for the decline of the PPD must be sought elsewhere in the rapid economic and social changes taking place in Puerto Rico.[27] The narrow victory of the PNP in the 1968 election came, as one of the leading luminaries of the PPD, Professor Luis Agrait, admitted, as a "complete shock" to the PPD. It also shocked American political scientists, who had, as late as 1965, predicted that the long dominance of the PPD might become institutionalized into a one-party system, as in Mexico.[28] Yet defeat could have been foreseen and, with hindsight, seems almost a natural consequence of the "new society of the 1960s."

The catastrophic economic and social conditions in Puerto Rico during the 1930s, when production was falling off and 60 percent of the population was unemployed, provided the circumstances for the rise of the PPD. Muñoz Marín's achievement was to harness the discontents of landowners and small farmers, displaced by American sugar corporations, and the workers exploited by these corporations, to the populist program of the PPD. The party's program was a cry for social justice for the *jíbaro* dispossessed by the sugar barons, and for the sugarcane workers, the artisans, and the small industrial working class. To a society in despair, Muñoz gave hope: "A vote, only one vote I ask of you.... will you deny me your vote to a man who asks nothing, who asks nothing for himself; to this man whose sole wish is that when he dies Puerto Ricans will get a little more bread, a little more justice, a little more happiness?" The 1940 and 1944 campaigns emphasized that Muñoz and the PPD represented "the people" against those who denied them justice — the mainland sugar corporations whose dividends went up as wages sank. This gave the campaign speeches of Muñoz an anti-imperialist tinge that appealed to the Nationalists.

In the *política del pueblo* of the Populares once in power, an active government would engineer a new prosperity. The PPD substituted the paternalism of a people's government for the idealized, mythical paternalism of the old, now ruined, hegemonic landowning class whose sons would run the new concern. The PPD, it is important to realize, never professed to alter the class structure of capitalism; it merely claimed that a state legitimized by the vote of *all* the "people" would ensure social justice for *all* classes — "justice," wrote Géigel Polanco, one of the architects of the party's program, "to correct the excesses of economic individualism." The liberals of the nineteenth century declared themselves the guardians of "the great Puerto Rican family" against metropolitan Spain; in 1940 and 1944, Muñoz Marín was the guardian of the "people" against the "excesses" of American imperialism.

It was not until the 1960s that it became evident that the social base for the populism of the PPD was collapsing. The electoral strength of the PPD had been eroded by the very success of the industrialization it had fostered. The party's emblem was still the subsistence farmer of the interior — the *jíbaro* in his straw hat. Yet in its enthusiasm for industrialization, the PPD had presided over the rapid decline of the agricultural sector of the interior that had constituted its electoral stronghold. The *jíbaros* had migrated en masse to towns of the periphery in search of a better living. The PPD proved incapable of refurbishing its populist image to attract the new urban electorate of a town like Bayamon on the outskirts of San Juan — in 1950, a town of 48,000 with 1,700 cars; by the 1970s, a city of 140,000 with 27,000 cars.[29]

It was left to the pro-statehood PNP to mobilize this new electorate, drawn from those jealous of their recently achieved middle-class status and determined to preserve it. This group included the more affluent of the emigrants who had prospered on the mainland and returned to Puerto Rico. To these emigrants American citizenship — which would be guaranteed in perpetuity by statehood — was "the supreme gift" of 1917. Citizenship had enabled them to work in New York and return to the island with their savings, settling in new residential suburbs like Levittown where their life-style was the envy of those who had stayed behind. To rally this electorate, the PNP beat the anti-Communist, anti-Cuban drum. This was not merely a warning against the suicidal folly of independence; it implied that the PPD was "anti-Yankee," an ally of the *independentistas,* and soft on Communist and Cuban subversion.

It is not surprising that PNP candidate Luis Ferré, a conservative Catholic industrialist, should have won the votes of the prosperous inhabitants of the new suburban communities and of the new generation of bright executives — "the most sophisticated and educated electorate in Puerto Rico"[30] — who had grown up beside the old professional class, mainly composed of government servants, who had traditionally voted PPD. What is surprising is the PNP's success in exploiting the discontents of the unsuccessful: the urban poor, who would be expected to have found little to attract them in a candidate who attacked government paternalism in the name of free enterprise. In wooing the poor, Ferré concentrated on the PPD's indifference to their discontents — for example, on their resentment of the PPD's housing policy, which proposed moving them from their communities to faceless housing developments. Minor local PPD politicians and campaign managers, who had not made the grade in the party, saw opportunities in the PNP, which flattered the young whose allegiance the PPD was in the process of losing. For Sánchez Vilella, youth was a "valuable patrimony" that had been somehow mislaid by the party in the 1960s. If the party in power offers little, then the poor, who think in terms of immediate benefits and short-term gratifications, turn to an opposition that offers more; this is especially true in the case of local leaders, who get out the vote and must have something to promise their clients. Ferré's local leaders in the slums promised everything: streetlamps, public telephones, better buses, Christmas presents for the poor, a municipal orchestra, trees in the plaza, higher salaries for municipal employees, homes for the aged, and flood control.[31]

It was Ferré's knowledge of these local concerns that gave him victory in the poorer districts of San Juan.[32] Oscar Lewis observed how Ferré and the PNP courted an electorate that the PPD had neglected and of whose concerns it appeared to have remained in ignorance:

"My mama," says Felícita, an inhabitant of La Perla, the slum settlement under the walls of old San Juan, "has always spoken to me well of Ferré....He's not like Muñoz Marín...he [Muñoz] pays attention only to rich people and to Populares. It was Ferré, who brought running water to every house in La Esmeralda...and paid for it out of his own pocket.... Ferré gave wood to the people to fix their houses and build new ones....[During the campaign] Ferré promised to come to La Esmeralda (i.e., La Perla) on a certain day and came right on time. He came in shirt sleeves and old shabby shoes. He went around the neighborhood...and all the way down on the beach. The beach was full of garbage and stuff and people kept saying, 'Come walk up here on the cement.' He answered, 'No, I'm going this way. These people here are poor, just like me. I feel for them because I know they need help. I hope this year you'll vote for me so that I can keep all my promises. If I don't, may I lose the next election.' Truly, people felt so happy during that meeting.... Ferré promised that if he won, he would build a housing development, but not on the outskirts of the city like those of Muñoz Marín. Ferré would build houses right here in La Esmeralda so that people can live near their relatives and in their own neighborhood.... Muñoz Marín hadn't come down to La Esmeralda in about eight years.... And then he showed up about fifteen days ago, just because it's election year....He didn't hold a meeting, but only visited his Populares here. He didn't go down to the beach the way Ferré did to mess up his shoes with the shit there. Ferré is my man. He gave us a big dinner with loads of food."[33]

Not only had the PPD failed to gain the support of the new urban poor, it lost its monopoly on working-class and union support that it had enjoyed in the 1940s. Muñoz Marín had absorbed and castrated the militant unionism of the old General Confederation of Labor (CGT). The "new unionism" was increasingly independent of, if not hostile to, the PPD, which seemed to the new generation of union leaders more concerned with manipulating labor in the interests of capital than fighting labor's battles. Once again the policies of the PPD had undermined its electoral base. The government it had dominated since 1944 had become the biggest single employer on the island, the patron of a large sector of the working class. Yet it was a PPD governor who, in 1973, called out the National Guard to control the striking public servants of his own government. In the election of 1976, the PNP exploited the workers' discontents, promising them the establishment of a federal guaranteed minimum wage.

Ferré cultivated the urban poor as Muñoz had once rallied the *jíbaros* simply by listening to their problems and promising to solve them. At the same time the PNP was seen as the party of "security" by the middle and upper classes. The election of 1968 set the pattern for the future: the PNP increased its votes both in the richest and poorest districts of San Juan.

The PPD had dug its own grave. Its policies had forced the growth of a society to whose aspirations it could not respond as it had responded to the aspirations of Puerto Ricans in the 1940s and during the best years of Operation Bootstrap. The

rural populism of the 1940s could not be effective in an urbanized society, nor could the party continue to be sustained by
the rapid economic growth over which it had presided in the
1960s. By 1968, Ferré attacked the PPD as an exhausted and
obsolescent party whose electoral slogans offered "more of the
same." In 1982, PPD *frondeur* Severo Colberg demanded that
the party, which had betrayed the legacy of Muñoz, leave its
"indolent policy."[34] It had become, to a perceptive journalist,
"a seaworthy but aging freighter,"[35] covered with barnacles,
plowing the water rather than slicing it.

6.

THE STATEHOOD PARTIES

Only the Congress of the United States can admit a territory as a state of the Union. Before it so acts, Congress has to satisfy itself that two main conditions have been met: the inhabitants of the prospective state must have democratically chosen statehood in a legitimate act of self-determination and they must be economically strong enough to bear the financial obligations — in the form of federal taxes — that statehood will bring. While opinion may differ as to what constitutes a democratic decision of the prospective citizens of a new state (i.e., on the size of the majority vote necessary) and what constitutes the degree of wealth necessary to support statehood, and while the terms of admission may be and have been varied to suit individual circumstance, Congress has never failed to weigh these two conditions before admitting a territory to full statehood. Thus, if those who seek statehood for Puerto Rico are to succeed, they must show that their demand is based on the exercise of the right of self-determination by the Puerto Rican people — that is, on a vote of a clear majority.[1]

Apart from the Socialists, those parties that have advocated statehood — that is, the entry of Puerto Rico into the Union as a state — as the solution to the status question and as an escape from the colonial closet descend from the Republican party formed by José Celso Barbosa in July 1899.

The United States appeared to Barbosa, as it did to many of his contemporaries, the greatest free democracy on earth, a model of liberty, untarnished. Many Puerto Rican politicians had been annexationists, seeking in union with the United States an escape from the bondage of Spain; in 1899 almost all were supporters of statehood. Barbosa is distinguished by the consistency of his political trajectory: his defense of statehood when others wavered and moved toward independence or autonomy.

Barbosa, a black from a poor home, was trained as a doctor in the post-bellum North. Ironically, it was not at the University of Michigan, where he studied, but in colonial Puerto Rico that he experienced racial prejudice: his American qualifications were rejected by the local Spanish medical board. His case was taken up by the United States Consul. Critics reminded Barbosa that his enthusiasm for America entailed the danger of importing American racial intolerance into Puerto Rico. He dismissed such criticism by the assertion that racial prejudice could only be created by Puerto Ricans themselves, stating "There is no threat, no danger from outside."

Rather than the *collective* liberty of a free nation, Barbosa wanted his people to enjoy the *individual* liberties of United States citizens under the Constitution. In 1969, Luis Ferré, the pro-statehood New Progressive Party (PNP) governor of Puerto Rico, could still echo Barbosa: "The full recognition of liberty as the base of society arrived on our tropical beaches [with the United States invasion] on July 25, 1898." But Barbosa, it must be remembered, had come into politics when Puerto Rico was still a Spanish colony as a Republican autonomist, a disciple of the Spanish Federal Republican Pi y Margall, whose proposal for a Spanish federal constitution was based on a genuine "pact" (i.e., contract) between two sovereign bodies, which gave much more power to the component units than was available to a state of the Union. Like Muñoz Rivera, Barbosa saw the United States as "a republic of republics" and Puerto Rico as "an *autonomous* republic within the American Federation [emphasis added]." The mystique of statehood, at least in its early years, rested on a misinterpretation that allowed Barbosa to fit the old autonomist dream into the reality of the American Constitution.

Later, statehooders would emphasize the flexibility of the constitutional conventions governing the admission of new states.[2] But critics of the present-day PNP program for statehood maintain that it contains conditions for admittance to the Union — for example, insistence on Spanish as the official language in Puerto Rico and a transition period in which Puerto Rico would enjoy economic advantages denied to even the poorest state — that may, in the eyes of Congress, stretch to its limits the Constitution's doctrine of equal treatment for all states.

This exposes the fundamental weakness of the statehooders' position. Statehood can be granted only by the Congress of the United States, which has been reluctant to settle the status question in a permanent form. Further, as a condition to the granting of statehood, there must be what President Reagan has called a "substantial majority" of Puerto Ricans demanding it; the democratic premises that governed previous admissions to the Union allow no other course. In the imperialist world of 1898 – 1900, Congressional granting of territorial status as a prelude to statehood would have been regarded as an act of generosity as meeting the demand of the Puerto Rican people themselves insofar as they were represented by the island politicians. In the era of decolonization and self-determination, it might have been legally possible to bring Puerto Rico into the Union by congressional fiat without the approval of the "substantial majority." But it would not merely be a departure from all previous precedent, it would be politically unfeasible.

Statehooders have not always recognized this dilemma. In 1945, the president of the pro-statehood Republican party claimed that the granting of statehood was not to be viewed as a congressional favor but as a duty to U.S. citizens, which Puerto Ricans became in 1917. It was "a moral obligation which Congress must recognize and fulfill."[3] It was at this time that a highly emotional argument entered the statehooders' armory: Puerto Ricans had paid a "blood" tax to the United States in World War II; they had a right to representation in electing the president and the Congress that declared the war in which Puerto Ricans had died.[4] But Congress has never adopted this view and has never favored statehood as the *only* "dignified" solution to the status issue.

The statehooders have consistently failed to rally the majority in Puerto Rico that might force the hand of Congress. While it is not constitutionally correct, as Governor Towner asserted, that to be admitted to the Union the demand for statehood must be "practically unanimous," it must be substantial. And while it may be, as Senator Howard Baker is said to have asserted, that in the American system a majority is a majority of one,[5] it is hard to believe that his fellow senators would admit Puerto Rico as a state on a handful of votes. Statehooders themselves talk of "breaking the 60 percent barrier,"[6] but as the election results since 1968 have shown, there is no present prospect of achieving such a result.

The argument of statehood presented by its supporters was that it provided the only "dignified" solution through which "second-rate citizenship" in a colony could be exchanged for "first-class citizenship" in the Union. It was the emotional satisfactions of statehood as evinced in a jingle of the 1950s that supporters hoped would convince Puerto Ricans to back their cause with their votes:

> Puerto Ricans love the flag too
> For we are Americans the same as you
> But as we gaze at the forty-eight stars
> None do we see that we can call ours
> Why can't the stars be forty-nine
> Let us share in the burdens of state
> Give us a star on that rampart of blue
> Full rights as Americans in all things we do.
> Give us a voice in deciding our fate
> Let us share equal in the burdens of state.
> Keep us not helpless with no vote of acclaim
> Make us Americans not only in name.

This was not to be the case. One explanation for the early failure of the statehooders to attract support lay in the nature of Puerto Rican political mores. Before 1940, Puerto Rican political parties were formed and held together by strong, charismatic leaders. But if the party *caudillo* disappeared, the party would disintegrate, torn by the consequent wars of personalist politics. The party's hold on public opinion would thereby come undone. This happened to the Republicans once the austere, dedicated, and authoritarian Barbosa died in 1921.[7] Just as statehooders had made little impression on opinion in the United States, so their party, in tatters, was in no position to create a majority for statehood in Puerto Rico.

The elections of 1952 and the advent of Commonwealth represented the nadir of the statehood movement. Statehooders won only 13 percent of the vote against the PPD's 65 percent. With the *independentista* PIP capturing 19 percent of the vote, the *Partido Estadista Puertorriqueño* (PEP), as the heirs of Barbosa then called themselves, sank to the level of third party on the island. The PIP became the official opposition in the legislature. Yet, by 1968, Ferré, president of the pro-statehood New Progressive Party (PNP), was elected governor of Puerto Rico. How did the statehooders' decline and dramatic resurrection occur?

In the 1930s, the statehood Republican party, in an alliance with the Socialists, held power, but the alliance discredited Republican statehooders and Socialists alike. It was an unholy combination, which appeared to be the instrument of a political and economic elite that sought power merely to maintain its members' economic privileges. In 1940, Muñoz Marín and his newly formed, disciplined, and popularly based PPD exposed the Republican party's slender social base and the factiousness of its leadership, which would paralyze the party for a decade.[8]

The statehood Republicans were less concerned with pressing for statehood in Washington than with hanging onto power and patronage in Puerto Rico; they made little use of their formal connection with the mainland Republican party to transform what they regarded as a moral obligation into an act of Congress. Bill after bill proposing statehood ran into the sands of congressional indifference. For the most part, these bills were formal exercises that did not receive the concerted and sustained lobbying effort necessary to win support;[9] they were always opposed by Senator Tydings and Representative Vito Marcantonio, both proponents, for differing reasons, of independence.[10]

The resounding victories of Muñoz Marín would convert the statehooders of the *Partido Estadista Republicano* into an impotent minority. The creation of the Commonwealth in 1952 threatened to postpone indefinitely the realization of the "supreme aspiration [statehood] of the Puerto Rican people." The decision over whether to participate in the referendum on Public Law 600 divided the party, driving it to an internal struggle that came near to destroying it. After innumerable rowdy assemblies that often degenerated into shouting matches, the old, patronage-oriented leadership of Celestino Iriarte was supplanted by that of García Méndez and Luis Ferré. Both rejected the *caudillismo* of Iriarte and wished to reorganize, democratize, and revivify a party that seemed to belong to a vanished age when politics were the preserve of a selfish oligarchy. Their nascent populism rested on their claim to represent "ordinary citizens," even though Ferré was the richest man in Puerto Rico, with an industrial and financial empire extending from Venezuela to Miami, and García Méndez was chairman of a large sugar refinery in Mayagüez.

When Ferré campaigned for governor in 1968, his program included the traditional praise for statehood: "In American citizenship and statehood resides the secret of the true liberty for Puerto Ricans, liberty which means the redemption of Puerto Ricans from misery by the participation in the riches, power and grandeur of the United States." Ferré's was an appeal for harmony between beneficent capitalism — its "high moral mission" untrammeled by the state intervention of the PPD — and labor. This was combined with a populist assortment of promises for economic benefits for every sector of the population.[11] Seen by his supporters as a combination of Abraham Lincoln and Henry Ford, Ferré was to be the driving force behind the revival of the statehooders' fortunes in the 1960s.

In 1952, with the establishment of Commonwealth, this renaissance of the statehooders' fortunes appeared a distant prospect. Commonwealth implied the rejection, at least for the foreseeable future, of what Muñoz had once called the two "classical" solutions: statehood and independence. But from the outset, statehooders argued against Commonwealth as camouflaging a continuing "colonial" status, as an ambiguous arrangement that provided no permanent solution to the constitutional status of Puerto Rico: "We have maintained that the Free Associated State cannot be by its very nature a final status. It is not and cannot be, whatever the amendments and colouring with which the colonial artisans (*artesanos*) seek to endow it.... We support a referendum which presents the two national formulas of liberty: statehood and independence."

It was easy for the statehooders to capitalize on the constitutional ambiguities and the "colonial" nature of Commonwealth. But the economic success that Commonwealth brought gave the PPD its most telling argument against statehood, which was presented as the road to economic ruin that would bring back the still-remembered poverty of the 1930s. "Under statehood," declared Muñoz Marín, "the Puerto Ricans will die of hunger."[12] If Puerto Rico became a state, it would lose the privileges that had been instrumental in generating the new prosperity and that depended on what Muñoz maintained was the "unique" relationship with the United States established by Commonwealth. Moreover, as a state, Puerto Rico would be subject to substantial federal taxation that could turn economic success into disaster.

The statehooders fell back on the argument of dignity. As late as 1960, Ferré shrugged off the estimate of the Budget Bureau that statehood would cost Puerto Rico $188 million a year in federal taxes by declaring that "if statehood costs $188 million it must be wonderful." This was to apply to statehood the rhetoric of José de Diego in defense of independence: that dignity was desirable in itself, whatever the economic cost. Nor should Congress shrink from bestowing statehood because the new state might constitute a financial liability for the American taxpayer by demanding more in federal aid than would be compensated by federal taxes. "Do we have to pay our way

144 THE PUERTO RICAN PARTIES AND STATUS

in?" Governor Romero told a Yale audience. "It's not a matter of purchase. It's a matter of political rights. We didn't ask to be made U.S. citizens, but as citizens of a democratic nation we are entitled to the right to vote and to representation."[13] Statehood, its supporters are apt to assert, is a moral imperative regardless of its cost to Puerto Rico or to the United States; it cannot be refused if the U.S. citizens of Puerto Rico, by their votes, choose it.

To meet Muñoz's argument that statehood will be a costly enterprise for Puerto Rico, statehooders stand his argument on its head. It is Commonwealth, not statehood, that threatens the economic future of the island. Far from threatening ruin, they see statehood, which would provide a secure political climate for investment, as the only safeguard for *future* prosperity: the tax holidays that brought investment under Commonwealth were as impermanent as Commonwealth itself. The ambiguities of Commonwealth threatened the maintenance of the growth it had created. "The sense of political insecurity growing out of the neither fish nor fowl status of the island [i.e., Commonwealth] is the major barrier," Senator Chavez of New Mexico argued in Congress, "to the investment of capital in the island."[14] This was to be a major theme in the statehooders' economic program.

Statehood, they argued, would ensure not only that the lifeblood of private investment would continue to flow to the island but also the continuity of federal transfers critical to sustaining the standard of living of Puerto Ricans—particularly vital to the poor among them—and the economy of the island itself. Under Commonwealth, Puerto Rico received payments from the federal treasury only at the discretion of Congress: some programs were not extended to Puerto Rico, others cut back. As a state, Puerto Rico would be eligible for all federal progam grants which would be secure in perpetuity. This was the linchpin of Romero Barceló's campaign for governor in 1976: "Statehood is for the Poor." Since then, Romero has toned down this emphasis on welfare payments. Presenting Puerto Rico as a perpetual mendicant does little to gain a sympathetic hearing for statehood in Congress.

To its adversaries, statehood entails not merely economic disaster but what they term cultural genocide. English will drive out Spanish; the island culture will be swamped by the American way of life. Although many early statehooders were ruthless Americanizers, the PNP rejects with indignation the charge that it is indifferent to Puerto Rican culture. Puerto Rican culture, argues Governor Romero, is "irreducible... our people are not assimilable" — a remarkable admission from a statehooder.[15] "Our Nation," writes his predecessor, statehood Governor Luis Ferré, "the United States. Our *patria*, Puerto Rico." "The heart's affection for one's place of birth" — the *patria* — can be contained within the larger loyalty to the nation. To consecrate this union, Ferré invented the term *jíbaro* state: the *jíbaro* state will have Spanish as an official language, acknowledging the enduring presence of the *patria* under statehood.

Statehooders insist that Puerto Rico will be a Spanish-speaking state: with a Spanish-speaking electorate there is no realistic alternative. It is the constant accusation of their opponents that it is the culture of Puerto Rico, including everything from family mores and food to literature and the protection of Taino Indian archaeological artifacts, that is endangered by statehood. The PPD claims to have saved that culture from extinction through the creation of the Institute of Puerto Rican Culture (ICP). Statehooders, though, regard the ICP with suspicion, viewing it as a bolthole for the *independentistas* in the PPD and as a relic of the bad old days when the *populares* claimed a monopoly over every political appointment.

It is difficult to estimate the electoral consequences of the PNP's alleged indifference to Puerto Rican culture as the depository of Puerto Rican identity. The PNP tends to be dismissive of the PPD's concern with protecting Puerto Rico's culture. Statehood, PNP Governor Romero claims, will not prevent him from eating rice and beans. To the PPD, this only shows his vulgar incapacity to grasp what is meant by the concept of "culture" as a coherent whole—a concept that owes much to the writings of the anthropologist Ruth Benedict.[16] In contrast, Ferré favors the concept of a wider "universal" culture as opposed to the narrow "chauvinism" of the ICP, which, with its folkloric enthusiasms, presents an Indian drinking coffee out of a gourd as the symbol of Puerto Rican "culture." To many voters, Ferré must have appeared a go-ahead politician, freed from anthropological backslidings and fervor for the Spanish inheritance. A substantial minority, however, defend Puerto Rican culture as a part of their own identity, the only defense against the destruction of their "personality" by wholesale Americanization.

When the statehooders appeared before the Status Commission of 1964–66, the pessimism and disarray that had pervaded their efforts in the early 1950s was vanishing. Statehood appeared a possibility; Commonwealth had not become fixed as the final solution to the status question. Muñoz himself had admitted in 1950 that "socially and politically" the island was capable of becoming a state. In 1966, the Status Commission concluded that statehood was both a dignified solution and constitutionally possible. Further, it estimated that by 1980 Puerto Rico would reach a level of economic well-being capable of sustaining statehood. This estimate, paradoxically, was a tribute to Commonwealth. It was the success of the Commonwealth's economic policies that had seemed to bring Puerto Rico within striking distance of statehood.

Moreover, the most serious argument against statehood —

that Congress would not admit as a state a territory separated physically from the mainland and containing an indigenous, non – Anglo-Saxon population — had lost much of its strength with the admission of Hawaii and Alaska as states. Neither of the new states was contiguous to the United States, and Hawaii was a racial hodgepodge. Statehooders were jubilant.* Puerto Rico could become a fifty-first state.

The statehooders had been spurred into action by the introduction of the Fernós-Murray bill of 1959, intended to "perfect" Commonwealth by granting Puerto Rico increased autonomy in a new compact of association with the United States. For the first time, statehooders organized Puerto Ricans in New York. *El Diario*, the local Puerto Rican newspaper, printed the results of a survey for statehood that showed overwhelming support among New York Puerto Ricans. The spearhead of the campaign against the Fernós-Murray bill was a nonpartisan association called Citizens for State Fifty-One. The statehooders viewed the bill as a double threat: improvement of Commonwealth would strengthen its claims as a permanent solution; the bill was, they argued, "the first formal attempt to close the door on statehood forever." Even worse, perfection of Commonwealth might be the first of a series of steps along a road that would end in independence. Statehooders always maintained that the PPD contained crypto-*independentistas* who might come to dominate the party.

The statehooders' protests brought home to Congress that Muñoz Marín was no longer leader of a people united in their enthusiasm for Commonwealth. "I came here," Representative O'Brien told the press on leaving the island, "believing that the

---

*The PPD was quick to point out that this jubilation was based on a misreading of the processes by which Hawaii had become a state. Hawaii had been an incorporated territory since 1900, and as early as 1940, 70 percent of Hawaiians had voted for statehood in a yes/no referendum; by 1958, opposition to statehood was virtually nonexistent. Between 1953 and 1958, Congress held twenty public hearings on Hawaii's status and the House of Representatives passed two statehood bills (1947 and 1953), both defeated in the Senate.

majority of Puerto Ricans preferred Commonwealth. Now I know that an awful lot of them want statehood." Nor was this all. The failure of the Fernós-Murray bill proved that Congress was reluctant to accept culmination that would remove what Muñoz considered the "colonialist" residue from Commonwealth status. That Commonwealth, as it stood, seemed no longer to satisfy its chief architect could only strengthen the statehood ground swell.

With the PPD on the defensive after the defeat of the Fernós-Murray bill, Ferré saw the opportunity to mobilize opinion. In December 1959, the statehooders held a successful mass rally.[17] In 1965, the *Movimiento Democrático Estadista* was formed, with the intention of combining the democratic tradition of social reform with the movement for statehood. Ferré made inroads in the working-class areas by touting statehood as the "redemption of the workers," as it would gain for them the federal minimum wage. While the PPD was feeling the strain and the diminution of enthusiasm that was the product of a generation of uncontested rule, the PER was campaigning in a novel field—the university. The PER founded both student and faculty organizations, the latter (AUPE) led by one of the most radical statehooders, Orestes Ramos, who would later become a PNP senator. Under new leadership, the statehooders shed their old elitist image with its focus on control of federal patronage and defense of the economic interests of the island bourgeoisie.

The growth of statehood sentiment persuaded Muñoz Marín to stage the plebiscite of 1967: victory would give the PPD a mandate to "culminate" statehood and legitimize Commonwealth as a *permanent* solution. Whether to participate in the plebiscite or to boycott it divided the statehood party once more. Ferré was for participation: 1967 would not, he argued, be a "once and for all choice"; it would be the first of a series of plebiscites that would demonstrate the growing strength of the statehood movement. The old guard opted for abstention. Ferré's newly formed *Estadistas Unidos* attracted the young, enthusiastic statehooders.

Ferré's tactic was triumphantly justified by the showing of the *Estadistas Unidos* in the plebiscite: the party won 39 percent of the vote, more support than a statehood party had ever won in a general election. Success gave Ferré the leadership of the statehood movement. In the election of 1968, Ferré was elected Governor of Puerto Rico as president of a new statehood party — the PNP.

The electoral triumph of November 1968 was not a victory for *immediate* statehood. Most of those who voted for Ferré must have known that statehood represented his ideal; but, like Muñoz in 1940, Ferré had insisted that statehood was not an issue in the election. It would come only as the consequence of some future plebiscite, as public opinion was convinced of its desirability. The election was fought on the PPD's record in government, and on its failure to solve the problem of poverty. Puerto Ricans were confronted with the strange spectacle of a multimillionaire industrialist protesting that his political opponents had become the allies of big business and claiming that he was the messiah who would lead the underprivileged to a "new life."[18] Nor would the PNP have won without the divisions in the PPD itself after Muñoz's retirement from the party leadership. Statehooders had always prophesied that once Muñoz retired, Commonwealth would lose its glamor and appeal: "After Muñoz's career is over Commonwealth will dissolve into nothing. The only person holding this chimera together is Muñoz himself."[19]

The statehood tide was stemmed in the elections of 1972 with the victory of Hernández Colón and the Populares. Without a majority in the Senate, Ferré's government had been "sterile."[20] The return of Romero Barceló and the PNP to power in 1976 represented less a resurgence of statehood than dissatisfaction with Hernández Colón's austerity program — above all his "vampire" taxes — and his attempt to hold down wages in an effort to deal with economic problems. It was under these circumstances that Romero's *Statehood for the Poor,* published in 1973, gathered popular support, less because it was a powerful plea for statehood than because it concluded that statehood would ensure the economic well-being of the underprivileged by securing federal handouts in perpetuity and without the ceiling then imposed on some grants to Puerto Rico because it was not a state. Equal treatment as a state would bring money as well as dignity.[21] The PNP's populism was displayed in attacks on the "rich industrialists who had thrived on the excessive tax exemptions" that were a feature of Commonwealth status and that were proclaimed by the PPD to be essential for Puerto Rico's continued prosperity. It was on these nouveaux riches, not the Puerto Rican poor, that the burden of federal taxes brought by statehood would fall.

Romero Barceló interpreted his victory as providing the basis for a new drive for statehood: statehood was "a goal which can and will be achieved." His case for statehood was based on the traditional argument that Commonwealth status was a "myth" concealing "candy-coated colonialism." A recent United States Supreme Court judgment, *Harris v. Santiago* (May 27, 1980), proved that Puerto Rico was "after all nothing more than a territory under the territorial clause of the United States Constitution, regardless of the name under which its local government functioned"; that is, territory subject to the absolute powers of Congress under Article IV, Section 3 of the United States Constitution. As for independence, Romero argued in an article in *Foreign Affairs* (April 1981), it was a legitimate and constitutionally permissible escape from colonialism but not an *acceptable* alternative to statehood. Only an exiguous minority of Puerto Ricans wanted it and its economic consequences would be disastrous; it was an alternative only "in the event that the door to statehood were to be closed forever."[22]

That door was now ajar. The political conditions for success existed. Romero's support for Jimmy Carter in the Democratic Convention had broken the exclusive, pro-Commonwealth alliance between the national Democratic party and the PPD. Carter had repeated in his July 25, 1978, proclamation that he would respect the democratic self-determination of the Puerto Rican people should they choose statehood; shortly afterward and for the first time, Congress, in a joint resolution, made the same promise. For Congress to deny statehood to a Spanish-speaking state, Romero argued, "would contradict everything the United States has stood for in the world community. How, I ask, could America preach democracy and human rights anywhere on earth after having flatly denied political equality to a community of its own citizens?" Once granted by Congress, he believed statehood would be accepted by opinion in the island. Puerto Rico was a stable democratic society; if Congress gave in to the minority of terrorists favoring independence, it would surrender democracy to the rhetoric of fanatics.

In order to refute the PPD's insistent assertion that statehood, by removing tax concessions, would stunt Puerto Rico's growth, Romero modified the notion of Statehood for the Poor. It was not, he argued, merely that statehood guaranteed federal largess; this would be to continue the degrading dependence generated by Commonwealth. "We need statehood," he said, "precisely to become *less* dependent on federal transfer payments, not more so." It was the uncertainty inherent in Commonwealth that inhibited long-term investments that would strengthen Puerto Rico's economy: "With statehood, the risk obstacle would disappear, and this in itself would help to counterbalance the loss of corporate tax exemptions, because the more secure an investment is, the less return is demanded on it." Statehood had made American businessmen "aware of Hawaii." It would do the same for Puerto Rico.

The assertion that statehood would provide more security for American investment than Commonwealth was guesswork, resembling the Byzantine arguments bandied between the PNP and the PPD as to the effects of the impact of federal taxation. The emotional core of the statehood case, as always, was the dignity of first-class citizenship and the justice of being treated on an equal footing with fellow American citizens. It was a demand for *active* citizenship, for participation in the decision-making process of American democracy in Congress. Statehood, it is true, also would bring material benefits. *All* federal programs would apply to Puerto Rico and grants could not be cut down by the exercise of what the governor called "geographical discrimination." Eight representatives and two senators would be able to steer toward Puerto Rico official contracts "and other activities which find their way into the home districts of members of Congress." Thus, in the long run, all statehooders' arguments turn on the assertion that equality of treatment as a state is preferable to the special status of Commonwealth, both in terms of dignity and material welfare. Statehood would bring Puerto Rico, through congressional representation, within the American decision-making process; its demands will receive greater attention with greater leverage than that provided by resident commissioners and visiting *políticos* seeking favor by assiduous, but not always effective, lobbying.

What distinguished the statehooders of the PNP from the Populares was their optimism. Commonwealth was fading and statehood advancing; they were on the side of history. In

Romero's 1980 campaign propaganda, a graph illustrated the rise of the PNP: it depicted a secular trend, an irreversible growth of statehood sentiments.

The statehooders' output of scholarly and legal studies on the preconditions and constitutional processes necessary to attain statehood represented a growing conviction that Congress would overcome its reluctance to admit a Spanish-speaking state. Statehooders had long argued that Congress, as a consequence of the concept of the equal-footing doctrine, was obliged, at least morally, to grant statehood. Now, change both in American society and in the international climate seemed to ease the way:

Once the irreversible tide of decolonization begins to sweep the American territorial system, the force of history, the demands of the colonial masses, national and public opinion, international pressures, moral arguments and political considerations will expedite a solution to America's colonial problem and the *end* to the existence of second-class citizenship before the end of this century.... After all, the concept of statehood, like American democracy, is not static. As the nation undergoes change, inclining towards a more pluralistic, just and egalitarian society, the right of membership in the national community must necessarily expand to include all American citizens living in the overseas possessions. In this context, statehood, as a legitimate source of equal rights, could be the wave of the future and a "quantum" leap in a people's long road to freedom.[23]

On the eve of the expected 1980 electoral triumph of Romero and the PNP, statehood appeared not merely a constitutional and legal possibility, as the Status Commission of 1964–66 had recognized, but a practical possibility; the rise in the statehood vote would leave Congress with no decent alternative but to admit Puerto Rico as a state of the Union. PNP intellectuals and lawyers prepared briefs on the constitutional problems involved in the admission of Puerto Rico as a state. The campaign of 1980 had been fought on the cry of "Statehood Now"; following victory, a PNP majority could hold a plebiscite which, it was assumed, would endorse statehood. Congress would live up to the promise of the Joint Resolution of 1979. Reluctance on the part of constitutional purists on Capitol Hill could be overcome, the statehood legal historians argued, by the adoption of the Tennessee Plan, by which Puerto Rico's elected representatives would form a convention in Washington to demand statehood on the very doorstep of Congress.

The electoral defeat — for such it was — of November 1980 meant the end of "Statehood Now." The chances of at least satisfying the essential condition that Congress demanded, a "substantial majority" for statehood had faded away. The graph of pro-statehood votes had flattened out. Disappointment encouraged division. These divisions, as always, represented personal rivalries outwardly visible in different political styles. As Romero's "brutal" style had paid no electoral dividends, so Hernán Padilla's low-key "pragmatic" politics seemed to single him out as the more suitable gubernatorial candidate for 1984.

If the Puerto Ricans had failed to live up to the expectations of the PNP, there were signs that Congress would not live up to the expectations aroused by its Joint Resolution of August 1979. Here again, optimism seemed misplaced. It was not that congressmen objected to statehood for Puerto Rico as such, as an abstract concept — probably none did. It was the *terms* that the Puerto Rican statehooders imposed as a condition of statehood — above all a transition period in which Puerto Rico would be temporarily exempt from full federal taxation — that troubled the minds of the strict constitutionalists in Congress.

Senator J. Bennett Johnston (Democrat, Louisiana) was such a constitutionalist. Congress would not abandon its power to set the terms for admission to the Union. Even though these conditions, as statehooders argued, were flexible and could be adjusted to the particular conditions of the prospective state, there could be no blank check to satisfy the economic and cultural demands of the Puerto Rican statehooders. "The plenary and exclusive authority" of Congress to admit states, Johnston argued, could not be short-circuited or limited. The 1979 Joint Resolution of Congress to respect the self-determination of the Puerto Ricans did not commit Congress to accept "some unstated change," some predetermined kind of statehood.[24] To suggest that it could be otherwise was mischievous, a mere exercise in "semantic gamesmanship," a ploy that would not succeed in its object: to placate Latin American opinion and the members of the United Nations Decolonization Committee.

It is a consistent technique of Puerto Rican politicians, thwarted by the deafness of Washington to their demands, to attempt to bully where they cannot persuade. Statehooders have consistently tried to bully Congress with the specter of independence as the "refuge of dignity" should statehood be denied. In 1978, Governor Romero Barceló declared that should Congress reject statehood; then he and his party would unite "to the movement in favor of building an independent Republic."[25]

That this threat has a long history in the statehood movement[26] reveals that both statehooders and *independentistas* share a political logic: they each view their solutions as final and permanent, whereas they regard Commonwealth as transient. But this alliance of political logic stops there; it does not work in political practice. It does not prevent *independentistas* from voting for the PPD — as many did in 1980 — in order to preclude an overwhelming victory for statehood that would forever block the option of independence. Nor does it restrain PNP attacks on *independentistas* as a minority or utopia-mongers or, worse still, as Castroite fellow-travelers and Communist "subversives." But the two causes are bound together by the desire for a final, clearcut solution.

It is clear from the electoral stalemate of 1980 that only a prolonged period of political education can shift the balance of Puerto Rican politics. All the political parties went back to the drawing board. The statehooders have initiated a process of educating the electorate, which includes ten-week training sessions for instructors — "missionaries," as Romero calls them — who will preach the gospel of statehood.[27] Given this effort in political proselytizing, the status issue, far from receding, can only become more important. The PPD must hold onto its vote if Commonwealth is to endure. The statehooders must break the electoral barrier to secure a "substantial majority" if they are to convince Congress to end what they regard as Puerto Rico's colonial captivity by admitting Puerto Rico as a state. In the last instance, statehood is based on the right of self-determination of peoples, including their democratic right to belong to whatever nation state they choose. It was for this reason that the statehooders supported the British in the Falkland Islands dispute: the 1,800 kelpers scattered on sheep farms, 8,000 miles from their metropolis, had an indefeasible right to remain British.

It is one of the more profound paradoxes of Puerto Rican political history that the Socialist party, with a working-class base, became the ally of a statehood party that favored annexation by the capitalist metropolis. This is one of the most dramatic indications of the political distortions inflicted by the status issue. In 1930, Santiago Iglesias, the founder of the Socialist party, led it into an alliance with a Republican party whose leaders then represented the business elite of the island — the sugar interests, with their long history of stubborn resistance to working-class claims, and the hard-faced bosses of the needlework shops of Mayagüez.

If the alliance with the statehood Republicans in 1930 appeared inconsistent with the working-class traditions of socialism, Iglesias's support of the American connection is understandable. Iglesias, a Spanish immigrant who had formed the first labor union in Puerto Rico, was imprisoned in San Juan jail by the Autonomist government of Muñoz Rivera when the Americans invaded. It was the American military authorities who released him from prison. To Iglesias, American rule, from the outset, was preferable to persecution by native politicians. Like Barbosa, a black who professed to represent the "humble" to the "oligarchic" wing of the old Autonomist party, he valued American liberties.[28] It was under the protection of the American Army that, in July 1899, he founded the Free Federation of Workers (FLT).

Trade unions, which had been illegal in Puerto Rico under Spanish law, became legal under American law. It was as a result of an appeal by Iglesias in 1901 that Spanish laws were declared null and void when in conflict with federal laws, one of the most significant court decisions for Puerto Rico. Iglesias wanted not only the protection of American laws but also the protection of the American Federation of Labor (AFL). Following an unsuccessful strike in 1901, he sought outside help. He went to New York to learn English, supporting himself as a carpenter. He was met by Samuel Gompers of the AFL at Washington Station. "The joy of Iglesias at this reception," remarks his biographer, "must have been immense." An unknown labor leader from an unknown island "was received personally, by the officials of the most powerful and respected workers' union in the world.[29] Here stands revealed one of the psychological stimulants of Americanism.

The American connection was to govern the subsequent

history of the labor movement in Puerto Rico. Iglesias became president of the Puerto Rican branch of the AFL. As such, he deserted the revolutionary European model that he had brought from Spain for the reformist American model. Gompers's patronage brought advice, strike funds, an interview with President McKinley, and a letter from Theodore Roosevelt; Gompers himself visited Puerto Rico in 1904, reporting on the "terrible conditions" of the workers.

Iglesias consistently used his Washington connection and the influence of the AFL to give support to American governors sympathetic to labor and to undermine those, like Governor Yager (1913 – 21), who sided with the local sugar barons and employers. His enemies were not the "Yankees" but the island *políticos*. According to Iglesias, they were "more inhumane than the pirates who sailed in the Caribbean…. They are directly responsible for converting Puerto Rico into a cemetery of the living." The *independentista* intellectuals, especially that hero of modern *independentistas* José de Diego, were members of an "oligarchy who raise obstacles in the path of the progress and the welfare of the people in the name of the independence of the country."[30] Iglesias viewed American citizenship as vital to the survival of the labor movement in its battle with the island oligarchs. Thus Iglesias, like Gompers, was a strong supporter of the Jones Act.

This did not mean that Iglesias had sold out to the American capitalists. He intended to use the individual liberties guaranteed by the American Constitution to combat American economic domination of the island. The Foraker Law, which limited the size of sugar plantations to 500 acres, would be enforced; there would be a tax on corporate profits that otherwise could drain the island of capital created by Puerto Rican workers; loans from the United States would finance hospitals and schools to provide free secular education. Much of this would become part of the PPD's program in 1940. It had been learned by Muñoz Marín as a follower of Iglesias in his self-imposed exile in New York.

Iglesias regarded the status issue as irrelevant to solving Puerto Rico's pressing problems of poverty and unemployment. He viewed statehood and independence as "conventional lies which divide the workers and distract the people from urgent social and economic problems." Yet as resident commissioner in Washington (1933 – 39), Iglesias presented a bill to Congress demanding a plebiscite on statehood, and he opposed the New Deal in Puerto Rico as, of all things, a "socialist" proposal.

How had this transformation come about? Unlike Gompers, who rejected the formation of a labor party on the mainland, Iglesias always considered *political power* essential in Puerto Rico, where organized labor was weak and "pure and simple unionism impossible" — a belief enforced by the habitual hostility to labor of Puerto Rican politicians.[31] In 1915, Iglesias refounded a Socialist party. He had no thoughts of transforming capitalist society, he merely wanted to give labor more muscle within it. During the campaign of 1924, the Unionist party of Barceló and a section of the Republican party formed a coalition called the Puerto Rican Alliance; Iglesias regarded this as a dictatorship of the rich, "a type of government," he wrote to Gompers, "like that of Mussolini." In opposition, the Socialists formed an electoral alliance with the dissident Republican Martínez Nadal, called the Coalition. The results of this alliance were fatal to the Socialist party. Nadal was a convinced *estadista*; Iglesias therefore became involved in the status issue, which his party had hitherto regarded as an irrelevance, while the Republicans showed no enthusiasm for the Socialists' labor legislation.

Some Socialists regarded Iglesias's alliance with a bourgeois party, engineered for the sake of his own political power, as a betrayal of the workers, during the bitterest and fiercest strikes in Puerto Rican history. Iglesias was accused of being "tied to the wagon of the bourgeoisie," cooperating with the governor and the employers to secure settlements acceptable to both. In 1934, the leadership of Iglesias's Free Federation of Workers sought to persuade striking sugar workers to accept a settlement negotiated with the Association of Sugar Producers; in 1937, the dockers sought the support of the Congress of Industrial Organizations (CIO) to fight settlements which favored the shipping companies, negotiated by the FLT and the AFL. *Afirmación Socialista* and the Socialist youth protested against the "treason" of these sacrifices made for the sake of political power and industrial peace. "The Red Flag has lost its color,"[32] they cried. Meanwhile, dissidents were expelled from the party by an authoritarian leadership. Dominated by "newcomers," who were professional negotiators more than labor leaders, the Socialist party was losing all contact with its grassroots membership. The disillusioned deserted the party. The Coalition had been a disaster.

It was Muñoz Marín who was to implement Iglesias's program after 1940. The Socialist party, its leadership bitterly divided after Iglesias's death in 1939, itself died. In 1952, with 3 percent of the vote, the party was dissolved.

Its legacy is nevertheless important and still influences labor politics in Puerto Rico. Iglesias sought to train the Puerto Rican working class to use government agencies to settle labor disputes in the reformist tradition of the AFL. Iglesias insisted that permanent union with the United States — finally in the form of statehood — was a necessity for the working class. He resolutely opposed Tydings's independence bills as "suicidal."

In the eyes of the left-wing, Marxist *independentistas,* this separation of the working-class movement from the independence movement constitutes the historical crime of Iglesias and has led to an underestimation of his early services as the creator and inspirer of a working-class movement.[33] Marxists maintain that only if the class struggle and the struggle for independence are united can they triumph.[34] The workers must be persuaded to see the connection between colonialism and the oppression they themselves suffer and join the forces of national liberation. Santiago Iglesias rejected Marxism and the Leninist critique of imperialism. In the reformist socialism he had learned from Samuel Gompers, the "abuses" (Iglesias's own word) of capitalism could be remedied within the system by reliance on the liberties secured in the Constitution of the imperial metropolis itself.

7.

THE INDEPENDENCE PARTIES

To the advocates of independence, the Popular Democratic Party (PPD) and the New Progressive Party (PNP) are "colonialist," committed to the defense of union with the imperialist metropolis and to the proposition that the economic well-being of Puerto Ricans depends on the maintenance of that union. In the lexicon of the independence movement, Commonwealth status is colonialism in disguise; statehood represents outright annexation.

The rhetoric of the independence movement can be sampled in the prologue, written by *independentista* Margot Arce de Vazquez, to the works of Bishop Antulio Parrilla, S.J., himself a supporter of independence and a prominent participant in demonstrations against the American military presence in Puerto Rico:

Under the mask of that juridical fiction called the Free Associated State and of an economic progress that reaches only a minute section of the population, is concealed the harsh reality: a reality that can be described by saying that Puerto Rico is a colony of the

United States, the richest and most powerful neo-capitalist empire in the world. As a consequence Puerto Rico finds itself underdeveloped, exploited and poor. Eighty percent of her wealth has passed into the hands of absentee American corporations which make no contribution to our Treasury and whose greed is attracted by a cheap labor force.[1]

Juan Antonio Corretjer, admired as a poet even by his political enemies, is committed to the armed struggle against the United States. In his view the reformists who once supported autonomy under Spain and are now the champions of Commonwealth have injected a "lethal poison" into the political life of Puerto Rico; their mission has been—and still is—to "serve the Empire" by supporting a policy that ensures American domination by clothing it with a specious respectability, tying the Puerto Rican nation "to the chariot of imperialism." Corretjer believes that Puerto Rico, though consistently betrayed by its leaders, has a right, like all other nations, to independence.[2] Reformism has "short-circuited" that right. Corretjer was a friend and admirer of the Nationalist leader Pedro Albizu Campos and second in command of the Nationalist party. The Nationalists, once the most serious threat to the American presence in Puerto Rico, have ceased to exist as an organized political force. But an understanding of the history and nature of the Nationalist movement is essential to comprehending the psychological roots of *independentismo* in its more radical forms.

"The political personality of Pedro Albizu Campos is, in reality, the contemporary history of Puerto Rico. With the passage of time the true significance of his patriotic activity grows, giant-like, and the relevance of his thought and his action begins to grip the hearts of our youth. His shadow today rests not only upon his beloved island but takes on a continental and universal significance."[3] This claim is made for the leader of the Nationalist party, who died in 1965 after twenty-five years in American prisons on charges of advocating the overthrow of American rule by violence. His followers are now divided, some belonging to an exiguous minority of terrorists, others scattered among the radical movements in the island.

Founded in 1922, the Nationalist party was committed to the sovereign independence of Puerto Rico; it languished until Albizu Campos became its president in 1930, injecting it with his radical nationalism.

Like so many Third World nationalist leaders, Albizu Campos attended a "colonial university." At Harvard, he met sympathizers with Irish nationalism, and the Irish road to national independence became and remained a model to him, assuming particular importance when the Nationalists failed, in the election of 1930, to gain sufficient support to promise any future as a parliamentary party. Misreading Irish history and misunderstanding the mass support for Irish nationalism that derived from the congruence of Catholicism and national sentiment, he attributed the winning of Irish independence to the "blood sacrifice" of the martyr rebels executed after the Easter Rebellion of 1916. His most significant and lasting contribution was to revive the tradition of Ramón Emeterio Betances, one of the few Puerto Rican separatist leaders who advocated independence from Spain before 1898, by setting Puerto Rican nationalism in a Caribbean and Latin American context.[4] Albizu Campos held that it was essential for the continued independence of Latin American nations that the United States be "booted out of the Caribbean.... Our cause is the cause of the continent." In 1925, he went on a tour of Latin America to win converts for the liberation of Puerto Rico, a nation that, during the nineteenth century, had missed out in the great continental independence struggle against Spain.

Emphasis on the international dimension of Puerto Rico's

fight for independence diverted attention from the Nationalists' lack of domestic support. The 1932 election was presented to Albizu's followers as a test of whether democracy could exist in the colony; once failure proved it could not, Albizu rejected the electoral battle as "a periodic farce to keep the Puerto Rican family divided."[5] This was a relapse into the political traditions of Spain, to Albizu the admired "mother country," whose values stood in stark contrast to those of America's "materialist" democracy. Those Spanish parties, particularly the Republicans, with no hope of winning elections, boycotted them by an operation known as the *retraimiento,* or withdrawal from politics. They then blamed the system for denying them a voice.

Rejecting the electoral road, the Nationalists fell back on the Irish model: "blood sacrifice." Independence would be forged in a "frontal assault" on American imperialism, which was equally determined to persecute nationalism out of existence. The assassination of the chief of police, Colonel Francis E. Riggs (February 26, 1936), was vengeance for the killing of Nationalist students. The two Nationalist "executioners" of Riggs were, in their turn, killed by the police. At their funeral, Albizu delivered his most famous oration: "There is only one entrance to immortality," Albizu declared, "the gate of courage which leads to sacrifice for the supreme cause. There must be sacrifice for the independence of the country."

The peculiar psychological foundations of Albizu Campos's brand of nationalism is the subject of César Andreu Iglesias's novel *Los Derrotados* (*The Defeated,* written in 1956), the story of the pathetic failure of a Nationalist group of amateur terrorists to assassinate an American general and blow up a U.S. Army petrol dump. Nationalism is presented as a mystique, a religion of blood sacrifice; two of the women Nationalists are *santas,* emotionally moved by the Sermon on the Mount as the creed of a dedicated elite of "chosen ones" converted to the "transcendental beauty of heroism." Don Pedro (Albizu) is worshiped as the poetic messiah whose messages from prison recite the martyrology of those who have died in "divine violence" and whose death announces "the hour of sublime sacrifice." His followers reject "this putrefying society" where men are "enslaved by monthly payments" for the car. They wear black ties to symbolize their mourning for their lost freedom.

It is important to realize that for the Nationalists this freedom was lost in 1898, hence the mystical attachment to a simple rural world of paternal coffee planters and independent *jibaros*, destroyed by the advance of American capitalism and the import of canned foods. The "traitor" Muñoz Marín, who had won the *jibaros'* vote, destroyed the very basis of their existence by welcoming American investment and the way of life that came with it. The hatred of the Nationalist conspirators is poured on the "traitor" Muñoz and the Americanized consumer society he had brought into being; their contempt is reserved for the *independentistas* of the Puerto Rican Independence Party (PIP) who think that national freedom can be won through the electoral struggle "without the fight, without sacrifice, without blood." In a rotten society, death is the only escape for the "individual touched by the divinity of heroism." That heroism would bring no immediate and tangible results was of no importance. Nationalists were in love with the grave and at the same time inspired by a naive optimism: Albizu sought to finance his activities by selling bonds that would be redeemed by the Republic of Puerto Rico.

César Andreu Iglesias was a Marxist. While in his novel he writes with sympathy for "the mad ones" and shares their violent anti-Americanism — all Americans appear as gross caricatures represented by drunken sailors staggering about in Old San Juan — as a Marxist he considered their philosophy of individual heroics profoundly mistaken. The "chosen ones" were sacrificing themselves for nothing in a political and social vacuum. For César Andreu the strike alone is the mass action that will bring independence: "From small fights you go to major battles. Without the people nothing is possible. You must know them and understand their drama." The Nationalists, as a self-chosen elite, nostalgic for a paternalist past, indifferent to and ignorant of the concerns and demands of the working classes, must fail; the future lay in an alliance of nationalism and socialism. Throughout his book, the Nationalists talk of their "movement," never of a party. The similarity, if not sympathy, with contemporary Fascist movements — particularly with the Spanish Falange during the Civil War of 1936 – 39 and under Franco — is the most disturbing aspect of Albizu Campos's political philosophy. Not all members of his National Army of Liberation were unsullied idealists.

Nationalist violence flared up at the height of the depression of the 1930s and again in the 1950s. In October 1935, there were clashes between the police and students, followed by the linked reprisals of the Nationalist assassination of police chief Riggs and the subsequent murder of the assassins by the police. The young Nationalist assassins were canonized as martyrs by Albizu. On Palm Sunday, 1937, a parade of Albizu's Liberation Army was caught in police cross-fire, which killed twenty. This was the "Ponce Massacre," and it has been regarded by Nationalists as a determined attempt to destroy their movement.[6] On October 30, 1950, the Nationalists mounted an uprising in the island; it lasted seventy-two hours and left thirty-two dead: they included twenty-one Nationalists, nine policemen, and one National Guardsman. Two days later, two New York Puerto Ricans attempted to kill President Truman. On March 1, 1954, four Nationalists managed to get a gun into the House of Representatives in Washington; five congressmen were wounded. Albizu praised the gunmen's "sublime heroism."

In the short term, violence was politically counterproductive. It put all the Nationalist leaders behind bars, leaving the movement without direction. Albizu himself was in prison from 1937 to 1943, from 1951 to 1953, and again from 1954 to 1964. Yet violence appeared the only course left to a movement that could gather no mass support. Albizu was a Nationalist leader during the years of the Great Depression, of massive unemployment, and falling wages. Yet he made no serious attempt to mobilize working-class discontent. His appeal to the workers was based on denunciations of the activities of American banks and attacks on the sugar barons. But, given his conviction that independence must be the platform for *all* Puerto Ricans, he could not base his movement on the claims of *one* class. In 1934, he responded to the sugar strikers' call to lead their movement,[7] but this did not signal the advent of revolutionary alliance between socialism and nationalism.[8] In 1935, Corretjer, secretary general of the Nationalist party, confessed that Albizu's "privileged intelligence was not that of a working-class revolutionary. Our history would have been different and better had Albizu been a Communist."

But there was a deeper reason for the Nationalists' failure to mobilize working-class discontents than Albizu's view of demands for higher wages and better working conditions as irrelevant to the national struggle. His nationalism was culturally conservative, harking back to the "old collective felicity" that had been destroyed by the barbarians in 1898, and romanticizing Puerto Rico's Spanish past. His famous speech in 1933 on the "day of the Race," celebrating the Hispanic heritage, was a poetic justification of the Spanish contribution to Latin American culture: Puerto Ricans were, via Spain, the heirs of the humanist civilizations of Greece and Rome, and Puerto Rico was a Catholic civilization. To Albizu, Puerto Rico was ethnically, culturally, and *religiously* a nation crushed by the materialism of the Protestant barbarians. Albizu held firmly to the view that Spain had granted its colony national independence in the Charter of 1897; American sovereignty was illegitimate because it rested on a treaty between Spain and the United States that was made without consulting and over the head of what was already, in international law, a sovereign nation. This piece of juridical casuistry — for such it was — remained his basis for denying the legitimacy of the American presence in Puerto Rico.

In his later years, Albizu's nationalism came to resemble the anticolonialism of Frantz Fanon, the ideologue of the Algerian nationalist revolt against France. Central to it was the conception that colonialism rested on the cooperation of the colonial bourgeoisie;[9] entrapped in the toils of dependent capitalism, the colonists consented to the presence of and cooperated with the agents of the metropolitan power. Shed of its backward-looking, reactionary character, Albizu's doctrine, which had led him to sympathize with fascism, could become absorbed into modern, Marxist-Leninist anticolonialism. As he repeatedly stated, the only people who benefited from Puerto Rico's economic integration with the United States were the mainland investors. This view was based on the assumption that Puerto Rico was a naturally rich country and that its misery resulted from the "confiscation" of its wealth by U.S. capitalists; once the expropriators had been expropriated the Republic of Puerto Rico, in possession "of all its material riches," would flourish. According to Albizu, the "fear of independence" on the grounds that it would bring economic disaster was a baseless propaganda ploy of the "annexationists."

For a brief moment in the early 1930s, it appeared to some that Albizu Campos, with his metallic oratory, might become the charismatic leader of an independent Puerto Rico. But it was Muñoz Marín, not Albizu, who would become the messiah, leading his people *from* independence *to* acceptance of Commonwealth. To Muñoz, the *patria* of the Nationalists was an abstraction, the quest of intellectuals steeped in an outdated romanticism. The reality was the *patria pueblo*—the real people of Puerto Rico who demanded, not the emotional satisfactions of independence, but bread and work. The "people" responded by voting for Muñoz and Commonwealth. "The nation," Albizu wrote, "consented to its own material and moral dismemberment." This seeming betrayal was inevitable: democracy cannot function in colonial regimes.

Hence, Albizu rejected the plebiscite of 1952 as a "farce." Only *after* a transfer of power to a Puerto Rican Republic could the people express their true opinion. Albizu's insistence on the complete withdrawal of the United States as a prior and necessary condition for the exercise of self-determination, together with his insistence on the necessity of placing the Puerto Rican status issue in an international context, is the main political legacy of the protomartyr of nationalism.

Albizu Campos was active in Puerto Rican politics for only six years; little seems to remain of his movement. A handful of faithful followers appear annually before the Decolonization Committee of the United Nations to denounce "American imperialism" for imprisoning "freedom fighters." Some, like Lolita Lebron, imprisoned for participating in the 1954 gunning down of congressmen and released by President Carter in 1979, seek to maintain the religious mysticism of the earlier generation; the more pragmatic survivors appear on platforms pleading for a united *independentista* front. But they are symbols rather than political organizers.

Yet Albizu's uncompromising nationalism, and his bitter anti-Americanism that went beyond accusations of cultural genocide to embrace physical genocide (the birth-control programs of the colonial governments were presented as a deliberate attempt to destroy the Puerto Rican nation),[10] remain a disturbing ingredient in Puerto Rican society. At a time in the 1930s when a generation of Puerto Rican politicians appeared incapable of rising above their petty concerns, Albizu Campos kept alive the ideal of independence and appeared, even to many who rejected his teachings, as having salvaged the dignity of Puerto Ricans. His rejection of American "materialism" salves the consciences of those perforce enmeshed in it. Even those who regard his legacy as illiberal and disastrous — "a philosophy of the grave" that condemns deluded enthusiasts to the useless sacrifice of their lives — cannot always bring themselves to condemn him.

Albizu's legacy of violence has come to rest with the young. While there is a tradition of political violence enshrined in the martyrology of the Nationalist movement, violence has no roots in Puerto Rican society as it does in Northern Ireland or the Basque provinces. Even so, the seeds of violence, once sown, can germinate in a society and sprout when those societies fail to provide the material benefits their political, social philosophies profess to provide. Terrorists are exponents of a *politique du pire*. Economic collapse, they argue, as in the 1930s, will show that colonialism is not merely spiritually and morally degrading; it cannot, in the long run, sustain, in purely economic terms, a dignified life. When this comes about, the democracy with which the metropolitan power has endowed its colony can be, in the jargon of terrorists, "destabilized."

Since it was clear that "democracy" would reject the independent Republic, Albizu Campos and his movement abandoned the "electoral path." But two other parties that reject permanent association with the United States and advocate creation of an independent republic participate in elections. They are the *Partido Independentista Puertorriqueño* (PIP) led by Rubén Berríos Martínez; and the *Partido Socialista Puertorriqueño* (PSP) led by Juan Mari Bras. Berríos is a law professor, a product of Yale and Oxford, and, like José de Diego before him, a compelling orator. Mari Bras is also a lawyer; his Castilian accent and didactic Marxist-Leninism mark him as a member of the bourgeois intelligentsia and would seem to alienate him from the workers whom he seeks to bring into the "struggle for national liberation."

The PSP's attacks on American imperialism and its exaltation of the Cuban Revolution are contained in the weekly *Claridad*, on sale all over the island. The PIP rejects the Cuban model and its anti-Americanism is less strident. It hopes to secure from Congress independence accompanied by a transitional period in which favorable economic concessions will ensure the economic viability of the infant republic. The PSP sees independence as the fruit of a revolutionary, anti-imperialist struggle, though, at the moment, that struggle must be conducted by participating in "colonial" elections and by forming popular fronts to resist "annexation."

If, as I shall argue, there is a widespread but latent feeling of a separate *puertorriqueño* identity, why has it not been translated into a powerful political movement dedicated to independence? Since 1952, when the PIP gained 19 percent of the vote with two senators and four representatives in the local legislature, the fortunes of the party have gone into decline. By 1960, it had lost its position as an official party because it lacked the votes required to register; in the elections of 1980, it attracted, with the PSP, a mere 5.7 percent of the votes.[11]

Independentistas argue that the PIP's poor showing is the product of fear: fear for the future of an independent Puerto Rico generated by persistent propaganda that argues that an independent Republic is doomed to economic decline and political disaster; and fear, in the present, of repression of *independentistas* by a "colonial" regime. Bishop Antulio Parrilla, S.J., talks of the "socialization of fear," "the culture of silence." Above all is the fear of losing American citizenship in a community where unrestricted emigration to the north has become a way of life for many Puerto Ricans, coupled with the fear of losing American investments, which are the lifeblood of the economy.

Without the constitutional link with the United States — which provides a protected market, an escape valve for the unemployed, and federal bounty — the opponents of independence argue, the standard of living on the island would sink to that of a banana republic with the per capita income of the Dominican Republic or Haiti. To meet this threat the PIP now argues for a lengthy transition period before full independence; it claims that it is the moral duty of the United States, in order to compensate for its "plunder" of Puerto Rico since 1898, to grant transitional terms that will allow the independent Republic of Puerto Rico to become, with time, a viable nation state. This is the island version of the politics of guilt reparations, sought in the United States by the blacks for their slavery and by the Indians for their loss of territory.

The political disasters implicit in independence depend on the model that its opponents adopt. In the 1950s, Trujillo's dictatorship was held up as a warning of the fate of independent Caribbean ministates. Once the Cuban Revolution lost its democratic bloom, the unpleasant nature of a one-party state was trumpeted by the anti-Castro Cuban exiles; to follow the Cuban model would entail the advent of shortages and rationing and a dependence on the Soviet Union more humiliating than dependence on the United States. Equally unpromising was Manley's Jamaica with its alleged combination of political gun-toting and empty shops — the latter the consequence of Manley's repudiation of the capitalist world and of U.S. support.

Both Cuban "oppression" and Jamaican "chaos" were widely reported in the Puerto Rican press during the election campaign of 1980.

There is a generalized fear that the dignity of independence may be purchased with the sacrifice of the comforts of the consumer society ensured hitherto by the American connection. The precondition of a successful independence movement would seem to be the gigantic task of changing the nature of Puerto Rican society. A large sector of the population must be weaned from a yearning for cars and color television; housewives must reject the vision of the good life portrayed in the store windows of that palace of consumerism, the air-conditioned shopping center of the Plaza de las Americas.

Repression has always been a favorite explanation for the political impotence of independence movements in colonial societies. The general will for independence, they argue, is not allowed to express itself, because those who share it are afraid to vote or to declare their allegiance to the independence parties. In the 1950s, this was a valid argument. After the Nationalist uprising of 1950, PIP militants who rejected the "armed struggle," including then party leader Gilberto Concepción de Gracía, were arrested and held for questioning.[12] Outrage at infringement of civil liberties is less valid when PIP leaders are now arrested for illegal acts committed during their campaign of "pacific militancy" in their struggle against the "institutional violence" of a colonial regime. For example, the occupation of U.S. Navy land in Culebra in the 1970s — an action for which party president Rubén Berríos Martínez was sentenced to imprisonment — was clearly illegal, as are actions in support of squatters whose settlements are in breach of the law, however unjust that law may be. It is a consistent practice of independence movements in colonial nations to "test" the colonial regime by actions that are illegal and that will force the government to try and imprison those who undertake them. This gives the movements valued publicity and news coverage. Since the laws the protesters violate are chosen for their unpopularity, punishment for breaking them exposes the "brutality" of the colonial regime.

At the present, though, the PIP does not suffer from repression. Its propaganda circulates freely; it fights elections as a legal party; its campaign funds are provided by a government subsidy; its leaders appear on television; it is not harassed by the police unless illegal acts are committed or encouraged; and its militants are usually provided with passports to visit Cuba. Hence the charge of more subtle forms of persecution in the form of job discrimination: it is said that employing an *independentista* may embarrass a firm that has connections with the government; that employers are provided with blacklists by the Federal Bureau of Investigation of the Commonwealth police, based on telephone tapping; that *independentista* professors of the University of Puerto Rico are not promoted in the university, a charge difficult to believe given their prominence in the social sciences.

That there is some substance in such charges is undoubted, though, as in all societies, those who fail to find jobs through their own shortcomings are apt to attribute their failure to external forces. There is a good deal of evidence that questionable police procedures are employed against the PSP. This is not surprising any more than that the British police keep tabs on sympathizers with the Irish Republican Army. The PSP's rejection of the "armed struggle" has been ambiguous in contrast to the resolute legalism of the PIP with its firm and repeated commitment to the "electoral struggle."

Since the PIP cannot convincingly argue that it is only the fear of repression that accounts for its poor electoral performance, it blames its lack of electoral support on its inability to compete equally with parties whose electoral coffers are regularly replenished by rich supporters and the fact that the media are controlled by its political enemies — particularly Cuban exiles who display a ferocious hostility toward the independence movement.[13] It is not so much that the media engage in political propaganda campaigns against the independence parties but that they saturate society with the values and the attractions of the American way of life, sapping the vitality of the "national" culture without which the independence movement loses its raison d'être.

One of the more convincing explanations of the PIP's electoral defeats is what has been called the *posibilista* reaction of the electorate. Since 1968, Puerto Ricans, like voters elsewhere, have tended to vote against governments in power.[14] "As it normally does, the electorate has gone back to the *posibilista* reaction," wrote Noel Colón Martínez, the defeated PIP candidate for governor in 1972; "Ferré had to be turned out and he could only be defeated by Rafael Hernández Colón [the PPD candidate]. Ideas, principles, hopes of a real and permanent change were buried by the necessity of defeating a bad government."[15] Defeat of the PIP, whose followers — *pipiolos* — deserted the party ticket to vote for Hernández Colón, did not, it was argued, signify the demise of the party. The faithful would resurrect it. Nevertheless, the pattern was repeated in 1980. The election of that year was fought, Berríos maintains, on a "stop Romero" campaign. Once again, the PIP suffered the *posibilista* effect. Hence the desertion of all but hard-core militants to the PPD as the best instrument to defeat the "annexationists" of the PNP. "We were reduced to the rock bottom of the party."[16]

"Fear" of independence, the multiplier effect of "repression," and the *posibilista* reaction of the electorate are all external deterrents to voting for *independentista* parties. They enjoy common currency in minority parties as explanations for electoral defeat. But some blame must rest with the PIP itself, which has been consistently weakened by its own tactical ambiguities, by its domestic squabbles, and by its failure to expand its social base beyond a core of middle-class intellectuals. These failures are exacerbated by the presence, on its left, of a party — the Puerto Rican Socialist Party (PSP) — that seeks to combine the class struggle and the political demand for independence within the overall scheme of Marxist-Leninist anti-imperialism. All this has led to periodic spasms of desertion or expulsion from the PIP of those who have "put themselves outside the party."

The history of the PIP — in particular its foundation and the crisis of 1970 – 73, which resulted in domination of the party by its present leader, Rubén Berríos Martínez[17] — explains the party's internal difficulties.

While the present-day *independentistas* claim descent from the heroes of the independence movement against Spain, and celebrate every year the *Grito de Lares* (the short-lived independence uprising against Spain in 1868), the founding father of the present party was José de Diego. De Diego was a florid poet and orator who parted company with Muñoz Rivera's Unionist party on the issue of independence. De Diego's Mazzinian eloquence set a tone that has never vanished from the *independentista* repertoire; his legalist tactic — "fighting within the regime against the regime" — remains the strategy of the PIP.

Consciously or subconsciously, de Diego realized that support for independence came from elite and middle-class intellectuals like himself. As the lawyer of a sugar company, and as a resolute and doctrinaire defender of laissez-faire economics, he was hostile to the working class and opposed every law that would improve working-class conditions. For many years, the *independentistas* presented independence in the liberal rhetoric of nineteenth-century nationalism, which had little popular appeal; nor did they make a serious attempt to organize a mass party. The desirability of and necessity for independence were, to them, self-evident truths.

But the problem was not only that the cause of independence lacked working-class support. Unlike the nationalist movements of nineteenth- and early twentieth-century Europe, independence also failed to become the rallying cry of a liberal bourgeoisie. What Marxists call a "national bourgeoisie" did not emerge to challenge the metropolitan power. By the 1960s, local exponents of dependency theories regarded the Puerto Rican bourgeoisie as agents of metropolitan capitalism, a "lumpen" bourgeoisie of technocrats serving the great American corporations, while Puerto Rican society as a whole was enmeshed in the pursuit of a pale island imitation of the American way of life and engaged in an orgy of negative saving sustained by easy credit.

The more immediate origins of the PIP lie in a nonparty group, the *Congreso pro Independencia* (Congress for Independence, or CPI), founded in 1943. Besides a handful of Communists and assorted *independentistas,* it included members of the PPD, since Muñoz Marín had not publicly rejected independence and the CPI in return disowned any notion of founding an independent party. By 1945, Muñoz was moving toward the Commonwealth solution and had come to regard the CPI as a dangerous antiparty in embryo and as an attempt to "sabotage" the PPD. It was Muñoz who forced the formation of the PIP by declaring, in the "Ukase of Arecibo," that membership in the CPI was irreconcilable with membership in the PPD. PIP leader Concepción de Gracía was a former Nationalist. The bulk of his party was made up of PPD sympathizers who were disillusioned with the "treason" of Muñoz and by his betrayal of the ideal of independence for the sake of Commonwealth.

From the beginning, the PIP was caught in ambiguity. While it accepted the electoral struggle and rejected the violence of the Nationalists, elections were guided by the constitution of 1952, which the PIP considered a farce, a cloak for continued colonialism without a shred of legitimacy. Thus de Diego's tactic was revived: "within the regime against the regime." "In its struggle," declared Concepción de Gracía, "our party will use all the working tools which the colonial regime puts in its hands to liquidate that regime."[18] Hence the contortions. While the PIP refused to elect members to the Constituent Assembly of 1950, it participated in the election of 1952 under the rules of a constitution drawn up by that assembly. At first the PIP refused to accept campaign contributions provided for parties by law in 1957; in 1959 it agreed to accept them.

The image of ambiguity was evident in the party's relationship to the heritage of the Nationalist party, with its mystique of voluntarism and blood sacrifice. Many PIP militants were former Nationalists; in the early years, the party leaders constantly asserted reverence for Albizu Campos. "If it was not for the *entronque nacionalista* which governs the heart of every *independentista*," declared Berríos Martínez, "the imperialists would have destroyed our country years ago....In 1946 the PIP succeeded in embodying in its aspirations the virile and uncompromising frontal fight inherited from the Nationalist party." The PIP rejected the armed struggle of the Nationalists; but tributes to Albizu were, to its enemies, proof that it was a party of violence.

Thus, once again, the contradictions. The PIP took no part in the Nationalist uprising of 1950; yet, after the deaths of young Nationalists, it could not condemn the attempt. Instead, in its Declaration of Aguadillas, it declared the government of

Puerto Rico guilty of provoking the uprising by "seeking to impose on the Puerto Rican people a political measure, with the name of Constitution, which defrauds the legitimate rights of the people and tends to validate the colonial system... this outrage to the dignity of the Puerto Rican people has led one of the most pacific peoples on earth to a state of unrest and protest which has culminated in the present revolutionary movement."[19] Muñoz immediately insisted that this was to support "assassins"; that the PIP, by refusing to participate in the referendum on Public Law 600, still held to the Nationalists' "criminal force of bullets." The image of tolerating violence was pinned on the party.

This image was not altogether without foundation. Although the leadership stuck to legalism, the younger militants were critical of the party's immersion in "electoralism" and "parliamentarianism." Given the diminishing returns of the "electoral way," they questioned the point of playing politics in a colony. The poor electoral performance of *independentismo* merely served to strengthen the argument of its adversaries that the Puerto Rican people decisively rejected independence. In 1959, those *independentistas* who saw no future in fighting and losing elections hived off to form the *Movimiento pro Independencia.*[20]

The divide between the militants and the legalists overlapped another rift in the party. In the 1970s, a group calling themselves the *terceristas* (third party) made an attempt to "unite the party on the left," taking the Cuban Revolution as their model, seeking to combine the struggle for national independence with the class struggle.

As the *terceristas* moved leftward, Berríos was moving in the opposite direction. He increasingly toned down the socialism of the party's 1970 program, emphasizing *democratic* socialism and pleading for a "Puerto Rican socialism" that would owe nothing to the foreign models so dear to his opponents. Without attacking the Cuban Revolution in toto, he dissociated his party from any connection with it. By 1980, he was reassuring American businessmen that the PIP constituted no threat to humane capitalism. The party lost its militant leftists; Carlos Gallisá, for one, formerly an ally of Berríos, believed that the rightward drift would turn an independent Puerto Rico into a "tropical Republic" ruled by a Creole bourgeoisie.[21] Only the resolute adoption of a true Socialist line, in alliance with the anti-imperialist liberation struggle, could broaden the base of the PIP beyond its middle-class, professional core—something that Berríos' vague "Puerto Rican socialism" could not hope to achieve.

In the Puerto Rican context, Marxist-Leninist socialism, Berríos argued, could only lose votes; his opponents held that his socialism was mere rhetoric, that his obsessive concern with the primacy of nationalism and his defense of Puerto Rican culture hid a failure to realize that the proletariat must be brought into the struggle for independence and given a decisive voice in an independent Republic. As César Andreu Iglesias had long argued, the true supporters of independence were those who suffered in their bones the "objective" results of colonial oppression.[22] The PIP must include the workers in a multi-class party or perish.

Berríos viewed the *tercerista* line as a challenge to his leadership while the *terceristas* considered Berríos the *caudillo* of a centralized party. A postmortem into the PIP's electoral disaster of 1972 reported that "the militants are completely cut off from the process of decision-making in the party."[23] A party that had been founded to reject the *caudillismo* of the PPD itself had become an authoritarian, centralized organization.

The fight between Berríos and his opponents — including the defeated PIP gubernatorial candidate Noel Colón Martínez

— was bitter and public.[24] Colón Martínez was accused of fomenting faction and seeking the support of "ultra leftists"; Berríos was accused of "fascism" and "*caudillismo*," of rigging the choice of delegates to an assembly at Mayagüez (September 1973) that would decide the issue between the "authoritarian centralizers" and the "democrats."

The Mayagüez assembly came out for Berríos. The defeated hailed his victory as the triumph of a "competent tyrant," a "megalomaniac" who meted out "Justicia a la Rubén" to his rivals. Berríos had, his critics maintained, personalized the ideological struggle in the party, imposing his own version of "revolutionary discipline" to destroy democrats and leftists alike, reducing the party to a "skeleton" as a result. The PIP had fallen into the old pattern of Puerto Rican politics set by Muñoz Marín. As with Muñoz, Berríos's democratic rhetoric cloaked a *caudillo*. "One does not enter into a dialogue with factions," he stated, "one crushes them." This was the language of the Ukase of Arecibo, which had driven Muñoz's opponents out of the PPD. But Berríos has neither the accomplishments nor the prestige of a Muñoz, only his oratorical talents and his imposing presence. The conflict between the ideal of intraparty democracy and the tradition of personal leadership may recur.

While the electoral performance of the PIP, under the leadership of Berríos, slightly improved in 1976, it sank again in 1980. Berríos explains this failure as the legacy of the ideological struggle of the early 1970s: the party lacked an "organized structure" to fight elections. "Now that struggle is over and the party is clearly defined . . . the gospel has been preached and now we must organize the church."[25]

Under Berríos, the PIP shed its pro-Cubans and "ultra leftists," who joined the PSP or one of the many Marxist-Leninist "grouplets." It has achieved unity, discipline, and respectability. The present program of the PIP for the creation of an independent, democratic Socialist Republic is reasoned and moderate in tone, far removed from the Marxist-Leninist, anti-American rhetoric of the PSP.[26] Berríos's emphasis on the party's links with the Socialist International and the non-Communist left in Latin America—he is a vice president of COPAL, the Permanent Conference of Latin American Parties, a post in which he takes great pride—contrasts with the PSP's close alliance with Cuba. The PIP expects independence to come peacefully, as part of a negotiated settlement with the United States. Such negotiations will be eased, Berríos argues, by a "favorable international context," but beating America with the Cuban stick does not help.[27]

The thrust of the PIP program is economic and social. Independence is not only a matter of dignity. It is necessary "to tackle at the root the dire economic and social problems from which Puerto Rico suffers." Colonialism has produced a stagnant, dependent economy, an island polluted by American absentee-owned factories—like many protest movements the PIP has its ecological wing. Such an economy can only support a "dependent, ambivalent, and impotent society," its impotence evident in widespread mental illness, drug addiction, and the collapse of the family.

The PIP considers the sole remedy for economic stagnation and social collapse to be political independence. Only control of the main instruments of economic policy—tariffs, the monetary and taxation systems, immigration, and shipping—will provide the tools for a new "model of development for Puerto Rico." This new model will be based on a "vigorous and rational system of import substitution" combined with a redistribution of income by a progressive income tax and a capital gains tax.

The "new model" echoes an optimism about Puerto Rico's economic potential as an independent state that runs through the independence movement and was embedded in Nationalist economics. It must perforce be optimistic about the riches that will be brought to the Republic of Puerto Rico through the control of its own mineral resources (one of the main planks of the PIP program), about the agricultural potential of the island and its prospects as an export economy in a competitive world market, and about its prospects as a recipient of funds from international agencies like the World Bank.[28]

This optimism reflects the difficulties inherent in the creation of a viable economy in a Caribbean ministate which constitute the main problem for the independence movement. It has only to look at the floundering economies of the new nation states of the former British Caribbean. This accounts for the PIP's insistence that independence be achieved through a negotiated settlement, as an "orderly, rational, and responsible" process. Immediate severance of the economic bond with the United States would condemn the new Republic to ruin. The PIP considers it is the moral obligation of the metropolitan power to make reparation for its past exploitation of Puerto Rico by granting favorable terms to cushion the economic shocks of independence. These would include access to mainland markets for a period of ten years, while the American tariff levels are reached by annual 10 percent increases; a quota for Puerto Rican immigrants; and the establishment of a Fund for the Development of Puerto Rico, an indemnity for the profits the metropolis has extracted from its colony.[29]

For all its "realism" and its emphasis on the "new model of development," the core of *independentismo* is what is called the "preservation of our way of being" (*manera de ser*). Economic viability is a necessary condition for the existence of a nation state. And while the PIP's program reflects Berríos's pragmatism and economic sophistication, its rhetoric still rings with the echoes of de Diego. A national theater is, it would seem, as important as a national economy; control over television, which floods the island with programs of "violence, cultural assimilation, individualism [sic] and the excess of consumerism" all hostile to "the ethical and moral values of our people," as important as control of the economy.

Much of the PIP program reflects the self-conscious puritanism characteristic of the independence movement, with its insistence that the shortcomings of all urbanized, industrial societies were introduced into a formerly "healthy" society by American influence. In the new Puerto Rican Republic, pornography would be eliminated; drug addiction, "the symbol of a sick society," would be treated in clinics and the young encouraged to participate, instead, in manly sports; saving would be stimulated by the reduction of official cars and foreign travel of local *políticos*.

Independentistas no longer believe, as they did in the early days of American rule, that the deluge of American "culture" is a deliberate design on the part of the new masters to destroy Puerto Rican "nationhood" at its roots. They now view the shortcomings of the American attitude to Puerto Rico as shortcomings of political imagination, a failure to realize that a Puerto Rican "nation" exists. Americans cannot bring themselves to recognize that the present relationship between the island and the United States is a *colonial* relationship; the various constitutional arrangements adopted since 1898 — from "unincorporated territory" to Commonwealth itself — hide from American eyes the fact that they possess a colony. Since Americans do not believe they own a colony, they cannot embrace a policy of decolonization. But constitutional cosmetics are wearing thin. *Independentistas* argue that international opinion, especially that of Latin America, and the demand for independence in Puerto Rico itself will increasingly put pressure on the United States to decolonize via a grant of independence. If it does not decolonize, the opportunity for a peaceful settlement will vanish, leaving only violence. Like the statehooders, the *independentistas* argue that the forces of history are on their side; but since statehood is a "monstrosity" tantamount to the political murder of a nation, independence is the only option, the necessary solution to the status problem.[30]

Unfortunately for the PIP, the Puerto Ricans do not follow the march of history when they vote. In the 1930s, the Spanish Socialist Luis Araquistain was puzzled by Puerto Rico: he had no doubts but that the Puerto Ricans *were* a nation, yet, he concluded, they had not found, like their fellow Latin American nations, a political form to contain their nationhood.[31] *Independentistas* would argue that this discrepancy between national sentiment and its political expression persists, and that its explanation is to be found in the spread of the habits of a consumer society introduced into the island by its foreign masters, in the attractions of a way of life that is dependent for its survival on the American connection, which, so those who enjoy the consumer society believe, cannot be severed without the prospect of economic disaster. In Berríos's dramatic phrase, "there is no massive support for independence in Puerto Rico because the economic addict has been led to believe that his fix will be discontinued should he demand his inalienable rights." What the present program of the party seeks to achieve is the continuation of the fix until the addict has become strong enough to do without the drug: a negotiated settlement that will assure a favorable transition period, providing the economic subsidies that will relieve the patient of withdrawal symptoms.

While the PIP served as the party of the liberal bourgeoisie, the PSP became the home of the radical petty bourgeoisie.

While the nationalism of the liberal bourgeoisie retained a nineteenth-century flavor, the radical bourgeoisie found new prophets — Frantz Fanon and American radicals. Above all, the PSP found in Fidel Castro its *lider maximo* and in Cuba a new model. For the PSP, the Cuban Revolution transformed the independence struggle in Puerto Rico, placing it in a new, more favorable international context. If nothing else, this context provides the dignitaries of a small political party with trips to conferences in foreign parts and all its members with the solace of international flattery that compensates for insignificance at home.[32] "Today," declared the First International Congress of Solidarity with the Independence of Puerto Rico, meeting in Havana, "Puerto Rico is a priority item on the agenda of the men, women and children of the free world."

The PSP is the heir of the *Movimiento pro Independencia* (MPI), founded in 1959. In its origins, the MPI was an all-party movement, a small and ill-assorted collection of the disillusioned, from Trotskyites through members of the old Communist party to bourgeois Nationalists and *independentistas*. All were weary of the "opportunism" of the PIP, which was committed to the compromises of the legal struggle, and despaired of a labor movement increasingly invaded by "business unionism" on the American model and which accepted the existing colonialist/capitalist structure. The "historical mission" of the Socialist party had ended in disaster: the FLT — the old Socialist Federation of Trade Unions — had proved a "bureaucratic corpse"; the CGT, the militant Confederation of the 1940s, conquered by the *políticos* of the PPD, had become the instrument for ensuring the social peace necessary for the success of Operation Bootstrap.[33]

It was the aim of the MPI and the PSP to win the working class over to the independence movement, a task in which the Nationalists and the PIP had signally failed. They thus hoped to convert nationalism into a revolutionary movement of national liberation under the control and leadership of the radical bourgeoisie.

The MPI, however, still moved in the shade of the Nationalist mystique of violence, now validated by the success of the Cuban Revolution, which was seen as a triumph of a dedicated band of freedom fighters. It talked of a "prerevolutionary situation" that could be exploited by "answering the violence of the regime with the violence of the proletariat" that, in turn, would provoke a brutal repression by the metropolitan power. This was Fanon's thesis: the creation in a colony of a revolutionary conscience by violence. "The greater the repression, the greater the militancy."[34] That the theories of Fanon and the Cuban model of revolution do not fit a society where there is no alienated and oppressed peasantry, as in Algeria, or rural proletariat, as in Cuba, is concealed in the violent anti-Americanism that was to become the stock-in-trade of the PSP.

To the orthodox Marxist César Andreu Iglesias, the advocacy of violence was a lapse into "infantilism." To Iglesias, PSP leader Mari Bras had fallen, like Albizu Campos before him, into Blanquist heresy. Iglesias did not believe that the revolution of independence could triumph through action by a minority. It had to have the organized support of the mobilized popular masses: "It will not be the product of select minorities nor of individual acts of violence nor of diplomatic negotiations. National independence must be the work of the whole people." But the legacy of Nationalism and enthusiasm for foreign models — from Cuba to China — found its outlet, Iglesias believed, in a naive and dangerous penchant for violence now called "the armed struggle" for independence. It was Mari Bras's defense, in 1970, of the assassination of an American sailor as "an act of war" and an important "stage in the escalation of violence" that drove César Andreu Iglesias out of the movement.[35]

While Mari Bras cannot disown acts of terrorism and publicly denounce the "armed struggle," he is aware that the "revolutionary vanguard" cannot operate in a vacuum; it must enjoy the support of "the revolutionary masses." In other words, the PSP must seek to make inroads among the working class. Although the insight of Mari Bras into the working-class mind and its aspirations is markedly inferior to that of César Andreu Iglesias, he has exploited every opportunity to create a proletarian following.

The labor struggles of the 1970s, the PSP calculated, opened up the possibilities of infiltrating the trade unions, mobilizing them for the independence struggle. But the "new syndicalism" of the 1970s was not revolutionary — it was a reaction to the recession. The appeals of Mari Bras for a general strike fell on stony ground. The penetration of existing unions by the PSP, its attacks on those who resisted its control, its activity in strikes where it encouraged violence, all brought against the unions the charge that they were "infiltrated" by "subversives," allies of Cuba and Communism.[36] The PSP's attempt to organize a united trade-union movement under its influence failed; instead, the PSP acquired — and not merely in the propaganda of the government — the reputation of the Communists: its members were considered ruthless manipulators, out to control every organization it sought to bring into the struggle for independence.

While the PSP failed to organize a mass working-class party committed to independence and revolution, converting a "patriotic" into a "revolutionary" struggle, it has, in recent years, acquired a new role and a new salience in Puerto Rican politics. Mari Bras has not disowned the armed struggle as a legitimate weapon, but he now views it as a weapon that can be taken up or abandoned as circumstances demand. Circumstances now demand that it should not be the preferred political tactic of the PSP. In 1968, the MPI declared an "electoral strike," boycotting what it considered a "colonial" election. By 1980, the PSP — which evolved from the MPI in 1971 — had become an "electoral" party, legally participating in elections. The PSP, Mari Bras argues, must use and exploit "bourgeois colonial liberties." They provide a convenient opportunity for propaganda and proselytism, both to expand and to publicize a new strategy.

This strategy is based on two assumptions. The first is that the advance of the statehooders has "polarized" politics and threatens "annexation." Statehood, therefore, must be resisted by an "anti-annexationist" front capable of defeating the PNP in elections (the threat in 1980 was an electoral triumph for Romero) and of resisting the "annexationism" detected in Mrs. Kirkpatrick's speech of July 4, 1982, in San Juan, when she praised the absorptive qualities of U.S. federalism. "We must stop playing politics," the PSP concluded, "and join our forces to battle against Washington's annexationist desires."

The second assumption is that independence cannot be achieved by the efforts of the *independentista* parties alone: a broader "anti-annexationist front" must be the basis of a new force in Puerto Rican politics. The PSP now has a respectable image as an "electoralist" party participating in elections and proposing the union of all those who reject the annexationism of the PNP in an anti-colonialist Popular Front of the "people of Puerto Rico." Since the term Popular Front raises the specter of Communist manipulation of the innocent, the new alliance is called a United Front.[37]

The PSP weekly *Claridad* devotes much attention to politicians who are seen as possible figureheads of the anti-colonialist coalition — Severo Colberg and Sánchez Vilella, for example. They can be used by exploiting their support of greater autonomy as the first stage on the road to independence. At times, Mari Bras seems himself to be speaking the language of the radical autonomists of the PPD: autonomism, he asserts, is the Puerto Rican tradition par excellence and its strength must be

recognized. The PSP considers the creation of an anti-colonialist coalition, including bourgeois elements, to be justified
by Castro's strategy of "uniting forces" in the first stage of the
revolution.

To the PIP, the new strategy of the PSP and the alliance of
Mari Bras with the "progressive autonomists," as the radical
autonomists of the PPD are termed in the present lexicon of
Puerto Rican politics, represents the desperate opportunism of
a small, weak party doomed to electoral defeat: the PSP "con-
fuses its own survival with the fight for independence."[38] The
results, the *pipiolos* of the PIP argue, are disastrous. The past
reputation of Mari Bras as a resolute *independentista* sanctifies
the autonomism of the Populares. Their action at the United
Nations in 1978, when they presented a joint resolution that
included free association as a proper form of decolonization,
threatens to legitimize free association as an acceptable alternative to independence. Moreover, the PSP's old image has
not been erased from the minds of Puerto Ricans; to a middle-
class electorate, the PSP's close cooperation with Cuba makes
independence itself look like a perilous alternative.

While the two independence parties are bitterly divided,
both parties base their strategies on the assumption that the
PPD is in the process of decline and that embedded in its ranks
are those who maintain a hankering for independence. Berríos
believes that the disillusioned Populares must gravitate to the
PIP. It must fight both the "colonialists" of the PPD and the
annexationists of the PNP. The United Front, which the PSP
advocates, can only come about when all *independentistas* have
joined the PIP. It alone can provide the axis of the independence struggle; it alone is the true depository of the *independentista* tradition.

The influence of the PSP is based more on its paper *Claridad*
than on its membership. *Claridad,* which claims a circulation

of 20,000, skillfully exploits minor local issues, and its sports pages are excellent.[39] It also maintains a never-ending offensive against the world capital of imperialism, the United States. Since Vietnam and the ravages of the oil crisis, that capital is itself in crisis. *Claridad* portrays Puerto Rico as the "principal colony of the greatest colonial power in all history" and claims that in Puerto Rico "the colonial system has entered into an irreversible crisis." The installation of a Democratic Workers Republic in Puerto Rico will entail the collapse of capitalism in the United States itself for which the Puerto Rican Revolution will provide "the indispensable prerequisite."[40]

It would be a profound mistake to dismiss the PSP and the PIP as insignificant because they together muster only a mere 5 or 6 percent of the vote. These two political parties keep the idea of national independence alive as a persistent factor in the political life of Puerto Rico. Both parties are anti-American. Both have organized demonstrations against the Reserve Officers' Training Corps (ROTC). Both keep up a consistent campaign against the presence of the U.S. Navy in Vieques. But the PSP's anti-Americanism is much stronger than that of the PIP. The PSP denunciations of the United States as guilty of physical as well as cultural genocide are much more virulent than those of the PIP. Whereas the PPD dismissed President Reagan's statement in January 1982 in support of statehood as a damp squib — "more of the same," in the words of Rubén Berríos — to Mari Bras it was a new and brutal attack on Puerto Rico's self-determination to be resisted by a new anti-annexationist front. Whereas the PIP is wary of Cuba and openly hostile to the Soviet Union, the PSP's support of Cuba and the Soviet Union has been unfailing. To an intelligent Marxist like José Luis González, this support represents the genuflections to its paymasters of a parochial intelligentsia devoid of any independence of thought.[41] The "electoral" strategies of the PSP ended its monopoly over the radical left, which it had enjoyed in the 1970s. To the small revolutionary groups that splintered off from the PIP or the PSP, the latter is seen as a "bourgeois" party eager to form ad hoc alliances with other bourgeois parties. According to Luis Angel Torres, formerly of the PIP and in 1981 leader of a newly formed Marxist group, the Socialist Workers Movement (a combination of the Socialist Revolutionary Party and the Socialist Populist Movement), the PSP is "an exponent of petty bourgeois socialism... characterized by its dissociation from the workers' struggle... willing to eliminate the Marxist-Leninist basis of its program."[42] Furthest to the left of this mishmash of "grouplets" — representing every shade of revolutionary thought from orthodox Marxist-Leninism to Maoism, Trotskyism, and anarchism — is the PRT, which is the political front for the Borinquen Popular Army or *Macheteros* — a clandestine group of terrorists.

All these groups reject the "electoral" strategy of the PSP. Their view is that "colonial" elections are a "manipulated farce" and that participation in them serves only to support the claim that a colony is a free society. They argue that "the revolutionary movement should not participate in them [the elections] since this would only legitimize colonialism through elections mediatized and controlled by the very enemy we are fighting."[43] By voting, these groups claim, the backyard politicians (*políticos de patio*) of the PPD and the PNP give a patina of democratic respectability to the annexationism that has been the hidden leitmotiv of U.S. policy since 1898. They consider annexation a strategic necessity for the United States, given the "decadence" of imperialism in the Caribbean. With the Empire in crisis, the "Cuban path" — i.e., the armed struggle of the workers for independence — is seen as the only tactic. The operative political philosophy of the more revolutionary groups is Marxist-Leninism, as interpreted by Caribbean-born Frantz Fanon. Only the revolutionary struggle itself can create a revolutionary consciousness in a proletariat that the PSP failed to mobilize, as had the PIP before it: "The party [PSP] has not reached the masses and the masses have not reached the party."

The PSP, in its thrust for what it calls a "regroupment of forces" (*reagrupamiento de fuerzas*), is seeking to regain its leadership of the left and to regain the allegiance of the splinter groups of young radicals. "Unity on the left" will find its expression in a renovated PSP, resolutely Socialist, but prepared to acknowledge its past "arrogance," when it pursued the old Communist tactic of penetrating and then seeking to master every radical organization. Mari Bras confesses that the "Achilles heel" of the party has been its "organizational weakness" and failure to build up a mass following.[44]

The "armed struggle" of the "grouplets" somehow must be tailored to fit the *mass* struggle of the new anti-annexationist front. In the effort to win broad public support for this strategy there can be no public alliance with the terrorist *Macheteros,* by definition a clandestine organization. Yet they cannot be disowned: a United Front must recognize the legitimacy of the armed struggle when appropriate as well as the truths of "scientific socialism." This is a tall order. Unity, therefore, is possible at present only on a series of separate issues. For example, all those who reject annexation, which Mari Bras sees as a present peril, can combine to protest the presence of the American Navy in Vieques — an issue to which *Claridad* devotes a great deal of space — or to celebrate the *Grito de Lares*.

The PSP is therefore confronted with the difficult task of combining "unity on the left" with its plans for a broader alliance with the bourgeois "progressive autonomists" in order to push autonomy toward independence and to resist the electoral advance of the annexationists. For Mari Bras, the road to independence is long and will be achieved only by a United Front that will recreate the strength of the independence movement in the 1930s. But the United Front does not appeal to the recruits the PSP is seeking through "unity on the left," who are impatient of "electoralism" and enthusiasts—most of them —for the "armed struggle." Since the "armed struggle" cannot be rejected, it must be tailored to fit the *mass* struggle of which the United Front is an instrument.

Two questions must be asked. Under what conditions would the *independentistas*—particularly the PSP—cease to walk the legal road? How serious a threat is posed by political terrorism?

On the *independentista* left the tradition of the armed struggle is well established. Every year it celebrates the *Grito de Lares*; the martyrs of Nationalism are still remembered and its prophet revered. "Annexation" would only fortify that tradition. Outbreaks of terrorism, both on the island and in the cities of America, will almost certainly be a consequence of statehood and of the negotiations that precede its grant. Terrorism, Rubén Berríos once stated, is the "ultimate veto." The United States will be confronted with the situation that it has not encountered in any other state of the Union: a state in which a determined minority committed to the achievement of separation by terror may well be able to count on *enough* support for it to operate.[45] In Mao's famous phrase, the fish (i.e., guerrilla fighters) must have water to swim in, the water being sympathizers on whom they can rely for support and protection.

It is the embittered members of the PIP and the old militants of the PSP who will provide the necessary sympathy and logistic support for terrorism. It is inconceivable, for example, that Mari Bras would hand over a Nationalist freedom fighter to the police. While respectable members of the PIP are unlikely to engage in gun-running, it is improbable that they will help the FBI or provide recruits for the National Guard.

This does not mean that the fifty-first state, as *independentistas* argue, will find itself with a Quebec embedded in it; it does mean that the FBI will have a difficult and disagreeable task on its hands. Still, Puerto Rico has become much less of a revolutionary society than it was in the 1930s. Whatever the defects or ambiguities of the Estado Libre Asociado de Puerto Rico (ELA) may be, even its statehood opponents must recognize that it has defused a dangerous situation; only a spectacular reversal of the economic prosperity the island has enjoyed can alter this. Further, terrorism is at a logistic disadvantage in a small island. With no frontier to skip over — as in the Basque Provinces or Northern Ireland — and no inaccessible Sierra Maestra as a refuge, terrorists are left to the mercies of a police trained in modern methods of counterinsurgency, backed up by 10,000 National Guardsmen, who will not throw their hands in as did Batista's army. It is reported that the Venezuelan guerrilla leader Douglas Bravo chided *independentistas* on their failure to engage in armed resistance; he was silenced when shown a map of Puerto Rico.

There are terrorists who will not wait for "annexation" to carry out sabotage, acts of incendiarism directed against American concerns, and murder of American servicemen. The *Macheteros* — the group responsible for destroying nine National Guard planes in January 1981 — base their strategy on the view that the United States, alarmed at the spread of Castroism in the Caribbean, will annex Puerto Rico and that resistance can only be conducted through "politico-military violence" that will force America to negotiate with the independence parties. On the mainland, terrorism is organized by the *Fuerzas Armadas de Liberación Nacional Puertorriqueña* (FALN), who claim to be an army of national liberation entitled to the privileges of prisoners of war under the Geneva Convention — a claim supported annually at the hearings of the United Nations Decolonization Committee. Since 1974, mainland terrorists have been responsible for over 100 bomb outrages and five deaths.

As in all terrorist movements, recruits come mainly from the sons of middle-class families. Puerto Rican terrorism combines the belief of Albizu Campos that national liberation will be the work of a dedicated elite with the tactics that are the common currency of international terrorism: the destabilization of democratic institutions by forcing democratic governments to adopt methods of repression incompatible with their liberal premises. Thus it is no proof of the existence of democratic freedom that the proponents of the armed struggle can propagate their views in *Pensamiento Crítico*. Limited tolerance is viewed as a trick characteristic of bourgeois, imperialist democracies: it must be exposed by forcing dissidence to the critical point where repression is invoked. Hypnotized by the Cuban and Nicaraguan revolutions, convinced by Fanon's strategy that a revolutionary national consciousness may be forged through the anti-colonial struggle itself, the terrorists continue to apply these foreign models to a complex open society quite unlike prerevolutionary Cuba or Algeria. There is no hard evidence that they receive outside support or training. On international standards they are, as yet, amateurs.

Nevertheless, just as it is an error to dismiss the "electoral" independence parties as of no importance because their electoral performance is so poor, it is equally an error to dismiss the terrorists because their operations so often fail to stir anything but resentment among Puerto Ricans. Terrorism can poison the political atmosphere, as the Cerro Maravilla episode proves: allegedly, with the governor's connivance, two young terrorists were shot by the police at Cerro Maravilla. The subsequent investigations divided Puerto Ricans between those who accused the police and the governor of murder, and those who condoned, if they did not approve, the shooting of the "subversives." To those with latent *independentista* sympathies, the young terrorists are a symbol of resistance to "American imperialism" and to its island representatives: the "Fascist" politicians of a "murderous regime."[46]

Part III

THE NEW COLONIALISM

8.

THE ECONOMY AND
ITS CRITICS

The long-term interests of the United States in Puerto Rico
are clear: the maintenance of a stable and friendly democratic
society. Although the positive connection between economic
growth and the advance and consolidation of democracy is by
no means as evident as politicians and political scientists
once imagined,[1] a stagnating economy, or one in which the
growth rate is declining, would place strains on any political
system. A modicum of prosperity provides a necessary, though
not a sufficient, underpinning of a democratic system. The
political instability of the newly independent African states is
in no small measure a function of their lamentable economic
performance.

The general proposition that prosperity underwrites political
systems, and the lack of it undermines them, has a particular
application in Puerto Rico. While the island elite sees the status
issue as a political issue, most Puerto Ricans view the legitimacy
and desirability of Commonwealth and association with the
United States as deriving rather from the indisputable economic benefits that the policies pursued in the 1950s and 1960s

brought with them. In the first year of American occupation, Elihu Root argued that if the Puerto Ricans were "left in huge and hopeless poverty they will be discontented, intractable and mutinous."[2] An impoverished island economy cannot provide a firm basis for a stable political system, let alone for a democracy, and grinding poverty and massive unemployment provide a breeding ground for radical politics and for anti-American feeling.

Such was the case in the 1930s. From Eleanor Roosevelt on, every American who visited Puerto Rico was appalled at its poverty, particularly in the slum areas of San Juan. Yet the conditions the slum dwellers sought to escape by leaving the sugar plantations of the countryside for the capital were even worse: villages surrounded by human excreta because only half the houses had even primitive latrines; malaria still a killer among an undernourished population; three-quarters of the children under fourteen years of age with no shoes. Scarcely surprisingly, the workers sought consolation in cheap alcohol.[3] In January 1935 Secretary of the Interior Harold L. Ickes observed, "There is today more widespread misery and destitution in Puerto Rico than at any previous time in its history."[4]

No one did more to reveal the plight of Puerto Rico in the 1920s and early 1930s than the young Muñoz Marín. Written during his bohemian period in New York, when he was known in Greenwich Village as a littérateur of Socialist leanings, his articles, now classics of political journalism, were a savage indictment of the social and economic results of American rule: "the ghastly spectacle," he wrote, "of wealth drained from a starving population into the richest country on earth is sanctimoniously set down in official reports as a favorable trade balance." This sorry state was the result, Ickes argued, of the workings of what he called the "laissez-faire economy" that came with the American occupation; American capitalism had converted Puerto Rico into a fief of the great absentee American sugar corporations. It had become the poorhouse of the Caribbean. The poverty of Puerto Rico was, therefore, the creation of an outside agent, the foreign devil in the form of the Yankee exploiter to whose interference with their "natural development" so many Puerto Ricans attributed — and continue to attribute — their plight. Scarcely surprisingly, anti-American sentiment waxed strong.

Yet it was the American connection that was to provide the escape from poverty. Laissez-faire capitalism on the American model became a lifeline, the devil a fairy godmother. The Populares (PPD) realized by 1947 that their original program of agrarian reform and government-sponsored enterprises could not provide a decent living for more than a small sector of the population; moreover, both the industries and the farms set up under government auspices were economic failures.[5] The PPD's emphasis shifted from its reliance on the public sector to stimulating the private sector, from redistributing existing wealth to the creation of new wealth through a process of incentives to induce industrialization. This shift entailed the promotion of private investment in factories. "For Puerto Rico's development to take place," Muñoz Marín is purported to have said, "we must allow three hundred sons of bitches to become millionaires." Since local entrepreneurs, with few exceptions, remained addicted to their family traditions in business, the only millionaires who could be courted were on the mainland.

The "millionaires" were to be attracted to invest in what Fomento, the government agency responsible for development, termed "Profit Island USA." Fomento offered a series of advantages, derived from the special nature of Puerto Rico's political relationship to the United States, a relationship that its architects called a "unique mixture" of economic integration combined with fiscal autonomy. Integration came through Puerto Rico's duty-free access to the huge mainland market. Fiscal autonomy came in the form of certain exemptions from federal taxes on corporate profits remitted to the United States for companies investing and setting up factories in Puerto Rico. Since the Commonwealth government also granted such companies a ten-year exemption from local taxes, the financial advantages of setting up business in Puerto Rico were considerable.

These advantages, which were the core of "Operation Bootstrap," later to be called the "Commonwealth model," did not derive from Commonwealth status as such. Free access to the American market dated back to 1902, and the exemption from federal taxation on remitted profits was a concession granted in 1921 to "overseas possessions," of which Puerto Rico was one, in order to favor American businesses in the Philippines over foreign competitors. This concession was granted by Section 262 of the Internal Revenue Code. The term "Commonwealth model" is justified in that it was the economists of the PPD who saw the possibilities — one might argue late in the day — of combining these federal concessions, which antedated Commonwealth itself, with exemption of new manufacturing enterprises from all Puerto Rican taxes.

There were other incentives that attracted mainland investors. Fomento provided factory buildings and the Government Development Bank offered low-cost loans. Puerto Rico also offered a common currency and a familiar legal framework — not inconsiderable advantages, as companies investing elsewhere in Latin America have discovered. The political presence of the United States insured them against the risks usually associated with foreign investment: there was no danger of expropriation. Moreover, they would find in the island a "docile" labor force requiring wages considerably below those of workers on the mainland. These advantages of tax exemption and cheap labor more than offset the costs of transporting Puerto Rican products to the mainland. The millionaires came. Teodoro Moscoso, appointed general manager of Fomento in 1942, became the messiah of a Puerto Rico prospering under the laissez-faire capitalism that Ickes had denounced and Muñoz castigated.

The early successes of the new policy were spectacular. Operation Bootstrap appeared as an exciting experiment in setting an underdeveloped economy on the path to prosperity within the framework of a representative democracy. At the height of Operation Bootstrap in the 1950s, one factory was established every day on the island. In constant 1954 dollars, Puerto Rico's per capita income almost quadrupled between 1950 and 1973. Between 1929 and 1933, per capita income had sunk from a poor $122 to a miserable $86; in the Depression years, only the food and clothing supplied by the public works financed by the Puerto Rican Emergency Relief Administration (PRERA) and the Puerto Rican Reconstruction Administration (PRRA) staved off total disaster.[6] But the 1950s and 1960s were years of rapid growth, of optimism and confidence. By 1968, Puerto Rico's per capita income was the highest in Latin America. Missions from Third World countries descended on the island seeking the counsels of Muñoz Marín and Teodoro Moscoso.

Industrialization by invitation did not imply the acceptance of market forces as the *sole* instrument for the redistribution of social goods. The experiments of the 1940s had been accompanied by investment in education and medical services that had permanent and beneficial effects on the quality of life in Puerto Rico: in thirty years, life expectancy rose by thirty years; enrolment in secondary schools more than doubled. Puerto Rico today is much closer to U.S. standards in education and health than it is in terms of per capita income. These advances represent a striking increase in human capital that critics of Commonwealth sometimes forget.[7] The shift of the 1950s was not to laissez-faire but to a form of welfare capitalism. By the 1960s, the planners had created a unique economy — a fully open economy subject to a degree of central planning that would have been unacceptable in the United States. Here was one of the most striking differences between the island and the state of the Union.[8]

What was remarkable was that all this was achieved in a typical Caribbean ministate with a poor resource base and no Trinidadian oil bonanza in sight. Puerto Ricans had only to look at the standard of living in the neighboring Dominican Republic, far more richly endowed by nature, to appreciate the advantages of the American connection and the way it had been exploited by Commonwealth.

The Status Commission of 1964 – 66 endorsed the achievements of Commonwealth. The economic progress that Commonwealth status and the Commonwealth model had secured provided "the most likely way to meet the economic development of the Puerto Rican economy over the next twenty years." But twenty years have elapsed and the Commonwealth model has ended with falling growth rates and mounting unemployment.

The optimism and dynamism of the early years have vanished. Critics talk of the "exhaustion" of the Commonwealth model, asserting its incapacity to deliver the goods it once provided. And just as Commonwealth status and the fortunes of the party that supported it had been buoyed by economic success, now pessimism about its present performance has both sapped enthusiasm for Commonwealth status and weakened the electoral support of the party — the PPD — that brought it into being. The critics' *Schadenfreude* reveals their motive: to discredit a political system they dislike and to denounce American "colonialism" in Puerto Rico by proving that it has brought, in the long run, a stagnant economy.

While it was an exaggeration to speak of the "exhaustion" of the Commonwealth model, the world recession of the mid-1970s exposed its weaknesses. The most striking of these was its failure to cure the chronic sickness of Puerto Rico: the structural unemployment that besets all Caribbean countries.

Its economic medicine, the policy of industrialization by invitation, had been the main thrust of Operation Bootstrap, but it never really succeeded. From the outset, spectacular increases in the gross national product (GNP) failed to provide jobs for those extruded from a declining agrarian sector. Between 1950 and 1977, a dramatic increase of 309 percent in the GNP provided only a miserable 24 percent increase in employment. To Eric Williams, himself a practitioner of industrialization by invitation in Trinidad, the weakness of the Puerto Rican model was evident as early as 1961. It was disturbing, he found, "that despite the tremendous development of Puerto Rico's economy within recent years, the Puerto Ricans had not been able to make any real dent in the unemployment problems."[9]

Moreover, a change in the pattern of investment — which reflected changes in the preferences of mainland investors — combined with new developments in the productive process itself, threatened to make industrialization by invitation even less capable of providing something approaching full employment.

By the late 1970s, the chief instrument used by the Fomento to encourage investment by U.S. corporations in Puerto Rico was the tax concessions allowed by Article 936 of the Internal Revenue Code,[10] which replaced Article 931, itself a lineal descendant of the 1921 concession to companies operating in overseas possessions. Article 931 had allowed American businesses established in Puerto Rico to escape U.S. corporation tax if, after the ten-year exemption from Puerto Rican taxes had expired, the company liquidated its operations in Puerto Rico and brought its profits home. This concession was unsatisfactory to Puerto Rico: it encouraged small family businesses and fly-by-night companies — particularly clothing concerns — to make a quick profit and leave without any lasting benefit to Puerto Rico. The substitution of Article 936 for Article 931 was perhaps the finest achievement of Puerto Rican lobbying in Washington. It allowed Puerto Rican subsidiaries of U.S. companies operating in Puerto Rico to repatriate their profits to the parent company subject, after 1978, to a Puerto Rican tollgate tax, which was so adjusted as to encourage local investment.

But the strategies pursued under Article 936 accelerated changes in Puerto Rico's manufacturing sector that made the economy even less capable of absorbing the tide of unskilled workers that flowed from the rural backwaters of the interior to the coastal towns. The early factories were in the "traditional" sector — textiles, leather, and clothing, for example — that was labor intensive and that paid low wages. These enterprises became less competitive in a difficult and unstable market, especially as other areas, including Puerto Rico's Caribbean neighbors, began to offer labor at far lower wages. As a consequence, labor-intensive industries stagnated while a new wave of sophisticated, capital-intensive concerns started up: petrochemicals, pharmaceuticals, and electronics. They employed a relatively skilled, well-paid labor force; they were attracted less by an abundance of cheap labor than by the tax advantages offered by Article 936, including the possibility of transferring — to the discomfiture of the United States Treasury — intangibles (e.g., research and development costs) to Puerto Rican subsidiaries.

Petrochemicals had proved a bad start.[11] But pharmaceuticals and electronics prospered, and by 1982 there were ninety-two pharmaceutical plants employing 11,000 workers in Puerto Rico.[12] Capital-intensive, they created a high-wage enclave with a large proportion of unskilled labor left outside on its margins. Abandoning the notion that Puerto Rico could remain a supplier of cheap labor to traditional industries, it was on drugs and electronics that Fomento pinned its hopes. It was idle to expect that capitalists would invest in order to satisfy the particular needs of Puerto Rico by establishing labor-intensive industries in order to cure chronic unemployment, particularly as the tax incentives served to cheapen capital relative to labor. In the capitalist system, you take what you can get. Puerto Rico was following the same path as Hong Kong, Taiwan, or Singapore: starting out as traditional low-wage economies producing low-grade consumer goods, they were forced to modernize to survive in the international market.

Neither the older, traditional manufacturers nor the new, sophisticated industries could solve Puerto Rico's historic problem of unemployment. Like most Caribbean societies, where migration is a long-established tradition and a way of life, Puerto Rico exported its unemployed. As American citizens, Puerto Ricans had unrestricted access to the United States. Encouraged by cheap air fares after 1945, they flocked to the farms and cities of the Northeast — by the 1950s, at a rate of some 60,000 a year. Only this migration, which brought a third of its population to the mainland, saved Puerto Rico from massive unemployment. Migration to the United States was a safety valve that concealed the central failure of the Commonwealth model. But it worked only as long as a prosperous mainland economy could absorb immigrant labor. In the recessions of the 1960s and in the deeper recession of the 1970s, the safety valve closed, and a process of return migration brought some of those without jobs on the mainland back to swell the ranks of the unemployed in Puerto Rico. By the 1980s, with over 20 percent of the work force out of a job, the underlying weakness of the Commonwealth model was exposed. It had produced a raft of well-paid workers floating on a sea of unemployed.

These developments illustrate the inescapable fact of Puerto Rican economic life: the policies pursued since 1947 engendered an "open" export economy, one typical of Caribbean ministates in that such economies are exposed to the ups and downs of the world market. Puerto Rico is unique in that its open export economy became closely integrated with the national economy of the United States, of which it is a depressed regional economy.

Like other Caribbean islands, Puerto Rico depends on the competitiveness of its exports in the international market and on the readiness of outsiders to supply investment capital. In Puerto Rico's case, exports represent 80 percent of its GNP. The international market for Puerto Rico means the United States, which, at the height of Operation Bootstrap, absorbed 90 percent of Puerto Rico's exports and has supplied 90 percent of its capital investment.[13] Thus, where a similar open economy might be dependent on a variety of markets for the purchase of its exports, the supply of its imports, and its capital requirements, Puerto Rico is tied to one country. Where other Caribbean countries might blame the capitalist world in general for their plight, for Puerto Rico the North-South dialogue had only one participant. There was only one benefactor, one villain.

This means that shifts in the world economy affect the island via the U.S. national economy: when the economy of the mainland prospered, Operation Bootstrap "worked." Recession after 1973 hit Puerto Rico as it hits poor regional economies of the United States:[14] investment withered away; factories closed down. The giant U.S. corporations regard their

Puerto Rican operations as part of their overall operations, not as particular contributions to the economy of Puerto Rico. When markets shrink and interest rates rise, the weak go to the wall. In 1982, Union Carbide closed its polyethylene plant in Peñuelas. "The market was down," explained its general manager, "so it was natural that the highest cost plant would be closed." His major consideration was that energy costs on the island were much higher than on the mainland.

Since investors behave in Puerto Rico as they would anywhere else in the world, including the U.S. mainland, the question arises as to the benefits that U.S. investment has brought to Puerto Rico. Critics of industrialization by invitation maintain that the profits of investment flow outside the island. Many companies in older industries often repatriated their profits and shut up shop in Puerto Rico after the ten-year tax holiday expired; modern corporations seek to escape U.S. tax by investing their profits elsewhere.[15] This revived the old charge — made with justification against the sugar barons of the 1920s and 1930s — that those who invest in Puerto Rico are absentees. That investors place their profits where it suits them is not surprising: after all, no one investing in Florida is compelled to keep his profits in Florida. The unfairness lies elsewhere. Florida businessmen pay local taxes. American firms operating in Puerto Rico are exempt from local taxation: they therefore "rob" the Commonwealth Treasury, which provides the infrastructure for their activities, of the tax base to finance it.

It is to meet the charge that U.S. companies repatriate profits or reinvest them elsewhere that recent Puerto Rican administrations have made efforts to encourage mainland investors to invest at least a portion of their profits in Puerto Rico. Governor Romero Barceló and his financial advisers claim success in the instituting of a modest tollgate tax on repatriated profits that will provide Puerto Rico with a more substantial tax base for local infrastructural investment. His 1978 tax law is also designed to encourage long-term investment in areas of high unemployment.[16] Whether the new strategy will produce a substantial local tax base and encourage a substantial investment in local productive industries to counterbalance repatriation of profits is at present unclear.

Critics of industrialization by invitation and of the behavior of American companies have to answer this question: What alternative to dependence on "foreign" investment was or is available to Caribbean island economies with poor natural resources, inadequate or negative rates of saving, and small domestic markets? "Industries from the States did not come to the island as colonial exploiters. We begged and beseeched and cajoled industry to come. Sure we offered them high tax advantages and high profits and low wages. So what? They rescued the island. Does life-saving have a price?"[17]

The price is that paid by all regional economies of the United States and by all countries that rely on international capital to finance their development: a portion of the profits will inevitably escape the region or country whose labor helps to generate it. In Puerto Rico that portion is indisputably large. It is the "leakage" of remitted profits to the mainland from the island that creates the gap between the value of what is produced on the island (its gross domestic product) and the total income available to its inhabitants (the gross national income). The recent widening of that gap, which has to be plugged by federal transfers, the Kreps Report of the U.S. Department of Commerce concludes, provides "the clearest evidence of Puerto Rico's close and growing dependence on external sources."[18]

Much is made, for polemical purposes, of the issue of the repatriation of profits. The issue is not how much profits are repatriated, but rather how much new investment is made, whether by reinvesting profits earned in Puerto Rico or by new investment. There has been a substantial decline in real investment in plant and equipment from its peak in the early 1970s. In constant (1954) prices, the decline was from a level of about $600 million a year to $400 million, which has been the prevailing level since fiscal 1977. It is irrelevant from an economic standpoint whether this decline resulted from high repatriation of local profits or from low investment from new sources. What is critical is whether there are ample opportunities for profitable investment.

There are two principal reasons why there is a scarcity of profitable investment opportunities in Puerto Rico today: the cost of petroleum and the cost of labor. Of these, the cost of petroleum is the more important. The Puerto Rican economy is virtually 100 percent energy-dependent on imported petroleum, compared with about 20 percent for the United States. Puerto Rico is therefore no longer competitive in petroleum refining and petrochemicals and it is less competitive than previously for industries in which electric power is a significant cost. It was the high cost of energy, considerably in excess of costs on the mainland, that caused Union Carbide to close its Peñuelas plant.

The era of low manufacturing wages, which once encouraged investment in the traditional industries — apparel, shoes, and so on — has passed. Wage rates for factory workers now average over $4.50 an hour. For many years, hourly wages in Puerto Rican manufacturing plants have been far above those of their competitors in underdeveloped countries and are now in the neighborhood of 80 percent of the U.S. level in labor-intensive industries in the southern states. Thus, Puerto Rico's labor-intensive industries still have a labor cost edge in the U.S. market, but in recent years an increasing share of the U.S. market for, say, apparel has been taken by Far East producers, who have lower wage costs. There has been no great change in the wage competitiveness of Puerto Rico in the past decade, but the strong labor cost competitiveness of the Far East had already brought an end to growth in its traditional labor-intensive industries.

This matter of competitive investment opportunities is the basic issue for small and developing economies. It lies at the heart of the virtual disappearance from Puerto Rico of sugar, coffee, and tobacco as export industries as well as of the stagnation of its labor-intensive manufacturing industries.

Lacking a substantial resource base, Puerto Rico's opportunities for competitive export manufacturing lie only where manufacturing costs are below those in the United States. These opportunities can vanish. Thus, the United States granted Puerto Rico a quota for imports of foreign oil when the price of foreign oil was below that of domestic crude. Using this advantage, Puerto Rican planners hoped to refine foreign crude and use the by-products to establish a petrochemical complex. Before these linkages could be developed, the price of foreign crude rocketed. By the 1980s, the Commonwealth Oil Refining Corporation (CORCO) was bankrupt, its vast modern plant at Guayanilla run by a skeleton staff. The hopes of a petrochemical industry employing 20,000 had been swept away by international price movements and the advantages granted by the United States proved of no avail. Peñuelas has become an industrial ghost town inhabited by the unemployed for whom playing dominoes has become a surrogate for productive work.

The devices adopted to deal with the crisis of the 1970s, which was marked by the slowing down in the rate of investment and mounting unemployment, were to alter the nature of the island's economy in two ways.

First, to stave off unemployment, the government of Hernández Colón in 1974 borrowed heavily in New York's capital market to finance jobs in the public sector. An unmanageable public debt and price inflation were the inevitable results. On the advice of Professor James Tobin of Yale, these excesses were abandoned for an austerity program; the short-term price paid for this conventional medicine was labor unrest and strikes in the public sector and the electoral defeat of the Populares in 1976. The enduring legacy was the enlargement of an already oversized public sector, with a resulting decline in its productivity and efficiency.

The second transformation was a dramatic increase in reliance on federal transfers to support the sagging economy. As fixed investment dropped, federal expenditures rocketed by 10 percent each year in the 1970s. Moreover, it was federal transfer payments that closed the widening gap between the GDP and the GNP created by the repatriation of profits by U.S. corporations. Payments from the federal treasury to Puerto Rico can therefore be seen as a sort of compensation for exploitation.

Federal transfers—both in the form of program grants, such as those for education or urban improvement, and in the form of grants made directly to individuals, such as food stamps—came to play an increasingly significant role in sustaining the island economy. In 1950, they represented a mere 9 percent of the island's GDP; by 1980, federal assistance accounted for 29 percent and over 60 percent of Puerto Ricans were receiving food stamps. By providing extra purchasing power, federal transfers play an important role in maintaining domestic demand. It can be argued that rather than relieving unbearable suffering for the poor, they produce a beggar economy, in which workers prefer to remain idle and live off federal handouts. "Profit Island USA" threatens to become "Welfare Island USA."[19]

The increasing importance of federal transfers is only one aspect of the economic effects of the political relationship between Puerto Rico and the United States. Also to be considered is the impact of federal legislation and policies that govern vast areas of the island economy—for example, pollution controls, shipping costs, and the regulation of air transport. The complaint is that federal legislation, in the making of which Puerto Ricans play no constitutional role, and administrative policies, which they have little opportunity to influence, are tailored to American circumstance and do not "fit" Puerto Rican conditions. The underlying assumption is that this legislation and these policies are addressed to the social and economic problems of the mainland; but, the argument goes, the United States is a rich society with pockets of indigence whose economy, temporarily lamed by recession, is fundamentally sound, while Puerto Rico is an indigent society whose fragile economy supports a standard of living still well below that of the poorest American state.

The long struggle of the PPD to avoid the application of federal minimum wage legislation to Puerto Rico is a classic illustration of this conflict of interests. To the architects of Operation Bootstrap, the fact that wages in Puerto Rico were below mainland levels was a prime incentive in the campaign to entice investors to locate their factories and provide employment in Puerto Rico; the spread of U.S. minimum wage levels via the Fair Labor Standards Act threatened the whole structure, as it would drive away potential investors by cutting their profit margins. When the act was applied to Puerto Rico in 1938, so drastic were the results (it was held responsible for the destruction of the needlework industry in Mayagüez) that a separate system for establishing wage levels for individual local industries was established in 1940.[20] Thereafter, PPD governments sought to maintain the differential minimum wage rates because they believed the alternative was a fall in invest-ment and a consequent rise in unemployment. "It is irrational and cruel," argued Teodoro Moscoso, chief architect of indus-trialization by invitation, in testifying before the Ad Hoc Com-mittee in 1976, "to provide higher and higher minimum wages for fewer and fewer people. Social justice for the employed without considering the unemployed, or future entrants to the work force, is not social justice."[21]

The PPD's struggle to maintain differential minimum wages and the right of the Commonwealth to set its own wage levels, irrespective of federal legislation, has been lost. As early as 1970, Puerto Rican manufacturing wages, as we have seen, were within striking distance of the poor South, and by 1982 island minimum wages were adjusted to the level set by the federal Fair Labor Standards Act.[22]

While it would be idle to deny that the prospect of the imposition of U.S. minimum wages exercised *some* influence on local wage levels, Puerto Rico could not remain, as it had been in the early 1950s, a low-wage economy. All other similar countries have seen the incentives to industry provided by low wages vanish with the growth and development of their econ-omies. The problem for the Populares was to increase mini-mum wages on an industry-by-industry basis as fast as this could be done without causing unemployment. Because it could not do so, the job loss from high wages has been very high.[23]

The attempt of the PPD administration to control Puerto Rican wage rates illustrates one of the conflicts between what the PPD perceives as the interests of the island economy and federal legislation.

It is a long-standing complaint that federal legislation forcing Puerto Rico to use American ships in its trade with the United States means that it must pay high American rates, subsidizing

U.S. shippers at the cost of raising the cost of living in an island that imports most of its food. Federal standards of pollution, it is maintained, are too strict for a developing economy that cannot afford to scare off investors by complicated and expensive requirements. Likewise the matching funds requirement of some federal programs forces the Commonwealth to spend money on "luxuries" — for example, special education programs for the disadvantaged — when the need is for basic education. Some of these arguments are suspect. It is, for instance, by no means certain that the repeal of federal legislation that restricts U.S.-Puerto Rican trade will bring cheaper shipping costs in the long run.[24]

The measures proposed by the Reagan administration have revived, in an acute form, the conflict between national policies and Puerto Rican needs. Critics maintain that Puerto Rico has suffered from the application to its dependent economy of the dominant economic philosophies of the mainland. Cynics might argue that Puerto Rico must take the rough with the smooth. While the island suffered the ravages of laissez-faire in the early years, later policies conceived in the interests of the nation as a whole have brought benefits to Puerto Rico. Thus Muñoz Marín saw the possibilities held out by the New Deal; President Johnson's Great Society brought federal largess. The food stamp program, conceived to help the urban poor and the mainland farmers, poured money into Puerto Rico. Now, with a change in the economic policy adopted by the president, this favorable relationship has been reversed. Whatever else supply-side economics, welfare cuts, and New Federalism may accomplish in the way of U.S. economic recovery through a revitalized private sector, they penalize the poor and the poor regions.[25]

Cuts in federal payments must fall disproportionately on an economy that derives 30 percent of its GDP from federal transfers. The most serious short-term damage will be inflicted by changes in the food stamp program. The Reagan administration raised the level of eligibility for food stamps, and payments —made in the form of a block grant—will be cut by 25 percent by the end of 1983. Puerto Rico remains the largest recipient of food stamps, proportionally, in the program; this island of three million inhabitants received more than 10 percent of all federal food stamp payments, important not only for the direct relief of suffering in a region with a level of unemployment much higher than that of the mainland, but also because, together with other federal transfers, these payments maintain demand.[26] The damage is compounded by the axing of programs like the Comprehensive Employment and Training Act (CETA); however limited its successes as a training program, it provided jobs for 20,000 Puerto Ricans and balanced the budgets of hard-pressed municipalities.[27]

Governor Romero and his financial advisers do not reject the premises of the new U.S. economic policy; they too believe in the promotion of private-sector economic activity by reducing taxes to stimulate growth.[28] Just as Reagan has retreated from the excesses of the welfare state and government interference in the private sector, so Romero claims to follow in his footsteps as fast as local circumstances allow. Indeed, he claims he led the way in departing from the economic and social philosophy of the PPD: "In the past," Romero explains, "there has been too much dependence on the accustomed government paternalism. Citizens and entrepreneurs turn to the government to solve their problems or difficulties of their own making. This practice must now end."[29] According to Romero, the New Federalism and cuts in welfare handouts will present Puerto Rico with "the challenge of strengthening the economy with a stronger effort on our own with less help from the federal government."

He may well be right. The massive recent inflow of federal funds was used for consumption rather than for productive investment that might have helped to cure massive unemployment in Puerto Rico.[30] It has induced a false sense of well-being in a stagnant economy.

The Romero administration, however, lacks the courage of its own convictions. It espouses equal treatment on equal footing with a state of the United States only when Puerto Rico has something to gain — for example, on Medicaid, when Puerto Rico's share is cut, and in Supplemental Security Income, when it gets nothing. However much Reagan's policies may promise a long-run recovery for both the mainland and the island, in the short run, across-the-board equal application of these policies to Puerto Rico produces acute withdrawal symptoms. Puerto Rico's resident commissioner in Washington has prophesied economic collapse and social revolution, with Puerto Rico becoming "the biggest slum area of the Caribbean, something similar to the South Bronx."[31] Romero therefore pleads for retention of the advantages given by special, unequal treatment — above all the maintenance of the tax concessions of Article 936 — even though these advantages are endowed by a status (Commonwealth) that he regards as colonial and that the coming of his own preferred status (statehood) would reduce to zero. While statehood is the ultimate haven, the governor's former economic adviser argues "the island must make the most of the advantages that the current political system offers its economy."[32] Like all Puerto Rican politicians, Romero is willing to use Puerto Rico's indeterminate status to get the best of both worlds. However much he trumpets the virtues of "stronger effort" on the island, salvation, as always, will come from Washington. Where once Puerto Rico boasted of its achievements to the world, it now displays its poverty to soften hard hearts in the Reagan administration.

As in every aspect of Puerto Rican affairs, an "objective" assessment of the economy of Puerto Rico is thwarted by mutually exclusive perceptions. To those Americans who are not radical critics of their own society, and to supporters of Commonwealth and statehood, Puerto Rico has been rescued from abysmal poverty and the fate of its less fortunate Caribbean neighbors by the American presence. Supporters of Commonwealth are sometimes critical of that presence, but still maintain that it is Puerto Rico's unique connection with the United States, established in 1952, that remains the essential condition of prosperity. To the radical critics of the American connection, it has turned Puerto Rico into a faltering open economy, dominated and plundered by American capitalists: "an extreme example of imperial domination" resulting in "inhuman conditions."[33] The *independentistas* argue that the policies pursued since 1947 have "distorted" Puerto Rico's economic development, creating "an extreme vulnerability to outside forces and decision-making units."[34] They view the bankruptcy in 1980 of CORCO, the largest single investment ever made in Puerto Rico, as symbolizing the collapse of a misconceived illusion: that American capitalists, seeking their own profits, could make Puerto Rico prosper.

This criticism is, in effect, a criticism of the operation of free-enterprise capitalism, free trade, and unrestricted international investment as a recipe for the development in poor societies. As in most of Latin America, it takes on a virulent anti-American tinge, because the United States is the most powerful capitalist nation. In Puerto Rico, it is far and away the largest investor and the largest supplier of consumer goods; the American presence is proclaimed from every billboard advertising the virtues of Winston cigarettes or Coca-Cola.[35] The radicals view the whole history of Puerto Rico since 1898 as an illustration of the evils of American exploitation. This interpretation depends on the assumption that some "normal" and beneficial development was interrupted and "distorted" by the American presence.

That the first years of American rule were years of acute distress in Puerto Rico — produced by dislocations resulting from change in the metropolitan market and heightened by the most disastrous hurricane the island had experienced — cannot be denied. Nor can the radical transformation that came with the invasion of American sugar capital, which forced Puerto Rico toward a dangerous reliance on a single crop in a volatile market.

The emotional appeal of the attack on American capitalism depends on an idealization of social conditions before the American conquest and on an optimistic view of the prospects of the Puerto Rican economy in 1898. It is probable, before the Americans came, that patriarchal, face-to-face relationships on relatively small coffee and sugar haciendas did something to mitigate the harsh face of the poverty and uncertain employment that existed in Puerto Rico. But the patriarchal society also was cruelly exploitative.[36] Poverty was there, even if, as in all economies with a sizable subsistence sector, it was masked by the possibilities of raising food on small plots. Unemployment or chronic underemployment probably affected over half of the work force; an undernourished and illiterate population, riddled with disease, had a life expectancy of thirty-five.

Nor were the prospects of the economy encouraging. Puerto Rico was a high-cost producer of coffee and sugar, but both crops were faced with severe competition from large units of production in Brazil and Cuba.[37] By 1898, Puerto Rican sugar producers had embarked on a process of concentration and mechanization in order to survive; American technology and American capital simply hastened this process, emphasizing the defects of the old society, the exploitation of the labor force, and the cultivation of export crops for the international market, creating an economy that produced what it did not consume and consumed what it did not produce.

In the early years, the American government had no solution to the evils of poverty and unemployment in the colony other than to plead for limitation of the uncontrolled growth of the population, which, governor after governor insisted, condemned the islanders to perpetual penury by dissipating the wealth conveyed by American capital.[38] That the application of laissez-faire economics brought disaster to a poor colonial economy by the 1930s is evident. Nevertheless, the adoption of more positive policies during and after the New Deal saved Puerto Rico from the poverty that afflicted other overpopulated Caribbean islands. Puerto Rico's economic resurgence in the 1950s and 1960s depended on the common market that came with American rule. Whatever the social, political, and cultural consequences of that rule, its material results to date have been, on the whole, beneficial.

This conclusion is unacceptable to many Puerto Ricans. The application of dependency theories — particularly as evolved by Latin American writers such as Celso Furtado, Osvaldo Sunkel, Anibal Pinto, and Enrique Cardoso — has become an essential element in the Puerto Rican nationalist and *independentista* ideology. These theories take on an explicit anti-American edge. Thus to deny the destructive impact of the United States on the Puerto Rican economy and the consequent dissolution of an integrated society and culture is to exhibit a "lack of a world historic view," a failure to appreciate that incorporation into the world of capitalist imperialism *must* result in an exploitation of the natives more ruthless than that experienced before their countries entered that particular stage of the historical process. What should have been an independent economy pursuing its "normal" development became a dependent colonial economy, its destiny as a "nation" compromised by the conquest of 1898. Dependence was reinforced by Operation Bootstrap, which made U.S. investment become the life blood of the economy and colonial status an economic necessity. Operation Bootstrap is therefore seen as a Machiavellian device of Muñoz Marín to thwart independence as an option. Severance of the political tie by an independent republic would spell economic ruin.

Dependency theorists argue that, sooner or later, the performance of a dependent economy will falter and that the consequent social conflicts must be mastered by force. Since these conflicts have not erupted in Puerto Rico, dependency theorists argue that the Commonwealth model was saved from the social disaster implicit in dependency by food stamps, which relieved distress and maintained a minimum level of demand, and by expansion of the public sector, which alleviated unemployment — one remedy dependent on federal doles, the other on federal programs. Thus supported, Puerto Rico could stagger on as a beggar economy. Wrongly conceived in the first place, it was saved for a long period after 1947 by the safety valve of emigration to the mainland.

Even if the Commonwealth model, relieved of those it cannot employ by emigration and preserved from collapse by the *mantengo* of welfare payments, can provide the modest continued growth that would stave off catastrophic unemployment, this would only be, critics argue, at the cost of increasing dependence and an ever-widening gap between the rich and poor. At present, 55 percent of Puerto Rico's domestic income goes to the top 20 percent of the population; the lower half is left with only 15 percent. Those who praise Puerto Rico's economic progress, the dependency theorists maintain, fail to distinguish between mere growth, as measured by traditional indicators such as increases in the GNP, and true development, measured by such factors as income distribution.[39] Puerto Rican planners of the Moscoso school had been obsessed by the wrong statistical yardsticks and blinded by faith that spectacular increases in Puerto Rico's GNP would enrich society as a whole.

These arguments were among those deployed by the *independentistas* when they appeared before the Status Commission of 1964–66. While the arguments have not changed, they have, especially in the hands of the economists of the PSP, been radicalized. Such is the case with the "labor surplus" argument, which holds that Puerto Rico is a victim of the international division of labor under capitalism.[40] This view brings Puerto Rico into the same category as Mexico, the Dominican Republic, or Haiti. The argument runs thus: the advance of American imperialist capitalism destroyed the old, precolonial economies, creating a vast "reserve army" of unemployed. When the metropolitan economy needs cheap labor, such as during World War II or the boom of the 1950s, the barriers to both legal and illegal immigration are lowered; in recession, the immigrants are extruded (for example, in the depression of the 1930s, Mexicans were ruthlessly deported) or an attempt is made to halt immigration (as has happened recently with Mexican labor).

"The problem of Puerto Rican migration," argues Manuel Maldonado-Denis, "should be seen as a problem that transcends the relationship between Puerto Rico and the United States, to become a problem...that hinges upon mass migratory movements within the context of the international division of labor in capitalist countries."[41] Emigration is seen not as an individual choice but as an economic necessity; in the capitalist system, Marx insisted, men enter into necessary relations that are independednt of their individual wills. The pool of unemployed, created by the impact of American capitalism on the island, provides cheap, nonunionized labor for mainland employers.

But there is one essential difference that makes Puerto Ricans a special case among Hispanics. As American citizens, they cannot be extruded by force. They can only be extruded by the fluctuations of the economy; hence the return migrations of the recessions in 1963 and in the 1970s. Once there is a threat of unemployment on the mainland, there is no point in staying in what many Puerto Ricans regard as an uncomfortable if not hostile environment. With a depressed island economy, Puerto Rico may cease to be a refuge, and the "dream" of returning home may fade at the very time that the "dream" of making good in New York has vanished.[42]

It is the present plight of the Puerto Rican economy that feeds the *Schadenfreude* of the critics of the American connection. The case of these critics is as irrefutable as it is irrelevant. Puerto Rico, just like any other Caribbean economy, cannot go it alone. However much the rhetoric of native politicians may strive to conceal it, all are doomed to dependence on the outside world, on an external benefactor — whether it be the Soviet Union, the United States, France, or Great Britain. Cuba is exceptional only in that it does not export its surplus labor. In the past four decades, Puerto Rico has been a manufacturing export economy, dependent on the international market, in which the United States is the largest importer of Puerto Rican manufactured goods, and on "foreign" investment from the capital market of the mainland, which financed 90 percent of Puerto Rico's industry.[43] While dependence on the U.S. market has diminished, the optimistic prophecy of the American economist Werner Baer, delivered at the height of Operation Bootstrap, that there appeared "a good probability that Puerto Rico's economic growth will become substantially self-generating," remains unfulfilled.[44] Recession in the Western economies in general, and in the United States in particular, has brought to Puerto Rico the zero growth, faltering investment, and mounting unemployment that afflict all the weaker economies of the capitalist West and that hit those of the Caribbean particularly hard. Tourism, on which Caribbean planners set such hopes — and of which, in Puerto Rico, the Caribe Hilton Hotel is the monument and the "Miamiization" of the Condado beach strip the end product — is in the doldrums; with less money to spend, tourists seek the cheapest places in the sun, and they are not now to be found in Puerto Rico.

Puerto Rico must not only survive the short-term shock of Reagan's policies but, in the long run, make certain that the end of the U.S. and world recessions brings the end of recession in Puerto Rico. This is the aim of the "New Strategy" of the PNP and the Fomento, a strategy that is not as novel as its proponents claim. PPD planners were long aware of the shortcomings of the old investment pattern in which traditional industries, paying low wages, served unstable markets; they were unfortunate in that their bet on heavy industry — petrochemicals — was ill-timed. As in similar economies — Taiwan, Singapore, or Hong Kong — Puerto Rico's future lies in high-technology industries. Encouragement of these industries, according to José R. Madera, the present head of the Fomento, will make Puerto Rico "the technological axis of the regional [Caribbean] economy while maintaining our position in the United States."[45] Whether such efforts can fulfill the dream of Muñoz Marín — a country with only 5 percent of its people out of a job — remains doubtful considering that Puerto Rico's competitors are prepared to work very hard and that international capital (U.S. capital included) moves quickly to where productivity is highest. Even to maintain unemployment at 10 percent for the next decade, the economy must supply 1.3 million jobs.

The "New Strategy" recognizes that the abject state of agriculture is the scandal of Puerto Rico's economy. Neglected in the drive for industrialization at all costs, unprotected against the invasion of the products of agribusiness on the mainland that are standard products preferred by supermarket chains, agricultural performance is abysmal. It is argued that where the marginal utility of labor in agriculture is zero (that is, where there are too many "useless" laborers on the land), the removal of the unproductive surplus of laborers will increase agricultural productivity. But while 140,000 laborers left the sugar estates and the subsistence farms of the interior, in the last decades productivity has remained stagnant and land has reverted to waste and fallow. Curiously, there is now a shortage of labor on the land; laborers and smallholders, in the hope of someday getting a job in town, prefer to remain idle, living off federal doles. The idealization of the *jibaro* in the literature and in the mythology of the PPD has not made the prospect of life on the land an attractive option to existence on the margins of the cities' consumer society. This is not to argue that a return to subsistence farming provides a remedy for the poor performance of the agricultural sector or that an agricultural revival can ensure the revival of Puerto Rico's economy as a whole. A return to the spectacular growth of earlier years is probably impossible. For better or for worse, Puerto Rico is part of the international market economy with privileged access to its American sector, above all for the investment capital that American corporations can provide. Operation Bootstrap, by its very name, tended to conceal this dependence; impressive though the achievements of its planners were, Puerto Rico did not so much pull itself up by its own bootstraps but rather was hoisted up by massive injections of capital from the United States. The resurgence of Puerto Rico was a reflection of the golden era of the capitalist West in general and the 1960s boom of the mainland. When the boom turned into recession, recession came to Puerto Rico with a drop in investment.

If Puerto Rico is to take advantage of a renewal of economic growth in the Western economies, if it is to use the advantage it now enjoys in order to attract investors, then it must ensure that investment is profitable. But there are signs that the productivity of capital is falling. The depressing alternative to dependence on the continued investment of the U.S. corporations is dependence on federal funds. Welfare, not work, will sustain the economy.

This dependence on federal transfers is a significant change from the early, successful days of Operation Bootstrap, when Puerto Rico enjoyed the rewards of seizing and exploiting the advantages that few of its competitors could offer investors. But by the 1960s, when the Commonwelth strategies were being presented to the outside world as models for economic growth, these advantages were diminishing as other countries began to offer similar attractions. When Puerto Rico's economy should have been analyzed as a problem, it was presented to Latin America as a showcase.[46] The plan that rescued Puerto Rico from its condition in the 1930s as one of the poorhouses of the Caribbean no longer works miracles; Puerto Rico now survives with the aid of a series of props provided by the United States.[47]

Puerto Ricans perpetually fear that these props will be removed, whittled down, or offered to their competitors. Puerto Rican economists prophesied that the General Agreement on Tariffs and Trade (GATT) tariff reductions of the 1960s would destroy the traditional industries on which the island was then largely dependent; they had a case. Now they fear that Jamaica will catch the eye of the administrators in Washington as a new candidate for special favors in the attempts to prove that the export of "our way of life" is the best means to resist the spread of Castroism in the Caribbean.

Rather than reliance on "artificial" props, Governor Romero and his economic advisers preach — but do not always practice — the gospel of self-reliance, which requires a drastic alteration in the existing structure of the economy and in the life-style of Puerto Ricans.

The special advantages of "colonial status" and the federal lifeline have provided the easy way out for Puerto Rico, diverting its inhabitants from the harder task of producing more and saving more than they do. For a time, Muñoz Marín and his party succeeded in creating something resembling a revolutionary society. Puerto Ricans were willing to sacrifice present satisfactions for future rewards, even individual benefits for the benefit of society as a whole, driven by what has been called "a collective will to achieve."[48] Those days are gone. A society saturated by the commercial advertisements of stores and supermarkets, where consumer credit is easy to come by, overspends. Even so, the underlying frustration of that society is that the economy does not provide many Puerto Ricans with the money to buy the products they now consider necessities. In 1929, Muñoz argued that the "modest security" of the old society had been replaced for Puerto Ricans by a "vision of opulence"; that "the margin between what they have and what they can get has widened enormously."[49] The sad fact is that in the new society of the 1980s, the margin is still wide for many Puerto Ricans, particularly for all those who remain outside the limited high-income enclaves created by American investment. Social justice demands that those at the edges of society do not remain parasites, but to provide them with useful jobs is a daunting task for a fragile economy.

9.

THE NEW SOCIETY

What kind of society have the economic developments of the past decades brought to Puerto Rico? How stable is it? What foundation does it provide for a democratic, open society?

The critical date is 1956. In that year, for the first time, the proportion of the gross national product (GNP) derived from manufacturing overtook that produced by agriculture. In 1950, 36 percent of the labor force was engaged in agriculture and only 9 percent in manufacturing; by 1980, a mere 5 percent made their living in agriculture while manufacturing employed 20 percent of the labor force. An agricultural society, with a weak manufacturing appendage of workers in small concerns — the needlework sweatshops of Mayagüez are a classic example — had become, in two decades, an industrialized society, with an agricultural appendage struggling to survive.

By the 1980s, therefore, Puerto Rico was confronted with the problems that face all underdeveloped economies that have undergone rapid industrialization: problems brought by the massive migration to the cities — or rather to *the* city, San Juan — of which the most striking early result was the creation of slum shantytowns. The culture of poverty that these shanty-towns generated became familiar to Americans in Oscar Lewis's

La Vida, which describes life in La Perla, the sprawling settlement under the walls of the old town of San Juan. Thus, rapid industrialization presented the Commonwealth government with huge tasks in social services and housing.

More significant than the emergence of a lumpenproletariat — attracted by the prospect of urban wages that they often failed to obtain — was the rise of what has been termed a new middle class accompanied by a change in the composition of the working class. At the risk of oversimplification, the "traditional" Puerto Rican society that survived into the 1930s can be described as a two-class society: the agricultural mass — sugar workers and subsistence farmers — and the amalgam of professionals and landowners who constituted the political and social elite. Industrialization spawned a more diversified society. In the process, the native landowning elite was weakened almost to extinction, the sugar workers became a less significant sector, and artisans were increasingly transformed into factory hands. This had significant effects. In the 1930s, the sugar workers, who were concentrated on the great sugar plantations, were unionized and militant; in the 1980s, a work force scattered in factories and small enterprises, of which only 14 percent is unionized, is relatively impotent.

The view of present-day Puerto Rico as a three-class society — "the rich," "the middle class," and "the poor" — is generally accepted. "The simple vision of a three-class system" concludes a survey conducted in the mid 1970s "appears well rooted in the perceptions of people."[1] Between 1953 and 1963, the gross domestic product (GDP) per capita increased by 68 percent in real terms. The share received by the top and bottom segments fell by 5 percent, while the bulk of it was enjoyed by the "new middle class" between these two extremes, itself divided between a "rich" upper middle class (there is no aristocracy) and the more humble lower middle class.[2] It is the upper middle class that sets the social values of Puerto Rico as it moves toward "the life-style of the most urban affluent segment of our society."

No doubt the picture of Puerto Rican society composed of benevolent *hacendados* (estate owners) and their grateful dependents, each accepting their mutual obligations in an unchanging and unchangeable social framework, is the creation of those who regret — and resent — the passing of a way of life unadulterated by Americanization. Both the *jíbaro* and the *hacendado,* protagonists of the two-class society, survive in literature, not in life: now the *jíbaro* typically seeks to leave his plot for the city and the *hacendado's* son seeks government or business employment while he studies accounting rather than writing poetry.[3] Nevertheless, there can be no question that the "peaceful revolution" of the Popular Democratic Party in fostering a more diversified society (PPD) has broken the hold of what has been called Hispanic fatalism: the acceptance of one's lot in life as given, as unimprovable. The deference paid to social superiors that characterized the old society has been replaced by the quest for individual welfare.[4]

The possibility of movement toward a more abundant life, at least in terms of the material possessions of modern society, accounted for the sense of optimism that was the striking characteristic of the early years of Commonwealth. In the late 1950s, the most detailed and sophisticated survey ever conducted in Puerto Rico revealed that people were overwhelmingly confident about their individual prospects in life.[5] "The generalized euphoria of the population is truly spectacular"; all classes shared "an unmistakable note of hope and of possibility." Only 15 percent of a sample of 1,000 were "seriously disgruntled." What was still, by American standards, a poor society, where sharp differences in income persisted, nevertheless appeared a satisfied society. There was no detectable class consciousness, no class war; in spite of blatant socioeconomic divisions, "there was much more class amity than hostility."[6]

An earlier generation of social scientists, working for the Brookings Institution in the 1930s, when chances of better jobs in Puerto Rico were minimal, noted "submissiveness to misfortune and a lack of class feeling" on the island. This docility may have contributed to "class amity," but it does not account for the "euphoria" of the late 1950s and early 1960s too well attested to be dismissed. Has this "euphoria" survived? Has it been weakened by a continued failure of the economic system to provide jobs? Do Puerto Ricans still feel that the political system satisfies their needs?

While the dynamism of the great days of Commonwealth has been eroded, confidence in a better future, in *personal* terms, still appears to permeate Puerto Rican society.[7] But the old confidence, so marked in the 1950s and 1960s, in the efficacy and honesty of the political system in dealing with the problems confronting Puerto Rico has diminished.[8] The present sense of disillusionment with politics and politicians is not exceptional; it is a feature of many new democratic societies. It is that the old confidence was unique.

From the election of 1940 to the retirement of Luis Muñoz Marín from the Senate in 1968, Puerto Rico possessed a father figure. Puerto Ricans voted, election after election, to keep Don Luis and his party in power. "Without votes," Muñoz wrote in his memoirs, "there was no power. Without power the reforms that were necessary would not be realized." Muñoz and the Populares possessed for two decades both the votes and the power. Thus equipped, the government's achievements in economic development were matched by its achievements in education and social services; it got things done in a way that the congressional system in the United States could not match.

No one who knew Muñoz or who has read his memoirs can

doubt the sincerity of his democratic convictions. He himself saw the perils of unchallenged one-party domination and sought to cure its defects. Nevertheless, his domination persisted. Puerto Rican political culture shared with other Latin American nations a toleration of authoritarianism and a faith in charismatic leadership.

What was normal in other democratic systems had been abnormal in Puerto Rico. The "normalization" of politics that came with the establishment of a competitive two-party political system after Muñoz's retirement in 1968 engendered a loss of faith in that system as an efficient mechanism for distributing the scarce resources of a poor society. Cynicism, familiar in other societies, replaced mystique. In a recent survey made in the late 1970s and admittedly imperfect, nearly half the respondents believed that "politics merely create discord"; that politics have "become so complicated that I can't participate"; that the government should help the poor, yet it "is more concerned to help the big corporations." Nearly three-quarters of the respondents held that election campaigns were sources of violence and that it would be "better to limit them"; that politicians are in politics merely for their own profit. The father figure has been replaced by "a tiny group who manipulate the people in order to cling on to power."

Before 1968, a major charge levied against the political system by Muñoz's critics was that politics were not competitive: political life and, above all, political patronage and *mantengo* were the monopoly of a single party — the PPD. Party funds were swollen by the levies on civil servants whose promotion prospects depended on loyalty to the party. The university was a PPD monopoly; schoolteachers were a corps of paid PPD propagandists.

Now the charge is that the coming of competitive politics has spawned a race of petty politicians; that political life reverted to the patterns of the pre-Muñoz era, when rival clans struggled for power as an end in itself and for a sufficiency of government appointments to provide pasture for the party faithful to feed on. What was once political patronage in the hands of a single party has become a sordid spoils system operated by two parties: with the New Progressive Party (PNP) victory, the defeated claim that the university is turning into an *estadista* fief; when the PPD regained control of the legislature in 1980, its clerks and porters were sacked en masse.

While the father figure has gone — his funeral rites in 1980 were a massive national mourning — personalism remains, in this small community, the dominant political style. Institutional mechanisms require the oil of personalism to work. The most paradoxical feature of Puerto Rican politics is that, while centralization has, over the years, left the mayors with little power and less money, they are, nevertheless, a major channel of communication with the political machine, "a sort of shock absorber" between the citizen with a problem and the government bureaucracy. In a survey commissioned by the PPD government in the late 1970s, while nearly 90 percent of Puerto Ricans could name their mayor, a mere 30 percent could name an islandwide politician — a complete reversal of the situation in European democracies.[9] The mayor of a large town will see two hundred or so of his constituents every week. All mayors agree that the only way to get things done — a bridge, a new ambulance, jobs under federal programs like the Comprehensive Employment and Training act (CETA) — is to make a personal visit to the government agencies. For the citizen with a complaint, the function of his representative or senator is less to make laws that implement programs than to badger civil servants for individual benefits.[10] This, it may be argued, is a common feature of all democratic systems, not least of the United States; but in small Antillean societies it is a fact of everyday life where intense personalism compensates for lack of faith in institutionalized politics. It would be idle to expect that democracy in Puerto Rico should function as it does in Germany or France.

Whereas the educated are clearly aware of the defects of personalistic paternalism, the poorer classes still cling to it. "You don't look a gift horse in the mouth" (*a caballo regalado no se mira al colmillo*). Hence the general acquiescence in the legitimacy of a system in which the government provides *mantengo* — the bundle of social services and relief payments that sustain so large a proportion of the population — and jobs in the public sector that employ 29 percent of the Puerto Rican work force. This will only change when the services rendered by government are regarded, not as bestowed from above, as gifts from the mayor or the local legislator, but as the legitimate rights of citizens;[11] when jobs are distributed for capacity and merit rather than as rewards for political fidelity. So rooted is the acceptance of political patronage that promotion by merit is regarded as a social solecism, as something not quite "fair."

How democratic, then, is Puerto Rican society? Its critics deny that there is a truly democratic political culture or that the democratic freedoms written into the Constitution can be effectively exercised. In 1957, an enquiry by the U.S. Civil Rights Commission concluded that, in the words of its organizer, "the majority of the Puerto Rican people are ignorant of the fundamental democratic processes and are inhibited in the use of the rights guaranteed by the Constitution and the laws."[12] Puerto Rican democracy, presented to the outside world as the exceptional case in Latin America, was therefore "a mere facade without real content"; the showcase was empty.

Later enquiries noted an improvement as regards respect for civil liberties but still revealed that Puerto Ricans confused authority and power and regarded acts of the government that breached the most elementary civil rights as, if not legitimate, then acceptable: for example, it was regarded as normal that Communists be denied jobs and imprisoned and their papers suppressed. Such surveys provide a picture of Puerto Ricans as natural authoritarians, satisfied with a government that provides jobs and lulls the population at large into supine, soulless acquiescence with large doses of *mantengo* (of which the politicians in power are the visible providers) and who allow their civil rights to be grossly and systematically violated by successive governments in order to suppress the opinions and activities of those who oppose them. Puerto Ricans are therefore, it is held, denied the essential instruments of a democratic policy: the possibility of presenting, by public political action, an alternative to the government in power.

Naturally enough these charges are made by those who have suffered for their opposition: intellectuals, professionals, and university professors of *independentista* convictions. The charges of violation of civil rights have been sustained by the bar association, the Colegio de Abogados, an *independentista* stronghold. The advocates of independence have suffered the most, and their complaints have a nationalist anti-American passion. They claim that they are "persecuted" under federal laws, investigated by a federal agency (the FBI), and tried in federal courts, which they profess to see, wrongly, as instruments of the U.S. government. It was federal customs officers, acting on information provided by the FBI under Sections 587 and 305 of the Tariff Act of 1930, who searched Mari Bras's luggage for seditious literature: "the Immigration and Customs agents constantly are humiliating and maltreating members of the Pro Independence Movement that [sic] travel abroad."[13] Washington has withdrawn passports from prominent pro-Cuban intellectuals.[14] Proponents of the armed struggle view the federal grand jury as "a rubber stamp for prosecuting attorneys," and an FBI instrument for extracting information, using the threat of prison sentences, from those who refuse to testify. They argue that President Reagan is personally directing an offensive using the excuse of "antiterrorism" in order to reduce to impotence all those who oppose the U.S. presence in Puerto Rico.[15] It is characteristic of the obligatory optimism of revolutionaries that the *Liga Socialista* sees in a campaign against the grand jury system a means to create the "effective support in the popular masses" that they so singularly lack.[16]

Many alleged infringements of civil rights arise out of the federal government's response to breaches of laws. The subsequent court cases provide publicity for the *independentista* cause; needling the Americans is part of an old political game that goes back to 1904. Thus, for example, Rubén Berríos Martínez defied a United States Treasury ban on travel to Cuba to attend the Caribbean Games. He cannot lose. If he is imprisoned, it proves the "system" is tyrannous; if he is not prosecuted, the "system" is exposed as suffering from a lack of self-confidence.[17] Similarly, the staging of demonstrations on United States Navy-owned land is both a protest and a provocation.

In all societies where terrorism and sabotage are threats, police are inclined to bend the law. For instance, the infiltration of political party meetings and the use of informers — alleged infringements of civil rights — are the normal response of security agents to organized terrorism. Some practices are questionable; for example, the close questioning of objectors to military service in order to elicit their political affiliations and the gathering of information from professors on the political reliability of student applicants for federal employment, particularly, it is alleged, in the University of Puerto Rico's Department of Social Sciences, which is regarded as a seedbed of sedition.[18] More serious is the supposed existence of files and blacklists drawn up by the FBI with the help of the Commonwealth police: in the 1960s, blacklists apparently included those who had ceased to be *independentistas* in the 1930s. The alleged resulting difficulties encountered by known *independentistas* in obtaining employment, which extend to the university and the private sector, are bitterly resented.[19]

Persecution was at its height in periods of Nationalist agitation (in the 1930s and 1950s) when, it must be remembered, the Nationalists mounted what they hoped would be an island-wide revolution, and in the years immediately after the Cuban Revolution of 1959, when it must also be remembered that a minuscule group regarded the Cuban armed struggle as a tactic applicable in Puerto Rico. The charge of Communism was extended to embrace *independentistas* of all shades; in 1959, the Committee on Un-American Activities visited the island convinced of the existence of a Communist plot involving a supposed liberation army two thousand strong. Its hearings were booed and the chief justice of Puerto Rico protested that the committee lacked "the moral authority to operate in the island."[20] In 1966, the FBI reported that "chronic riots at the University of Puerto Rico are attributed to agitators following instructions from Cuba's government-controlled subversive student organization . . . .Incendiarism and other acts of terrorism have been accompanied in the past by bloody Communist-led student riots."

This overreaction was more an American than an island phenomenon. Muñoz Marín asserted, time and time again, that "Castro Communism" constituted no threat to Puerto Rican democracy; anti-Communist hysteria, on the other hand, *was* such a threat. Hoover's allegations about the activities of "a violent revolutionary minority" that "would accept help from anyone, particularly Fidel Castro," were dismissed by the *San Juan Star* as ridiculous.

Like every other feature of the political landscape, the civil rights issue was transformed by the PNP victory in the elections of November 1968. Since that date a powerful opposition has watched over the party in power; every doubtful or improper action of the police in support of the government became front-page news, castigated as incipient Fascism. For example, newspaper exposure of PNP Governor Romero Barceló's supposed involvement in a clumsy police action, which ended with the shooting of two young *independentistas* at Cerro Maravilla, contributed to his poor performance in the 1980 elections. While there is no "quality" press, the political information in most Puerto Rican papers is superior to that supplied by the popular press in the United States or Britain. Far from being concealed, political and financial scandals are the stuff of Puerto Rican investigative journalism.

It is scarcely surprising that democracy in Puerto Rico is not as firmly rooted as in older democratic societies. What is surprising is that its roots in a society that has enjoyed effective suffrage only since 1940 are as strong as they are. Further, problems such as police brutality are not unknown in democratic societies like Great Britain or the United States; this does not mean, however, that they are not serious problems and that they are not more serious in relatively new democracies.[21] It is idle, however, to maintain that Puerto Rico is not an effective democracy. Honest elections, on which the legitimacy of a democratic system rests, take place in spite of the baffling complexity of electoral laws and the political nature of the bodies that supervise them. There has been a steady improvement in the protection of the voter's rights.[22] In spite of continued public accusations of fraudulent electoral practices, politicians admit in private that fraud on any appreciable scale does not take place. Puerto Rico has come a long way since 1940 when *jíbaro* votes could be bought for a dollar or a pair of shoes.

While there may be a certain Latin American style in Puerto Rican politics, this does not necessarily mean, as was so frequently asserted in the early days of American rule, that Puerto Ricans are unfit for self-government; nor does it deny the self-evident proposition that peoples learn the discipline of self-government only by its exercise. But the vindictiveness of local politics, which sometimes verges on political cannibalism, is not without its dangers for democracy, and some pessimists even view it as a prelude to civil war.[23]

Santiago Iglesias was not the only labor leader to believe that workers fared better under the protection of federal laws than when left to the mercies of the Creole bourgeoisie: "It is not necessary to argue," wrote Socialist Eduardo Conde in 1915, "whether the Americans are worse or better than Puerto Ricans in power. But at least with them we have the liberty of protesting their errors which we cannot do with Puerto Ricans, because in so attempting they will beat in our ribs and we will lose our liberty."[24] "If Puerto Rico should become an independent Republic," argues Felícita in Oscar Lewis's *La Vida*, reflecting an argument that is still common coinage among statehooders, "people would be strung up on lamp-posts along the streets and everybody would be dead."

Would Puerto Rican judges, appointed by partisan Puerto Rican politicians, better protect individual liberty than the judges of the much abused federal courts? One *independentista* asserts that Governor Romero "only respects civil rights because the federal authorities are watching him."[25] Suppose that Puerto Rico had become an independent republic with its own army. Would it have been spared those military interventions and army takeovers that have distorted and still distort the political life of so many Latin American nations? Puerto Rican politicians are not above exploiting, for partisan purposes, situations that might erupt in violence. Even the respectable

PPD backs and encourages the shanty settlers of Villa San Miedo to resist eviction by policemen who are trying to enforce the law.

Puerto Rican politics do not resemble those of an American state. They are the politics of a self-absorbed island community, conceived — even by statehooders — as a unique world with its own rules of the game. Rather than a state of the Union in embryo, Puerto Rico is a city-state, torn as were city-states in antiquity and in Renaissance Italy by the feuds of political clans, feuds fostered by the intimacy of a small society and fueled by the status question. Entrenched behind their status preferences, political clans advance into battle with each other to defend irreconcilable dogmas. Status politics, Muñoz Marín concluded at the end of his life, had sapped the political energies of Puerto Rico, diverting them from the real problems of the island.

It is not the absence of institutions such as a free press and an honest electoral system that constitutes a danger to Puerto Rican democracy. Nor can it be argued that the electorate is alienated from the political system: the enduring feature of Puerto Rican political life is the persistence of a very high level of electoral participation—about 80 percent. It is truly remarkable that the rural poor and those subsisting precariously on the margin of urban society use their vote, even if they do so less because they see the political system as an instrument for solving their pressing problems than because they believe that voting for a patron will engage his personal influence on their behalf. In Puerto Rico, where the voluntary associations, which de Tocqueville portrayed as a redeeming feature of American democracy, are weak, politics constitute a main tissue of society; but they hold it together much as an unhappy marriage is sometimes held together by quarrels between spouses. Mutual abuse is the stock-in-trade of the local *políticos* and it spreads downward. "No politics here" is the admonition exhibited in working-class bars. The most depressing feature of Puerto Rican politics is not any lack of commitment to democratic institutions, but the factious behavior of politicians who man those institutions; it is depressing because, presumably, they act as they do because they believe that such behavior is what their electors expect of them.

IO.

CONFLICTS AND CONFORMITY

In his attempts to force the Reagan administration to maintain the existing rate of federal payments, Puerto Rico's resident commissioner in Washington asserts that substantial cuts in welfare threaten social and political revolution in Puerto Rico and would turn a peaceful island into "another Cuba." Where is the material for such a conflagration? Is there a revolutionary lumpenproletariat? Is there a national bourgeoisie ready to undertake the first stages of the anticolonial revolution? Is there a coalition of the "forces of progress" that will tread "the noncapitalist road to socialism" that Soviet theorists see opening up in societies such as those of most Caribbean islands and that has been adopted as a model by some of the islands' leaders and intellectuals? Is there a militant proletariat prepared to form the revolutionary vanguard? Are the students of the University of Puerto Rico, as J. Edgar Hoover and the FBI feared, capable of staging bloody affrays under the guidance of Cuban experts? Is there an oppressed ethnic group ready to stage a Puerto Rican Watts?

As in most societies, the racial issue in Puerto Rico is clouded by euphemisms. Certainly Puerto Rico is not a racial paradise, as some of the propagandists of the island as "a showcase for democracy" profess. Racial discrimination exists, complicated by a confusion between the simple white/black dichotomy supposedly imported from the United States and the traditional, complex, native color scale.[1] The surveys conducted by Eduardo Seda Bonilla, a Puerto Rican sociologist much concerned with the racial issue, reveal discrimination in job opportunities — especially in white-collar occupations — in choice of marriage partners, and in social life in general (particularly in clubs and university fraternities). Attempts to hide racial origins, he argues, produce the psychological disturbances of "cryptomelanism" — the fear of losing one's "white" identity — exaggerated by internalization of the racial dualism of the United States, for whom all shades of color identify one as black.[2] "All Puerto Ricans are niggers" is written on the front page of Pedro Juan Soto's novel *Usmail,* published in 1979 but describing the situation in the late 1930s. It is the story of the struggle for identity of the illegitimate son of a black woman and a U.S. relief administrator. In the end he establishes that identity by killing an American serviceman. For Bonilla, Puerto Rican racial democracy is a myth hiding a "situation of infamous exploitation."

This attempt to present Puerto Rico as a society with a *severe* racial problem seems to be misguided. That racial discrimination exists cannot be doubted, but neither can it be doubted that Puerto Rico has no racial problem comparable to the problems of the United States and Great Britain. This is in sharp contrast to the former British Caribbean, where there are few aspects of West Indian life that race and color do not significantly touch. American rule, whatever its defects in Puerto Rican eyes, has never been marked by the combination of snobbery and color prejudice that made social life grotesque in the British colonies.[3] There is no public discrimination on grounds of color, and since 1943 racial discrimination of any kind has been illegal.[4] While there are some concentrations of blacks — the town of Loiza Aldea, for example — there are no black ghettos; the more exclusive suburbs tend to be white, but the slum settlements are racially mixed. Data on delinquency in the slums of San Juan are largely color free, a sharp contrast to the situation in continental U.S. cities.[5] Blacks are not molested and picked up by the police just because they are black, a practice that in Britain turns the assumption that blacks are inclined to crime into a self-fulfilling prophecy.[6] Blacks behave politically like slum dwellers in general: they tend to vote for the PNP. They have not been exploited by a revolutionary movement.

Puerto Rico constitutes what the Dutch sociologist H. Hoetink defines as a "segmented society." As a result of the importation of black slaves for a plantation economy — a late stage in Puerto Rican development—the white segment is dominant and sets the desirable "somatic norm," that is, the ideal physical type, which is devoid of Negroid features. Only a minute number of upper-class women exhibit marked Negroid features,[7] and marriage between a white woman and a black man is still a social solecism.

Nevertheless, there is a gradual process of "whitening," a movement, slow as all such movements are, toward a racially homogeneous society. In Puerto Rico, as in all Antillean countries colonized by Iberians, the "somatic norm" is more "liberal" than in the colonies of the Protestant powers of northwestern Europe or in the Deep South of the United States, partly because the Iberian ideal phenotype is darker than the Anglo-Saxon. This permits a less formidable "somatic distance" and the growth of an intermediate segment of mulattoes who, once they are "culturally" assimilated and economically well off, can merge with the dominant white segment to cushion the clash of colors. Racial statistics reflect the fact that Puerto Ricans would class as "white" those who in the non-Iberian colonies or in the United States would be classed as "blacks"; hence the black population in census data steadily diminishes. Blacks are not considered a threat; nor, as is true also in the Dominican Republic, are they bearers of an independent black culture hostile to the white world. There are very few significant African survivals, and such survivals as there are — apart from music and a widespread practice of spiritism — appear exotica, carefully cultivated by enthusiasts.[8]

Puerto Rican society is not free from racial prejudice and the pathological frustrations racism engenders. Racial jokes abound. A black senator is told after a car crash, "You look pale." "Get a photographer, quick," is his reaction. Prejudice still imprisons the majority of blacks in low-status occupations. But given a degree of what sociologists term "intersegmental mobility" (i.e., a black can "become" a mulatto and a mulatto can enter the white segment), it is not a racially explosive society. Of this, the casual observation of the behavior of the students in a university library or of the passengers in a downtown bus provides, at least, superficial proof.

The social alienation of the lumpenproletariat, of which disadvantaged blacks constitute a significant section, is expressed not in collective political action nor in mob violence against "white" civilization, nor even in the internecine gang warfare characteristic of Puerto Rican youth in New York. It finds its expression in deviance and delinquency: hence Puerto Rico's high levels of drug addiction and alcoholism, and the frequency of unstable consensual unions, which result in single-parent families in a society that professes to set great value on family life. More than anything else, the collapse of stable family life accounts for the high rate of juvenile delinquency, especially in San Juan, where 72 percent of burglaries and 85 percent of all cases handled in the courts are brought against youths under the age of seventeen.

High rates of juvenile delinquency have a profound effect on Puerto Rican society. Robbery, with or without violence, car theft, and attacks on stores have come to obsess Puerto Ricans, who lock themselves in their barred, fortresslike homes. Every political party promises to reestablish law and order.[9] In the early stages of the 1980 electoral campaign, crime and its prevention appeared as more salient issues than status.

Puerto Rico exhibits, in almost all respects, an extreme case of a Western malaise that afflicts societies that set material success as their goal yet block its attainment because they cannot provide the young with jobs. In Puerto Rico, two out of every five youths between sixteen and twenty-four years of age are *permanently* unemployed. In 1979, the Governor's Labor Advisory Council considered "the structurally unemployed" youth as "an economic and social disaster." Their numbers have mounted steadily since then, and crime rises *pari passu* with unemployment.

That crime and vandalism, like drug addiction, are seen by *independentistas* as imported from America, a perversion of a formerly sound society made sick by "foreign" influence and the psychological traumas that are a concomitant of political subjection, does not make crime in Puerto Rico a form of political protest or some popular instinctive revolt against Yankees.[10] Crime is on the increase in Western, urbanized societies.[11] It is not anti-American — most criminals commit crimes to attain the material products of American civilization. It falls into the pattern of that short-range hedonism of the poor, of which gambling is a less harmful manifestation. Politicians are seen, not as the oppressive representatives of an unjust society, but as potential providers of immediate benefits. The poor of the housing settlements and peripheral slums of San Juan have been organized as voters, not by parties that present some hope of a dignified society, but by politicians who offer a bandstand or a new sewage system.[12] In 1968, the poor were mobilized, not by a Puerto Rican Eva Perón, but by Luis Ferré, a middle-aged industrialist. But if the Puerto Rican "shirtless ones" were to become an explosive political force, they probably would be led by an island Eva Perón rather than a Puerto Rican Fidel Castro.

Labor unions have played a prominent part in the recent history and political culture of the former British Caribbean. Unions were the power base of the politicians who came to rule the new nations: Alexander Bustamante and Norman Manley in Jamaica. The neo-Marxists of the dependency school see in a militant proletariat of the Latin American periphery the motor of revolutionary change, the vanguard of the anticolonialist struggle that a bourgeoisie subservient to the metropolitan powers will never undertake. Puerto Rican unions have not followed the pattern of the former British colonies; nor do they seem likely to take up the role of a revolutionary vanguard.

Like every other feature of Puerto Rican life, trade unions have been influenced by the American connection. Santiago Iglesias, correspondent and admirer of Samuel Gompers, affiliated the Puerto Rican unions of his Free Federation of Workers (FLT) with the American AFL; the AFL provided organizational expertise, strike funds, and the ethos of "business unionism" until its pursuit of industrial peace was challenged in the sugar workers' strike of 1934.[13] The militants, many of whom were Communists who rejected Santiago Iglesias's version of "business unionism," broke away to form the General Confederation of Labor (CGT).[14]

By the 1940s, the labor movement was badly divided. The militants of the CGT, struggling with the AFL and its political ally the Socialist party, found in the populism of the PPD a temporary resting place. But by 1946, Muñoz Marín saw that his industrialization program demanded a manageable labor force just when the Communists abandoned their support of the PPD, now denounced by the party as the heresy of "Browderism."[15] The function of the unions, according to Muñoz, must be "to cooperate in the development of the country";[16] organized labor must now find its "indispensible defender" in the PPD government. The CGT split, and its non-Communist sector came under PPD control.

Whereas in the 1930s it appeared to workers that higher wages came from strong union pressure on employers, it was now apparent that wage increases resulted from negotiations between union leaders and government agencies.[17] Organized labor had been domesticated and governmentalized. The gains achieved by the new labor bureaucracy in the form of wage increases and the housing and social services that were part of the Populares "silent revolution" combined to make militant unionism less attractive to the majority of Puerto Rican workers—and just at the time that "Communist" unions were under attack on the mainland. The Taft-Hartley Act of 1947 not only put Puerto Rican independent unions at a disadvantage compared with those affiliated with the AFL, but also strengthened employers' delaying tactics.

In the postwar years, the union world became one of confusion and conflict. The unions that had originally joined the CGT were "independent" unions, both in the sense that they were sympathetic to the cause of independence and independent of the AFL. Industrialization by American companies saw the advance of the American unions affiliated with the AFL — the "internationals," so called because of their Canadian affiliates. The internationals, which were often very successful in negotiating favorable wage settlements in their early years, were accused by radicals of preempting the local left's leadership role via the "Yankeephile short circuit."[18] What is certain is that engaged, as they have been, in a campaign of "union piracy" against the independent unions — at their zenith the internationals captured about two-thirds of the work force — their presence has had a divisive effect.

The "internationals" are strongest in the private sector, but the government is the largest single employer in Puerto Rico, and the unionization of government employees is a critical issue. In recent years, strikes by the independent unions in the public sector have been characteristic of union activity. They reached unprecedented levels, on Puerto Rican standards, between 1970 and 1977.[19] That these strikes became a bitter struggle between Governor Hernández Colón and the unions shows the degree to which the PPD has lost its old hold over organized labor.

Early union history shows that weakness breeds violence: without substantial strike funds or industrial muscle, violent, short strikes are often the only way a union can get results. Violence is characteristic of even the strongest union, UTIER (the light and power union). In the 1978 strike, there were 270 acts of sabotage, "massive acts of vandalism" in the face of which UTIER remained "passive and encouraging." Violence resurfaced in the summer strike of 1981. Rather than submit to defeat, UTIER leader Lausell declared, "we are not going to allow anything to remain standing."[20] Yet UTIER lost the strike. Highly paid and highly politicized, by Puerto Rican standards, the strikers were presented in the press as selfish and vicious enemies of the people. As on the mainland, recession and the fear of dismissal weakens unions: UTIER lost 800 members after a strike in 1981.

Like American unions, and unlike the British unions, Puerto Rican unions have no formal commitment to a political party. Hence union leadership can change from party to party. The Pharmaceutical Union presidency, for example, passed from the PSP to the PNP. Politicians are naturally aware of the electoral advantages of deals with union leaders, and the independence movements seek to make the independent unions an instrument for their fight against "colonialism." Union rivalries severely limit their success. Federico Quiñones Rodríguez, a professor at the Institute of Labor Studies, a disciple of Ramos Antonini of the PPD but a member of the PIP, finds Rubén Berríos a "clean" fighter and Mari Bras of the PSP a sectarian operator.[21] The PSP's belief that unions must accept the leadership of the radical bourgeoisie, if they are to be effective, offends working-class leaders.[22] Moreover, the political commitment of the leadership does not carry with it the commitment of the members. While the leaders of the independent unions may be figureheads in the anticolonial struggle, the membership may vote PPD or PNP. No *independentista* political leader has built up a solid union base.

At the moment, the union movement is weak and divided. Only 14 percent — which reflects a decline of 6 percent in the past decade — of the labor force is unionized, and unions are particularly weak in the private sector where the pharmaceutical companies, which pay the highest wages, resist unionization. Only those unions that do not involve interstate commerce (for instance, the bus drivers union) can enforce a closed shop. Weakness is compounded by the disarray created by "cannibalism" — the union organizers' determination to absorb as their personal fiefs other unions, however remote their trades may be.[23] Trade unionism has become a jungle in which union organizers seek to "steal" other unions rather than recruit the nonunionized. All attempts to revive an islandwide federation have failed. The attempt to form a single island union in 1972 fell prey to the "sectarianism" of the PSP; the later attempts to create a united front tied to the Latin American Christian Democrat unions have yet to show any strength. Division is a manifestation of the Puerto Rican disease and is denounced by the far left who seek to organize a single island federation in order to infiltrate and control it: "We are specialists," they maintain, "in displaying our diffferences." The recession has further weakened a movement consisting of five hundred local unions, of which only a handful have any industrial muscle. This "archipelago" of "economist" unions, interested solely in their separate concerns, watch the general crisis of the economy as "spectators."[24]

The weakness of the unions in the dynamic years of Operation Bootstrap is understandable. Individual prospects were so bright that collective action seemed irrelevant. Now that the rate of economic growth has slowed down it might seem that collective action would become more important to a new generation that does not fear a relapse into agrarian poverty and that compares earnings, not to the abysmal pittances of the 1930s, but to mainland wage levels.[25] The "new unionism" of the 1970s seemed to reflect a change in attitudes, to represent a challenge to the alleged passivity of the internationals and to exhibit new levels of militancy evident in a series of violent strikes. Hopes of a *politically* radical unionism revived in the leadership of the PSP.[26] But the new unionism has died away with the recession; the present weakness of Puerto Rican unions is a mirror image of the present weakness of American unions.

Every survey of Puerto Rico — the first was taken in 1926 – 27 — shows a working class deeply conservative in its views and strongly authoritarian in its attitudes. While the old acceptance of a hierarchical society has vanished and while there is a general perception that "the rich" exist — and are envied — there is little class consciousness. In a newly industrialized society there is no working-class culture in the sense that it exists in European societies. The Puerto Rican poor set extraordinary store by education because they see it as a means of aspiring to the life-style of the middle class—impregnated, as it is, with the values of the American mainland.[27] If the pro-Americanism of the labor movement under Santiago Iglesias has weakened, workers tend to see the status issue as an irrelevancy, the pet concern of an intellectual elite bred in what was called by the Socialists in the 1920s the "House of Luxury"—the University of Puerto Rico.[28] "Independence for whom?" asked Iglesias. He did not believe that it was for the workers.

In many Latin countries, both in Europe and America, where trade unions have been domesticated, it is the university students who, if they do not constitute "the vanguard of the revolution," can discredit a political system by taking to the streets. Student trade union demands for better facilities and instruction are used by a minority of activists to politicize the campus.[29] The ultimate goal of the activists is to form an alliance with the working class; they rarely succeed. Student revolutions remain a petty bourgeois affair, reflecting the social composition of the student body.[30]

The student troubles of the 1970s in Puerto Rico may be seen, in part, as a case of continental mimicry, an island replica of Berkeley and Kent State. But the University of Puerto Rico (UPR) at Río Piedras occupies a unique place in island society, a place that has no counterpart in the larger society of the United States. Moreover, UPR has always been regarded by the opposition as an area where "the new anticolonialist conscience" can be forged. The two major parties of the island view higher education as the ideological preserve of the party in power; the chancellorship is regarded as a political prize.[31]

Under the long reign of Chancellor Jaime Benítez, that prize went to the PPD. Benítez's conception that UPR should be a *casa de estudios* ("a house of learning") as the only device to create a first-class university, was dismissed either as an irrelevant intellectual luxury for a developing nation or as a subterfuge to close UPR to politicial activists among the independence groups. Nor was Benítez sympathetic to the idea of student participation; little effective came of proposals, in 1966, to increase student representation. By 1970, it appeared to some professors and students that the university was run by the administration in the interests of the dominant party — after 1976, the PNP.[32]

There was, in 1971, a great deal of political activism, brought about by a backlog of frustrations sharpened by more recent events: the triumph of the "annexationist" PNP; the dismissal of liberal Rector Abraham Díaz González, an admirer of the radical educational reformer Ivan Ilich; the accidental shooting of a student, Antonia Martínez, immediately elevated to the status of a Nationalist martyr, for whom a mass was celebrated by *independentista* Bishop Antulio Parrilla Bonilla, S.J. The immediate cause of the worst outburst was a fracas in the UPR students' center between supporters of Muhammad Ali and Frazier that developed into a stone-throwing scrimmage between the cadets of the ROTC and those who saw in the existence of the ROTC on campus a symbol of the American military presence in Puerto Rico and an onslaught on university autonomy.[33] The police were called in to reinforce the university guards. The police commander was killed, together with an ROTC sergeant. The police, who got out of hand, arrested people at random and beat up some of those detained at the police station — until the arrival of the PIP lawyers. The press highlighted the police casualties; the opposition made much of police brutalities.[34] After 1971, campus violence died down, as it has on the mainland. The subsequent repression was fierce; but the closed-circuit televisions installed in university buildings after the riot have vanished; the gun emplacements are now used as monster flowerpots. Student agitation subsided. This may be partly due to the cessation of the Vietnam War and to the sobering effects of increasing difficulties in obtaining jobs after graduation. The rapid expansion of the university (from 5,000 in 1940 to over 50,000 in the 1980s) has changed its class composition. In the 1930s, Antonio Pedreira, the writer then a professor at UPR, despaired of the frivolity of the well-heeled sons of the rich; now, to the despair of those who have sought to implant Ortega y Gasset's ideals of a general education and share his scorn for "specialization," the mass of lower-middle-class students are more concerned with qualifying for jobs than with organizing demonstrations. Militancy may also be dampened by an evangelical revival that affects all denominations. When I was at UPR in 1980, the majority of student meetings were of religious groups and the graffiti in lavatories concerned the love of Christ.[35] It was particularly noticeable that PIP-organized protests against President Carter's selective draft were vastly less dramatic than the corresponding protests on the mainland. In May 1980, it seemed as if the student protests were phenomena of a past era: "the student struggle exhibits signs of acute weakness" was the verdict of a student militant.[36] But as any university administrator knows only too well, it is impossible to predict when some new issue may rekindle the fires of protest.

They were rekindled in the autumn and winter of 1981–82. The UPR troubles provide a classic example of a confrontation rooted in a genuine student grievance but engineered and politicized by a determined and able student leadership faced with an unyielding administration. A report of the Middle States Association had criticized UPR as run-down and academically weak. To improve standards, the PNP-dominated Council of Higher Education, to which the university's chancellor is responsible, raised fees by a modest amount. This was a necessary, reasonable step, as fees had remained at the same low level for thirty years. The university was "broke."[37]

On the ground that the new fee levels penalized all poor students — since many of them were financed by federal basic education grants, this was an exaggeration—the student union organization controlled by the PSP (the FUPI) organized a strike supported by the radical professors. The administration dug in its heels; the rector excluded from the campus those who refused to pay fees and banned demonstrations. When student gangs engaged in violent harassment of lecturers, who continued teaching those students who refused to strike, the riot police were called in and the university closed.[38]

The strike leader was Roberto Alejandro Rivera, a Marxist who saw the university as the "soft belly" of the system, as an arena for an exercise in heightening the revolutionary consciousness. The significant feature of the strike was that it revealed an alliance between the Catholic left and the Marxist-Leninists — Mass was celebrated outside the university gates. Alejandro Rivera was too able a leader to jeopardize a united student front by monopolizing the protest movement for his own party, a splinter group of the PSP. Neither the PSP, which controlled the FUPI, nor the PIP played an active role in the strike.

This did not prevent political interpretations. For the PNP, the strike was "Communist inspired"; on the most popular television program, a PNP speaker waved a student pamphlet on homemade bombs. *Claridad* responded by printing photographs of police beating up students. All sense of proportion was lost. To those on the left, the administration, acting under orders from Governor Romero, had converted UPR into another Auschwitz; to those on the right, the university was about to be subverted by Cuban agents.

The situation hardened: the administration refused to talk; the strikers stuck to their demands; the majority, who wanted to resume their studies, and the professors, who wished to teach, were caught between two immovable objects. Well-intentioned attempts at mediation failed — the administration even rejected the efforts of the conservative Cardinal Aponte. The dispute ended in the peace of exhaustion, serving only to deepen the mood of frustration and irritation.

For lack of authoritative studies, the influence of religion — a significant aspect of Puerto Rican society — as a force for conformity or protest remains a matter of guesswork. This influence is particularly important since there is a religious revival that corresponds to, and, in many cases, is supported by, the religious revival on the mainland.

There is no doubt that the early missionary campaigns of the Protestant churches after 1900 made for acceptance of the new regime, nor that Catholicism, disestablished and impoverished by the new masters, kept alive a sense of separate identity (the local Catholic clergy were pro-Spanish). This latter function was lost as the hierarchy itself became Americanized. Now the picture is confused and fluid. In the 1970s, the American Catholic Archbishop of Puerto Rico disciplined *independentista* priests and ordered the cathedral bells to be rung on the Fourth of July. His Puerto Rican successor celebrates Mass in sympathy with striking university students. Bishop Froilan of the Protestant Episcopal Church is an *independentista* sympathizer.

The fundamentalist evangelism of preachers like Rashke, who attracts vast crowds with his crusades against pornography and Communism, makes for conformity and reinforces the conservatism of audiences that include members of the middle class; the same must be said of the formal Catholicism of the *haute bourgeoisie*. More interesting is the influence of the Pentecostal churches and of sects such as the Mitas, both originally rooted in the working class but now making some headway in the middle classes. The Mitas were founded by Juanita García, daughter of a *hacendado* of Arecibo. She claimed to be the immortal abode of the Holy Spirit (she died in 1970) and considered herself a man, using the masculine form *contento* to describe herself as "happy." The Mitas are now a highly organized community with their own savings banks and commercial enterprises. The weekly service of their white-clad congregations is televised on Puerto Rico's Channel 11. Both the Pentecostals and the Mitas preach the gospel of self-improvement and self-discipline, campaigning against drink, drugs, and the cinema. Since they represent 10,000 votes in the city, they are courted by establishment politicians like Celeste Benítez, PPD candidate for Mayor of San Juan.

Protest comes less from religious sects with roots in Puerto Rico itself than from those linked to the world outside. Catholicism, like all the churches undergoing a process of spiritual renewal evident in the proliferation of small study groups and the propaganda of "charismatic" Christianity, is no longer a bulwark of the status quo. The Latin American theology of liberation, which has provided two Jesuit ministers for Nicaragua, has its Puerto Rican exponent in Father Samuel Silva Gotay: the European Marxist-Christian dialogue is supplemented by dependency theory, which adds the colonial struggle of the exploited periphery to the class struggle.[39] During the university protests of 1980 – 81, the youth section of Catholic Action combined with the Marxist left, their leader proclaiming in *Claridad* that there was nothing "contradictory" in the alliance. The union was symbolically consummated when Alejandro Rivera, the Marxist leader of the students, was married by a Jesuit priest.

Bishop Antulio Parrilla, S.J., represents an older tradition.

The Nationalist movement of the 1930s had strong Catholic overtones, since Catholicism was the faith of Spain and the spiritual bulwark against the intrusion of Anglo-American materialism. The bishop has a regular column in the PSP newspaper *Claridad*, where he combines a Catholic condemnation of birth control with the standard Nationalist argument that family planning is an American device deliberately introduced in order to destroy the Puerto Rican nation; he is a consistent campaigner against the presence of the United States Navy, which he claims represents the imperialism that resulted in My Lai.

Protestant groups are connected with mainland religious, pacifist movements: like Bishop Parrilla their particular target is the American military presence, above all the naval bombardments of Vieques. They also have connections with ecological protest movements, and argue that American corporations pollute Puerto Rico because they would not dare pollute the mainland. The Ecumenical Movement of Puerto Rico (PRISA) supports the independence movement in toto. Together with other ecumenical movements, it published a pamphlet entitled *Puerto Rico: A People Challenging Colonialism*, a more convincing and better-documented onslaught on American imperialism than any publication of the local independence movements.

In recent years, the religious movements in Puerto Rico have favored quietism and conservatism: the Mitas, like the Pentecostals in many Third World countries, aim to foster in the poor and disadvantaged those virtues that will earn them a respectable place in society. They link the psychological and emotional release found in traditional spiritualism—apparently a growing "sect"—and revivalism with the gospel of self-help. It is these sects that may have absorbed and neutralized the belief in spirits and sorcery once widespread in the folk religion of the rural interior.

The *explicit* religious protest movements are more often con-

nected with the so-called historic churches that have no connection with folk religion. They are important, not because
they rally large numbers to the causes they proclaim, but because they give an emotional force and a certain spiritual legitimacy to the protests of the independence movement. Status
invades all; even religion is its instrument in debate. Hernández
Colón of the PPD laments that without the enlarged political
autonomy he advocates, Puerto Rico lacks the legal powers to
prohibit abortion, a practice repugnant to the traditional faith
and mores of the island. Religious leaders join with *independentistas* and the progressive autonomists of the PPD in condemning a recent bill proposing the Sunday opening of stores
as an insidious concession to materialism and the American
way of life, as a threat to the "moral, religious, and cultural
value of the island."[40]

The transformation that came with industrialization was neither immediate nor painless. Old cultural patterns agonize and
die slowly. In the years after the conquest, the political elite
chafed under American rule but proved unable to articulate an
alternative to it. The generation of 1898 never mastered the
invader's tongue — Muñoz Rivera is described in Washington
as "struggling forcefully with his English grammar."[41] To the
amalgam of estate owners and professionals that constituted
this elite, the invader's concepts of business and of entrepre-
neurship were foreign. Although by 1959 Puerto Rico had
reached a level of industrialization comparable with that of the
mainland in 1910, its business community moved in the simpler
world of a small domestic market and family concerns. In the
1950s, an American social scientist noted "the persistence of
the habits of a family-centered, clearly stratified society"; that,
as far as business methods were concerned, "many aspects of
the inherited [Spanish and Latin American] culture have not

been deeply affected by mainland contacts"; that "some of the most important traits of the hereditary culture have only been slightly modified by over half a century of relationships with the United States."[42] Local businessmen failed to see the connection between high wages and high productivity; they saw no advantages in economies of scale and fought profitable amalgamations of struggling family firms; only a few sent their sons to study engineering or business administration in the United States.

By 1980, the presence of the large American corporations on the island had broken down these resistances; unable to beat them, the Puerto Rican business community had no alternative but to join them and become their servants or attempt to follow their example, as Luis Ferré did successfully. To follow their example was not easy. The advance of the large chain stores — Pueblo, Sears, Roebuck — crippled the old, largely Spanish, wholesale merchants; the local banks struggled to maintain their operations against the vast resources of American banks. The one field that was open to local capitalists was real estate speculation and construction: hence the animus against the Cuban exile community, which was in direct competition in these fields. Cubans also have come to dominate many new ventures in the television and film industry. In the words of a road contractor, driven out of business, they are the "Jews of Puerto Rico." It is hard to resist the conclusion that their less successful Puerto Rican competitors still retain "some of the most important traits of the hereditary culture." That culture, which Cuban exiles have largely sloughed off, does not favor the energetic entrepeneur and, as Ralf Dahrendorf has argued, "economic performance and cultural values are linked.[43]

The most solid social support for the PNP comes from the Cuban exile community, many of whom are members of the prosperous former middle class who have fled the perils of socialism in their home island. With very few exceptions, the Cuban exiles are the new 100-percent Americans, the preferred targets of the Marxist-Nationalist left, which views them as arch-reactionaries for whom "the day will arrive when they will be tried as traitors to the *patria*."[44] Scarcely surprisingly, the Cuban exiles vote for the party that is resolutely hostile to Cuba, remembering the expropriations and the sentences of People's Courts in the early days of the revolution. Their twenty thousand-odd votes are critical to the PNP; without them, Romero would not be governor of Puerto Rico.

Neither is it surprising that the independence parties have not succeeded in capturing a mass following in the new society of the 1980s. Their vote has fallen steadily. They have failed to produce a proletarian leader, nor have they captured the vote of what Berríos Martínez defines as the new working class, which is, in effect, the lower middle class and the skilled workers. *Independentistas* are apt to refer to a "false middle class," a "lumpen bourgeoisie" that fails to fulfill its role as a national bourgeoisie; its members' lavish use of credit and complete immersion in the consumer society accounts for the negative saving in Puerto Rico. Their ideals are reflected in the names of their residential suburbs: Golden Gates, Highland Park, Beverly Hills, Hyde Park.[45] The clubs they join — the Lions and the Elks — conduct their meetings in English. English is the essential tool of social mobility in a world dominated by American concerns. It is this lumpen bourgeoisie that is the despair of the *independentistas*.

The members of the lumpen bourgeoisie do not hesitate to embrace the life-style of the mainland; they see in U.S. citizenship the "supreme gift" of 1917. It is the American presence that guarantees protection against a Cuban-style revolution: they support the PNP because statehood guarantees that presence in perpetuity. They are haunted by a vague fear of "Communism," by the vision of empty shops in Manley's Jamaica, by concern that independence will bring "Cubanization." They attack the presence of pro-Cuban "subversives" in the university. When the activities of Professor Lima—a mathematician of muddled Marxist inclinations, who had visited Cuba—were protected by the UPR authorities, outraged conservatives released a flood of protest in the press.[46] "This gentleman should be sent to Cuba with the Communist Fidel Castro. Together with him should go the Rector, Jaime Benítez." Benítez can scarcely be classed as a dangerous radical. Puerto Rican conservatives frequently excel their mainland counterparts in their practice of paranoid politics. It is not only the lumpen bourgeoisie who are scared when the PNP beats the anti-Communist drum, an exercise in which Governor Romero frequently indulges. Its sounds are intended, not only to present the *independentistas* as dangerous Cubanizers but to slander the establishment *populares* as soft on Communism. "A lot of people round San Juan," reports the repentant prostitute of the slums of San Juan to Oscar Lewis, "are saying that some of the big shots in the Popular Party, Muñoz Marín himself, even the Mayoress Felisa [Gautier] are half-Communist. I've heard businessmen in San Juan say so, and the man in charge of Joe's place."[47]

Apart from the modest inroads the two *independentista* parties have made in the trade union movement, the *independentistas* remain a small but articulate section of the urban bourgeoisie. The PIP vote in new urbanizations, where the PNP is also strong, is twice the national average. There reside the "Jacobin professionals" of the party — the lawyers who control the Colegio de Abogados, university professors, and those schoolteachers who have abandoned the traditional loyalty to the PPD. They set its tone. Berríos Martínez himself is a lawyer and university professor. But the Jacobin professionals are immersed in a conservative society. "Puerto Rico," writes an American journalist with long experience there, "is essentially — and largely has always been — a conservative island in lifestyle and everyday ideology."[48] Such a society does not breed radicals.

It is the narrow social foundation of the independence parties that makes the intellectual elite such an important component within them, and this in a society where intellectual and artistic achievements enjoy a higher, if sometimes excessive, prestige than in the United States or Great Britain. The overwhelming majority of writers sympathize with the cause of independence; it may be that their writings are a form of salving the conscience of a movement that can show little in the way of political success. "While this group exists," argued René Marqués, himself a distinguished novelist, "the Puerto Ricans can hold on to the illusion that they are preserving their heritage in the face of the invasion of North American culture and the signs of assimilation in every aspect of life."[49]

To support this illusion is no easy task. Intellectuals feel that, even if respected for their talents, they are surrounded by a hostile universe. Overwhelmingly, they are supporters of some brand of independence: hardly a single writer of importance supports the status quo; the PNP are viewed as craven Americanizers; the PPD's defense of "puertorricanism" is an imperfect bulwark against Americanization. Many despair at the essential frustrations of their lives; there is only minimal electoral support for independence and they cannot sympathize with the mystique of the armed struggle. They become *realengos* — stray sheep in a country without a future — with sniping at *norteamericanos* their only relief.

II.

CLASH OF CULTURES

It is a revealing, if uncomfortable, experience to travel daily in a San Juan bus and listen to the conversation of the passengers: the word "Puerto Rico" crops up time and time again. In an evening's viewing on television, "Puerto Rican" and "Puerto Rico" occurred forty-five times in the commercial advertisements, a sure sign that their incantation elicits a powerful response in a market of three million consumers. Copywriters, after all, do not waste their employers' money. They are appealing to something that exists: a sense of cultural identity — evident in every aspect of life form child-rearing to poetry — a local patriotism that is distinct, say, from the sometimes abrasive assertions of Texan self-confidence. One is the reaction of a poor, small society that sees itself besieged by the culture of a great power; the other the local pride induced by size and wealth, but a pride that can be accommodated within the greater pride of the American nation.

The statehooders of the PNP maintain that the sense of Puerto Rican identity can be contained within a larger American patriotism. "We Puerto Ricans may speak Spanish," argues Luis Ferré, "but we are American and we think American."[1] All other parties make the defense of Puerto Rican culture a center of their programs; a culture distinct from that of mainland America. Existing in embryo under Spanish rule, it is held that Puerto Rico's cultural identity was finally forged in the long struggle *against* Americanization and American values. In a survey made in the early 1970s, an overwhelming majority of middle-class schoolteachers saw the mainland, which most of them had visited, as a distinct society. The distinction was perceived as cultural—"a different way of life." Statesiders "don't like us." Their language and customs, from food to sexual mores, "are not ours." They are "strangers."[2] In this sense, Puerto Rican "culture" is not the creation of an envious intellectual elite; it is the common property of many Puerto Ricans. While it is the folk culture that may constitute the most lasting barrier to the assimilation and internalization of American values, it is the elite culture that stands in the front line of the battle against Americanization. It is the intellectuals who have discovered—or created—a national identity based on the postulate that a Puerto Rican culture exists, an overarching sense of values held in common that is more than a provincial edition of mainland culture; indeed, to radicals it is its antithesis.

Compared with most Latin American nations, the historical and cultural roots of national identity in Puerto Rico are weak. Latin American nationalisms are rooted either in the nineteenth-century struggle for independence, which created both a national consciousness and national heroes — San Martín, Sucre, or Bolívar — or in the sense of continuity with the great pre-Columbian civilizations conquered by the Spaniards — the Incas in Peru or the Aztecs and Mayas of Mexico. These essential ingredients are lacking in Puerto Rico. Ramón Emeterio Betances, the apostle of Puerto Rican independence in the final years of Spanish rule, could lead no struggle to match the long and bloody separatist wars of Cuba; as he himself confessed, when conspiracies against Spanish rule failed, "the Puerto Ricans do not want independence." The modest ball park of the Taino Indians cannot match the majestic temples of Mexico or Peru; in any case, unlike those countries, the indigenous population of Puerto Rico has vanished.

The Puerto Ricans make the best of what they have. Celebration of the *Grito de Lares* has become the ceremonial setting for the annual delivery of rhetoric by the independence movements. The *Grito,* that ill-organized and easily suppressed revolt against Spain in 1868, is seen by Nationalists as indubitable proof of the existence of a "nation" conscious of its true destiny — independence. It is the island version of the Latin American wars of liberation.

Heroic efforts have been made to elevate the Taino Indians of Borinquen (the Indian name for the island after which the "national" anthem is called *La Borinqueña,* and after which restaurants and stores in the Puerto Rican quarters of New York are named) into bearers of a distinct and important indigenous civilization. The Tainos are presented as exponents of a gentle culture, superior in its simplicity to that of the Western conquerors, and yet which, destroyed by the Spanish Conquest, contained within itself the seeds of a culture as advanced as our own.[3] The television civilization of modern Puerto Rico, argues a pamphlet published by the Communal Division of the Department of Education, should not forget its roots in the *cultura propia* of the Indians: they were "the most advanced sculptors" in pre-Columbian America; they used snuff and tobacco for religious purposes "not as a frivolous vice"; their medical treatments are being rediscovered by modern science; in their body painting, by means of clay disks, was "latent the art of printing." They were peaceful when European Christians were killing one another. Above all, they were self-sufficient economically — they imported no food — and independent politically: "an independent nation not dominated or intervened (*intervenida* — the catchword of anti-imperialists) by any foreign power."[4]

Finally, there is the search for a Caribbean identity. It was Betances, the separatist patriot, who conceived of Puerto Rico as a Caribbean nation, a component part of an Antillean federation within the larger Latin American community. Caribbean unity has proved to be a weak plant. Even within the British Caribbean, federation failed and Caricom, which brings together the former British colonies, falters, and falls into ideological factions. The disparate languages and cultures of the islands are an inheritance of attachment to distinct metropolitan powers. Jamaicans speak English and play cricket; Puerto Ricans speak the Spanish of the first conqueror, Ponce de León, and play baseball and basketball, the legacy of the last of the Caribbean imperialists. The two main avenues of San Juan are called Ponce de León and Roosevelt.

The essential flaw in the search for a Caribbean identity is that, in the islands of the former British Caribbean, national consciousness is rooted in the oppression by whites of a black population — the descendants of slaves. It is not only that Puerto Rico and the Spanish colonies were never slave societies to the same degree as Jamaica or Barbados, where independence has brought black political, if not social, supremacy. It is that the Creole *independentista* intellectuals were the descendants of the masters, not of the slaves.

The whole history of Puerto Rico was conditioned by the fact that in 1898 there was a resident educated white elite in situ to whom Puerto Rico was "home," whereas in Jamaica or Barbados there was no such resident elite possessed of pretensions to culture. The Jamaican resident whites were "remittance men to whom oligarchy was the sole compensation for exile."[5] It was the Puerto Rican white elite, equipped with a provincial edition of Spanish culture, that led the resistance to American governors and to Americanization. José de Diego, to many *independentistas* the founding father of the modern independence movement, was called the "Knight of the Race," but that race was the Spanish race. Scarcely surprisingly, those dismissed as "nigger Socialists" (*la negrada socialista*) by the white Creole elite showed little enthusiasm for independence and preferred to vote for the black leader Barbosa and statehood.

The poet Luis Palés Matos (1898 – 1959) incorporated black rhythms in his poetry and argued that Puerto Rican culture could only resist the advance of an amorphous Americanization by returning to the vitality of its black roots. More recently, the poet and novelist José Luis González has made powerful pleas for the incorporation of the Afro-Antillean heritage into the independence movement in order to broaden its social base.[6] But whereas the Jamaican elite have been forced, by sheer demographic pressure, to accept Garvey, a prophet of black nationalism, as an official national hero, it is inconceivable that the Puerto Rican elite would accept a national identity based on *négritude*.

"We are and shall be for a long time," wrote Salvador Brau (1842 – 1912), one of the few Puerto Rican intellectuals with a genuine feeling for the underprivileged, "a people in the process of formation."[7] According to the *independentista* version of history, it was the American conquest of 1898 and the forcible imposition of a foreign culture that prevented the modest provincial edition of Spanish culture, which had supported the autonomist movement of the late nineteenth century, from developing into full-blown national consciousness. The American occupation, wrote the historian and essayist Tomás Blanco, was "the dissolvent of the progressive crystallization of our people."[8] Puerto Rican cultural growth had been truncated. (This is the Puerto Rican equivalent of the Cuban doc-trine of "frustrated revolution," according to which the fulfill-ment of the ideal of José Martí (1853 – 1895), the prophet of Cuban nationalism, for an independent republic was frustrated politically by the Platt Amendment and economically by the invasion of American capital after 1898. Goliath was victorious until a David arose in the person of Fidel Castro.)

The fathers of the independence movement recognized that the culture truncated in 1898 was the property of the elite, without roots in an illiterate population. Nor did the literary figures of the time find themselves at ease in the culture that later writers were to praise as essentially Puerto Rican. The *jíbaro* was not the representative of a submerged nationalism but a brutalized and shifty peasant in a rural backwater devoid of intellectual distinction or social grace. The *Memorias* of the poet-dramatist Alejandro Tapia y Rivera (1827 – 82) present Puerto Rico as a sick society "eaten up with moral inertia, indifference and egoism." All of them, as members of a liberal bourgeoisie, saw Spanish rule as "barbarism," and many of them welcomed Americans as representatives of the most pro-gressive and democratic nation in the world.

How, then, are we to account for the reversal of cultural alliances that had taken place by the 1930s? Enthusiasm for America soon evaporated. It could only have been sustained by the rapid grant of statehood, which would have made Amer-icanization *at that time* compatible with political freedom and personal dignity. Enthusiasm was followed by a period of cultural depersonalization and self-questioning in the face of a powerful society that held Puerto Rican culture to be of no account and denied Puerto Ricans "American" liberties. By the 1930s, Puerto Rican writers had turned to an idealized Puerto Rican past in a defensive reaction against the brutalities and absurdities of official Americanization. Politically, apart from needling the American governor by passing bills he was forced to veto, there was little to be done. It was left to the intellectuals — and most Puerto Rican politicians were intellectuals, many of them poets, almost all of them lawyers with literary inclinations — to seek and find a barrier against Americanization by fostering the myth of a Puerto Rican culture superior to the materialism of the invaders of 1898; the myth of "our happy society" (in the phrase of Albizu Campos, the nationalist martyr-hero) broken by "northamericanization." It was this "happy society" that had appeared to Brau and Tapia as brutish and oppressive.

This defensive reaction has been explained in terms of the disillusionment of the island intellectual and political elite, displaced by the American presence. But it represented more than the sour grapes of the sons of landowners impoverished by the decline of the coffee estates and the advance of the American sugar corporations, and of disappointed *políticos* who had ceased to be the *caciques* of their municipalities. It was a reflection of a Latin mood. Latin American writers had been pessimistic about the future of their nations and hypnotized by the cultural and material achievements of American and European civilization as superior to "decadent" Latin cultures. But North American values came to Puerto Rico precisely at the time when the belief that Latin American values were inherently "inferior" was weakening. In 1900, the publication of Rodó's *Ariel* and the poetry of Rubén Darío represented, in their different ways, a recovery of self-confidence in distinctive Latin American values. José Enrique Rodó (1871 – 1917) was the lay preacher of a spiritual anti-imperialism; the Nicaraguan poet Rubén Darío (1867 – 1916) was the apocalyptic prophet of a fabulous Latin American future.

Thus it was that the visit, in 1914, of a Latin American poet, the Peruvian Chocano, inspired Luis Llorens Torres (1878 –

1944) — perhaps the most widely read of Puerto Rican poets through his poems exalting the beauty of the island — with confidence in "the vitality of our race" that "our" Latin America "is one."[9] Puerto Rico could not become an appendage of the northern colossus. Its inhabitants formed a separate race. The *jíbaro,* whom the liberals of the nineteenth century had either pitied because of his destitution or despised on account of his passivity and ignorance, became for Llorens "the soul of our race." The patriotism of Llorens is lyrical, but he was closely involved with politicians, like Matienzo Cintrón, who chafed under American rule. In 1914, at Muñoz Rivera's request, he wrote a poetic drama on the *Grito de Lares,* symbol of Puerto Rican separatism:

"El grito de Lares/se va a repetir/y todos sabremos/vencer o morir."

Exaltation of "our history and our race" was nevertheless tinged with pessimism. "Our people are incapable of understanding heroism... they do not feel the dishonor of slavery, like dogs loving their chains."

It was this despair of the present that led Puerto Rican intellectuals to search for a Puerto Rican "personality" in the past. This quest for the historical Puerto Rico reached its most typical expression in Antonio Pedreira's *Insularismo,* published in 1934. Pedreira (1898 – 1939), a popular professor in the Department of Spanish Studies at the University of Puerto Rico, wrote *Insularismo* in response to a questionnaire put out by the periodical *Indice* in 1929. "Do you think," it asked, "that our personality as a people is completely defined? Is there a way of being (*una manera de ser*) indisputably and genuinely Puerto Rican? What are the defining marks of our collective character?" After four hundred years of Spanish rule and three decades under American government "Are we or are we not? What and how are we?"[10]

Pedreira sought the answers by searching the past, "the point of departure for the investigation of the national character of our people." What he found was not reassuring: weakness, docility, a cloud of rhetoric developed to hide facts from colonial governors but that now hid the unpleasant face of a society incapable of collective action, a country "without epic grandeur." He recognized the nineteenth-century emergence of a Puerto Rican "personality," a process of differentiation within Spanish culture. When cut short in 1898, Puerto Ricans were left "without a compass," wavering between what he called "civilization" (i.e., American culture) and culture proper, which, for Pedreira, was the product of the Spanish humanist tradition. Puerto Rico was still in a state of cultural shock. The amputation of 1898 left Puerto Rico "the corpse of a society that has not been born."[11] It was the task of the young generation to heal the wound and to salvage the cultural identity of Puerto Rico.

The melancholy pessimism and elitism of Pedreira's search for national identity in the preconquest past stand revealed in the work of a major novelist, René Marqués (b. 1919). Whereas the liberal writers of the nineteenth century had denounced the oppression of the rural patriarchs, Marqués sees in the society they dominated the "distant liberty of his people" (*la libertad tan lejana de su pueblo*). In his novel *La Víspera del hombre*, Marqués's anti-Americanism, his intransigent *independentismo*, ends in existentialist despair: "The problem was not to seek a meaning in life but to live it without hope of finding a meaning."[12] The Indian resistance to the Spaniards was futile: in a folk story, the Indian prince is killed by Spaniards after the exhaustion of love-making; all his mistress can do is bite the hand of the Spanish captain responsible for the prince's death. The *Grito de Lares* was betrayed by "a few informers.... Instead of fighting, the Puerto Ricans cry (*gritar*). That's why it's called the Cry of Lares."[13]

Pedreira had discovered a consciousness of separate island identity that he called *insularismo* (islandness) or *Puertorriqueñismo* (Puerto Ricanness). It was the weakness of the *puertorriqueño* renaissance of the 1930s that its most respectable element — in terms of culture in the narrow sense — was the exaltation of the heritage of a former master, Spain, against the impositions of a new master, the United States. This is evident in the nationalism of Albizu Campos: unlike its Irish model, it lacked deep *independent* cultural and religious roots; there could be no Puerto Rican counterpart to the Gaelic League. According to Albizu, Puerto Rico had inherited the Christian culture of Spain. The *independentistas* inherited the rhetorical patriotism — purely Spanish in its style — of de Diego, which had as little relation to the realities of Puerto Rican life as his laissez-faire philosophy had to the social problems of the Puerto Rican economy.[14]

To most American observers and administrators, Puerto Rican "culture" was a poor thing, a transient impediment to the Americanization that it would, in the long run, be unable to resist. By the 1930s, such optimism about Americanization could no longer be sustained. By the 1950s, Puerto Rican "culture" had not merely survived, it had been institutionalized.

This was the work of the Populares. Muñoz Marín was at the same time an admirer of (most) American values *and* a defender of those of Puerto Ricans. He thought that the two cultures could be reconciled. The Commonwealth was the political incarnation of this cultural syncretism: the danger lay in the weakness of the Puerto Rican input. It was to secure the preservation of the popular culture of Puerto Rico that, in 1955, the Legislative Assembly, on Muñoz Marín's initiative, set up El Instituto de Cultura Puertorriqueña — the Institute of Puerto Rican Culture (ICP). The ICP, in the words of its first director, Ricardo Alegría, was:

To be a counterweight to decades of ignorance and abandon in the conservation and promotion of our cultural values... there was a necessity to oppose a conscious cultivation of these values to decades of prejudicial and on occasion openly hostile influences; it was necessary to fight against the sociological conditioning deeply embedded in our colonial society which has induced many Puerto Ricans to systematically despise all that seemed genuinely native and to overvalue, out of all proportion, that which was, or appeared to be, exotic.[15]

The provenance of this exoticism was clear. For Alegría, the cultivation of Puerto Rican culture was an anti-American operation, something that went beyond the reconciliation that Muñoz Marín hoped to achieve and that reflected the *independentista* leanings of Alegría.

From its beginnings, the ICP was seen by statehooders as the creation of the PPD, a sop given to the residual *independentistas* within the party. While its crusade to save Old San Juan from speculation and ruin and its preservation of archives are uncontroversial, its efforts to foster a distinct Puerto Rican culture were and are dismissed by its critics as manifestations of a provincial chauvinism. Within the PPD elite itself, Jaime Benítez upheld the values of "universal" culture, of which Puerto Rican culture was a part — an emphasis that led to his estrangement from Muñoz Marín. To the statehooders of the PNP, "universalism" had a different use; it was a concept that lay at hand to combat the work of an organization — the ICP — that was the creation of its political enemies and provided jobs for PPD intellectuals whose anti-American prejudices were evident and whose activities were defended by the *independentistas*. Universalism, by which the intellectuals of the PNP meant Western values as mediated by America, could be used if not to deny the existence of a specific Puerto Rican culture, at least to denigrate it. The nature of Puerto Rican culture, therefore, became the football of party politics.

This partisan definition of culture is revealed by the recent history of the ICP. As assimilationists, the PNP must regard

Americanization as a desirable goal and the ICP's attempts to defend a Puerto Rican *national* culture as misguided. As if to demonstrate the irrelevance of the ICP's activities, Governor Romero has appointed a woman scientist as its director; she has embarked on what *independentistas* regard as a campaign of "cultural genocide," dismissing staff members devoted to the work of the institute and "crippling" some of its activities. The PNP government has set up its own Performing Arts Center devoted to the presentation of universal, international culture. Its opening ceremony was greeted as a day of mourning over the holocaust to which Puerto Rican culture and the ICP were being subjected by the rabid assimilationists and annexationists of the PNP. The PNP view the defenders of the ICP, who talk of the "dissolution of the national character of our culture," as an exiguous minority of unemployed malcontents, an elite who set themselves up as "super Puerto Ricans,"[16] and who will use "any conduct for the release of their political passions."

The *independentistas,* while they defended the ICP against the attacks of the PNP, regard Muñoz Marín's defense of Puerto Rican culture as "deficient," a piece of window-dressing designed to fit the ambiguities of Commonwealth status; as "a convenient amalgam of cultural nationalism and colonial assimilation"[17] fabricated to "mask official fear of nationalist or nationalistic sentiments" whose emergence would "embarrass the development of the colonial New Deal" (i.e., Commonwealth).[18] As for the "universalism" of the PNP, the *independentistas* consider it as nothing other than Western culture as represented by the United States; its adoption brought Puerto Rico into the cultural cold war in which, as a Latin American nation, it should be neutral. To René Marqués, both the *puertorriqueñismo* of the Populares and the "universalism" and cosmopolitanism of the PNP seek to conceal the existence of a conflict between two irreconcilable cultures.[19]

12.

AMERICANIZATION

Diffuse, riddled with ambiguities, and tinged with melancholic self-doubt as it was, the cultural identity created by the intellectuals of the 1930s was, above all, an anti-American construct. If the Puerto Ricans were docile, the Americans were barbarians; if the Puerto Rican intellectuals were meandering along the paths of Ortega y Gasset's elitism or looking back to a Christian and Spanish humanism that had lost touch with the modern world, American social scientists were apologists for a soulless civilization. The resurrection of the pre-1898 past, the obsessive concern with the discovery of a Puerto Rican identity, and the later onslaughts on the credit-card consumer civilization were all reactions against the processes of Americanization. As in colonial societies in general, every movement from folklore to ecology, every aspect of culture from poetry to social science, comes equipped with a peculiar cutting edge directed against the metropolitan power.

If the reaction was often violent, so was the process of cultural assimilation subsumed in the concept of "Americanization." Rejected as full members of the American political community, consigned as political orphans to the limbo of an unincorporated territory, from 1898 to the late 1920s the Puerto

Ricans were the objects of a campaign of cultural assimilation — above all evident in the enforcement of the use of English in the educational system — on a scale practiced by few other imperial powers.

By the 1930s, the campaign had failed. But just as what Salvador Brau had called the "process of formation" of a national consciousness was truncated and frustrated by the invasion of 1898, so for the second time the recovery of identity, subsumed in the *puertorriqueñismo* of the 1930s, was now threatened by the integration of an increasingly urbanized and industrialized economy into that of the mainland. The instrument of Americanization was no longer the public school. It was the multiple store stocked with imported food and consumer goods, the car, and the television set. In order to vitalize the economy, it had been argued in the depressed 1930s, Puerto Ricans must feel the need for houses, better food, and for "some of the trinkets and unnecessary things of modern civilization."[1] The "trinkets" have come to stay to seduce Puerto Ricans by the garniture of the American way of life.

The Americanization campaigns of the early years can best be understood in the light of the unstated premise of American actions after 1898. Rather than a policy they constituted a drift, but a drift toward a haven: cultural assimilation with the United States, which was to be either a preparation for acceptance as a state of the Union or the essential condition for a generous grant of autonomy, for a "Canadian" solution. This was a gigantic task. The immigrant in the United States, argued Governor Theodore Roosevelt, Jr., could attune to the new life in which he was immersed, but "it is another matter to try, with a handful of officials to change an entire people in the land where they have been born." The "resolute attempt to stamp out local customs and culture and to substitute English for Spanish" failed. Its result was that the United States, a country that was "doing its level best at considerable sacrifice and expense to aid the Puerto Ricans," was accused of tyranny.[2]

The problem was that the Puerto Ricans, mostly illiterate and poverty-stricken as they were in 1898, were not in American eyes fit for either self-government or membership of the Union. The island must first be turned into a prosperous English-speaking community. While this can be seen as the hubris of a nation supremely confident in the universality of its values and achievements, it was not an ignoble aim. It represented a more enlightened conception of the white man's burden than British policy in the West Indies. Yet, from the first years, Americanization was regarded by all but the island Republican party as a brutal and misguided attempt, in the name of progress, to force Puerto Ricans into an alien mold; by the Nationalists and *independentistas,* it came to be seen as, at best, inspired by a desire to make Puerto Rico a suitable location for the operations of American businessmen, or at worst, as a deliberate policy of "cultural genocide." From the outset, American intentions were distorted by *independentistas* to fit the purposes of incipient nationalism as they were later to be presented within the rusty framework of Marxist-Leninism. For years, the liberal bourgeoisie had pressed the Spanish government for a university in Puerto Rico; the request had been refused as dangerous and unnecessary. The Americans founded a university. For what purposes? In order, writes a radical critic of American policies in Puerto Rico, "to create a better living environment for metropolitan investors and the colonial officialdom." American doctors wiped out endemic tropical diseases. To what end? "To create a healthier and therefore more productive labor force."[3] Puerto Rico *must* be presented as "an extreme case of imperial domination."[4] Propaganda passes as history.

This clash of American intentions and Puerto Rican resentments was particularly evident in three spheres: educational policy, where the aim of the United States was to create an English-speaking colony; the activities of the American Protestant missions; and the legal reforms of the early years.

The concern of the Spanish authorities in education was conditioned by the belief that education was politically dangerous: rather than educate Puerto Ricans in Puerto Rico, the elite was to be educated in Spain.[5] The educational record of the Catholic Church was lamentable and that of the native municipalities, manned by the oligarchy that provided the island's intellectual and political elite, even worse. This neglect genuinely shocked Americans who came to administer Puerto Rico, but they saw educational improvement not as an end in itself but as a tool for Americanization. For the first American Commissioner, "Czar" Martin S. Brumbaugh, "the open door to the Federal Union is the free public school:" "The spirit of American institutions and the ideals of the American people, strange as they do seem to some in Porto Rico, must be the only spirit and the only ideals incorporated in the school system of Porto Rico."[6] To implant this spirit and these ideals it was imperative that English should become the major language of instruction in the public schools.

General Easton, who had reorganized the school system, and whose first act was to order 4,000 copies of Appleton's *First Reader in English,* believed that the Puerto Ricans would be "passive and plastic"; an early commissioner of education dismissed Puerto Rican Spanish as a "patois" with no powers of resistance. This was the grand illusion of the Americanizers. By 1929, the whole school system was bankrupt. Lessons in English were a *via crucis* to teachers; to schoolboys they were a mumbo jumbo doled out from primers based on American life.[7] The system had met with fierce resistance in Puerto Rico, particularly from Muñoz Rivera, engaged in the game of colonial politics: he introduced bills in the Puerto Rican legislature against English only to see them vetoed, as he knew they would be, by the governor. Education, complained the commissioner of education in 1915, had become "the football of certain political agitators who would have people believe that the scheme of education now in force is . . . the thin entering wedge to destroy the personality of the people of Puerto Rico."

But to American commissioners of education, Puerto Rican schoolchildren possessed "an inalienable right to learn the English language." English opened the road to advancement in the new world. English, daily shaving, and decent dress "as our brothers on the mainland" were "things indispensable for success," explained Commissioner Juan B. Huyke in his *Counsels to Youth*. "You have before you a splendid future" that "depends on love of and confidence in America."[8] There was the prospect of teaching Spanish in mainland schools. A Puerto Rican was employed in the U.S. Consulate in Lisbon. This now reads like a joke in poor taste. Yet the well-intentioned educational advisers who descended on the island from Columbia University insisted that to deny Puerto Ricans the English language was to deny them opportunity.

The reforming zeal of American educationalists, and the onslaughts of commissioners on municipal inertia and on the use of the educational system as patronage for party members, were regarded as the policy of a colonial power engaged in a deliberate process of denationalization. American teachers were regarded by Puerto Ricans as clumsy intruders at best. In contrast, Commissioner Brumbaugh saw them "as a solemn and sacred sacrifice for the Americanization of the people of Puerto Rico. They are true patriots and are worthy of the highest commendation."[9]

The patriots failed. The "patois" remained the language of

Puerto Ricans; the Status Commission of 1964 reported that "the number of Puerto Ricans who can be described as bilingual is small."[10] Yet as long as the United States appointed the education commissioner, and therefore controlled the educational system, enforced bilingualism remained official policy. As late as 1937, President Roosevelt wrote to the commissioner he had appointed: "It is an indispensable part of American policy that the coming generation of American citizens in Puerto Rico grow up with *a complete facility* [emphasis added] in the English tongue" — this in order that they should understand "American ideals and principles."[11]

Bilingualism via English as a language of instruction was abandoned only when Puerto Rico acquired control of its educational system. In 1948, Muñoz Marín, as the elected governor, appointed a commissioner of education committed to the restoration of Spanish as the language of instruction, with English as a second language. It meant the end of what the Liberal leader Barceló had denounced as a form of "false and unhealthy Americanization." The decision that was to be of cardinal importance to the whole future of Puerto Rico was a result not of the coming of Commonwealth in 1952 but of the abandonment of control over domestic issues implicit in the Elective Governor Act of 1947.

With the American teachers came the church militant: the Protestant pastors to whom Puerto Rico was a providential mission field. If Catholics had preached "the true Doctrine of Christ," declared an Evangelical journal in 1901, "God would not have permitted the crowning victory of 1898";[12] the Catholics had built no schools and shunned the rural backwaters. The conversion of a race sunk in "superstition" was undertaken by the Protestant churches of the mainland, which supplied the funds and the mission supervisors. By the 1960s, possibly 20 percent of Puerto Ricans belonged to some sort of non-

Catholic church, and a tripartite society was reflected in religious affiliation: the upper classes remained Catholic; the "historic" Protestant churches, especially the Methodists, were strongly represented in the middle class; the Pentecostalists and later new popular revivalist cults like the Mitas won their converts among the working class.

Protestant pastors, like schoolteachers, have been seen by radical *independentistas* as agents of Americanization, as the ideological instrument of imperialist expansion, as "armies of peace" that divided the island into campaign districts as in a "military" operation. This is a characteristic misrepresentation of American intentions; the division into mission districts was a commonsense device to prevent competition between denominations. The Protestant missionary effort was often crude, its insensitivity to local conditions symbolized in the pitched roofs and gables of the pastor's house which stood out in a tropical landscape as exemplars of an alien architectural tradition. Nor could missionaries and pastors refrain from attacks on Catholicism and the exaltation of the Protestantism of the mainland as the faith of a superior culture. They were fervent supporters of the benefits of American citizenship as part of a progress from darkness to light. The Jones Act of 1917, which granted American citizenship, an evangelical periodical claimed, should be enshrined in "letters of gold." It was believed that the assumption of Protestant American mores would regenerate the nation. Redemption, in Christian theology an individual process, came to embrace the redemption of a whole people. The adoption of prohibition, before it was enforced on the mainland, by a major rum producer in 1917 was extraordinary proof of the influence of the Protestant churches and their detestation of alcohol, even if their campaign had little practical effect on the drinking habits of Puerto Ricans.

The Protestant churches, with their zeal for education — particularly of women — did much for Puerto Rico; while often narrow-minded themselves, they broke down a lethargic and conformist Catholicism. The Catholic Church itself renewed its lost vigor; but since the bishops were Americans, this seemed to suggest that Catholicism, too, had joined the church militant of Americanization. In the early years, the financial necessities of the Protestant churches turned Puerto Rico into a religious fief of the mainland; however, by the 1940s, the churches increasingly relied on local funds and local pastors, a process that began with the Pentecostalists and the Adventists and later spread to the "historic" churches.[13] In a curious parallel, the search for church autonomy corresponded to the quest for political autonomy.

With the American soldiers, teachers, and pastors came the American lawyers. They, too, believed they were bearers of a progressive and modern legal philosophy; they, too, were resented as obtuse blunderers, who, bred in the common law tradition of the Anglo-Saxon world and knowing no other, failed to appreciate the merits of the civil law tradition embodied in Spanish legislation. American carpetbaggers who came to the island between 1899 and 1904 could not practice, ignorant as they were of Spanish law; they became a pressure group for the Americanization of the legal system and the extension of federal jurisdiction. The Insular Commission of 1899 recommended total Americanization of the "barbarous" Spanish legal system.[14] The Codifying Commission of 1902 implanted American criminal law and procedural rules; the Civil Code remained based on Spanish law but was interpreted, up to the American Supreme Court, according to precedents derived from what Puerto Rican lawyers stigmatized as a confused, uncodified jumble compared with the clarity of Roman law.[15] They viewed the American legal system as a "joke…unworthy of a civilized people."[16] The American attitude, reflected in the *San Juan News,* was precisely the opposite: everything that differed from the American system was worthy only of rejection. The clash of cultures was complete.

The Americanization of the early years, an effort in transculturation on a scale matched before modern times only in Alsace-Lorraine and Finland, has left an important legacy. Though it was abandoned, the memory of its excesses still nourishes the historical vision of the independence movements and fuels the emotional indignation of anti-imperialists. Moreover, the processes of Americanization illustrate means by which certain social groups, or sections of them, became vehicles of anti-American sentiment. The initial resentments of local lawyers — and the vast majority of local politicians were lawyers — over the imposition of elements of a "foreign" legal system are still echoed by *independentistas,* who have made the bar association (the Colegio de Abogados) a forum for the expression of anti-American sentiments and a factory for the manufacture of legal arguments against statehood and Commonwealth to be presented to the Decolonization Committee of the United Nations. From the time of its installation, local lawyers objected to the setting up of the District Court of the United States in Puerto Rico as "the ruin of Puerto Rican institutions... the beginning of the juridical death of Puerto Rico."

As in so many spheres, institutions that should remain outside politics have become politicized by the unresolved status issue. As we shall see, in the judicial review of the electoral process in decisions over contested seats, the PNP supports the American Federal Court, the PPD the Commonwealth Supreme Court.[17] To *independentista* lawyers, the clash of jurisdictions is a source of confusion and sterile conflict. The outraged indignation of the defenders of a legal system attacked as "barbarous" in 1900 still persists. Even if the Puerto Rican legal system must learn from other legal systems, it is a mistake to argue, they claim, "that only Americans can think."[18]

Since the 1940s, Americanization has no longer been imposed from above; indeed, the Status Commission of 1964 claimed that it was U.S. policy to foster "Puerto Rico's cultural autonomy";[19] Americanization is an attitude that seeps up from below. Its instruments are the American supermarket and television; its missionaries, the emigrants returning from the mainland. The whole weight of a powerful and assured "civilization," in Pedreira's phrase, threatens to overwhelm Puerto Rican "culture." Above all, the adoption of the American way of life has become a vital necessity to "get on" in a society and economy dominated by American business. Membership in American-based clubs like the Elks or the Lions is the door to promotion for the bright executive. Assimilation becomes a voluntary act. Because it is voluntary, it represents, to *independentistas,* a threat more insidious than the deliberate Americanization of the early years; it is as if the forcible feeding had been replaced by a gluttonous appetite for poisonous food.

Hence, the animus of the *independentistas* against the use of English as the language of instruction in private schools: with the end of Americanization in the public schools, the battle was transferred to the private sector — the fee-paying private schools — where the middle class, as practitioners of voluntary Americanization, send their children. Most of these schools were established by American Catholic Orders, above all in and around San Juan, and they expanded rapidly between 1950 and 1970. The teaching was predominantly in English and the textbooks largely American.

The private schools are seen by *independentista* intellectuals as a conscious, politically inspired attempt at Americanization;

as providing, via English as the language of instruction, the essential condition for absorption of Puerto Rico as a state of the Union; as a deliberate attempt to destroy the cultural foundations of Puerto Rican identity and the Spanish language by enticing Puerto Ricans to abandon them. "This type of school will slowly convert English into the language of culture, reducing Spanish to the status of a folkloric idiom to be used only in the family," declared Eladio Rodríguez Otero, a wealthy lawyer, businessman, and leading Catholic layman, who led the fight to secure Puerto Rican rather than American bishops and who was president of the Ateneo, the literary society that, like the bar association, is an *independentista* fief. Ricardo Algería, director of the Institute of Puerto Rican Culture, in a speech to the Schoolteachers Association — a receptive audience, since the state teachers were extremely hostile to the private schools — insisted that the emphasis on English was politically inspired.[20]

The debate illustrates the paranoia of *independentistas,* for whom educational policies, like everything else, must be construed in terms of conspiracy theories. The Catholic schools taught classes in English less because they regarded English as an instrument of Americanization than because teachers coming from the mainland knew Spanish imperfectly, if they knew it at all; now that Catholic schools increasingly employ native Spanish-speaking teachers, it is only the most expensive schools that retain English as the language of instruction. Nor was English inflicted on the unwilling. Parents demanded intensive teaching of English, since command of the English language was the essential tool of social mobility in a business world dominated by stateside firms. It is America's economic presence, rather than its political presence, that dictates the patterns of everyday life.

Nothing is more striking than the extreme sacrifices, out of all proportion to those made in Western Europe, that even lower-middle-class parents will make in order that their children learn English at private schools and crown their educational careers by attendance at a stateside university. The majority of Catholic schools, especially since they increasingly have to employ lay teachers, charge substantial fees; they are therefore confined to the elite and to those who wish to join the elite. The mark of "belonging" is a mastery of English. Given that the state secondary schools are often markedly inferior to the private schools, both in discipline and in the quality of education they offer, Puerto Rican society, like British society, is divided between those who have been privately educated and those who have not.[21] This is apparent in the proportion of privately educated pupils who go on to study in the university. It is a myth that "most" Puerto Ricans can "get along" in English. With few exceptions, only those who have been privately educated handle English with ease; a linguistic division corresponds to a class division.

Americanization has produced an island that is neither a mirror image of America nor an essentially Latin American Caribbean society like the Dominican Republic. Puerto Rico is a cultural hybrid, its inhabitants victims of an all-pervasive cultural schizophrenia.

Nemesio R. Canales (1878 – 1923), a satirical writer of great power, is an early example of the cultural ambiguity — often unperceived — that has come to haunt Puerto Ricans. He had nothing but scorn for the vulgar provincial culture of the turn of the century in what he called "this miserable island." Nevertheless, confronted with the "involuntary" submission to the United States he claimed, "We are a cultured people," literate, with roads and railways. Yet the schools, the roads, and the railways were the creation of the invaders. He felt passionately (and wrote bad novels to prove his point) on the subjugation of women in the "macho" world of San Juan; yet it was the Americans who brought with them coeducation for women. He saw Puerto Rican society riven by the shock of "the new [American] customs and our ancestral barbarism." It still is. The disturbed personalities produced by that shock, Nemesio Canales asserted, found their outlet in violent crime that was, he alleged, novel in Puerto Rican society.[22] This diagnosis of the etiology of crime as the consequence of the disruption of a "healthy" society by the shock of conquest and the importation of the conqueror's way of life was to have a long life in the Puerto Rican anti-American tradition.

The anti-Americanism of Puerto Rican intellectuals represents the cries of pain of a marginated intellectual, provincial elite that is conscious of the poverty of the university's libraries, its lower salaries, and its lack of graduate schools, and that feels crushed by the superior academic resources of the mainland. Hence the occasional outbursts against stateside social scientists who, on their visits to the University of Puerto Rico, are regarded with a mixture of awe, envy, and suspicion and whose vaunted empirical studies are seen as justifications of the "colonial" status quo, contributing nothing to the peculiar problems of Puerto Rico nor even to those of society in general: "The vast social science research on Puerto Rico conducted by most North American investigators" writes a UPR professor "has contributed very little to a real understanding of our society."[23] Stateside social scientists are criticized as having no understanding of or sympathy for Puerto Rican culture. The pioneer study, *The People of Puerto Rico,* under the direction of the American anthropologist J.H. Steward, by its emphasis on the existence of separate subcultures, ecologically determined, denies the presence of an overarching, "typical" national culture confronting the overwhelming influence of American power.

To Puerto Rican patriots this is unacceptable. Social scientists from the mainland are thus considered the lineal descendants of the missionaries of the early years of the colony; it is now the accepted wisdom among Third World radicals that American sociology and anthropology have replaced Protestant theology as a tool of American imperialism.[24]

We must return to the plight of Nemesio Canales. Puerto Rican social scientists may quote, with approval, Merton's aphorism — "I know what I say is true but I don't know if it is significant" — to prove the apparent futility of American social science but they can neither blind themselves to its achievements nor invent some native alternative to this imported soulless science. University textbooks in all fields are largely American, either in English or in translation. As sociologist David Lowenthal observed of small Caribbean societies, it is difficult for them to generate an independent intellectual universe since they lack a sufficiently wide supportive market. It is remarkable that Puerto Rican intellectuals have nevertheless created and maintained such a universe.[25]

The present position of Puerto Rican culture is perhaps best described as one of unstable hybridization. To the despair of economists, alarmed at the negative savings rate, Puerto Ricans run into debt in order to acquire the material products of American civilization. "Everyone is up to their neck in debt," says Adela in Pedro Juan Soto's novel *Ardiente suelo, fria estación* (1961). "They've just got to have a house, an automatic washing machine and a car." Yet all surveys indicate a persistence of "traditional" patterns in family life. The influence of the American cinema and television, dominated by American products, is prodigious. Yet the peak viewing time is devoted to Spanish-language Puerto Rican or Mexican situation comedies. Does this mean that American productions are not in accord with the values, mores, and tastes of Puerto Ricans?

Television advertisements pay homage to Puerto Rican traditions but the Taino Indians and *jíbaro* families are seen consuming American products whose English names break harshly through the Spanish dialogue. Does this represent a paradoxical triumph for the ICP campaigns in support of Puerto Rican culture, in that no product can sell unless it has a Puerto Rican wrapping? Or does it signify the ultimate triumph of American consumerism over a folk memory of a vanished past, an island edition of the commercial use of the Wild West?

Iris Chacón and Danny Rivera, the two most popular singers, profess occasional *independentista* sympathies; the group of musicians and singers *Haciendo punto en otro son,* with its Latin American rhythms and protest songs, attracts enthusiastic audiences. Jacobo Morales has made an excellent film and runs a satirical television show that is as un-American — if not anti-American — as can be imagined. But can these performers adequately defend, at a popular level, Puerto Rican culture against the overpowering influence of the American cinema and pop culture? Puerto Ricans often display the dualism that permeates the whole society. They may indulge in fierce assertions of independence that make Puerto Rico and its concerns seem the center of the world or subside into an inferiority complex with disturbing personal manifestations. The "vacillation" that Antonio Pedreira attributed to miscegenation is the acute symbol of a cultural ambiguity.

The hybridization of Puerto Rico, its cultural dualism, is revealed in the language itself.[26] Lack of linguistic security results in the use of stereotyped, colorless speech that can be frequently heard in middle-class milieus. In popular speech, Spanish is adulterated by Americanisms and becomes the mumbo jumbo used by the characters in the novel of Luis Rafael Sánchez, *La guaracha del Macho Camacho* (1976) — indispensable reading for those who wish to sense the texture of everyday life in San Juan, its vulgarity and pretensions. The attempt of some enthusiastic patriots to elevate this mishmash into a native tongue has rightly been dismissed by José Luis González as an absurdity.

The *coquí*, a noisy tree frog, is almost the national emblem of Puerto Rico. "Its haunting refrain," runs a publicity handout of the Puerto Rican Federal Affairs Administration, "is an eternal reminder that the distant past has been able to make its peace with the relentless encroachment of modern civilization." But the junction of the mainland "civilization" and what Pedreira called "culture" is imperfect. The joints show up. The clash of cultures remains unresolved: it is not surmounted by such devices as the amalgamation of American Christmas and the Spanish Feast of the Three Kings. Father Christmas and snow are exotica in a tropical island; that the woman mayor of San Juan brought Christmas snow from New York for Puerto Rican children would be comic were it not tragic.

Few Americans take seriously the claims of Puerto Rican culture. They arrive in an island where they are offered rum and Coca-Cola by English-speaking waiters and where they see bookshops crammed with American paperbacks. Puerto Rican culture appears to them a folkloric affair kept alive for the tourist trade. There is a minority who become 100 percent Puerto Ricans — a familiar and frequent phenomenon among expatriate intellectuals. For the majority, the concept of docile plasticity persists; in the long run, Puerto Rican culture will succumb to the superior strength, if not the intrinsic superiority, of the American way of life. This view, even when expressed by American scholars who are sympathetic to Puerto Rico and its problems, outrages the native intellectual establishment. Daniel Boorstin classified Puerto Rican culture as American with vague vestiges of the Spanish past, and Puerto Rico as a country without history. To René Marqués this was the verdict of a "beardless intellectual" after a three-week stay on the island.[27] When the American anthropologist Sydney Mintz questions the existence of a "unitary society with a unitary culture," he offends Puerto Rican susceptibilities. It was Alfred Kazin's on the whole sympathetic description of Puerto Rican intellectual life that sparked off a controversy to which the most perceptive contribution was René Marqués's *El Puertorriqueño docil,* a bitter essay in national self-criticism.

It is the sense of impotence in the face of the advance of creeping Americanization that leads to an overestimation of the values and achievements of the lost culture, a phenomenon characteristic of many nationalist protest movements: for example, José Campeche, who painted the first Puerto Rican bishop, is presented as "one of the most notable portrait painters of all time."[28] The traditional society, destroyed after 1898, is romanticized just as nationalist historians in India romanticized the Indian civilization that existed before the British arrived.[29]

According to this vision of the past, the Puerto Ricans living in shacks on sugar *haciendas* were poor in material terms but rich in the sense of secure cultural identity; now settled in their "comfortable little cement houses," open to "the infernal electronic invasion of privacy," they have become "apprehensive and anxious" beyond recognition.[30] The town square, now deserted, was once a popular university. The brutalities of rural life under the *ancien régime* are conveniently forgotten. The shiftiness with which the *jibaro* once faced his native landlord is transformed into a national virtue when he outwits the American; "Juan Bobo" (stupid John) becomes a national symbol.

Exaggeration of Puerto Rican virtues is matched by the attribution of the vices and malaise of Western urbanized society as such to a particular virus injected by North America. Reckless driving is a form of suicide in a society that years of Americanization have left devoid of meaning. Mimesis of the colonial power, it is argued, is a psychological necessity for colonial peoples. Crime and drugs are the expression of a youth that has deserted the old songs and the old customs for a soulless imitation of American youth.

It could be argued that the cultural issue is of little moment; that many American observers are correct in their view that Puerto Rican "culture" as the basis of a national character rests on an artificial construct of little intrinsic worth; that it is doomed to perish without social roots in a community where the vast majority has no access to a culture that is the creation of a leisured class of literary inclinations and where the lower classes are merely imitating the already Americanized life-styles of the middle class.

This is false — if for no other reason than that the disparity and ultimately irreconcilable nature of American and Puerto Rican culture will always be maintained by the cultural elite, since the maintenance of that divide is their raison d'être. Moreover, even if mass culture in Puerto Rico, as elsewhere conditioned by television, has little connection with the culture of the elite, that this mass culture is expressed in Spanish poses a problem for assimilationists.

The point that many analysts fail to appreciate is that, while it may be difficult to discover by scientific methods "genuinely distinctive character traits and values we may confidently call Puerto Rican" that apply *uniformly* throughout the island,* those traits and those values that exist, unoriginal and diffuse though they may be, are distinct from those of North America.

*Sydney Mintz argues (correctly) that culture is class conditioned and what have been taken as universal norms apply differently to what Steward, in his classic study of Puerto Rico, calls "differing socio-economic segments."

Puerto Ricans' culture may be a poor thing, but it is their own; less as an intellectual construct than as a bundle of attitudes, of feelings, that make the life of the tribe comprehensible to its members. Moreover, the tribe has preserved its own language. Forcible imposition in the early years of Americanization and its convenience in later years as a tool of social mobility have not made English the dominant tongue. Spanish remains the language of daily intercourse, of the popular press, of poets and politicians. It constitutes a serious obstacle to assimilation; it is significant that modern statehooders have had to acknowledge that Spanish will remain an official language if Puerto Rico becomes the fifty-first state.

As has every other aspect of Puerto Rican life, culture, too, has been politicized. In Puerto Rico, the very definition of culture is a political, not a scientific, enterprise. Mintz is scientifically correct in deploring the "disappointing fuzziness" of the notion of a Puerto Rican national character.[31] But, perhaps fortunately, politicians and peoples do not act on scientific principles. Politicization has made the cultural identity of Puerto Rico part of the pathology of island politics. Like everything else, it ultimately depends on the unresolved status issue: statehooders do not perceive a cultural barrier to assimilation. As the PNP conceives it, *jíbaro* statehood will allow Puerto Rican culture to continue to exist in a multicultural union. To the PPD, it is the existence of a Puerto Rican culture, defended by the ICP, that makes Commonwealth — which accommodates the coexistence of the two cultures — preferable to statehood, which sooner or later will destroy the weaker element. To the PIP cultural identity is a foundation of its claim for separation; it erects a Berlin Wall, separating two civilizations.

If there is no Berlin Wall, there remains a gap that many Americans do not perceive. When it is perceived, if at all, it is not because Americans are familiar with the Latin American residues on the island but because they construct a stereotype of Puerto Ricans from those who have immigrated to the cities of America.[32]

Puerto Rican society is divided not merely into two cultural camps. It is divided geographically. According to how one defines Puerto Rico, either two million or three million Puerto Ricans live on the mainland, nearly two-thirds of them in New York. It is not the purpose of this book to examine their plight, which is well-known, except insofar as it affects the relations between the island and the United States and the image that the continental Americans hold of their Puerto Rican fellow citizens.

The Puerto Rican community of the old *barrio* was overwhelmed in the 1950s by a massive influx of Puerto Rican immigrants who, driven by poverty, took advantage of their American citizenship and cheap air fares.[33] The immigrants settled in the poorest ghettos of New York, ousting the Italians from East Harlem and mixing with the blacks in the South Bronx. Some came as seasonal workers to the farms of New Jersey; those in the cities could find only semi-skilled work in the garment and hotel industries.

The immigrants suffered severe discrimination in housing and employment. Lumped together with other Hispanics and blacks, they fared worse than either group. By every yardstick — welfare payments per capita, school dropouts, and so forth — they ranked below blacks and the non-Puerto Rican Hispanics, and well below Anglo-Americans.[34] In spite of recent registration campaigns, they are underrepresented and underorganized politically. The massive postwar immigration and urban renewal programs broke up the old *barrio* in the north-eastern corner of Manhattan, with its vivid and active political life. It was only the need to grasp a share of the antipoverty programs of the 1960s that brought the Puerto Ricans as a community back into the political life of New York, largely to challenge the monopoly of the blacks.

Ramón Velez, "the anti-poverty czar of the Bronx," helped Hernán Badillo emerge as the political leader of the city's Puerto Ricans; in 1965, Badillo became borough president of the Bronx, and after failing in his campaign for the mayoralty of New York, was elected in 1973 to Congress. Admired by many in the Puerto Rican community as the orphan islander who had come to New York at the age of eleven to become a successful middle-class lawyer, Badillo is a reformist in the Democratic party tradition. He sees in the registration of Puerto Ricans their avenue to political influence as an ethnic group.

In spite of those efforts, and the increasing sense of communal identity evidenced in the annual Puerto Rican Day Parade (the *Desfile*), the Puerto Ricans do not enjoy the political influence their numbers justify. Their leaders find it hard to agree among themselves — Badillo is opposed to his successor in Washington, Congressman García. Even more difficult is the creation of a common front with other poor and disadvantaged groups—the blacks and the other immigrants from Latin America and the Antilles. The Cubans (80,000 odd in New York) often tend to tar the Puerto Ricans as "Communists." The blacks are held to have monopolized welfare organizations and affirmative action jobs and to be indifferent to the one issue that is central to Puerto Ricans and Hispanics in general: bilingual education. The black and Puerto Rican legislative caucus in Albany is frequently on the point of disintegrating into its two component parts: "I have a hard time just going to the meetings," complains Puerto Rican Assemblyman José Serrano of the Bronx. "There are always black groups talking about black issues."[35] In Florida, the tension between blacks and Hispanics results in open violence.

Emigration has produced two contrasting phenomena. Poor emigrants from the rural backwaters, however disadvantaged in New York, enjoy more of the material benefits of a consumer society than they would in Puerto Rico. It is natural that they should internalize some of the values implicit in American life-styles. Equally understandable is the violent reaction of the militant anti-Americans—second- and third-generation Puerto Ricans, the "Neoricans," of New York stimulated by the black revolution of the 1960s. This reaction is embodied in a search for a Puerto Rican identity by groups like the Young Lords, formed by young urban Puerto Ricans in 1969, for whom Albizu Campos was the Puerto Rican Malcolm X. Their con-frontation tactics — for example, sit-ins or disruption of the *Desfile* by chanting independence slogans — were in sharp con-trast to the legalism of Badillo, whom they despise as a "colonial mediator." Their militancy was carried into American univer-sities in the 1960s by a sudden enthusiasm, now on the wane, for Puerto Rican studies.[36]

So far, political apathy and the irrelevance of the independ-ence issue to the problems of Puerto Ricans in New York have defeated attempts to re-create the link between discontents of the mainland Puerto Ricans and the cause of independence. The Puerto Rican community, while it seeks to maintain con-tact with island mayors by organizing clubs celebrating the immigrants' hometown, sees that independence will do little to bring more hospitals, more welfare, or better bilingual ed-ucation to Puerto Ricans in New York or Philadelphia; for second-generation Puerto Ricans, who, unlike their fathers, have no intention of returning to die in Puerto Rico, these are the important issues to which the status of Puerto Rico is at most a tangential concern. The Young Lords, who took up the cause of independence, came to realize that the home front was where support could be mobilized. They formed the Puerto Rican Workers Organization to fight for the Neoricans.[37]

Radicals seek to reestablish the link between independence and local issues: resistance to colonialism in Puerto Rico and to exploitation on the mainland are part of a joint struggle against "imperialism." The slums of the South Bronx and of San Juan, as they see it, are the products of the same exploitative system. It is in the great cities of America that the Puerto Rican immigrant — and above all his children born in the United States — meets "imperialist capitalism" head on; hence "their extraordinary revolutionary potential" that can carry "the revolutionary struggle into the heart of the oppressor society." Like the Irish against the British and the Algerians against the French, they will be the "battering ram" against walls of the empire at its weakest points.[38] To the terrorists of the FALN, the armed struggle in Chicago, New York, and Puerto Rico is part of the same war.[39]

This apocalyptic vision of a Puerto Rican revolution in New York provides an emotional compensation for the evident lack of revolutionary elan in Puerto Rico itself. It is a deduction from the Marxist analysis of emigration as an involuntary act, a necessary consequence of the international capitalist division of labor. Immigrants are not attracted by a promised land but extruded from their homeland to provide cheap labor for the metropolis. Emigration has become central to the radical attack on U.S. imperialism in the Caribbean; to its Puerto Rican proponents, it is connected with an older thesis. Like the Nationalists before them, the new generation of Puerto Rican radicals see campaigns in favor of birth control and sterilization as "social practices which are an attack on Puerto Rican national integrity" by ensuring that the number of Puerto Ricans is actually diminished.[40] Now placed in the wider context of the Third World, birth control is viewed as a weapon of imperialism, used "to retard the world-wide revolutionary process." Malthus is brought in by the imperialists in order to defeat Marx. Emigration accomplishes the same ends as birth control: by removing a large number of Puerto Ricans from the island, it enfeebles and defuses local protest. In addition, it is deliberately encouraged by the Puerto Rican government to hide the failure of its economic policies to provide employment.

In spite of their sufferings it would seem that those immigrants who have settled in American cities do not become rabid anti-Americans, as radicals would have them become. Immigrants *are* forced out of Puerto Rico by poverty but it does not follow that they are potential revolutionaries; most of them wish to "make it" in America, even if they find the society that surrounds them uncongenial. Exploitation of their plight provides propaganda copy for *independentistas*, rather than recruits for the cause of independence and the anti-imperialist struggle.

This is not to argue that assimilation in American society is an easy process, particularly for Puerto Ricans who in Puerto Rico were considered nonblack and who now find themselves classed as blacks. Most poorer Puerto Ricans find Americans "cold" and "materialistic," bereft of those warm sympathies and family affections that they maintain are characteristic Puerto Rican virtues; this sense of isolation from the American mainstream leads them to revisit the island and to resist calling themselves "Americans."[41] It is those who adopt the garniture but who cannot assimilate the values of American life who suffer the emotional disturbances of a divided cultural personality. The classic delineation of the divided psyche is the anti-

hero of Pedro Juan Soto's *Ardiente suelo, fría estación* (1961).
Brought up in New York, he returns to Puerto Rico — "his"
country and "his home." He cannot adjust his life-style to the
island, and yet he despises the efforts of his contemporaries to
create the ambience and recapture the fashions of New York
in a seedy San Juan nightclub. Mocked for speaking bad English in New York, he is mocked for speaking bad Spanish in
Puerto Rico: "Well what can you do? You shut your mouth
and live in a no-man's land." He felt "the loneliness of feeling
unwanted in his own country." After "lovingly and earnestly"
— and unsuccessfully — seeking his roots in Puerto Rico, he
goes back to New York.

Soto is an *independentista,* and it is the *independentistas* who
insist on the destructive effects of adopting a superficial Americanization. The clash between the values, or lack of values, of
American urban civilization, as experienced in the ghettos of
the great mainland cities, and the "traditional" family values
of a Caribbean island results in the anomie that causes youth
to posture as "cool" and to take to drugs and crime.

This vision must be treated with caution. There is little
evidence of a wholesale Puerto Rican rejection of the American
way of life, nor are the psychological consequences of city life
confined to Puerto Ricans. Returning emigrants have difficulty
readjusting precisely because of their belief in the superiority
of life on the mainland: they create their own suburban enclaves
in such places as Levittown. A survey conducted in the 1970s
reveals internalization of dependency rather than its rejection:
65 percent believed that, but for the American connection,
"disorder" would reign in Puerto Rico; 75 percent believed
that Puerto Rican youth should serve in the U.S. armed forces;
60 percent believed that Puerto Rico extracted more profit than
loss from economic dependence on the United States.[42]

The key to this acceptance lies in the value placed by Puerto

Ricans on American citizenship. American citizenship brings with it welfare payments and the right of unrestricted entry into the labor market of the mainland. But to many Puerto Ricans it also confers *dignidad,* the right of inhabitants of a Caribbean ministate to use the passport and enjoy the protection of the most powerful nation in the world. It is the loss of citizenship that is the stumbling block to independence.

"The political problem of Puerto Rico," wrote a correspondent in the *San Juan Star* in 1962, "is a very simple one that boils down to this. Americanism versus anti-Americanism." If the issue was this stark, it might be argued that, once it had been decided, then the political future of Puerto Rico also would be decided and the status issue resolved: either statehood for an Americanized Puerto Rico, or Commonwealth, or independence — both of the latter, in very different ways, determined to preserve a Puerto Rican personality. But the issue is not clear; there is a shifting balance, an indistinct frontier that divides slavish mimesis of the United States from rejection of its values, a gray area that is neither Puerto Rican nor American. "Self-determination" writes one of the most perceptive commentators on Puerto Rican affairs "in the last analysis, requires a clear definition of self."[43] If that clear definition was lacking in 1973, when this statement was made, it shows no signs of emerging a decade later.

Part IV

THE RELUCTANT IMPERIALIST

13.

AMERICAN INTERESTS AND ATTITUDES

Puerto Rico remains part of the United States because an overwhelming majority of Puerto Ricans vote that it should so remain. Only a massive desertion of voters to the cause of independence could secure a majority for separation. For its part, the United States is committed to union, though not necessarily to the present form of that union, because it cannot, on democratic principles, force separation on Puerto Rico. Independence is not something that can be administered like a pill. Self-government was not bestowed on Canada from above; it was earned from below.

There lies the essential weakness in the case for independence. Lack of domestic support forces the independence movements to concentrate on the mobilization of opinion outside Puerto Rico and to work so doggedly to interest the United Nations in Puerto Rico's status. Those who argue that the United States should "unilaterally give Puerto Rico her freedom right now" to avoid harboring "a suppurating sore for the next forty years"[1] neglect that, on present showing, this would amount to forcing Puerto Ricans to be free and to imperil their American citizenship. Only by arguing that the general will of the Puerto Rican people has been so distorted or suppressed by the "colonial" connection can a case be made for the United States sloughing off the responsibilities assumed in 1898. Just as Great Britain might like to "pull out" of Northern Ireland but cannot while it is pledged to continue union as long as a majority so desires, so the United States cannot "pull out" of Puerto Rico even if the island may come to be regarded as an expensive and embarrassing liability.

Apart from respect for the democratic will of the Puerto Ricans, the United States has a direct interest in retaining Puerto Rico. This interest derives from its larger interests in the Caribbean and Latin America.

U.S. interest in the Caribbean has veered from relative indifference to intense concern. It was, in theory, based on the application to the Caribbean of the Monroe Doctrine of "two spheres" — no European power should be allowed to intervene in the Western hemisphere. In the early years of this century, U.S. direct intervention, which kept American troops in the Caribbean until 1934, was aimed at establishing quasi-protectorates in an area where unstable and weak governments were considered unable to resist outside pressure. But by 1926, when U.S. marines landed in Nicaragua — to halt "Bolshevism" in the Caribbean[2] — there was not the remotest prospect of European intervention to justify invoking the moribund Monroe Doctrine.

The establishment of Cuba as a Soviet satellite has renewed these fears and reactivated the mechanisms of intervention in the Caribbean after a period of relative indifference. Hence that perfect failure, the Bay of Pigs in 1961, and President Johnson's expedition to the Dominican Republic to stave off a "second Cuba."

President Reagan's advisers fear more than a "second Cuba."

They already have potential second Cubas in Nicaragua and the People's Democracy of Grenada, and there can be no doubt that the Cubans have been active in forging links with the Caribbean left. With the Nicaraguan Revolution, the administration sees the whole Caribbean basin threatened by a domino effect with "Cuban"-style revolutions toppling unstable regimes. It holds that Havana, since 1978, has been actively pursuing a new policy: making aid to opposition parties in Central America and the Caribbean dependent on "unity of the left" and on committing that unified left to the violent overthrow of existing regimes.[3] After Nicaragua, El Salvador or Guatemala may go. Hence the administration's determination to "draw the line" at El Salvador and, by the Caribbean Basin Initiative (CBI), to remove the discontents that feed Cuban-style national revolutions. But as has been pointed out by Senator Zorinsky, among others, "Caribbean" is a misnomer. El Salvador does not touch the Caribbean; the Caribbean Basin Initiative "is little more than a cover operation" to increase aid to El Salvador.

The underlying fear that haunts some American policymakers is that an independent Puerto Rico itself may become "another Cuba." This is not a present danger: the Puerto Rican Independence Party (PIP) rejects the Cuban model and the Puerto Rican Socialist Party (PSP), which embraces it, is a minuscule party on bad terms with the PIP. Although Puerto Rico is a conservative society imbued with democratic values, with independence, its opponents maintain, there is no real security against "Cubanization." Senator Orestes Ramos of the New Progressive Party (PNP) argues that those who, like Rubén Berríos Martínez, now support a peaceful negotiated settlement with the United States for the installation of a democratic republic will be "pushed aside" once the republic is installed. The senator maintains that it is the pressure of business interests, which are fearful for their investments under a radical socialist regime, on the national administration that will force statehood as permanently precluding independence and the dangers of a drift toward Cubanization, which well-intentioned citizens of a small Democratic Republic would be unable to resist.[4]

"I think," Henry Kissinger is reported as saying, "the United States has to hold onto Puerto Rico for strategic reasons."[5] These reasons appear compelling to the United States Navy. For Mahan, the late – nineteenth-century advocate of a strong American Navy, a naval base in Puerto Rico would protect the sea lanes of the Caribbean; above all it would secure the Panama Canal. Puerto Rico, Mahan argued, would play the role for the United States Navy in the Caribbean that Malta played for the British Navy in the Mediterranean. It can be maintained that the Panama Canal is no longer a vital concern today, as large aircraft carriers cannot use it. The Navy's case turns on the protection of sea lanes along which 50 percent of America's imported refined oil reaches the mainland from refineries on the Virgin Islands and elsewhere in the Caribbean. These sea lanes are vulnerable to an attack from Cuba, and their protection "has a very high strategic importance."[6] Protection can best be secured from Roosevelt Roads, the naval enclave on the eastern tail of Puerto Rico and one of the largest naval bases in the world; ships are not permanently stationed at Roosevelt Roads, but in a war it would be a valuable, if not an indispensable, base for bunkering.

The revision of the Navy's plans for Roosevelt Roads is a clear indication of the impact on defense planning of the Cuban Revolution, the 1962 missile crisis, and the fact that Cuba has become an "enormous training and intelligence base" for the Soviets in the Caribbean.[7] While Roosevelt Roads was enlarged during World War II to accommodate the British fleet should

Britain fall to Hitler, since then proposals were intermittently made to deactivate it. Now it has been developed into "one of the most exclusive and sophisticated control centers for weapons training in the world." The "Outer Range" — 194,000 square miles — provides "a realistic hostile electromagnetic environment" for training purposes that, according to the Navy, cannot be simulated anywhere else[8] — not least, as the Pentagon confesses, because at Norfolk or any other mainland base, jamming would interfere with statesiders' television. Conditions are so ideal for training purposes that "everything is working for you."[9] To the Navy, the Atlantic Fleet Weapons Training Facility, which is based on Roosevelt Roads and includes Vieques and the Virgin Islands, is irreplaceable. Even were this not the case, moving it elsewhere would mean sacrificing a capital investment that the Navy estimates at $1.5 billion.

The Navy professes to share the official policy of successive U.S. governments on Puerto Rico; it will accept any political status the Puerto Ricans themselves support. After all, independence would not preclude a status of forces agreement as in the Bahamas; statehood also is acceptable. But since, as the Navy's experiences in Trinidad have shown, arrangements with independent states are vulnerable to local attacks, and since Puerto Rican representatives in Congress might make trouble —Romero's attacks on naval bombardments of Vieques are a warning shot—it is hard to resist the conclusion that Commonwealth suits the Navy admirably.

It is not the American presence in Roosevelt Roads that at present sours Puerto Rican-U.S. relations; rather it is the use by the Navy of the offshore island of Vieques for target practice —the "bombardment" of Vieques.

The agitation against the Navy's presence and activities in

Vieques has been organized and orchestrated by the PSP and the PIP in collaboration with island protesters, particularly the local Fishermen's Association. Fishing has become one of the island's main economic activities since the decline of the sugar industry. The Navy's interference with fishing initiated the protests when, in 1978, fishermen sailed into practice areas. (The Vieques issue also involves older conflicts, including eviction of local inhabitants from land acquired by the Navy and the insecurity of resettled tenants.) The protest movement has supplied the remnants of the Nationalist party with a martyr in Angel Rodríguez Cristóbal, who was arrested for demonstrating on naval property in Vieques and then "assassinated" in a Tallahassee prison.[10] The Vieques "bombardments" are presented as a particularly violent example of American imperialism, evidence that the United States, with all its professed respect for human rights, has no regard for human rights in its "colony." The federal district court's authorization of the bombardments "against the small and indefensive [sic] island of Vieques," the mayor of Vieques protested to President Carter, constitutes a "great slap" to "your politics [sic] of Human Rights."

Vieques is, indeed, a "suppurating sore." It is a signal instance of American insensitivity that the agitation against the Navy's activities in Vieques is dismissed by the chief of staff at Roosevelt Roads as the work of the "subversives," whose names have been supplied to the Navy by the Federal Bureau of Investigation (FBI). Exploited and exaggerated beyond all reason by the *independentistas* and Nationalists as the Vieques issue is, the "bombardments" during target practice are considered abusive by Puerto Ricans as little inclined to subversion as Governor Romero himself. It is the governor who instituted a federal suit seeking an injunction against the Navy on the grounds that it is polluting the sea and has not obtained the necessary release from the federal Environmental Protection Agency. To the Navy the bombardment of Vieques is part of a greater scheme of things: the effective defense of the West by an efficient Navy. The Navy admits that the training is being conducted in an area where local protests will have no direct repercussions in Congress. It is this that fires the indignation of the Puerto Ricans: the Navy is treating Puerto Ricans, citizens of the United States, as it would not dare to treat the citizens of the mainland. It would smooth a strained relationship if the bombing were to cease, even if the removal of one grievance would result in agitation centered on some other activity of the Navy.

The *independentistas* exploit the local grievances of the fishermen and the other inhabitants since they see in Vieques an emotional issue around which anti-American feeling can be concentrated. Whether this protest movement should be openly "anti-imperialist" (and therefore become the property of "ultraleftists") or whether it should be a wider movement of all ideologies gathered on a common anti-American front, splits the protesters.[11] Verbal hyperbole — the mayor of Vieques talks of "the savage assassination of the life of our people" — is the stuff of all protest movements:[12] "The state of mind of the average citizen of Vieques can be compared with the state of mind of a citizen of Derry, North Ireland," writes a Catholic priest of the National Chaplains Association. Such gross exaggeration is only effective when it covers a real grievance commanding uncritical support beyond the organizations that manipulate indignation. Vieques is such a grievance. Car stickers proclaim its plight.

Compared with the Navy, the U.S. land and air forces are relatively insignificant in Puerto Rico, and both Army and Air Force strength has been reduced in recent years. With approximately 400 troops in Fort Buchanan, the American military forces are regarded less as an implement to be used in defense of American interests outside Puerto Rico than as a force symbolizing the American presence in Puerto Rico itself. Fort Buchanan is the organizational and social center of 94,000 veterans, many of whom are strong supporters of institutions like the American Legion. *Independentistas* regard such institutions, and the ROTC with its 2,000 cadets, as vehicles of Americanization. The National Guard (with about 10,000 men), formally controlled by the governor, is financed by the Department of Defense; it can, as it was in the hurricane relief operation in the Dominican Republic, be used directly by the president of the United States. Its function is, as its commander made clear, "to defend our democracy" against "Communism and subversion."[13] In turn, its installations are the target of terrorists.

The American military presence in Puerto Rico is considered by the anti-American lobby as a colonial garrison. Year after year in the United Nations, *independentistas* insist that U.S. troops—instruments of political oppression—must vacate the island before there can be any free exercise of the Puerto Ricans' inalienable right of self-determination in a plebiscite. The U.S. armed forces are seen as FBI agents in uniform rather than as military forces stationed in Puerto Rico under the common defense that links Puerto Rico to U.S. defense policies, just as the common market links it to the continental economy.

"Common defense" now means the *possibility* of a nuclear attack on Puerto Rico. The United States signed the Treaty of Tlalteloclo, which bans nuclear weapons in Latin America. It maintains that this multilateral treaty does not preclude the entry, for short periods, of nuclear-armed vessels to Roosevelt Roads. Since it considers Puerto Rico part of the United States and *not* an independent Latin American nation, this is logical enough.

It is surprising that the anti-American lobby has not exploited the wider implications of common defense in an age when antinuclear protest movements are gathering strength in Europe and elsewhere. The American military presence in Puerto Rico is seen in political rather than strategic terms. The reason must lie in the fact that the majority of Puerto Ricans accept that American citizenship, which they wish to retain, implies military obligations. There is no electoral mileage in concentrating on the strategic implications of common defense.

A society that fears "Cubanization" accepts that the Soviet Union is the enemy-in-chief and that Cuba, a Soviet satellite, should be properly reminded of the dangers of spreading subversion in the Caribbean by war games round the island involving NATO ships. Governor Romero acknowledges that Puerto Rico as a "land super carrier" is now a military target for the Soviet Union, but he does not want the Navy out of Roosevelt Roads since it "boosts island security"; Puerto Rico is "much better with those vessels around than without them."[14] Many Puerto Ricans would agree. "The most attractive feature of the statehooders," argues Rick Neale of the Puerto Rican Task Force, "is that they favor a strong defense posture."[15] So, odd as it may seem, complaints that U.S. target practice endangers the living of Vieques fishermen and disturbs the tranquillity of the island's inhabitants figure more prominently in anti-American propaganda than the potential involvement of Puerto Rico in a third world war. If the Navy left Vieques in peace, no doubt the attack would center on Roosevelt Roads; but *independentistas* see the bombing in Vieques as an issue that has immediate appeal — as always, overestimating the interest of the outside world in the plight of Puerto Rico. "The fight of the people of Vieques," writes an *independentista,* "is already known in the whole world." It is not.

The imperialism of the turn of the century was never solely a matter of what Kissinger calls "strategic reasons." It had a wider and, to it exponents, a nobler purpose: the gift of a superior civilization to what we would now call a part of the Third

World, the incorporation of a backward society into the value system of the Anglo-Saxon democracies. This *mission civilatrice* in the Caribbean now entails the defense of Western values threatened by the successful establishment of a Soviet-supported Socialist state in Cuba. To many American policymakers, Castro's Cuba was more than a direct political and strategic threat. It was a moral affront; it bred an ideological virus that could not be allowed to spread. The Caribbean became a battlefield between the democratic values of the West and Soviet totalitarianism.

In this battle, Puerto Rico is cast to play an important role: it was a "showcase of democracy," a proof that democracy and free enterprise could bring well-being and political stability, a model of successful economic growth exhibited to the Third World in general and to Latin America in particular. Puerto Rico, Reagan argued when he was a presidential candidate, was the pivot of a "worldwide tug of war...to show the world that the American idea can work in Puerto Rico is to show that our idea can work everywhere."[16]

At the outset, the Puerto Rican model suffered a serious drawback: the special and favorable economic concession that underwrote the growth of its economy could not be extended to independent nations that were not "part" of the United States and within a common market.[17] When it was proposed by the Reagan administration that these privileges be generalized in the Caribbean through the President's Caribbean Basin Initiative (CBI), the "showcase" itself was threatened. To encourage the maintenance of "stable" democracies, revivified by private investment and a modicum of aid, the privileges, once the unique possession of Puerto Rico, were to be extended by the CBI to its Caribbean competitors, which already enjoyed the additional attraction to investors of lower wages. The administration's policies were "contradictory": Reagan could not hold Puerto Rico up as a model and at the same time put it at a severe disadvantage. In the early stages of policy-making these contradictions escaped attention in Washington: only at a later stage were modifications made to accommodate Puerto Rico's special circumstances.[18]

The idea of Puerto Rico as "our show window looking south" was not merely an invention in an anti-Castro propaganda campaign. It had long played a role in America's Latin American policy. The phrase was coined by Theodore Roosevelt, Jr., governor of Puerto Rico from 1929 to 1933. He was the first governor to learn Spanish; he respected Puerto Rican culture as possessing a valuable and "distinctive characteristic." He grasped the connection between the performance of the United States in Puerto Rico and its image in Latin America: "on Puerto Rico," he wrote, "depends a great deal of our relationship with South and Central America."[19]

The notion of Puerto Rico as a happy mix of the Latin civilization of the South and the Anglo-Saxon civilization of the North, which could act as a "bridge" between the two, represented a diplomatic tool to be brandished whenever American policy went through one of its intermittent revivals of interest in Latin America. This was particularly evident in the Kennedy administration. Teodoro Moscoso was appointed coordinator of the Alliance for Progress, the most ambitious attempt to formulate progressive policy for Latin America; Professor Arturo Morales Carrión became a deputy secretary of state for inter-American affairs, one of the first major federal posts held by a Puerto Rican. The Puerto Rican experience, writes Arthur Schlesinger, Jr., "was an important source of ideas behind the alliance."[20]

The role of Puerto Rico in the Alliance did not yield striking results. I traveled extensively in Latin America in the 1960s. Puerto Rico was regarded by most politicians as a country manipulated by the United States; it did not truly belong to the family of Latin American nations represented in the Organization of American States. Muñoz Marín was seen, not as a Latin American, but as a friend of America whose knowledge of the continent did not extend beyond Betancourt's Venezuela. Teodoro Moscoso was consistently presented in Cuban propaganda as a *titere* (puppet) of the United States. Nor did advice, when heeded, always fit the peculiar circumstances of Latin America. An admirer of Betancourt and *Acción Democrática* of Venezuela, Muñoz wished to encourage, by discreet subsidies, the emergence of parties of the democratic left in other and similar Latin American countries. The Central Intelligence Agency (CIA) passed funds to the Chilean democrats. While "useful at the time," this established "bad habits and contained an awful potentiality for abuse."[21] Any influence Puerto Ricans possessed in the Muñoz period has gone: those politicians who now cultivate relations with Latin America are not members of the political establishment but *independentistas,* whose connections are with the anti-American left in Latin America. They are not available for bridge-building operations.

While Puerto Rico's role as a "bridge" in the Alliance gave it a prominence it had never possessed before, those Puerto Ricans who chafed under the dominance of the United States — rather than relishing their role as a useful link between the north and south of the continent — found, in the emphasis on Latin American identity, an emotional weapon *against* the processes of Americanization. Muñoz was ready to exploit the "showcase" theory in order to maintain the interest of U.S. politicians in the island's concerns, but he himself was unhappy with the "bridge" metaphor. A bridge, he once said, is something to be trodden upon.

One of the messages that travels across the bridge, from south to north, is that Puerto Rico should be an independent Latin American nation. In 1953, it was the Latin American vote that helped the United States achieve recognition by the

United Nations that, with Commonwealth, Puerto Rico had ceased to be a colony.[22] In the 1980s, most Latin American nations support the Decolonization Committee's efforts to force the United States to "decolonize" Puerto Rico. The U.S. delegation dismissed Latin American concern for Puerto Rican independence as "token politics" displayed by politicians bred in the rhetorical tradition of the independence movements of the nineteenth century and intent on cultivating an electorate that relishes mild doses of anti-Americanism. A spokesman for the U.S. delegation told me, in 1980, that "they [the Latin American nations] won't do anything." Nevertheless their actions constituted a "nasty nuisance."

It is idle to argue that, in order to improve its relations with Latin America as a whole, the United States should get rid of the "nasty nuisance" by forthwith granting Puerto Rico independence.[23] This it cannot do without a mandate from the Puerto Rican electorate, the results of which it is perilous to prophesy. Nor would the shedding of Puerto Rico noticeably facilitate the forging of a viable Latin American policy. With or without Puerto Rico, the paranoiac anti-Americanism of the Latin American nations — Mexico and Argentina, for example — will seize on any pretext to belabor even well-intentioned policies of the United States: the Venezuelan press, for example, referred to the Caribbean Basin Initiative as "exploitative." Latin American rhetoric is supplemented by that of Puerto Ricans; Severo Colberg of the PPD regards the CBI as devised to serve the political and strategic interests of the United States. The contradiction between the search for allies in an anti-Communist crusade and the liberal tradition of the United States is irresolvable. As Franklin Roosevelt discovered, the United States ends up supporting sons of bitches manning unsavory regimes because they are "our sons of bitches."

How do the demands and protests of Puerto Rico "get into" the American political system?

The official channel is provided by the resident commissioner in Washington. Elected at the same time as the governor, and on the same party ticket, the resident commissioner can speak but not vote on the floor of the House of Representatives and sit on House committees; there is no such access to the Senate, though proposals are under discussion that such a channel should be set up. The limited power of the resident commissioner depends on his contacts with congressmen and the information with which he is provided. Jaime Benítez as commissioner was an assiduous cultivator of friends on the Hill, though his disquisitions on what have been called the baroque qualities of the constitutional aspects of Commonwealth puzzled and sometimes wearied his audience and caused him to be dismissed by down-to-earth congressmen as "an intellectual with his head in the clouds." The present resident commissioner, Baltasar de Corrada, is respected, but his influence with a Republican Senate and a Republican executive is weakened by his Democratic affiliations.

To be an effective lobbyist, the resident commissioner needs to be informed, as he must act before the proposals of the administration take final form. This is frequently not the case. The block grant for food stamps was sent to Congress without any previous consultation with the resident commissioner. Baltasar de Corrada learned of the proposal as a member of the Committee of Labor and Education; on that committee the commissioner had "friends" and a vote that he could trade. On the Agriculture Committee, which deals with the food stamp program, Puerto Rico was without a voice, while the Senate committee dealing with the matter was chaired by Jesse Helms, a fierce critic of food stamps in general and of their extension to Puerto Rico in particular. It is at the committee stage that bills can be altered and the particular interests of Puerto Rico protected. The commissioner's effective action is limited, not

...ast because he is only granted the staff support that is provided for one congressman. Above all, he lacks the weight of
the two senators and seven representatives that would be
Puerto Rico's quota as a state. To oppose the administration's
food stamp proposals, Baltasar de Corrada had only the force
of his eloquence on the floor and the votes of his Democratic
friends. They were powerless to stop a budget reconciliation
bill that included the block grant.

As the history of the food stamp issue proves, it is more
important that Puerto Rico makes its wishes felt and protects
its special interests — and no issue is more important than food
stamps — within the administration before the resident commissioner and Puerto Rico's friends on the Hill attempt to
modify the administration's policies as they grind through
Congress and its committees.

The lobbying efforts of the resident commissioner are supplemented by the Commonwealth Office and the array of lawyers employed by the Commonwealth government in Washington; they are the most informed and influential figures in
Puerto Rican affairs. One such legal lobbyist is presented as
"very knowledgeable and knows his way around Congress"; as
a friend of Tip O'Neill, majority leader of the House, he is
considered worth $4,000 a month.[24] Each of the major Puerto
Rican political parties retains its own law firms in Washington
to handle cases of political interest — particularly electoral cases,
which, in 1982, involved whether the PNP or the PPD should
have a majority in the lower house of the Puerto Rican legislature. The size of disbursements to Washington lawyers to
fight political cases is a frequent source of acid comment in the
local press.

Until the establishment of Commonwealth in 1952, the presidents of the United States retained a direct role in the govern-

322   THE RELUCTANT IMPERIALIST

ance of Puerto Rico. At best, they saw themselves as paternal istic proponents of what President McKinley had called "benevolent assimilation." President Wilson was an educator: Puerto Ricans should learn as good pupils from a well-intentioned schoolmaster. At worst, presidents appointed party hacks as governors, using the island as a field for patronage or, like Harding and Coolidge, showing little interest in the island's affairs and slapping down any untoward claim for greater self-government.

The most momentous changes came with President Truman: the Elective Governors Act of 1947 and the establishment of Commonwealth in 1952. Truman was the first president to be influenced by the postwar enthusiasm for decolonization. He believed that the beneficent paternalism that characterized President Roosevelt's approach was no longer satisfactory for governing a colony that, President Wilson had acknowledged, constituted an international embarrassment for the United States.

Once Commonwealth status made it improper to treat Puerto Rico as a territory similar to the Virgin Islands or Guam, and once the instruments of "beneficent assimilation"—control of education, for example—had been transferred to the Puerto Rican government, it was no longer possible to have the handling of Puerto Rican affairs and the guarding of its interests centered in the Department of the Interior. On July 25, 1961, President Kennedy issued a memorandum to all executive departments explaining that the relationship between Puerto Rico and the United States was "in the nature of a compact" providing for "full internal self-government subject only to the applicable provisions of the Federal Constitution, the Puerto Rico Federal Relations Act and the Acts of Congress authorizing and approving the [Puerto Rican] Constitution." The Executive Order of May 29, 1934, which had transferred Puerto can affairs from the War Department to the Department of the Interior, no longer applied. "Matters affecting Puerto Rico should be referred directly to the Office of the President." When the State Department protested that the order "appears to grant the island the status of a foreign independent sovereignty," Muñoz quieted the alarmists; the order merely sought to establish "a uniform attitude in the Executive Branch."

The PPD hailed the president's memorandum as a victory for the diplomacy of Muñoz: Puerto Rico now had direct access to the White House. It was less a triumph than the solution to an intractable administrative problem. Where should Puerto Rico "go" now that it was no longer some species of a territory that could be dealt with by the Department of the Interior? The State Department dealt only with sovereign states. "It was the last thing we wanted," an official remarked. "It's bad enough to put up [sic] with Puerto Rico in the United Nations."[25]

The attention devoted to the island's problems became a function of the president's own interest and that of his domestic staff. Since there was still no one person responsible for Puerto Rico, the new arrangement, Teodoro Moscoso claims, "did not go far enough."[26] President Kennedy inherited President Roosevelt's concern and his friendship with Muñoz Marín, but his interest in Puerto Rico was primarily a consequence of his larger interest in Latin America. Muñoz tendered advice on the Alliance for Progress; Arturo Morales Carrión expanded the president's speech during the missile crisis of 1962 in order to appeal to Cuban and Latin American susceptibilities.[27] Even so, Kennedy's refusal to support the PPD's plan for a plebiscite in 1962 came as a disappointment. President Johnson was conscious of the old Democratic alliance with the PPD, but his domestic special counsel, who was responsible for Puerto Rico, had more important matters than the island among his daily

concerns. "Unless a special issue blew up I spent about tv
hours a month on Puerto Rico... unless someone has a speci.
interest he will be swamped by other duties."[28] President Nixor
had no special interest in Puerto Rico; President Ford's one
intervention — his rejection of the ad hoc committee's recommendation and his declaration of support for statehood —
seemed, for the opponents of statehood at least, to diminish
Puerto Rico's right of self-determination.

Before the Puerto Ricans voted in large numbers in the
Democratic primaries of 1976, no presidential candidate had a
direct political interest in Puerto Rico. Now the votes of Puerto
Rican delegates to the national party conventions stimulated
such an interest: Puerto Rico had become "organically" connected with national politics for the first time. This produced
a peculiar situation: the main engineer of the conversion of a
sector of the traditionally Republican statehooders to support
a Democratic candidate had been Franklin Delano López. In
return it was he who gained control over what was a vital
instrument in every Puerto Rican governor's political armory:
patronage and the control of appointments to federal jobs in
Puerto Rico. Governor Romero made his anger felt and López
was dropped after what has been described as a "bloody battle"
between Romero and Carter.

As defenders of Commonwealth, the newfound influence
of the statehooders in the White House alarmed the PPD; the
traditional support of Commonwealth was seemingly imper-
iled by the "alternative futures" option, which, backed by the
president, seemed to open the door to statehood. "We were,"
says Hernández Colón, "gravely concerned."[29]

In the 1980 national election, Governor Romero backed the
losing candidate. The Washington connection now ran
through loyal Republicans — Mayor Padilla, who was "more
in tune philosophically" with the Reagan administration and

Senator Luis Ferré, "a magnificent figure." The new administration's first contact with Puerto Rico was over the "dumping"
of Haitian refugees at Fort Allen. Romero, after "ranting and
raging," was surprised, according to Richard Neale, who as a
member of the Puerto Rican Task Force is in close contact
with island affairs, that "we did not intend to handle him like
Carter."[30] By accommodating the administration in its desire
to dispatch Cuban refugees to Puerto Rico, Romero hoped to
regain his "ear" in Washington.

That "ear" once more turned deaf over the Reagan administration's budgetary proposals. Puerto Rico had no influence
whatever in the Office of Management and Budget, which the
resident commissioner finds "the most difficult of all agencies"
— and the most powerful. Nor was he consulted in the initial
stages of the Caribbean Basin Initiative. Once these policies
were revealed, the commissioner protested vigorously and
Romero "screamed." Puerto Rican screaming gave birth to the
latest administrative improvisation, which attempts to reconcile the demands of Puerto Rico with those of national policies:
the Puerto Rican Task Force, whose chairman is Richard Williamson, special assistant to the president for intergovernmen-
tal affairs. It has one Puerto Rican member, resident in the
United States, and one member with sympathy for and knowledge of Puerto Rican affairs. As Romero confessed, the Puerto
Rican input came "from the outside."

The Puerto Rican Task Force is not a policymaking body.
Meeting every month or so, it is a collection of middle-level
bureaucrats who present the Puerto Rican position to various
government agencies and departments; thus, for example, the
Treasury was asked to "clarify" its intentions in regard to Section 936 of the Internal Revenue Code.

The Task Force was soon aware of the unease created in
Puerto Rico by the announcement of the Caribbean Basin

Initiative and the administration's budget proposals.[31] The proposal to grant other Caribbean rum producers free access to the U.S. market, the commonwealth government protested, was completely "unacceptable"; it represented "blatant discrimination." The Treasury delays in clarifying the tax concessions allowed by Section 936 were having a disastrous effect on new investment.[32] Where the Puerto Rican Secretary of State Quiros cajoled — largely by telephone — PPD Senate President Miguel Hernández Agosto threatened that ruin and social revolution would result from the administration's indifference to the effects of its policies on Puerto Rico.

To the administration, the Puerto Rican Task Force solved the old problem of how to fit Puerto Rico into national policies. It "has been and continues to be," claimed Williamson's executive assistant, "a vehicle for communication and cooperation between Puerto Rico and the Reagan administration." It did have some success in making Puerto Rico's voice heard in Washington. But since all administrations are apt to dismantle the ad hoc administrative creations of their predecessors, it is unlikely that the Task Force will remain as an effective vehicle. Even at present, its effectiveness is limited by the amount of time the department officials can devote to Puerto Rican business, and by interdepartmental frictions and personal rivalries between those who claim to have "a gut feeling" for Puerto Rico and those whose sole concern is to bring Puerto Rico into line with the administration's policies. Neale claims the Task Force occupies a third of his time, and he seeks "to spare Mr. Williamson as much as possible" of Puerto Rico's problems.

It was Muñoz Marín who brought to a fine art the cultivation of friends in Congress, the administration, and the American establishment in general; interested and influential congress-en were invited to Puerto Rico in the winter months. No subsequent Puerto Rican politician has enjoyed Muñoz's prestige, but the cultivation of friends in Washington remains an essential function of the resident commissioner and of Puerto Rican politicians in general, the more prominent of whom will have a "line" to an influential senator.

Members of Congress become involved in Puerto Rican affairs either through membership of committees or through the special interest of their constituents. Senator Bennett Johnston of Louisiana came onto the Committee on Energy and Natural Resources of the Senate, which now deals with Puerto Rican affairs, not because he was interested in Puerto Rico, but because he was the representative of an oil state. Once on the committee, he took his duties seriously, developing a skepticism about the constitutional proprieties of Congress changing Puerto Rico's status that alarms statehooders and supporters of improved Commonwealth alike. Senator Daniel P. Moynihan of New York is a defender of Puerto Rican interests, partly because, as ambassador to the United Nations, he had strongly opposed the efforts of the Decolonization Committee to decolonize Puerto Rico, partly because many of his electors are Puerto Ricans living in New York. Senator Edward Kennedy has strong ties with the *Populares* leadership: "the bond between us and Ted," claims Hernández Colón, "is very strong." Congressman Philip Burton was on the Insular Affairs Committee of the House: he claimed credit for bringing food stamps to Puerto Rico.

Though Puerto Rico has powerful friends in Congress, it has no caucus and no representatives and senators to trade votes.[33] Most members of Congress, however, are indifferent and not overzealous about devoting time to Puerto Rican affairs; in 1943, when Puerto Rico's status was under review, the House Committee on Insular Affairs had great difficulty getting a quorum.[34] Some few congressmen are hostile: in th. debates on the installation of Commonwealth, Senator Oli Johnston referred to Puerto Rico as "a giant incubator of people who do not understand American traditions or ideals but who are glad to qualify for American residence or American charity." Senator Jesse Helms proclaims that Puerto Rico deserves no federal aid because it pays no federal taxes.

However friendly a senator or representative may be, he is always subject to the pressure of his own electors, especially in an election year. The limiting case is when a Puerto Rican interest conflicts with that of a domestic pressure group. In 1973, Senator Bennett Johnston, on most issues a friend of Puerto Rico, was not prepared to abandon the defense of his home state's rice growers in order that Puerto Ricans might buy cheaper rice — a staple food of the island — on the open market. An exception which proves the rule was Senator Jackson's defense of the Mayagüez meat-packing industry in 1976. Mayagüez has a free trade zone, and Puerto Rican meat packers imported Australian meat, tinned it, and re-exported it to the United States, where it entered free of duty. Though Puerto Rican imports were an infinitesimal proportion of total U.S. meat imports, the Cattlemen's Association was up in arms. The Meat Import Act did not cover free trade zones. The Department of Agriculture issued an order to cover the Mayagüez imports under the Act, but the order was stopped by a court ruling. The Cattlemen's Association therefore proposed amending the Meat Import Act to cover free trade zones.[35]

Since 1976 was an election year, the Cattlemen's Association made it clear that those who opposed the amendment would suffer. When Senator Jackson, with Puerto Rico's interests in mind, opposed the amendment, the Cattlemen's Association contacted their local branch in Washington, the senator's home state. While the Association threatened "to give him trouble" ın the election, the senator, who was a brave man, persisted in his opposition. So did the Cattlemen. Jackson was saved because the amendment died away in the late-night convivial confusions at the end of the Senate session.

Given the selective inattention of the Congress and the president, the day-to-day government of Puerto Rico in the early years fell into the hands of bureaucrats, first into the hands of the Bureau of Insular Affairs, to whom the Puerto Ricans were "tropical dependent peoples" to whom the First Amendment did not apply.[36] After 1934, authority was transferred to the Department of the Interior. Insofar as there was a consistent policy, it was the accumulation of precedents and inertia, the disinclination to change existing arrangements that characterizes most bureaucracies. Muñoz found the War Department "conservative"; while the "liberal bureaucrats of the New Deal," he wrote in his *Memoirs,* "were an improvement," even they obstructed the Chardón plan for the restructuring of the sugar industry.[37] The plan was too imaginative, too bedeviled by legal problems, to appeal to civil servants. Routine was reinforced by prejudice. Bureaucrats wearied of Puerto Rican politicians. In this, they prolonged in Washington the exasperation of the early governors and American officials in Puerto Rico who found the local political factions unreliable, engaged in an unseemly scrabble for patronage and jobs.

Once the responsibility for Puerto Rican affairs was removed from the Department of the Interior, there was no single office coordinating policy, by picking out those aspects of the administration policies and Congressional legislation that affected the island, and guarding the interests of Puerto Rico. As federal legislation expanded after the war and federal grants-in-aid became increasingly important for Puerto Rico, so contact with government agencies became a growing concern for the government of Puerto Rico. Nonetheless, these contacts were often haphazard or even nonexistent.

Muñoz perceived the central problem: legislation and administration policies, conceived in the national interest of the United States, did not "fit" Puerto Rico. Most states contain a bundle of interests that usually, though not always, stretch outside the boundaries of a single state. For Muñoz and his successors, Puerto Rico has but one interest; it constitutes a special case. Bureaucrats and civil servants dislike special cases, especially when they entail a loss of revenue.

A striking example of the manner in which Washington bureaucrats make decisions that seem reasonable and proper on their criteria, but that may have crippling effects on Puerto Rico, is the Treasury's handling of tax exemptions granted to corporations that operate in overseas possessions. The Treasury was unhappy about the tax revenue that escaped it under Section 931 of the Internal Revenue Code, which covers corporations' exemptions on their operations in overseas territories, of which Puerto Rico is one. To its chagrin, Section 936, which, in 1976, replaced Section 931, did not net it more revenue from overseas corporations. Rather, the reverse was true.

A small compensation for Treasury bureaucrats was their power, under the 1976 Tax Reform Act, to report on "the revenue effects of the provision [i.e., the "tax expenditure" or taxes lost to the Treasury] *as well as* the effects on investment and employment in the possessions." [Emphasis added.] This allowed Treasury economists to conduct what amounted to an investigation into the economy as a whole; they did not like what they found. The tax concessions of Section 936 not only allowed investors to make vast tax-free profits by transferring intangibles (i.e., research costs, royalty payments, etc.) to their island subsidiaries; their Section 936 investments were made in such a fashion that they did little to provide jobs. They were ot cost effective if the primary aim of investment was to alleviate unemployment, still the scourge of Puerto Rico. The same investment that created one job in the capital-intensive pharmaceutical industry would provide eighteen jobs in the "traditional" labor-intensive industries such as apparel or leather. This was to assume that investors would still invest in traditional, labor-intensive industries, when it was only the new, capital-intensive, sophisticated industries that were attracting investment and providing employment. Between 1968 and 1978, employment in "traditional" labor-intensive industries declined by 16,000; it was the "cost ineffective" (on Treasury reasoning) pharmaceuticals that provided 8,000 new jobs.[38]

To the planners of Fomento, the implication of the Treasury's reasoning set the clock back to 1950 and condemned the island to a low-wage economy, but the expectations of its people had changed dramatically. Sophisticated, capital-intensive industries paid high wages for skilled workers; it was in these industries that the prospects of training and promotion were attractive to a population no longer willing to work for low wages in unstable, dead-end jobs with high worker turnover. This was, perhaps, one of the unfortunate effects of federal largess. Young Puerto Ricans, with a good education, preferred to stay on welfare payments rather than go back into agriculture or accept the low-paid jobs in "traditional" industries that had been so attractive to their fathers.[39]

Lack of normal representation in Congress, with the influence on policy that comes with it (exaggerated, no doubt, by statehooders who see a flood of defense contracts coming to a Puerto Rican state and the grant of economic privileges that no other state enjoys) forces Puerto Rican politicians to use a miscellany of approaches, from the supreme accolade of an interview with the president to a talk with a minor departmental official.

Looking back on the history of Puerto Rico's relations wi Washington, it is evident that they are muddled because con gressmen, and others, often are presented with diametrically opposite views from the two major Puerto Rican political parties: for example, the Commonwealth supporters' demand for control over immigration is opposed by the statehooders. According to one official who is deeply — almost passionately — involved in the plight of Puerto Rico:

The PNP and the PPD employ too many lawyers who give con-flicting advice.... They [Puerto Rican politicians] don't know how to play the game in Washington politics.... When they think they have a personal line to the White House, they drop everything else. When they don't have it they clamor for an institutional linkage through some sort of Puerto Rican office. They hold out the tin cup and when nothing is put in it fall back on their dignity and rights as citizens. Congressmen get muddled. It's not so much that they don't want to do what's right, they just don't know what "right" is and they've no Puerto Rican constituents to tell them what's "right." I wish to God that I didn't feel like a proconsul when I go down there.

"We just don't have a policy for our *territories* [emphasis added] and we ought to have one," says another official, "but it's hard because what might work in Micronesia won't work in Puerto Rico."[40]

The relationship between two societies is not merely a matter of the formal or informal political and administrative linkages that bind them together. When two cultures meet, each devel-ops a stereotype of the other. Sometimes these stereotypes are favorable and flattering — for instance, the European vision of the Chinese in the eighteenth century. More often they are negative. Such stereotypes can change, as the European image of the Chinese changed in the nineteenth century, but they tend to persist over time. The attitudes of presidents, congress-men, and civil servants reflect, to a greater or lesser extent, the stereotypes of Puerto Ricans that have developed since 1898.

Early attitudes varied from "benign assimilation" and pater-nalistic concern to outright prejudice. It was, for example, asserted in early congressional debates that Puerto Ricans did not merit self-government because they had not been manly enough to take up arms to earn it, as had the Cubans, by rising against Spain. "Such a race," argued Senator Henry M. Teller, "is unworthy of citizenship."[41]

Overt racism can no longer be paraded in public. This was not the case in 1900: District Judge Hamilton warned President Wilson that self-government must be administered in small doses "to a race of mongrels of no use to anyone, a race of Spanish American talkers."[42] To George Milton Fowles, who brought out a well-informed study of his country's new colony, Puerto Ricans were a race of stunted illiterates given to cock-fighting and concubinage, whose defects ranged from bad teeth to bad morals, "ruled" by a wealthy and "unsympathetic" land-owning class whose only desire was to "keep the masses poor and dependent."[43] General George W. Davis reported that "the vast horde of the ignorant" had no "conception of the duties of citizenship" and were "no more fit to take part in self-government than our reservation Indians."[44]

These prejudices became less strong with time, and there were always those who did not fully share them — President Wilson and Henry Stimson, for example — or who rejected them altogether and who, in the radical tradition, demanded the justice for Puerto Rico that prejudice denied. The Diffies' — fervent anti-imperialists — critical study of the economic consequences of colonialism in Puerto Rico, *Porto Rico: A Broken Pledge*, published in 1931, became something of a sacred text for American radicals.[45] Describing an economic structure that has long ceased to exist—an agrarian economy dominated by the great absentee corporations — an American scholar could, in 1982, still describe the Diffies' book as a "standard work."[46]

Puerto Rico's image in the 1930s was that of an island of slums, straw shacks, and disease, sunk in a hopeless poverty that could not be compared with even the poorest state of the Union; this poverty, American administrators were apt to assert, was self-induced, by a failure to control procreation and by a disinclination for hard work that was considered part and parcel of the Latin culture.

Operation Bootstrap substituted for this image of indolence and poverty that of a small community resolutely set on an approved course of self-improvement. Earl Parker Hanson's *Transformation: The Story of Modern Puerto Rico*, published in 1955, is a eulogy of Puerto Rico fighting its way out of poverty by its own efforts.[47]

These contrasting stereotypes and the attitudes they supported had one feature in common. They were based on the supposed behavior of Puerto Ricans in Puerto Rico. With the massive immigration after World War II, the focus of the image shifted to the mainland, especially to New York, where the Puerto Ricans were the most visible members of a growing Hispanic community. Even with the replacement of a belief in the efficacy of the "melting point" by a recognition of ethnic and cultural pluralism, it is hard for Americans to accept a community that seems to resist the processes of assimilation that absorbed previous waves of immigrants. It can be argued that it is too early to expect Puerto Ricans to follow the paths of Germans or Italians. Nevertheless, as the American Civil Rights Commission recognized, the road is likely to be a long one.[48]

Nor will it necessarily be shortened by bilingual education, however justifiable, whether by a liberal respect for cultural diversity or by a pedagogic concern for the education of a child whose mother tongue is Spanish. It is their incapacity to handle English, the language of social mobility, that keeps so many Puerto Ricans at the bottom of the ladder and from a fuller participation in political life. While Puerto Rican and Hispanic activists endorse an emphasis, in bilingual programs, on "maintenance" (i.e., the deliberate cultivation of the native culture and its traditions as a natural right) as opposed to "transition" (that is, the teaching of English as rapidly and efficaciously as possible), Americans often see this as a deliberate attempt to resist acceptance of American values: bilingual education, then, becomes a political and social rather than a pedagogical issue. Enthusiasts for bilingual education are often criticized by Anglo-Americans as members of a pressure group for whom bilingual education ensures jobs. Anyone who has taught in an American university will be conscious that bilingualism is supported by the students and teachers of Hispanic departments.

It is the supposed reluctance of Puerto Ricans to commit themselves to American values — a reluctance that they are assumed to share with Hispanics in general, and that distinguishes Hispanics, in the American popular mind, from previous generations of immigrants. "For the first time," the *New York Times* reported in 1978, "a major immigrant group is giving up on the American dream." This "refusal" on the part of Hispanics results, in part, from the state of the economy. The blue-collar jobs that were open to immigrants are steadily contracting. Earlier immigrants, often after a very difficult period of adjustment, could find steady employment in an expanding economy. Their modern successors cannot always do so: many are condemned to what radicals call "ghettoization."[49]

As with Mexicans, it is the proximity of the home country that combines with linguistic and cultural differences and precarious employment to weaken commitment. First-generation Puerto Ricans — and the same is true of Colombians and Mexicans—may not commit themselves to America when they can so easily return "home." Will second- and third-generation Puerto Ricans, born in American cities, commit themselves? If British experience with Jamaicans is relevant, then the answer is by no means certain when the host society is forced to substitute welfare payments for employment. Recent evidence seems to show that young second-generation Jamaicans, particularly those who are unemployed, reject Britain more radically than their parents. They consider themselves "Jamaicans," not British, and form their own subcultures, of which the Rastafarians are an extreme example.

While middle-class Americans tend to view Puerto Ricans as part of a Spanish-speaking community that survives on welfare provided by the taxes of industrious citizens, the urban working class tends to view them as shiftless and irresponsible, ready to accept low wages and to drive "native" Americans out of their jobs. Unions like the International Ladies' Garment Workers' Union (ILGWU) are accused of failing to live up to their liberal rhetoric; threatened by a shadow immigrant labor force, they have sought to keep Puerto Ricans out of the union. This reflects the debility and linguistic difficulties of the Puerto Rican community. "Eighty percent of our members speak Spanish," protested the Puerto Ricans in Local 132. "A meeting in English is a farce."[50]

Negative attitudes are intensified by apocalyptic visions of the Hispanicization of America and the incapacity to control illegal immigration. Rather than fellow citizens struggling for jobs, Puerto Ricans are seen as drug addicts and drop-outs whose leisure occupation is gang warfare. The sins of a minority are visited on the whole community. The violent rejection of the mores of America ("all this table etiquette and shit") by the Young Lords is not typical of a community that, however proud of its culture and tenacious of its life-style, wants to combine these with "getting on" in American society.

The constructive work done by community organizations to help Puerto Ricans overcome the problems of city life are overshadowed for many Americans by the verbal violence of the radicals, mostly second- or third-generation Puerto Ricans, who write their protests in English and who have been influenced by the militancy of the blacks. For other Americans, the image of Puerto Ricans had been tarnished by Oscar Lewis's widely read La Vida.[51] Intended as a serious study of the culture of poverty in the San Juan slum of La Perla and in the ghettos of New York, it has painted a picture of a nation of neurasthenics, prostitutes, and pimps.

Because of Americans' general ignorance of the island, an image of Puerto Ricans derived from crime and welfare payments statistics from the South Bronx is applied to Puerto Rico and Puerto Ricans as a whole. A common reaction is to wish that Puerto Rico did not exist; this, as much as liberal sentiment, accounts for the high and growing percentage of Americans who support independence. Others shy away from statehood, which will make Puerto Rico, with a per capita income half that of the poorest state, a permanent liability.[52] It is not merely the size of welfare payments to Puerto Ricans that creates prejudice; it is a deep-rooted fear of the seemingly uncontrollable demographic advance of the Hispanics. George Ball can talk of "the supreme folly of admitting Puerto Rico as a state," a step which he sees as strengthening a community whose resistance to assimilation threatens a precarious ethnic balance.[53] While Republicans may, for strategic reasons, and carried along by an old political tradition, favor statehood, they still may jib at a Spanish-speaking state, and a Spanish-speaking state is all they will get. Puerto Ricans fall into a conceptual limbo. They are not considered full-fledged Americans; nor are they thought of as members of a separate, self-sufficient community.

14.

PUERTO RICO IN THE UNITED NATIONS: THE ANTICOLONIALIST OFFENSIVE

The status of Puerto Rico is not only a subject of domestic debate and concern in the United States and Puerto Rico; increasingly it has become an issue with an international dimension, as the Cubans and their allies bring the status of Puerto Rico before the United Nations.

Every year, the United States is pilloried, as a colonial power, before the Decolonization Committee of the United Nations.[1] Its colony is Puerto Rico. The committee asserts the right of the Puerto Rican people to self-determination and has stated that the United States should transfer sovereign powers to the island in order to enable Puerto Ricans to exercise that right, free from the presence and pressures of the colonial power. Every year the hearings of the committee resound with the rhetoric of the Third World — forged and practiced in the meetings of the nonaligned nations—highly acceptable to most members of the committee. Rather than serious debate, the committee's hearings allow group after group hostile to the United States, from Freemasons to Charismatic Christians, to make its *acte de présence*. In 1979 and 1980, those groups expressed their grateful thanks to the Committee for allowing it the privilege of attacking the United States in public.[2] The United States was denounced as guilty of cultural genocide, even of the murder by "atomic radiation" of the Nationalist "martyr" Albizu Campos.[3] Emotional testimony also was presented on the "daily bombardment" of the island municipality of Vieques by the United States Navy and the persecution of *independentistas*, including the ambush of two saboteurs by police at Cerro Maravilla, resulting in their deaths.[4] Lolita Lebron, the Nationalist heroine, who had been imprisoned for the 1954 armed attack on Congress, testified. The Cuban ambassador, Raul Roa, demanded that those, like her, who were engaged in the armed struggle should be recognized as freedom fighters according to the General Assembly Resolution 3103 (XXVIII) of 1973, as "persons engaged in the armed struggle against colonial and alien domination and racist regimes," with the right to be treated as prisoners of war under the Geneva Convention.

The irritation that the hearings of the Decolonization Committee arouses in American breasts is understandable. A nation that prides itself on its liberal tradition does not take kindly to public accusations that it exercises "a constant, systematic and planned policy of repression" in Puerto Rico.[5] To an administration already obsessed by fears of a Castro-led, Communist takeover in the Caribbean, the committee presents a platform to the proponents of a war of liberation in the Caribbean and of terrorist outrages on the mainland. The trial in April 1980 of the Evanston Eleven — members of the clandestine terrorist group, the FALN — on a charge of opposing by force the authority of the government of the United States has, according to supporters of the *independentista* cause, "criminalized the very form of anticolonial struggle that this committee and the General Assembly have repeatedly endorsed." What to Americans are plain acts of terrorism, a representative of the Civic Committee in Support of Puerto Rican Prisoners of War presents to the United Nations as the work of freedom fighters legitimately engaged in putting into effect the right of Puerto Ricans to self-determination as recognized by the United Nations. They argue that those who have learned from the failure of the 1950 uprising in Puerto Rico and "from the liberation struggles in Cuba, Algeria and Vietnam and around the world the need for clandestine guerrilla action to provide the initiative and nucleus for a successful people's war"[6] are entitled to the protection of the United Nations in a just war.

The proceedings of the Decolonization Committee are regarded by American congressmen with indignation tinged with contempt. The United States was being traduced by its enemies — totalitarian enemies at that — led by the Cuban delegation to the United Nations. "We do not propose to be lectured by dictatorships on how to run a democracy." Those nations who are "looking to us for assistance" should take note that the United States regards the actions of the committee as a Soviet-Cuban ploy, and the United States is "increasingly angered by their efforts to meddle in our affairs."[7] These efforts were not merely an affront, they were a farcical exhibition of hypocrisy.

Until 1978, this "meddling" was more an annual irritant than a political threat, a ritual performance publicized by demonstrations of Puerto Ricans outside the United Nations building but scarcely reported outside the island newspapers. The committee's resolutions demanding that the United States decolonize Puerto Rico were dismissed by the United States delegation as a Cuban move, supported, year in and year out, by *independentista* organizations devoid of popular support and rich in rhetoric. The Cubans and the *independentistas* were unlikely to succeed in bringing the question of the status of Puerto Rico onto the agenda of the General Assembly. This was the central issue. In 1953, the General Assembly had recognized Commonwealth as a legitimate expression of the Puerto Ricans' rights of self-determination and thus removed the question of Puerto Rico from debate.

By 1981, constant dripping had worn away the stone. The Decolonization Committee went beyond its admonition that the United States should forthwith set about decolonizing Puerto Rico. It referred the "question of Puerto Rico" to be examined "as a separate item at its Thirty-Seventh session" by the General Assembly, where the decolonizers of the Third World were a force. The U.S. delegation could still dismiss the resolution as "a nasty nuisance," but there was more to it than that. The political tenacity of the Cuban delegation threatened to undermine the traditional stand of the United States on Puerto Rico — that is, to deny that an international body had any jurisdiction over Puerto Rico whose affairs were a domestic issue.

The first attempt to present the *independentista* case to the United Nations was made in 1953, when the *independentistas* realized that Muñoz Marín and Washington wished to get international recognition for Commonwealth status at the United Nations. This would be accomplished by a declaration that Puerto Rico's colonial status had ceased and that the United States, as the administering power of the territory, was no longer under any obligation to present an annual report to the United Nations on its administration, an obligation that

Article 73e of the United Nations Charter placed on all powers that administered a non – self-governing territory. This the United States delegation achieved in 1953 with General Assembly Resolution 748(VIII), passed on a favorable report by the Committee of Information on Non – Self-Governing Territories. The resolution affirmed that "in the framework of its Constitution and of the compact agreed upon with the United States of America the people of Puerto Rico have been invested with *attributes of political sovereignty* [emphasis added], which clearly identify the status of self-government attained by the Puerto Rican people as a status of an autonomous political entity." Puerto Rico, under its new Commonwealth constitution, enjoyed full internal self-government, had freely associated itself with the United States, and was no longer a dependent territory. The obligation to report under the Charter therefore lapsed. Puerto Rico was struck off the list of non – self-governing territories — the Charter's formula for describing a colony.[8]

Resolution 748(VIII) was greeted as a triumph by the United States and the Puerto Rican government, and it has remained the official position of the United States that it removed the question of Puerto Rico's status from discussion in the United Nations. Fernós Isern, who, as resident commissioner, had steered Public Law 600 through Congress, exulted: "the world's highest tribunal [had confirmed] that the relationship between Puerto Rico and the United States is one of free association."[9] Victory was all the sweeter in that the resolution was passed by the sixteen votes of the Latin American nations whom the *independentistas* were to court as potential allies against the colossus of the North. The Bolivarian tradition and the rhetoric of independence had been subdued by the pressure of the U.S. delegation.[10]

To the *independentistas*, who had picketed the United Nations building, the passing of Resolution 748(VIII) was a severe setback. It meant that in the view of the United Nations, Puerto Rico was no longer a colony, its people struggling for their freedom as an independent republic. Denied a hearing by the Committee of Information on Non – Self-Governing Territories, the Puerto Rican Independence Party (PIP) had presented its case in a long memorandum. The memorandum was a dissection of the official assertion that, by Public Law 600 and the subsequent plebiscites, Puerto Rico had exercised its right of self-determination and should therefore escape the jurisdiction of the United Nations. The whole process started by Public Law 600, the memorandum argued, was a "malicious fraud," "a political trick" to induce "a part of the people to vote in favor of the so-called constitution"; that constitution was a "mere colonial statute" that in no way altered the "absolute control of Congress over all Puerto Rican affairs," a piece of meaningless window dressing for foreign consumption that the assistant secretary of State for Latin American affairs confessed "will aid us very materially in our Latin American program."[11] That the colonial relationship between the United States and Puerto Rico was in no way altered by the "New Constitution" was demonstrated by excerpts from the debates in Congress, including Fernós Isern's statement that Public Law 600 "would not change the status of the island of Puerto Rico relative to the United States.... It will not alter the powers of the sovereignty acquired by the United States over Puerto Rico under the terms of the Treaty of Paris."

This did not alter the fact, however, that the Puerto Rican people *had* voted for Public Law 600 even if this was, as the memorandum argued, "in order that the formal consent of the Puerto Ricans may be given to their present relationship to the United States." This aberration of the general will was explained by the fact that "the colonial government presided over by Luis Muñoz Marín appealed to tricks, gross misrepresentations, falsehoods, bribes and coercion of all sorts to obtain at least a limited support for this spurious constitution." The referendum was taken at a time when Puerto Ricans were cowed after the Nationalist uprising of 1950; it was a plebiscite on the Nazi model, with opponents labeled as "subversives" or "Communists." The constitution satisfied none of the factors to be taken into consideration in deciding when a territory had attained a complete measure of self-government as set out in Resolution 567(VI) passed in January 1952.

"The wicked political comedy" mounted by Muñoz Marín had deceived the United Nations. The PIP immediately attacked Resolution 748(VIII) as lacking in moral force. The PIP claimed the resolution was based on lies peddled by the U.S. representative on the Committee of Information on Non – Self-Governing Territories; he claimed that "the Puerto Rican people held a national referendum to determine what kind of self-government they wanted. The question was whether they wanted to become (1) a state in our federal Union, (2) completely independent, or (3) a Commonwealth associated with the United States. They chose the last by an overwhelming vote." According to the PIP, this assertion was completely false. If the committee had allowed the PIP to testify, it would have realized the mountain of misinformation on which Resolution 748(VIII) rested.[12]

In their dismay at the adoption of the resolution, the *independentistas* could take some consolation. The debate on the resolution had not been the walkover that the U.S. delegation expected.[13] It was the first sign that the Third World would not accept the claims that Puerto Rico enjoyed the attributes of self-government. The Indian representative supported the *independentista* case; treaties between unequal states, he argued, masked colonialism. Moreover, the resolution made it clear that the United Nations *did* have competence to judge whether a territory had achieved full self-government and a subsequent resolution set out the factors that should guide its judgment. It was clear that Commonwealth status did not satisfy these criteria. By exploiting this contradiction the *independentistas* and their allies in the United Nations might hope to turn the triumph of 1953 into defeat, and to reestablish the "true" colonial status of Puerto Rico so as to lead the fight against it.

Not surprisingly, the *independentista* case made little headway. Decolonization was, in 1953, neither as fashionable nor as precise a process as it was to become by the 1970s. The United Nations' concern about implementing Chapter XV of its Charter and promoting the development and political freedom of non – self-governing territories was both tepid and intermittent. The United States could still bring out the vote in the United Nations, and the 1950s and early 1960s were the years in which the Commonwealth was presented as a great experiment in democratic development in the Third World, as a new and dynamic form of federalism. In April 1959, Muñoz Marín gave the Godkin Lecture at Harvard: "Breakthrough from Nationalism." Puerto Rico, he argued, had not merely ceased to be a colony. It was "more advanced" than the "Balkanized" countries that had achieved independence but could not escape from the narrow confines of nationalism to join the wave of the future: the "interdependence" embodied in the new relationship with the United States.[14]

The opportunity for internationalizing the colonial status of Puerto Rico that the *independentistas* had sought finally came in 1960. As the number of former colonies in Africa and Asia that had achieved independence and joined the United Nations grew, so it increasingly became the forum for the Third World's enthusiasm for decolonization.[15] The breakthrough was General Assembly Resolution 1514(XV) on the Granting of Independence to Colonial Countries and Peoples: "Immediate steps shall be taken, in Trust and Non – Self-Governing Territories or *all other territories that have not yet attained independence* [emphasis added] to transfer all powers to the peoples of those territories without any conditions or reservations, in accordance with their freely expressed will and desire... in order to enable them to enjoy complete independence and freedom." To implement the "speedy and total application" of the resolution, the General Assembly set up the Committee of Twenty-Four, later known as the Decolonization Committee.

A Second Resolution 1514(XV), passed the following day, recognized three ways by which non – self-governing territory could reach a "full measure of self-government": sovereign independence, free association with an independent state, integration with an independent state. According to these criteria, Puerto Rico had not reached "a full measure of self-government." As defined in the resolution, Commonwealth was not free association. The resolution stated that the associated state must be free "to modify the status of the territory which is associated with an independent state (i.e., Puerto Rico with the United States)."

This Puerto Rico could not do without the consent of Congress. Moreover, it could be maintained, although with less conviction, that Puerto Rico had not determined its constitution in 1952, as the resolution demanded, "without outside interference." Congress had modified the Puerto Rican constitution, even if those modifications had subsequently been accepted in a referendum — a referendum that presented the Puerto Rican people with only one choice, Commonwealth or nothing.

The Decolonization Committee injected new vigor into the process of decolonization and give the *independentistas* the in-

ternational forum they needed. As the independence movement grew steadily weaker in Puerto Rico itself, and the PIP
lost its position as the second party on the island (by 1960, its
share of the vote had sunk to a mere 2.8 percent), so pressure
in the United Nations became its major tactic, especially for
Juan Mari Bras, leader of the MPI (which he defined as a
"nonpartisan movement" of *independentistas*) and subsequently
founder of the PSP. "Our demand before the United Nations,"
he asserted, "is the *only legal way* that Puerto Rico has to obtain
self-determination and sovereignty." [Emphasis added.] For
Mari Bras, the application of Resolution 1514(XV) meant
only one thing: immediate, sovereign independence. This dubious proposition the *independentistas* sought to establish as
"U.N. law."

The midwives for the birth of national independence for the
Republic of Puerto Rico were to be Cuba and the nonaligned
nations, with the support of the Soviet bloc. It was Cuba that
possessed the political will to force the issue of Puerto Rico,
year after year, on the agenda of the Decolonization Committee. Even as a student, Fidel Castro had seen that Puerto Rico
was the "Achilles heel" of the United States and that the independence movement could be exploited to unmask the
United States as "the enemy of Latin American freedom."
"Everyone in Latin America," he told the General Assembly in
1960, "knows that the U.S. government has always laid down
the law that might is right, which it has used to destroy the
Puerto Rican nation and maintain its dominion over the island." Resolution 1514(XV) applied to "all other territories
which have not yet obtained independence." In the Cuban
view, these included Puerto Rico. At the end of a long speech
on Puerto Rico, Raul Roa, the Cuban foreign minister, concluded that it "is still a dependent territory placed outside the
jurisdiction of the United Nations by a clever stratagem," that

is, Resolution 748(VIII), passed when the United States and the Western powers still dominated the General Assembly.

This domination ended with the emergence of the Afro-Asian bloc. It was the aim of the Soviet Union, Cuba, and their *independentista* allies to secure the support of the nonaligned nations for the cause of Puerto Rican independence and then to use that support to force the Puerto Rican issue to the attention of the United Nations. The World Council of Peace, a Soviet-backed organization, meeting in Mexico City in March 1961, was the first body to "open our road to internationalize the Puerto Rican case."[16] More important, the Cairo Conference of Non-Aligned States of 1964, with Mari Bras in the wings, took up the issue of Puerto Rico. Strengthened by the Cairo declaration on Puerto Rico's right to independence, what Muñoz Marín called the "little game" of Mari Bras and Cuba, was to get the Puerto Rican issue on the agenda of the Decolonization Committee under Resolution 1514(XV) and, via its recommendations, refer it to the General Assembly. Thus, the triumph of the United States in 1953 might be turned into defeat.

By 1965, the lobbying of the *independentistas* and the pressure of Cuba to include Puerto Rico on the agenda of the Committee began to bring results. The Ghanaian ambassador, president of the General Assembly, maintained that the United Nations had a moral right to enquire into a state of affairs which puzzled him: "It is true that Puerto Rico is no longer a non – self-governing territory, but at the same time neither is it independent." The United States was successful in blocking the Cuban request to bring Puerto Rico's status to the General Assembly. But, if the road to the General Assembly was closed, the Cubans could still hope to force the Decolonization Committee to place the issue of Puerto Rico's colonial status on its agenda.

Its efforts succeeded in 1972 and 1973. The *independentista* case that, in spite of the 1953 resolution, Puerto Rico was a colonial territory "which had not yet attained independence" was given a full public hearing. The committee recognized Puerto Rico's "inalienable right to self-determination and independence in accordance with General Assembly Resolution 1514 (XV)." It agreed to keep the question under review, stating that no measures should be taken that might prejudice self-determination, and resolved that its Working Party should examine the procedures to be adopted with respect to the application of 1514(XV) to Puerto Rico.[17]

This was heralded as a "historic decision" by Mari Bras, as "a triumph of the anticolonial nations against the efforts of the United States to maintain a colonial ghetto in the hemisphere."[18] The "brutal pressure" of the United States had failed at last. On their return from New York, Mari Bras and Berríos Martínez were welcomed by crowds chanting "Yankee go home"; the Stars and Stripes were ritually burned.

The *independentista* euphoria of 1972 – 73 was short-lived: in 1975, the committee postponed the issue *sine die*. The "brutal pressure" of the United States was still effective. Having failed in the Decolonization Committee, Cuba took the issue of Puerto Rican independence to the meeting in Lima of the foreign ministers of the nonaligned countries: nine countries that had voted for postponement on the committee now voted for the "rapid decolonization" of Puerto Rico, and recognized the PIP and the PSP as the representatives of the Puerto Rican people. To *independentistas*, this was proof that "brutal pressure" had been exercised on the Decolonization Committee.

It was not until 1977 that the Decolonization Committee mounted a major onslaught on American imperialism in the Caribbean. The PIP pointed to President Ford's support of statehood in 1976 as proof of the persistence of the "dominance and arrogance of the old colonial powers." Ford's blunt refusal to accept the recommendations of the ad hoc committee was the "best evidence of the United States' notion of self-determination.... it is obvious that to the United States Government 'self-determination' as far as Puerto Rico is concerned means adjusting the aspirations and needs of the Puerto Ricans to the military and economic needs of the United States."[19] Mari Bras now demanded "the immediate, unconditional, and absolute recognition by the Government of the United States of the right to independence of the people of Puerto Rico of all their sovereign rights and powers from the Congress and Government of the United States, in accordance with General Assembly Resolution 1514(XV)."[20] This was to demand immediate independence and the "transfer of powers" — that is, the withdrawal of the United States from Puerto Rico. Once liberated from the American presence and the operations of what *independentistas* consider its repressive agencies, the Puerto Rican people would choose independence, even though every poll and election result seemed to prove the contrary. Nations, Berríos Martínez told me, do not commit suicide.

The majority of the members of the Decolonization Committee regarded its actions as a fulfilment of its duties and perceived the 1953 resolution of the General Assembly as implying that Puerto Rico was under the jurisdiction of the United Nations and thought that the resolution could, therefore, be reconsidered. The United States viewed Cuba as using the committee for its own *political* purposes, relying on the support of the Afro-Asian and Communist bloc. It dismissed the actions of the committee on three counts. First, the U.S. delegation argued that "in view of the self-governing status of Puerto Rico and the fact that the nature of its relationship with the United States is based on the free expression of the will of the Puerto Rican people, the United States government regards discussion of Puerto Rico's status in international forums, particularly in forums which deal with colonial issues, as inappropriate."[21] There could be no doubt but that the Puerto Ricans had exercised freely their right to self-determination.[22] Second, the U.S. position was that as long as Resolution 748(VIII) of 1953 of the General Assembly had not been reversed, Puerto Rico had been taken out of the jurisdiction of the United Nations. Last, the attempt to raise the issue of Puerto Rico's status either in the Decolonization Committee or in the General Assembly was regarded as "an act of interference in the internal affairs of the United States and Puerto Rico."

On all counts, the actions of the committee were considered *ultra vires*. In this the United States was supported by the two major Puerto Rican parties. Both parties passed a joint resolution (No. 452) condemning the committee's action in 1972 as "flagrant interference."[23] The PPD view was that Puerto Rico had democratically chosen Commonwealth in 1952. It therefore rejected "any outside intervention designed to impose on Puerto Rico terms which violate the free self-determination already expressed by the Puerto Rican people with regard to their destiny and political status."[24] According to the PNP, the United Nations had no right to interfere in the domestic concerns of the U.S. citizens. Governor Ferré said "the vote of the committee [in 1972] doesn't mean a thing." In 1965, he had written to the Cuban ambassador to the United Nations, stating that: "I condemn your intromission in affairs that only matter to the free American citizens of this island and the Congress of the Nation. You are the least indicated to talk about obtaining freedom to men who live under institutions that respect the dignity of the human being and enjoy civil rights to the utmost. Men like you, with blood on their hands, represent not the noble people of Cuba, but an assaulter that has established in our sister island one of the most odious tyrannies known."

The United States dismissed the committee's activities because it could not acknowledge that it possessed a colony. Such an assertion could only be the invention of its political enemies —of Cuba and the Communist bloc, together with the support they might rally in the Afro-Asian bloc for which decolonization was a passion. Such interventions would be treated with glacial indifference.

The U.S. case, it has been argued, went by default:[25] that case was that the overwhelming majority of Puerto Ricans still voted for parties supporting association with the United States, a proposition that its opponents sought to rebut by dissecting the results of the plebiscite of 1967 and by assertions of illegitimate U.S. pressure on the voters. Such arguments could convince only those to whom the United States was, by definition, the imperialist power par excellence. Nevertheless, since the United States cold-shouldered the committee and continued to intone the litany that the status of Puerto Rico was a domestic concern of U.S. citizens of Puerto Rico and Congress, Cuba was allowed to set the terms of discourse and, in some measure, to succeed in its endeavors to present its dubious interpretation of Resolution 1514(XV) as "U.N. law." Nor was the annual assertion that Puerto Rico was a colony without its effect on American opinion. "There is a colonial taint in Puerto Rico's status," argued an editorial of the *New York Times* in January 1982, "no matter how hotly Washington disputes the charge at the U.N."[26]

It was The Decolonization Committee that kept the issue of the status of Puerto Rico alive as an international concern. Every year, Mari Bras and Berríos Martínez, supported by a variety of independence organizations, argued the case for independence. Every year, the committee harked back to Resolution 1514 (XV), lamenting that the United States had taken no steps to implement the transfer of powers, *en passant* accusing the United States of political repression and military occupation. Yet nothing happened.

The U.S. delegation had nothing to fear from what remained a propaganda assault mounted by its enemies, the Soviet bloc and Cuba. Neither of the two main Puerto Rican political parties accepted the jurisdiction of the committee and had protested, along with the U.S. delegation, that Puerto Rico's status was a domestic concern of the citizens of Puerto Rico and the United States. But in 1978, their position changed dramatically. Both the PPD and the PNP came to the United Nations for the meetings of the Decolonization Committee.

In 1978, the PPD was in disarray and on the defensive. A statehooder, Governor Romero, had won the election of 1976 and threatened a referendum on statehood should he win the elections of 1980. The party was disillusioned by the failure in Congress of the ad hoc committee's recommendations for increased autonomy and reeling under the shock of President Ford's declaration of support for statehood. "We must strike back," they said. The old alliance between the Democrats and the PPD was in bad shape. President Carter's support, in July 1978, for Puerto Rico's right of self-determination and for "alternative futures" for Puerto Rico seemed less a harmless statement of democratic principle, or a rehash of President Eisenhower's declaration of 1953, than an indication that the White House was prepared to consider statehood as advocated by Romero. "Carter was playing dirty."[27] Battered and badly in need of a political pickup, the PPD saw in the United Nations and the hearings of The Decolonization Committee an arena in which to state in public its case for "culminating" Commonwealth by endowing it with greater autonomy.

The refusal of the United States to develop Commonwealth constituted "immorality"; the growing power of the federal government without a corresponding growth of the Commonwealth's own power threatened a relapse into colonialism: "It is precisely the absence of development and growth," the representatives of PROELA, the pressure group of the radical autonomists in the party, testified to the committee, "despite the persistent claims of the Puerto Rican people, that casts doubt on the validity of that status as a formula for the decolonization of Puerto Rico — and these doubts are felt in Puerto Rico, in the United States and in international forums." These doubts would be resolved if the United Nations recognized Commonwealth as a legitimate form of free association and insisted on its further development "until the maximum self-government has been achieved." Public protest at the United Nations might prove an effective weapon where commissions and representations to Congress had failed.

It was this strategy that led to a startling development: an alliance of the PSP and the PPD using the Cuban Mission to the United Nations to "resist the annexationist offensive" of Governor Romero.

At a luncheon on July 26, 1978, Mari Bras and Marco Rigau, acting on behalf of Hernández Colón, sketched out a joint proposal on the back of a table napkin; on August 6, eluding the police in a borrowed car, Mari Bras met Hernández Colón in the mountains at Aguas Buenas — a symbolic place, since it was there, in 1970, that the PPD had declared for a wider autonomy.[28]

The gist of the agreement was to present a joint resolution in the Decolonization Committee. Mari Bras insisted on the inalienable right of Puerto Rico to independence and the principle of the transfer of powers; Hernández Colón on the acceptance of free association, which implied the power to modify the existing Commonwealth status without denying the legitimacy of its origins. Mari Bras accepted the resolution because it included the central demand of the PSP — the transfer of powers. Without such a transfer, Mari Bras was convinced that the activities of the federal agencies and the police, from which he himself had suffered, would make a mockery of self-determination when exercised under "colonial" rule. But in order to rally the "progressive autonomists" of the PPD he accepted free association. Free association, he argued, was open-ended, acceptable if "the people wanted it" and could be later transformed into independence, a choice Mari Bras assumed "the people" would "sooner or later" adopt.

Once in New York for the meeting of the Decolonization Committee in August, the PPD delegation, after a disappointing interview with U.S. Representative to the United Nations Donald McHenry, made contact, via Mari Bras, with the Cubans. Hernández Colón was never forgiven for this by his political opponents. In the election campaign of 1980, photographs of Colón beside Castro were faked to present him as a fellow traveler.

The circumstantial alliance between Mari Bras and the "progressive autonomists" threatened to break down on the "transfer of powers." This was "the magic phrase," to Mari Bras, without which a resolution would be devoid of value. But for the autonomists of the PPD, to accept the point of view that without a previous transfer of powers the Puerto Ricans could not exercise their right of self-determination threatened to deny the legitimacy of Commonwealth itself, since in the plebiscites of 1952 and 1967 the United States had not withdrawn its agencies and military establishment from the island.[29]

The resolution adopted by the Decolonization Committee bridged the gap by including the demands of both the PSP and the PPD. It stated that self-determination should be exercised "in accordance with Resolution 1514(XV)" — the demand of the PSP — *and* that "any form of free association between Puerto Rico and the United States" was legitimate provided it was "in terms of political equality" recognizing "the sovereignty of the people of Puerto Rico."[30] This satisfied the radical autonomism of the PPD. Statehood was excluded, a "crushing blow" for the PNP; Commonwealth was no longer stigmatized as "colonial" — the word did not occur in the resolution.

In 1977, Hernández Colón had acted with the U.S. delegation. Now the bridge was broken. So was the bridge between Berríos Martínez and Mari Bras. Whereas to the PSP and the PPD it was essential to defeat the statehooders, for Berríos Martínez the main target remained the PPD and the main task to label Commonwealth as "colonial."[31]

The PIP viewed the acceptance of free association in the 1978 Resolution as nonsensical and dangerous. The recognition of free association implied that:

... a colony can exercise its right to self-determination by remaining a colony.... It must be clearly established that independence is the only decolonization formula that would be in keeping with General Assembly Resolution 1514(XV). It would be a negation of the purpose for which the Special Committee was established if the Committee were to lend itself in any way to an endorsement of colonialism by agreeing to a mere change of name, under the title of "free association," as a way out of the present colonial situation. We are, therefore, requesting the omission of any reference to the concept of "free association," of the kind included in the 1978 resolution, since this reference has only served as an attempt to confuse the issue of the alternative solutions to our country's colonial situation, for the benefit of the country which is intervening in our affairs.

... We cannot accept the notion that any people or nation can legitimately exercise its right to self-determination without and until it is sovereign or independent. Just as a slave cannot choose "freely" to continue to be a slave, a nation without sovereignty or independence, in other words a nation without freedom, cannot make free decisions. It is absurd to talk of the "free" decisions of a slave.[32]

The appearance of former Governor Hernández Colón was not the only novelty in 1978. The PNP had consistently refused to appear before the committee. In 1978, Governor Romero testified. Just as the PPD wished to legitimize Commonwealth, so the PNP wished to insist that integration (i.e., statehood) was a legitimate escape from colonialism. It would strengthen the case for statehood if the present Commonwealth status was presented in public as colonial. But this statement had to be made *without recognizing the jurisdiction of the committee* to which it was addressed. According to Governor Romero, "The fact that we are a colony does not give the U.N. jurisdiction since we already have the constitutional and electoral means to decide."[33] However much the governor may have wished to alert American opinion to the defects of the present status of Puerto Rico and to convince it that statehood provided the only dignified exit from the colonial closet, he could not fly in the face of the official U.S. position at the United Nations: that Puerto Rico's status was a domestic concern of a democratic society of U.S. citizens in Puerto Rico and Congress and therefore outside the jurisdiction of the United Nations.

Romero could scarcely have expected a sympathetic hearing in the committee or from the galleries packed with the New York *independentista* claque. He presented Puerto Rico as a fully functioning democracy, as the defeats of the government in power in 1968, 1972, and 1976 demonstrated. Where such freedom existed — and it did not in many nations represented on the committee, Cuba included — and where over 90 percent of the electorate voted for the continuance of an association with the United States, to impose independence via Resolution 1514(XV) would "represent colonial status," a denial of the right of the Puerto Rican people to decide their own destiny.[34] Nevertheless, he too criticized Commonwealth as a quasi-colonial arrangement, but added that "we are free" to opt for "the vestiges of colonialism which characterize our relations with the United States." The committee members turned off their microphones in horror. The Cuban ambassador, Raul Roa, denounced Romero as a "traitor... who preferred a degrading yoke to the shining star of liberty and dignity." In response to the PNP's charge of the absence in Cuba of the democratic freedom enjoyed in Puerto Rico, he retorted, "It is not necessary to defend the Cuban Revolution against the lesser servants of the United States."

As might be expected, the U.S. Mission (in a muddled press release) rejected the resolution of the committee as *ultra vires*, as "denying the right of the people of Puerto Rico to self-determination" — a right fully recognized by President Carter, in his July proclamation. Its position remained that the United Nations had no right to interfere in what was a domestic concern of the United States and Puerto Rico: "On the question of United Nations jurisdiction, the United States believes that the United Nations effectively discharged its responsibilities in the matter through its 1953 decision. Moreover, through their elected representatives, the Puerto Rican people have declined the Committee of Twenty-Four's [the Decolonization Committee] jurisdiction. Any review by the United States of its position regarding jurisdiction would of course take due account of the wishes of the Puerto Ricans themselves. That is the only position which would be consistent with our views on self-determination."[35]

The novelty of 1978 lay less in the resolution of the committee than in the hearings at which *all* the major Puerto Rican political parties, from statehooders to nationalists, expressed in public their demand for a change in the status of Puerto Rico. "The 1978 Committee hearings," argued an article in the State Department's *Open Forum*, "were important in demonstrating to the world more clearly than ever before that, whatever

Puerto Ricans may think about the United States, they are clearly dissatisfied with the current status relationship .... This mass of negative testimony materially undercut the support for our position in the committee to defer the issue."[36] Even if "the Puerto Rican people" could not make up their minds what *future* status they wanted (professing respect for the right of self-determination *and* the insistence that the status quo was based on the exercise of that right had allowed the United States to coast along since 1953), it was clear that no party in Puerto Rico accepted the *existing* status.

It was in 1981 that the Cuban delegation thought it had brought off the victory it had sought so long: the reversal of the 1953 triumph of Muñoz Marín and the United States, which had taken Puerto Rico off the agenda of the General Assembly of the United Nations. In the past, Cuba had sought to force decolonization by proposing the immediate application of Resolution 1514(XV), only to be confronted by the refusal of the United States to put forward, as requested by the committee in 1980, a plan for decolonization. Now, in its resolution of 1981, the Decolonization Committee recommended that the case of Puerto Rico be put on the agenda of the General Assembly as a "separate item."

Mari Bras exulted. Decolonization was in sight. His quest for a "consensus on decolonization" had brought "progressive autonomists" (themselves engaged in what Severo Colberg of the PPD called "clarifying the collective conscience" of Puerto Ricans) to see that action in the United Nations would expose the United States as "blind and deaf" to the Puerto Rican demands for the development of Commonwealth. The statehooders were outraged. They rejected "interference in a domestic issue."[37] The PPD and the PSP were in an unholy alliance with those (Cuba and Iraq) who wished to solve the

Puerto Rican question by "foreign intervention." The Puerto Rican people would reject both the "Socialist Republic" of Mari Bras and "independence disguised as free association" propounded by the "progressive autonomists" of the PPD.

Rubén Berríos Martínez of the PIP accepted the resolution without enthusiasm. It was "dangerous" to the cause of independence, since it recognized the legitimacy of free association, which the Cuban delegation admitted as possible, even desirable. To Berríos, the right tactic was to apply Resolution 1514(XV), with independence as the only solution. He was in danger of being acted off stage by Mari Bras with his appeal for an island consensus on decolonization.

The discomfort of the United States with the 1981 resolution was evident. It was "totally improper for the Decolonization Committee" to discuss "a purely domestic affair... removed [in 1953] from the competence of the General Assembly." "Right now [the Resolution]," a member of the U.S. Mission confessed, "is just a nasty nuisance; but if the Assembly acts it could become a political threat."[38] It was the aim of U.S. policy to remove that threat by blocking the issue of Puerto Rico from the General Assembly's agenda.

The political threat lay in the unpleasantness of being arraigned by the Third World delegations as a South Africa of the Western Hemisphere and in the complication the Puerto Rican question might import into the United States' already ragged relations with Latin America. The U.S. delegation dismissed Latin American interest in Puerto Rico as token politics: "In the end," a spokesman for the U.S. delegation told me in 1980, "they [the Latin American nations] will do nothing."

This is a half-truth. It is clear that the relationship of, say, Venezuela and Mexico with the United States is conditioned by more important issues — oil and immigration, for example — than the independence of Puerto Rico, and that even the grant of independence to Puerto Rico would remove an irritant rather than substantially improve the relationship between the United States and its Latin neighbors. But Puerto Rico remains an irritant. Off the record, the U.S. delegation described the passing of the 1981 resolution as a "Communist ploy." This it was in the sense that Cuba, as always, provided the necessary political will. Yet parts of the resolution were signed by Chile and Venezuela.

It is the attitude of Venezuela that was particularly illuminating. Mari Bras and Berríos Martínez had both canvassed in Caracas for Venezuela's vote. Venezuela is pursuing an active policy in the Caribbean and seeks a position of leadership in the Third World. In 1980, as a new member of the Decolonization Committee, it voted against the United States. In 1981, it supported those parts of the resolution that did not recommend reference to the General Assembly but that asserted the Puerto Rican people's "inalienable right to self-determination and independence."

Why did Venezuela vote as it did? President Herrera Campins's oracular statement makes it clear: "It's not that we don't like the boy, it's just that we don't have confidence in the godparents." The Venezuelan delegation had no wish to support the Cuban resolution; Cuba's pro-Soviet stance and its ambitions in the Caribbean had no attractions. But to support the independence of Puerto Rico was a cheap way to display Venezuela's freedom, as a Third World power, from United States' pressure and its fidelity to the legacy of Bolívar the Liberator. A month after the debates of the Decolonization Committee, Herrera Campins, who shares none of Romulo Betancourt's admiration for Muñoz Marín and the Commonwealth he created, welcomed the independence of Puerto Rico as a sovereign *Latin American* nation as the hope of *all* Latin Americans. If President Reagan is to implement his program for a Caribbean rescued from Castroism by private enterprise, he will need the cooperation of Venezuela, already a significant investor in the Caribbean. The "nuisance" of Puerto Rico can only complicate the president's endeavors.

Battle was joined when, at the November 1981 session of the General Assembly, the Decolonization Committee submitted an Omnibus Resolution (A/36/L20) that contained a request that Puerto Rico be put on the agenda of the General Assembly. The United States learned that the U.N. Secretariat would interpret a general approval of the resolution as instruction to put Puerto Rico on the 1982 agenda. This would represent a defeat of the position that the United States had maintained since 1953 — that Puerto Rico was not a concern of the United Nations.

The U.S. delegation reacted with the vigor characteristic of the Reagan administration. Ambassador Jeane Kirkpatrick made it clear to the nonaligned nations that, while abstention was understandable, a vote against the United States would carry penalties. The U.S. delegation immediatley submitted an amendment that the General Assembly make no decision on the recommendation concerning Puerto Rico. Whenever an amendment contains a matter of substance, the president of the Assembly postpones a decision to give member countries the opportunity to consult their home governments. The U.S. delegation immediately rallied its friends and threatened its enemies; it did not regard Puerto Rico as a matter of indifference. When it became apparent that the U.S. amendment would find cosponsors, a consensus was worked out through which the United States would drop the amendment and the president of the General Assembly would make a statement that while the committee had recommended the inclusion of Puerto Rico, acceptance of the Omnibus Resolution did not imply a vote on Puerto Rico.

The U.S. delegation had saved face: "Not a great victory but the issue was resolved to our satisfaction." It represented a moral setback for the Decolonization Committee; there had been a sign that it was possible, by resolute action, to resist the pressure for decolonization. It was, perhaps, a fortunate outcome of the United Nations itself. The United Nations had long lost its appeal to American public opinion; to force a declaration from the General Assembly that would have publicly condemned American rule in Puerto Rico and demanded an immediate transfer of power would have been an outcome that the United States would simply have refused to accept — encouraging those in Congress who would like to see the United States no longer burdened with contributions to an organization dominated by its critics.

The reaction of the General Assembly will depend less on what the United States does in Puerto Rico than on its policies elsewhere, particularly in Latin America. It can count on a certain ennui at the end of a decade of decolonization. The nonaligned countries cannot do anything but abstain — an attitude that the United States understands—or support Cuba, which the U.S. Mission resents. But it is open to question whether Cuba, the one country that has consistently shown the political will needed to force the Puerto Rican issue, year after year, onto the attention of the United Nations, will allow the cause of Puerto Rican independence to remain an obstacle in the path of some form of "tactical" rapprochement with the United States. Whether Cuban approaches, in the form of declarations of pacific intentions to visiting U.S. intellectuals, represent anything more than an effort to sow confusion in gullible minds must likewise be in doubt. What is certain is that the present U.S. administration rejects all Cuban hints of "mutual restraint." Reagan views Cuba as the carrier of a "Marxist virus" that may infect the whole Caribbean.[39] As long as the administration pursues a policy of inflexible hostility to Cuba, so Cuba will continue to embarrass the United States by arraigning it as a colonial power in Puerto Rico and as the immoral surviving representative of the imperialism rejected by the international community.

Part V

THE ELUSIVE
QUEST

15.

A CASE STUDY: 1980–82

This chapter describes the course of Puerto Rican politics, at times in some detail, from the election campaign of 1980 until the early months of 1982. Its intention is to give some insight into the political mores of the island and the effects in Puerto Rico of drastic changes, at least at the level of rhetoric, in the political landscape and the dominant political philosophies of the United States. It aims to convey the atmosphere of the election and of the subsequent political infighting and to examine the reaction in Puerto Rico to the policies proposed by the Reagan administration insofar as those policies were considered by Puerto Ricans as affecting the well-being of the island. The administration's proposals touched the raw nerve of Puerto Rico's relationship with the United States, reviving the latent paranoia that has haunted that relationship since 1900: that the interests of Puerto Rico count for little in national politics.

Nineteen eighty-one, Governor Romero announced, would be a year of decision. Having won the elections of November 1980, he would call a plebiscite that would settle Puerto Rico's "destiny"; the rising statehood tide, apparent since 1968, would drown both Commonwealth and the *independentistas,* leaving statehood as the democratic choice of the "Puerto Rican people." But this was not to be. The elections produced a legislature in which the Popular Democratic Party (PPD) won by the narrowest of margins; the governor himself was reelected by a mere 3,400 votes. The Puerto Rican electorate failed to respond to the governor's call to settle its destiny. He abandoned the plebiscite. "It is absolutely clear," he confessed, "that neither the legislative power nor the executive power has the electoral mandate to significantly alter our future destiny."[1] Far from leading Puerto Rico to its destiny, to Berríos Martínez of the PIP, master as always of the telling phrase, the elections threatened "four years of nothingness."

Given Governor Romero's drive for statehood — "the annexationist offensive" as it was termed by his opponents — status appeared an issue in the 1980 election; this had not been the case in 1976. "Status," the governor announced on October 5, 1980, "will be more important than in any other campaign." Each contender sought, and blazoned in the press, backing from leading congressmen, less perhaps because Congress must consent to a status change than because the word of a major American politician carries the psychological weight of a papal pronouncement in the political world of San Juan Washington watchers; it blesses him who receives, costing little to him who gives. Senator Howard Baker, who had come out for "statehood now" in the primaries, denounced the PPD's "New Thesis" as a step on the road to independence. "I do not see how Congress," House Minority Leader John J. Rhodes was quoted as saying, "could sympathize with these proposals" (i.e., the New Thesis). On the other hand, Senator J. Bennett Johnston's constitutional hesitations about *jibaro* statehood and *Washing-*

ton Post editorials served the purposes of the PPD. *Jibaro* state-hood was portrayed as a "false Utopia" that would never be turned into a reality by Congress.

The arguments of both parties not only tended to cancel each other out but must have left the electorate in a state of some confusion as to the economic effects of statehood or Commonwealth; and it was these effects that concerned most voters. What could the ordinary citizen make of Byzantine (and inconclusive) arguments about the effects of U.S. minimum wage legislation as opposed to the prospect provided by Puerto Rican control of wage levels? (The PPD argued that U.S. minimum wage legislation tended to make wages "stagnate"; the PNP argued that they benefited the workers.) The favorable or disastrous economic effects of statehood, Commonwealth, or independence are matters of dogmatic conviction to their committed upholders, rather than demonstrable propositions. As to federal payments — the handouts that played such an important part in the lives of Puerto Ricans — each party insisted that the status it defended provided the best lever for easing payments from Washington.

Though all but the most politically innocent voter must have realized that the way he cast his vote implied a status choice, no outside observer of the campaign, except in the last weeks, would have guessed that status was the main issue.

It was the Puerto Rican Independence Party (PIP) candidate for Guaynabo for the House of Representatives who declared that voters were not interested in status but in "security and honesty."[2] All parties stressed that it was their policies that would best provide security in the home and in the streets, as if stopping burglary, mugging, and car theft was the major issue for most Puerto Ricans.

Given the concern for "honesty" — rather than *dignidad*, the key word of the campaign — the campaign against Governor

Romero became obsessively concerned with two *causes célèbres:* Cerro Maravilla and the Calderón case. Properly exploited by his opponents, these would nail Romero as a politician whose authoritarian attitudes made him indifferent to civil rights; his attempt to halt investigation into his "crimes" by a gag order on the courts in the Cerro Maravilla case could, skilfully used, convert him into an island replica of President Nixon embroiled in a Puerto Rican Watergate. "Cerro Maravilla," senior PPD Senator Nogueras told me, "could cost us the election." (That is, if the revelations of police officer Andrades [see below] turned out to be true.)

Cerro Maravilla became a *cause célèbre* because of the alleged complicity of Governor Romero in the killing of two young Nationalist terrorists by the police in July 1978. Romero's opponents claimed that they had been led to their deaths in a police ambush by an undercover agent.

Immediately after the killings, Romero had, ill-advisedly and typically, greeted the policemen as "heroes." By November, their heroic qualities had been severely eroded by the investigative journalism of the *San Juan Star,* by the promise of sensational revelations of complicity from above by a police officer named Andrades, and by the evidence in suits brought against the police by the taxi driver who had been shanghaied into taking the terrorists from Ponce to Cerro Maravilla and the parents of the two terrorists — one of whom was the son of the distinguished Puerto Rican novelist Pedro Juan Soto. These suits, together with two innvestigations by the Commonwealth Justice Department and two federal grand juries, kept Cerro Maravilla on the front pages for months on end; it became a festering sore in Puerto Rican political life.

Two points were critical. Did the police fire two volleys, simulating that the terrorists had fired first when in fact they had been shot down in cold blood? Did the police, as Andrades asserted, act on orders from above and if so, how "high" was above?

It would be tedious to enter the labyrinth of conflicting testimony.[3] The point about this continued concern, the daily cliff-hangers in the press, is that Cerro Maravilla was the opposition's main instrument in the attempted destruction of Romero. Mari Bras, of the Puerto Rican Socialist Party (PSP), bought half an hour's radio time to present a minute dissection of the evidence in order to prove that Cerro Maravilla was but one episode in a deliberate campaign, mounted by the governor to intimidate prospective *independentista* voters by murder — "a prefabricated essay in police terrorism"; Romero was "the intellectual author" of a vulgar assassination plot. The high point came when Hernández Colón, in a television broadcast on October 15, publicly accused Romero of authorizing murder and then attempting a Watergate-style cover-up by consenting to the rigging of police evidence.[4] Romero dismissed Andrades' statements as "political soap opera" and stuck to his defense — more muted, it is true — of the police. His characteristic counteraccusation was that Hernández Colón was psychologically unbalanced.

One curious personal footnote to the Cerro Maravilla affair illuminates the capacity of Puerto Ricans to overestimate the interest in their concerns and the knowledge of them and the importance given to them outside the island. I was asked by one of Romero's opponents to "test the reaction of the [national] Democrats" to Cerro Maravilla. Would the affair, if properly exploited by Senator Edward Kennedy, not ensure the defeat of Romero's ally President Carter, whose attorney general was alleged to have kept the governor out of trouble in the federal courts? No one in New York — and only the lawyers concerned in Washington — had heard of Cerro Maravilla.

The PPD used the Calderón case as they had used Cerro Maravilla: Hernández Colón sought to brand Romero, if not as a criminal himself, then as an associate of criminals prepared to cover up their activities. The Justice Department rejected the testimony of a disgruntled policewoman and an imprisoned prostitute, which sought to establish that Calderón, the district attorney of Mayagüez, was an associate of the local Mafia engaged in the numbers game and drug trafficking, and whose capture in a police trap in the local Hilton Hotel had been prevented on instructions from above. The PPD put out a newspaper advertisement showing Calderón in handcuffs, and implying that Romero was his protector.

If the PPD tried to brand Romero as an associate of criminals, the New Progressive Party (PNP) had little moral ground for indignation. In the 1976 election, the PNP put out a poster headed "All the Governor's Men." A portrait of Hernández Colón was surrounded by a "rogues' gallery." It included his own brother, supposedly saved from bankruptcy by an opportune government land purchase; Teodoro Moscoso, accused of holiday travel at government expense; and PPD representatives, accused of luxuriating in expensive hotels — the return for political favors to their proprietors. Moreover, in the 1980 campaign, if the PPD showed Romero surrounded by shady associates, the PNP propaganda showed Hernández Colón hand-in-hand with murderer El Negro Tanco, once employed as a minor figure in a Hernández Colón sports program.

When Hernández Colón could not convincingly be exhibited as a friend of criminals, he was branded as the ally of revolutionaries. Posters showed him grasping the hand of PSP leader Mari Bras, ally of Cuba. The deal made between them in 1978, it was argued, was continued in their joint exploitation of Cerro Maravilla. They were, Romero claimed on television, *comparsas*, confederates in political crime. The PPD was not merely out to destroy Romero, it had formed an opportunist alliance with a party out to destroy democracy itself. A PPD victory would be the first step in the "Cubanization" of Puerto Rico. The PNP's television campaign was both effective and unscrupulous, not the least of which was one slot that gave the impression that the PPD had abstracted gold from the Treasury.

Neither Cerro Maravilla nor the Calderón case was used to exploit the status issue. In September, a wearying electorate — as on the mainland, campaigns are rituals that exhaust candidates and electorate alike — was galvanized by an issue that directly affected Puerto Rico and involved its relations with the United States. President Carter, faced in an election year with the hostility of his own electors to the Cuban and Haitian refugees, proposed to "dump" Haitian refugees, of whom there were some 8,000 in America, in Puerto Rico — where no one could vote in the presidential election. The site chosen was Fort Allen in southern Puerto Rico.

Governor Romero, while anxious to accommodate the president, soon sensed that welcoming the Haitian refugees would hand a weapon to his adversaries. He was immediately accused by the PPD of truckling to the president and hiding his subservience from the electorate;[5] if Puerto Rico controlled immigration, as the PPD's New Thesis demanded, undesirables could not be dumped on Puerto Rico by presidential order. The PNP countered that Carter could act as he did because, under Commonwealth (the PPD's creation), Puerto Rico remained a colony. Senator Orestes Ramos, a hard-line statehooder, claimed that Carter had sent the refugees "without the consent of our government." But Puerto Rico had no clout in Washington, which only statehood could confer. A president would have to pay attention to a state of the Union with more votes than those possessed by thirty-two of the states. By sending the refugees to Puerto Rico, claimed Hernán Padilla, PNP mayor of San Juan, Carter was reinforcing the theory "promoted by Fidel Castro" that the United States was an imperialist power and that Commonwealth status condemned Puerto Rico to the condition of "a weak colony." Berríos Martínez, president of the PIP, viewed the refugee episode as revealing "naked" colonialism.

Governor Carlos Romero claimed that he had acted as strongly as he could with the feeble weapons left to him in a constitution bequeathed by the Populares. He filed a suit in federal court; Judge Torruella, who had favored the Navy in Vieques, upheld Romero's resistance on the grounds that the refugees at Fort Allen would constitute a health and environmental hazard. "Carlos" (i.e., Romero) ran a full-page advertisement in the local newspapers; "supported by reason and truth, [he had] confronted the president of the United States in defense of the best interests of his people, ignoring the political demagoguery of the minority parties." He went to the courts and achieved a triumph for Puerto Rico, "a triumph for Democracy." Pedro Vázquez, Puerto Rico's secretary of State, ostentatiously absented himself from a Hispanic fund-raising dinner for Carter. Romero defended Vázquez. Puerto Rico, the colony, was reduced to such symbolic acts for want of the effective political powers that would come only with statehood. The president of the United States would not dare to treat Wisconsin or Florida as he had treated Puerto Rico, where there were no votes to lose.

The PPD sought to play on the Puerto Ricans' dislike for refugees, including the Cubans, who had become the "Jews of Puerto Rico" and who were, as it happened, enthusiastic supporters of statehood and the PNP. Demonstrations paraded against "Cuban worms"; "Puerto Rico is a great nation, not a garbage can."[6] To play on such sentiments was a tasteless gesture of electoral desperation. Could a country that had sought to "solve" its unemployment problem by exporting it to New York with dignity deny Cuban and Haitian exiles a temporary home in Puerto Rico?[7] The arguments between statehooders and the supporters of Commonwealth canceled each other out, and neither was convincing. Was Romero correct in arguing that statehood was the only real protection against a horde of Haitian blacks and Cuban delinquents? Would the power to control immigration into Puerto Rico, claimed in the PPD's New Thesis, ever be granted by Congress?

Electoral predictions based on the erosion of the social basis of the PPD, on its failure to replace rural populism by urban populism, and on the "exhaustion" of its model for economic development proved false. Voter loyalty remained strong, reinforced by the party's image as the heir of Muñoz. In the last days of the campaign, Muñoz's seventy-year-old widow made a series of emotional if rambling speeches consecrating his memory.[8] The wavering ranks of the faithful were rallied by the old cry of culture in danger: the PPD was the last defense against Romero's intended "destruction of Puerto Rican culture." Romero's appointment of a natural scientist and PNP militant to the directorship of the Institute of Puerto Rican Culture (ICP) was seen as a "political assault on the ICP" and as representing the determination of a minority to "thrust Americanism down the throats of Puerto Ricans," as part of a general offensive to destroy every institution that opposed "annexation," from the bar association to the Olympic sports committee.[9]

The "triumphalism" of the PNP, which one could not fail to notice, induced a certain defensive pessimism in the ranks of the Populares. The election result was, however, a qualified victory for the PPD. At least the "annexationist" offensive had been stopped short. The cross-voting of the PSP and the PIP, combined with an abnormal level of abstention by PNP voters in the urban districts, favored the PPD. The PPD may also have benefited from the fact that its majorities came from districts that were atypical of the island vote; it won six "at-large" seats (i.e., on an all-island vote), whereas the PNP gained only five. The PNP failed to deepen its 1976 inroads into PPD strongholds like Humacoa, Arecibo, and Guayama. Wise after the event, commentators pointed out that the closely contested Democratic primaries (in which Senator Edward Kennedy, favoring the PPD, was only narrowly defeated by Carter, the ally of Romero) should have been a warning that the PPD was still a strong force in Puerto Rican political life. During the campaign the PPD capitalized on "fear" of statehood as a leap into the unknown. Commonwealth was "a practical reality much more familiar than promised statehood."[10] The Puerto Rican electorate had shied away from a final choice. All PNP voters are not necessarily enthusiastic statehooders (in 1976, a poll showed 30 percent of them indifferent to statehood), but one section was far from indifferent: the committed statehooders of the Cuban colony. Without their numbers, Romero might well have lost the election.

No one could have guessed from the enthusiasm that accompanied his electoral caravan as it toured the island that Rubén Berríos and his party would go down to a humiliating defeat. Once more, it seemed, "psychological" *independentismo* could not be translated into votes, and the PIP was reduced to its middle-class core.[11] The most probable explanation for the poor showing of the PIP is that, in order to avoid victory for Romero and statehood, some *independentistas* voted PPD. Hernández Colón (October 13) appealed to *independentistas*. Only two parties, he told them, stood any chance of victory: to stop a plebiscite "managed" by the PNP, which, if won, would join Puerto Rico indissolubly to the Union, *independentistas* should vote PPD. Such defensive tactics were implied in some of Mari Bras's speeches; though his platform was that only the PSP could provide "a real opposition," he advised cross-voting to defeat the enemy-in-chief: "the Fascist clique of the PNP."[12] Given to conspiracy theories, the PIP, to whom the "alliance" of the PSP and the PPD in support of autonomy threatens to weaken a party committed to outright independence, argued that Washington, irritated at Romero's truculence over the Fort Allen issue, wished to bring him down by fostering an unholy alliance of Socialists and Populares.[13] Such are the intricacies of colonial politics.

It was not only the results of the election, which could satisfy no one, but the tasteless verbal violence of the campaign that flung Puerto Ricans into one of their periodic fits of self-doubt. "We are an anguished nation scourged by crime, corruption, degeneration, politicization, and *revanchisme*." Verbal violence there was; it lowered the whole tone of political life. On October 14, Severo Colberg, a powerful figure in the PPD, announced he would reveal three new "enormous" scandals. "Severo," replied Senator Nogueras of the PNP, "is a vile coward who can only live with other degenerates of his own species; that is to say he suffers from political homosexuality... a drunken politician."[14] The despair of reasonable men at these competitive exercises in character destruction was expressed by Fernando Picó, a Jesuit and nephew of one of Muñoz's most distinguished administrators: "It is a shame and an appalling measure of the vacuity of our political debate that one candidate calls the governor a murderer and the governor calls him a madman."[15] Romero was called a "Fascist," a Puerto Rican Hitler; Hernández Colón, a fellow traveler who fiddled with his income tax returns.

In no modern democracy are elections exercises in good taste, and a longer perspective might have shown that the old-time ritual physical violence of Puerto Rican elections had been replaced by a ritual slanging match, a verbal gladiatorial contest run by advertising agencies with the contenders publicized by their Christian names: "For Carlos [Romero] Puerto Rico is first"; "Puerto Rico believes in Rafael [Hernández Colón]." But laments for lost dignity and the more elevated style of the days of Don Luis Muñoz Marín or Don Luis Ferré — even Don Pedro Albizu Campos — should not hide the fact that Puerto Rico had become a two-party democracy and that the elections were peaceful.

The simple faith in the paternal leadership of Don Luis was not transferable to a lesser breed of politician; the monopoly of his party as the defender of the Commonwealth he had created had ended in 1968. Elections are now fought between those who seek the power to destroy and replace the heritage of Muñoz and those who seek to maintain that heritage and nourish its further growth. In other words, elections are not about what competing politicians seek to accomplish within the existing political system; they are about the nature of the political system itself.

This raises perplexing problems. Since 1968, neither of the two major parties has won an electoral victory decisively enough for it to claim that the status it advocates represents the democratic will of the Puerto Rican people. Moreover, the victory of the PNP in 1976 would seem to show that it is the economic performance of the government in power and the promises of the opposition that, as in all democratic societies, determine the choices of the floating voters and the tepid. It is therefore possible to imagine a situation in which economic catastrophe under a PPD government might hand to the PNP a handsome majority but which would not necessarily be an indication of widespread support for statehood. Fear of statehood as the unknown country from which there is no return, fear of the "destruction of Puerto Rican culture," and fear of loss of the economic advantages Commonwealth bestows might turn back the statehood tide in a plebiscite.

If the 1980 election campaign was conducted on the lines of what advertising men call a "knocking copy," postelectoral political activity descended into the jungle of tribal politics. To some observers, partisan passion seemed to threaten the continued credibility of Puerto Rican democracy. "A heavy stench of gunpowder," wrote one journalist, "is settling over the island."[16] This may be taken as yet another outburst of island self-denigration, an expression of the sense of frustration produced by the electoral stalemate. The postelectoral "crisis," however, was not the responsibility of the Puerto Rican electorate; it was the artificial creation of political leaders who, still breathing the heated atmosphere of a bitterly fought campaign, lost all sense of proportion, if not all sense of responsibility. It seemed as if the pattern of politics of the 1920s and 1930s had resurfaced: members of a political elite — "the elected buffoons of legislature," as one journalist called them — were pursuing their internecine feuds with no concern for the pressing problems of the island.[17] "What Puerto Rico needs," remarked Mayor Hernán Padilla, "is to depoliticize itself a little."

The battle was joined on the night of the elections. When Governor Romero claimed victory before the result was clear — in itself a provocative step — Hernández Colón appealed "to the trenches" should the Electoral Board certify Romero's election. Such ill-considered outbursts were to set the tone for his allies. When Judge Torruella of the Federal District Court overthrew a judgment of the Puerto Rican Supreme Court given in favor of the PPD, Severo Colberg declared "a state of permanent Puerto Rican rebellion without any concession to the forces of the annexationists."[18]

These belligerent postures were sustained for months by a
bitter battle that was a consequence of the extraordinary nar-
rowness of the electoral margin (0.48 percent) between the
PPD and the PNP. While the governorship remained with the
PNP, the PPD emerged as the majority party in the Senate;
the House was deadlocked at twenty-five PPD to twenty-five
PNP. Even the governorship was initially in doubt. Governor
Romero was not certified as elected until forty-four days after
the election. The final determination of seats won by a narrow
margin or where there were charges of electoral malpractice
was therefore a matter of political life or death for each party.
If the seats that were in doubt went to the PPD, then Romero
would be faced with the prospect of a hostile House that would
use every opportunity to discredit his governorship. With characteristic lack of scruples, the governor sought to put off the
evil day as long as possible.

The struggle for supremacy in the House involved the State
Election Commission, the Electoral Review Board, the Commonwealth Supreme Court, and the federal courts: the U.S.
District Court in Puerto Rico, the First Circuit Court of Appeals in Boston, and, in the last instance, the Supreme Court
of the United States. The decisions of all these bodies over
disputed counts and spoiled voting papers were challenged by
the losers on the ground that each was a tool in the hands of a
given political party. As for the Electoral Commission, which
certified elections, its administrator, who had a casting vote,
was an appointee of Governor Romero, while the Electoral
Review Board's president was, according to the PPD, blinded
by his "passionate" attachment to the PNP.[19] It gave the disputed seats to the PNP: this was Romero's "electoral coup."
The chief justice of the Puerto Rican Supreme Court was José
Trías Monge, former secretary of Justice under Muñoz Marín;
six of its seven judges had been appointed by PPD administrations; when the court decided in favor of the PPD, Romero
accused it of blatant partiality and appealed to the federal

courts.[20] The PPD, in turn, presented the federal courts as the "annexationist" instruments of statehooders, a claim that found justification in Romero's talk of "our" court.

In the following months, during the recount of the votes by hand and while the courts handed down their decisions, Puerto Ricans observed the daily changing fortunes between the two major parties for the control of the House. It was dramatized by journalists as a race — "PNP leading by a neck in District 35," ran a headline. The Electoral Commission, to the Populares an agency of the PNP, had certified the PNP candidates as victors in two districts by narrow margins. If its decision stood, then the PNP would have a majority of one in the House.

The contest over District 35 illustrates the points at issue. It involved the so-called *pavazo* votes, named after the peasant's straw hat, which is the emblem of the Populares. The voting papers in Puerto Rico are set up in columns, and a cross in the box at the top of each column elects the whole slate of one of the four parties. In the contested votes, some PPD voters had put their crosses, not in the box, but above the party emblem *outside* the box. The PPD appealed to the Commonwealth Supreme Court, which held that, since the voter's intention was clear, the votes were valid — a commonsense decision but one that was open to the charge that the court was making a law in favor of the PPD rather than interpreting the law as it stood. Immediately, the PNP appealed to the U.S. District Court, where Judge Torruella reversed the verdict on the grounds that it was a civil rights issue (and therefore subject to federal law) and that the counting of the technically questionable *pavazo* votes "diluted" the rights of voters who had voted correctly. The PPD appealed to the First Circuit Court of Appeals in Boston.

Two other cases raised the question as to whether the PPD could choose a replacement to a vacant seat in a party primary without a new election in which all the voters would participate. In District 31 (Caguas) the member had died, and Fernando Tonos, the newly elected member for an at-large constituency, was disqualified as under age; both were members of the PPD. To the PPD election by the party was a proper proceeding according to the Puerto Rican Constitution; the PNP protested that such a practice was unconstitutional according to the U.S. Constitution in that it denied electors their civil rights as voters. Both parties appealed to the courts.[21]

All these cases raised an issue that had long exercised the lawyer-politicians of Puerto Rico: the jurisdiction of the federal courts over the domestic political concerns of Puerto Rico.

The *independentistas* delighted in pointing out that the ultimate arbiters of the composition of the Puerto Rican legislature were the federal courts, staffed by judges appointed by the president of the United States. Professor Luis Agrait, a prominent PPD intellectual and journalist, argued that a Supreme Court ruling on District 31 would have "grave implications for the capacity of Puerto Rico to control its domestic political system."[22] To Mari Bras and Severo Colberg its jurisdiction was proof, in Colberg's words, that a "foreign agent" was "troubling" the life of Puerto Rico, "questioning the very essence of our status." Mari Bras believed Hernández Colón's readiness to appeal to federal courts was to submit to the "blackmail" of the "annexationist" PNP. The Populares, Mari Bras argued, should take on the fight with the jurisdiction of federal courts over the domestic constitution of Puerto Rico and thus "define the limits of autonomy."[23]

Given these outraged protests, the paradoxical result was that the "annexationist" federal courts finally decided against the "annexationist" party. To the chagrin of the PNP, their decisions gave its rival, the PPD, the vital majority.

As always, decisions of the U.S. courts were scrutinized as signposts on status, as if the status of Puerto Rico would be decided as a legal issue by the courts rather than by an act of political will on the part of the people of Puerto Rico and the

Congress of the United States. When the First Circuit Court of Appeals decided in its favor the PPD exulted: the judgment referred explicitly "to the compact entered into by the Congress and Puerto Rico." The ambiguities of the phrase "in the nature" of a compact had disappeared: Commonwealth was a *contract* between two sovereign bodies.[24] The U.S. Supreme Court gave the statehooders a crumb of comfort: it did not base its decision in the case of District 31 on the argument of Abe Fortas that the court should "accord special weight to Puerto Rico's unique autonomous status." Its decision applied to electoral practices in all states; it was a general judgment that took no account of Puerto Rico's unique status.

To a rational man, a legislature temporarily paralyzed in its lower chamber between two parties equal in strength would demand an experiment in what political scientists call "consociational democracy": in a society bedeviled with irreconcilably hostile subcultures—and certainly the two major Puerto Rican political parties form subcultures — the elite come to an understanding to save the system. They form what is called an "elite cartel" to get on with the business of government. In plainer terms, they seek some form of limited cooperation. When Romero proposed this, his "olive branch" was dismissed as the fraudulent offering of a "fascistoid," of a leopard who could not change his spots. Having failed by every means to get a majority in the House, he was talking the language of consensus politics but to cooperate with a "classic fascist" would merely aid his design of "subverting the constitution."[25] His inaugural address was boycotted by the PPD: senators and representatives went en masse to pay homage to Muñoz Marín's widow. Romero was not the legal governor of Puerto Rico, declared the PPD's then-President Hernández Agosto, but "commander of an army of occupation."[26]

Romero, no man to guard his speech, replied in kind. In seating a PPD representative before the court decision that gave him the seat was formally operative, the PPD leaders "had dealt contemptuously, scornfully, willfully, and intolerably with judicial edict.... They flout the law, the constitution, and the most essential principle of democratic government." If the PPD leaders had acted hastily, they were scarcely representatives, as Romero declared, of a "fanatically oppressive" party.[27] When the Senate refused to confirm his appointments, his reply was "never before in the history of our people have we seen action as irresponsible. The belligerent and cynical attitude of the PPD senators violates the trust of the people who elected them and shows their incapacity to carry out responsibility."[28]

This was the language of a temperamental authoritarian whose authority was challenged not only by his political enemies but within his own party. Romero had lost the party the election and might become a political liability. A rival, as journalists put it, was coming up on the outside track to challenge Romero as gubernatorial candidate in 1984 — Mayor Hernán Padilla, whose restrained political style was designed as a deliberate contrast to what he called Romero's "hysteria." Would the Puerto Rican electorate, still hankering after the charismatic leadership of Muñoz, accept the leadership of the would-be strongman of the PNP? Or would it prefer Padilla, the assiduous negotiator, expert at extracting federal funds for his near-bankrupt city? By November 1982, the rivalry was making the headlines: on December 19, Padilla announced that he "would be available in whatever way the people want me." He would be the candidate of the "people" against Romero, the ruthless master of the party machine.* The internal feuds and bickerings

---

*At a party meeting in Ponce on November 20, Romero challenged any prospective candidate for the governorship in 1984 to come forward; none did, and Romero was safely chosen president of the party. This, Padilla's supporters maintained, was the tactic of a "street fighter" to humiliate Padilla by crushing him with the weight of a party machine manipulated by government servants appointed by Romero. Padilla wanted the contest to be decided by a party poll. Romero dismissed polls as "unreliable"; Romero favored a party primary, which Padilla maintained would be controlled by the party machine. See *El Nuevo Día* for November 1982 and January 1983 and *San Juan Star,* December 20, 1982.

of both the PNP and the PPD were public property. Like the PPD, the PNP seemed possessed by an instinct of self-destruction, a determination to commit political suicide. Riven by rivalries, a divided party faces the uphill task of winning over an electorate, fearful of statehood as a departure from what exists and which does not share the determination of committed statehooders to solve the status question by ending what they regard as a colonial status that condemns Puerto Ricans to second-class citizenship. Colonialism breeds an inferiority complex, a supine acquiescence in the status quo among the mass of electors that the intellectual and political elite have failed to conquer. Wrangling over inessentials is the fruit of frustration. "Although our intellectuals and the educated elite recognize the gravity of colonialism," writes a young statehood lawyer, "it is no less certain that this same elite has failed in its intent to convince the mass of the electorate that the fundamental problem and the obstacle that impedes the rational solution of the problems of the country (*el país*) is precisely our inferior condition, our lack of political equality."[29]

A year after this election, the "clowns of the legislature" appeared more engaged in a combat between professional rhetoricians than in the task of legislating. The final arrangements that allowed the House to function came less as the consequence of political realism and reasonable compromise than as a consequence of bitter feuding within the PPD.

The relations between the defeated PPD gubernatorial candidate Hernández Colón and the president of the party, Hernández Agosto, were strained; even more strained were those between Severo Colberg, who acted as Hernández Colón's "political kamikaze," and Rony Jarabo, considered the hatchet man of Hernández Agosto. The ideological differences that underlay the alignments (Colberg's "radical autonomism" as opposed to Hernández Agosto's more conservative stance) were obscured by personal conflicts. Rony Jarabo's power in the PPD, the reward for his addiction to the chores of party organization, stood in the way of the long-standing ambition of Colberg to end his career as Speaker of the House. He was prepared to break party discipline to achieve it.

Colberg's first step was to unseat Tonos, the political ally of Jarabo and the youth candidate for the PPD, on the ground that he had misrepresented his age. This involved defying the PPD House Caucus, voting with the PNP, and denying his own party control of the House. Colberg claimed Hernández Agosto's men had "betrayed" a promise to elect him as House leader; Jarabo's supporters viewed Colberg as a "traitor" who, had he been a soldier, would have gone before the firing squad. The unedifying spectacle of these domestic feuds was laid before the people of Puerto Rico in a seven-day televised debate, giving "our illustrious legislators one more chance to display their amazing talent for coming to grips with the inconsequential issues of the day... little men fighting other little men for shabby prizes."[30]

Colberg, after voting with the PNP to unseat Tonos, came to an agreement with Angel Viera Martínez, House leader of the PNP, that gave Colberg the Vice-Speakership of the House and the prospect of becoming Speaker when the agreement expired in December 1981. Viera Martínez remained speaker in the meantime. This allowed the House to get down to business. Colberg, engaged in the pursuit of his own ambition, emerged, by the use of his single vote in a "hung" Assembly, in the unexpected role of the savior of Puerto Rican democracy. The aging representative of the generational revolt of the 1960s was greeted by Puerto Rican journalists and the weekly satirical television show *Rayos Gamma* as politician of the year; his backstairs deal with Viera Martínez was heralded as "historical and transcendental."[31] Democracy could function in Puerto Rico, not because politicians had come to their senses, but as a by-product of personal rivalries in the PPD and of the ambition of Colberg himself. He finally became speaker after another rowdy marathon debate, televised live.

In these heated postelectoral battles, it was scarcely surprising that no agreement could be reached on the status question. All parties favored some form of consensus on the procedures to resolve the status question, but the attempt to achieve a consensus degenerated into a game aimed at creating party capital and discrediting opponents. In May 1981, Hernández Colón proposed a meeting of all four parties to discuss such a consensus. The governor's reply was to propose a tripartite "Decolonization Commission" of the PPD, the PNP, and the PIP. Each party was to define the terms of its status option. This move was classed by observers as a classic checkmate in the chess game of Puerto Rican politics.

The PPD could not accept the exclusion of the PSP; its whole historical trajectory meant that it could not acknowledge that the term "colony," appearing in the committee's title, applied to the Free Associated State of Puerto Rico and that it could, therefore, be "decolonized." The governor, with the tactlessness that is his hallmark, pointed out to Hernández Colón that he was "fully cognizant of the precarious situation in which you and your party find yourselves with respect to Commonwealth status" and that to define it would split the party between supporters of permanent union and free association. Dropping the term "decolonization" as a concession to the semantic sensibilities of the PPD did not save the commission. The Tripartite Commission was stillborn; it served to drive parties back into the fortresses of their dogma rather than bring them together into an open discussion. Nor did the PNP proposal for a plebiscite — for or against statehood — rouse any enthusiasm in the PPD. Congress, Colberg argued, must decide *before* the plebiscite whether Puerto Rico could be a

Spanish-speaking state and recognize, among other matters, "our right to compete in international sporting events" as a "nation."

If the democratic institutions of Puerto Rico remained in place, the politicians who manned them earned little credit either in the election or during its contentious aftermath. The budget was endlessly delayed. The PPD was determined to efface its image of austerity (earned by Hernández Colón's "vampire tax" and his wage freeze for public servants in 1974) by raising the pay of policemen and schoolteachers. This was seen by Romero as an irresponsible exercise in vote catching —which it was, given the state of the Commonwealth revenues and the PPD's resolute refusal to sanction tax increases.[32] The exhibitions of degrading political spite in the legislature were televised; viewers saw the galleries chanting "drunkard" to Colberg and "thief, thief" to Viera Martínez. The representatives occasionally proceeded from insult to fisticuffs. Resident Commissioner Baltasar de Corrada in Washington despaired: "When I read about them fighting down there it makes me sick, literally sick."[33] Even worse, the elected representatives of the people were revealed as lining their own pockets and those of their relations and the party faithful at the expense of the taxpayer.* Relations between Speaker of the House Colberg and the press, anxious to expose scandals, collapsed in acrimony.**

*The so-called *nominas* scandal concerned the inflated office staffs of senators and representatives, the payment of large fees to party members no longer in the legislature as consultants, and the abuse of per diem payments and car allowances. The scandals started through a revelation by one of Colberg's staff that a representative had cut his staff salaries while retaining his wife on his staff at the old level.
**Colberg tried to block journalists' enquiries and sacked the staff member concerned with the leak — a clear indication that too much contact with the press would be punished. For the *nominas* scandal see *El Reportero,* April 13 and 19, 1982, and *El Mundo,* April 14, 15, and 23, 1982.

The most depressing reflection of the behavior of the "buffoons of the legislature" reeling, as journalists reported, punchdrunk (if not actually drunk) from "crisis to crisis" was that their conduct, presumably, was designed to give the electorate the spectacle it expected. It is a sad truth that in democratic societies the people get the politicians they deserve.

But it is important to realize that violence remained verbal and confined to the House; it did not, as the pessimists had prophesied, spill over into the streets. Hernández Colón's appeal "to the trenches" on election night, the subsequent rowdy demonstrations, and the barracking of the Puerto Rican Supreme Court justices by "Romero's bully boys" in protest against a decision in an election case in favor of the PPD were ugly incidents but not a prelude to civil war.

Do the public exhibitions of degrading and petty political spite threaten Puerto Rican democracy? It is unlikely that disillusionment with politicians and parties will, as some commentators argue, give rise to a third party. To use the cliché of the British Social Democratic Party (SDP), the breaking of the mold of Puerto Rican politics, by establishing a new party with a fresh approach to the status issue that could challenge the hold of the PPD and PNP on the electorate, may prove a difficult operation. The major parties have well-organized and well-oiled machines and are too tied to their status options to desert them, since they have no other raison d'être and no other signs of identity. It is left to the minority parties to propose unified fronts or third parties in the hope of attracting the deserters and the disillusioned as a way out of "the pathetic tribalism that immobilizes us."[34]

Into this scene of disarray and contention came rumors in January 1981 of the possible effects of the policies of the Reagan administration on Puerto Rico. As the policies took shape, so those effects appeared more alarming. Supply-side economics entailed corporate tax reductions on the mainland that would erode the comparative attractions of investment in Puerto Rico, a prospect further darkened by uncertainties surrounding the Treasury's intentions over Section 936 of the Internal Revenue Code, regarded as the essential instrument in inducing the U.S. investment on which Puerto Rico's economy had come to depend for its continued growth. The partial dismemberment of the welfare program of the 1960s and the New Federalism threatened the federal transfers that supplemented the Commonwealth budget and sustained the living standards of those whom the economy could not itself sustain. Finally came news of Reagan's Caribbean Basin Initiative (CBI): the advance of Communism in the Caribbean was to be halted by the creation of a new prosperity based on private investment, encouraged by granting to other countries the economic privileges that had hitherto been the exclusive prerogative of Puerto Rico.

For the Puerto Ricans, who for years had been engaged in continuous lobbying with the object of maximizing federal transfers (the resident commissioner had set his hopes on Medicaid), the Reagan cuts represented a drastic modification of a system on which they had come to rely. In a poor country, with a higher rate of local taxation than the mainland, how could the local revenues be generated to cover the expenses that the New Federalism would devolve on the states? The end of the Comprehensive Employment and Training Act (CETA) meant the end of 20,000 jobs and the impoverishment of municipalities, many of which were already on the edge of bankruptcy, unable to perform the few functions that a highly centralized government had left them, and whose budgets were balanced by federal grants distributed by the Commonwealth government. Above all, the conversion of the food stamp program into a block grant that would be reduced in real terms meant that a substantial proportion of the population faced hard times. As for Section 936, a chemical company that had already planned a plant in Puerto Rico withdrew its application, uncertain as to how a change in Treasury practice would affect the profitability of its investment.

The Reagan cuts and the application of supply-side economics were conceived in the interests of the national economy; the implicit corollary for Puerto Rico was that a healthy mainland economy could only benefit Puerto Rico in the long run, an assumption with little consolation for an island confronted with severe short-term problems. The Caribbean Basin Initiative was conceived in the interests of the administration's foreign policy; it was, the president announced, "vital to the security interests of the nation in this hemisphere." "New Cubas" must not arise, and this could only be prevented by sustaining pro-American democratic regimes in the region: "security, democracy and economic development are clearly linked together."[35] Economic development would come through what the president called "the magic of the marketplace"; "one-way free trade," giving the poor Caribbean economies duty-free access to the American market coupled with granting to investors the same tax credits for their Caribbean investments as they got for their U.S. domestic investments, would revivify the private sector of the struggling economies. A modicum of direct aid would help to meet their balance-of-payments difficulties.

While the administration argued that the long-term interests of the United States and Puerto Rico were identical and that a prosperous Caribbean could only benefit Puerto Rico, this was not apparent to Puerto Ricans. Their Caribbean neighbors were competitors for both capital and markets. Puerto Rico, a high-wage economy by Caribbean standards, had already seen some of its industries migrate to low-wage economies like Haiti or the Dominican Republic.

Even the modest proposal to grant tax exemption to conventions held in Jamaica would, it was argued, hit the none-too-healthy convention trade of San Juan. The New

Federalism, the governor had warned the president's office, would have serious effects on poor states, and Puerto Rico must be considered the poorest "state." Now the concessions in the CBI to other Caribbean rum producers would ruin an industry that employed 3,000 and provided the Commonwealth government with a tenth of its revenues. They were "completely unacceptable." It was all very well, the governor's former economic adviser complained, to "turn the Caribbean mini-states into mid-American Taiwans or Singapores; but it was doubtful whether Puerto Rico stood to gain by generosity to others."[36]

The ultimate impact of the Reagan cuts and the final shape of the Caribbean Basin Initiative, subject as it still is to amendment by Congress, are still uncertain.* Those Puerto Ricans who fear that the CBI will lame the Puerto Rican economy pin their hopes on the possibility of Congress destroying it. An editorial in the *San Juan Star* declared that this "would be one of the nicest things Congress has done for us for a long time." This is a counsel of despair and the genesis of the Caribbean Basin Initiative and the New Federalism have exposed the existing conventions that govern the relations among the government agencies. To Resident Commissioner Baltasar de Corrada, long familiar with Washington ways, the Reagan program merely repeats an old pattern. The Senate had omitted

---

*For the CBI in Congress see *New York Times*, August 16 and September 24, 1982; *Washington Post*, July 7 and September 24, 1982. There is considerable congressional opposition to "one-way free trade" as harming domestic producers. The cut in the U.S. sugar import quota for the year starting October 1, if it brings comfort to U.S. producers, can scarcely be reconciled with good intentions in the Caribbean. "To be sure, Mr. Reagan and Secretary Schultz have had their distractions in Lebanon. But that is precisely the persistent complaint of Caribbean leaders — that Washington is quickly bored with diplomatic initiatives in the region. Their cynicism can only grow if Washington lectures them on free market virtues while it acts to injure them with heedless protectionism." "No Sweets for the Caribbean," *New York Times*, September 25, 1982.

Puerto Rico from the Head Start Program: this showed "little concern for Puerto Rico." The framers of the CBI and the president's budget had not perhaps intended to punish Puerto Rico, but their failure to consult its representative in Washington certainly constituted inadvertence. The old paranoia surfaced. Puerto Ricans are obsessive Washington watchers; Washington bestows on Puerto Rico the occasional glance.

A well-used technique to force the attention of Washington on the affairs of Puerto Rico is to "scream"; "the wheel that squeaks loudest gets the most grease" is an old Spanish proverb. Baltasar de Corrada was an expert practitioner of the "cry wolf" school; his was the loudest voice denouncing what was, indeed, a "basic contradiction" in Reagan's policies. If Puerto Rico was to remain a "bastion" of the United States in the Caribbean, then "astronomical cuts" would defeat the president's purposes: the island's poor would "fall prey to some radicals who would like to force them [the poor] toward independence and communism"; Puerto Rico would become "another Cuba"; the administration "had better straighten out their policies in Puerto Rico if they want the peoples of the rest of Latin America to believe them." He prophesied massive emigration from an impoverished Puerto Rico to the mainland.[37] As a Democrat, the resident commissioner hoped that his concern would be shared by fellow Democrats who were opponents of the administration's policies: Senator Kennedy warned of grave consequences for the social and political stability of Puerto Rico; Senator Alan Cranston argued that the cuts were "very damaging to national security in the Caribbean."

Screaming is not the only instrument employed by Puerto Rican petitioners. There is the alternative of rallying friends, the strategy that Muñoz used to such effect. "Go to Washington," Mayor Hernán Padilla told the PNP mayors threatened with the loss of jobs under CETA. "He who doesn't travel doesn't get to first base."[38] The technique of those of his party who, like himself, had remained loyal Republicans was to "rekindle old friendships" rather than to indulge in political blackmail through prophecies of social and economic collapse. Luis Ferré and Padilla had good connections; Governor Romero, as a Democrat, lacked direct access to the White House and influence in the Republican connections. It was therefore Ferré and Padilla who lobbied in Washington.

The president's budget advisers, Ferré confessed, had "no political feel for Puerto Rico"; but talks in Washington in April would modify their views. "I know him [President Reagan] personally and talking face to face will help." From the days of Muñoz, every major Puerto Rican political figure had sought local prestige by boasting of his influence in Washington; Ferré was no exception, and his lawyer moved heaven and earth to get Ferré and Reagan photographed together during the 1980 campaign, to be displayed in the Puerto Rican press as proof of his clout in high places. Ferré did have influence in Republican circles, but in his face-to-face talk with the president, he found himself but one member of a Hispanic delegation.

By April 1981, it began to be apparent in Washington that the administration's policies were fueling a wave of anti-Americanism in Puerto Rico and embarrassing a pro-statehood governor.

Puerto Rico had not been consulted. The resident commissioner learned of the food stamp proposals from friends on committees on which he sat. Padilla relied on what he calls "third-hand rumors" that reached his office in Washington.[39] The administration's solution to what seemed another outburst of indignant protest over selective inattention was to set up a White House interdepartmental committee—the Puerto Rican Task Force — to examine the impact of the new policies on Puerto Rico. This represented the "special efforts" that Senator Howard Baker had promised his political friends and prospective voters in Puerto Rican primaries.

Organized in April, the task force got off to a bad start. The names of its members were kept secret in order to avoid lobbying by importunate Puerto Ricans. This was considered an insult. "Would they dare to do such a thing with Texas, Mississippi, the oil lobby, the milk interests?"[40] Some of its members seemed to share the views of Senator Jesse Helms, who dislikes food stamps in general and Puerto Rico's share of the program in particular. "How is it," he remarked on the Senate Agricultural Committee, "that you don't pay federal taxes but get $1 billion in food stamps? How do I explain that to my constituents?" One of the task force members told me that Puerto Ricans were spending food stamps on television sets: they must "be brought back to earth."

Mild concern was coupled with the conviction that the Puerto Ricans were indulging in an outburst of what Governor Rex Tugwell had once called the "colonial whine." The recipients of these outbursts in Washington argued that the Puerto Ricans protested too much. Instead of "griping" about the supposed catastrophic effects of the Caribbean Basin Initiative, "why don't they go along with the scheme and see what there is in it for them? They haven't a chance in hell of defeating a presidential initiative." Why not, therefore, use the CBI to extract concessions — for instance, the abandonment by Congress of the cabotage legislation that confined Puerto Rican trade with the mainland to American shipping or the grant of cheaper oil? In Washington Puerto Rican fears were dismissed as exaggerated. Jamaican rum was "different to the Puerto Rican product" and would not compete with it in the U.S. market; the Puerto Rican tourist industry "served a different market" from that of the old British West Indies;[41] no harm would come to Puerto Rico from granting Jamaica the tax relief for conventions that Puerto Rico enjoyed.

The gap of perception that had haunted the relationships of Puerto Rico and Washington had surfaced once more. The electoral slogan of Governor Romero encapsulated the Puerto

Rican perception: "For Carlos Puerto Rico is first." For congressmen and civil servants, it came far down on the list of priorities, a name at the end of the schedules of federal programs that could be struck off almost at will. To Puerto Ricans, the island and its concerns must be treated as a whole, a *Ding an sich,* a unique society with unique problems that it was the moral duty of America to alleviate. For Washington, the function of the task force was to fit Puerto Rico into wider policies by making a series of "pragmatic adjustments" at agency level. This was apparent in the language used by members of the task force: "an adjustment of the royalty payments under [Section] 936 will satisfy him [Carlos S. Quiros, the Puerto Rican secretary of State, one of the most diligent lobbyists of the task force]." The CBI would be modified so that it could be presented as a package deal that would give Puerto Rico, the most highly developed Caribbean economy, its modest place in the sun as the "center of a revivified region." In April, Governor Romero was willing to welcome the Initiative as "the best thing that had happened to Puerto Rico in the last twenty years."[42]

The atmosphere of peaceful adjustment of the early months of 1982 was shattered in July: the conflict between American policies and Puerto Rican needs surfaced in its sharpest form. The Republicans in the Senate decided to do something to meet the budget deficit in as politically painless a manner as possible; their device was to close every tax loophole. One such yawning loophole was Section 936 of the Internal Revenue Code. Long under attack by the Treasury, it allowed corporations with subsidiaries in Puerto Rico, above all the twenty pharmaceutical companies with plants on the island, to evade federal taxation on a colossal scale, estimated at some $400 million a year, or 10 percent of the book income of the pharmaceuticals. Senator Robert Dole presented a bill that would close the gap by preventing these companies from escaping taxation on the profits on intangibles (patents, development costs) transferred to Puerto Rican subsidiaries and by inflicting savage cuts in their exemptions on "passive earnings" — that is, Section 936 funds held in Puerto Rican banks. The Treasury would now decide what was a reasonable profit in terms of Puerto Rican production; to the governor's economic advisers this meant "the end of the 936 program."

Dole's amendment created panic in Puerto Rico. Section 936 had enabled Puerto Rico to pursue its drive for industrialization. "Without Section 936," Puerto Rico's Treasury secretary told the U.S. House Subcommittee on Banking, "Puerto Rico's economy as we know it would hardly exist." The island Treasury would be ruined: it would lose $50 million in local taxes, $80 million in tollgate taxes, and $240 million in employee personal taxes. Without 936, no one would invest in Puerto Rico: 15,000 jobs would be lost; industrial production would plummet by 25 percent; according to the Puerto Rican Treasury secretary the cutting back of tax-free "passive income" (i.e., Section 936 bank deposits) would "destroy our financial institutions." José Madera, head of the Fomento, found an "amazing lack of sensitivity" in Washington. The governor was outraged: Puerto Rico had not been consulted. The U.S. Treasury, after promising to help, did nothing to stop "one man" — Dole — from ruining Puerto Rico. The governor "screamed." After having come around in April to the view that the CBI might be "splendid" for Puerto Rico,[43] he now threatened with the only weapon at hand. In spite of his willingness to cooperate, "unless tax legislation can accommodate our industrial development program and establish investor confidence in Puerto Rico," there was nothing he could do to help the administration in the Caribbean.

The most intensive lobbying ever mounted in Washington

had failed to stop Dole, supposedly a friend of Puerto Rico. The campaign was renewed to get the Senate House Conference (to which Dole's amendment would go) to accept a compromise hammered out by the Puerto Ricans and the Treasury and now supported by the president. After an exhausting battle, the compromise was accepted, not least because Representative Charles B. Wrangel, with his New York constituents in mind, fought a heroic battle on Puerto Rico's behalf. The compromise, which cut back tax-free profits on intangibles and on Section 936 funds held in Puerto Rico on a less drastic scale than the Dole amendment, was hardly the Puerto Rican triumph trumpeted by the resident commissioner. But at least something had been saved. "We can live with it" was the unenthusiastic verdict of an exhausted governor. With some of the uncertainties surrounding Section 936 cleared away, the only large pharmaceutical concern without a plant in Puerto Rico decided to come to the island.

As always, what was viewed on the island as an attempt by the administration to make Puerto Rico pay for both its domestic and foreign policies, was seen through the lens of the status options.

The *independentistas* and the PPD indulged in a prolonged fit of *Schadenfreude*. Romero and the statehooders had been "caught with their pants down." Statehooders had always argued that under Commonwealth there was no security for a continuation of federal payments; that equal treatment as a state would mean the end of arbitrary cuts in federal programs inflicted on a nonstate like Puerto Rico. Now the administration was imposing cuts all around. For Berríos Martínez of the PIP, the New Federalism, "by making everyone pay for himself... shuffles all the cards in the statehooders' pack," leaving all the aces in the hands of the *independentistas*. Juan M. García

Passalacqua — a prolific political journalist, always at hand to paint a gloomy picture based on "inside information" — prophesied that the indifference of the administration meant that the United States was preparing to slough off responsibility for an expensive colony.

When in March the Puerto Rican legislature examined the implications of the CBI for Puerto Rico, the PPD poured salt on the statehooders' wound: the Reagan administration's proposals threatened "great economic and social instability." Romero's "statehood for the poor" now had a hollow ring: statehood would, in present conditions of welfare cuts, "finish off the poor."[44]

Only the enlarged autonomy of the New Thesis could save Puerto Rico from "shocks" and set it on the road to prosperity once more: powers to set its own tariffs to save its agriculture and to join the San José agreement that allowed independent Caribbean countries to get cheap oil from Venezuela. To the PNP, this exposed "the ambivalence of the PPD in that, on the one hand they ask for the powers of a Republic and, on the other, the benefits of a state."[45] The PPD "would have you believe that the only course to follow in addressing possible problems [raised by the CBI] is to give Puerto Rico more privileges resulting in a degree of autonomy unknown to the American Constitution.... Their proposals in this area are identical to the notions advanced recently by the Puerto Rican Independence Party."[46]

The statehooders' counteroffensive was the old assertion that Puerto Rico would not have been so savagely treated as a state, and that Commonwealth, according to the Fomento administrator José Madera, meant that the economic autonomy "exercised by the Puerto Rican government can be unilaterally revoked by Congress, partially or totally." "We are just a small piece in the puzzle," lamented the governor's economic adviser, a piece with no influence in Congress.[47] Statehooders could point to the benefits that, for example, Senator Baker had obtained for Tennessee in an atmosphere of budget-trimming: there was no senator to protect the interests of Puerto Rican rum producers. If Puerto Rico were a state, "it would be inconceivable that the administration would seriously consider a proposal that would destroy a major industry in the island." Luis Ferré quoted Senator Daniel Moynihan: "If the American citizens of Puerto Rico were represented in the Senate by two senators, legislation like this [the Dole amendment on Section 936] would not be approved or ever passed." What this argument failed to point out was that, as a state, Puerto Rico would not enjoy the benefits of Section 936 in the first place. The statehooders' argument was therefore, Miguel Hernández Agosto of the PPD insisted, a patent absurdity.[48]

At the same time that Romero was complaining of "geographical discrimination" over food stamps, and over the fact that Commonwealth left Puerto Ricans politically impotent as "serfs on someone else's estate" who must beg at Washington for "special treatment," it was "special treatment" that he himself was demanding. Romero, his opponents insisted, had attempted a deal with Washington that had come unstuck: he had supported the administration's policies in the hopes that they would be shaped to fit Puerto Rico's needs, above all in the critical issues of rum and Section 936. To plead for "special treatment" was to put his electoral survival above ideological consistency. A Puerto Rican electorate plunged into poverty by the ending of Section 936 and by the loss of a substantial slice of its rum exports would not reelect the governor and his party in 1984. All that his "truckling" to Washington had brought was Reagan's statement of January 1982 in favor of statehood and a photograph of Romero, Padilla, and Luis Ferré seated smiling beside the president in the White House.

The statehooders saw no ideological inconsistency in pleading for "special treatment." They could, and did, point out that the economic advantages of Commonwealth were in situ in all their essentials long before Commonwealth came into existence: Section 936, for example, had its origins in a revision of the Internal Revenue Code of 1921; exemptions from federal taxation and a common market dated from the first years of American rule. Since it was the economic policies of Commonwealth which had forced the economy of Puerto Rico along the wrong paths and had ended up plunging it into economic decline and an unhealthy dependency, the limbs of "special treatment" could not be suddenly amputated. The special concessions that Puerto Rico enjoyed must be used — wisely and well, not as the PPD had used them — to bring Puerto Rico out of a degrading dependency. Only as a healthy economy could Puerto Rico become eligible for statehood in the eyes of Congress: hence the necessity for congressional generosity during a transitional period.

This necessity exposes an enduring weakness in the statehooders' quest for full membership of the Union. The Status Commission of the 1960s predicted that by 1980, Puerto Rico would have reached a level of prosperity at least equal to that of the poorer mainland states. This optimism was misplaced; with a per capita income half that of Mississippi, Puerto Rico remains a long way from the economic threshold of statehood. It is the moral obligation of the United States, statehooders maintain, to see by special treatment that poverty does not deny Puerto Ricans the dignity of full citizenship and to help their faltering economy to reach the standards of well-being demanded of a prospective candidate for statehood. It is precisely the implications of this obligation that makes congressmen uneasy.

The first years of the 1980s have been years of muddle and frustration rather than years of decision, as Romero had claimed they would be. An electoral stalemate on the island has corresponded with changes in U.S. national policies that flung

Puerto Rico's relationship with the United States into confusion. These confusions were sensed by old Puerto Rican hands in Washington: "Psychologically the island is floundering with every rumor of change in federal policy, creating political pressures on the system."[49] The impasse created by Puerto Rico's ambiguous status, Senator J. Bennett Johnston declared, was "a political tragedy of profound proportions." Status had once more been brought to the attention of Washington by Puerto Rican reactions to the policies of the Reagan administration. But status had been, the senator added, "for some time a bomb waiting to explode."[50]

CONCLUSION

The immediate problem of Puerto Rico is not the state of its political relations with the United States but the state of its economy. It might seem that Puerto Rico is suffering the common fate of the Western capitalist world. If CORCO, the giant refining complex, is bankrupt, so is the German electrical giant, AEG-Telefunken. The structural unemployment in southern Puerto Rico is matched in southern Spain. Small businesses are going under in London as well as in San Juan. But the economy of a small island without a rich resource endowment is particularly fragile; if it is a "showcase of democracy," Puerto Rico is also a showcase of the impact of recession on an economy whose only resource is its people. Thus, although three-quarters of a century of American rule have integrated the economy of Puerto Rico into that of the United States, Puerto Rico, like its Caribbean neighbors, still faces some of the common problems of small Third World economies. Puerto Rico has avoided their fate because it has been propped up by access to American capital and the American market—advantages that other independent Third World countries do not enjoy. Additional props — federal transfer payments and unrestricted emigration — help hide the failure of these advantages to secure growth after 1974.

Remove the props provided by political association with the United States, and Puerto Rico's economy, if it did not collapse, would sink back to the level of the Dominican Republic.

Since the United States could not allow this to happen, a Puerto Rican Republic would demand large injections of foreign aid to replace federal transfers and special concessions to investors in order to maintain fixed capital investment at a satisfactory level. An independent Puerto Rico could not compete with Taiwan or Singapore in attracting investors by the availability of cheap labor, nor can there be any guarantee that it would benefit from loans by international organizations, as the Puerto Rican Independence Party (PIP) envisages. Having raised Puerto Ricans' living standards to a level higher than they would have achieved by their own efforts, the United States would be committed to sustaining those standards lest economic collapse turn an independent Puerto Rico into a "second Cuba."

Because the essential economic props are now provided as a result of Puerto Rico's political relationship with the United States, the prospect of some of them being knocked away by the policies of the Reagan administration has placed that relationship under severe scrutiny. Statehooders, encouraged by Ambassador Jeane Kirkpatrick's exposition of the expansive and accommodating qualities of American federalism, argue that only statehood and *complete* integration can save Puerto Rico, both spiritually — in Romero's phrase — and materially. The Popular Democratic Party, with its demand that Congress endow it with the instruments to control the economy, sees statehood as only reinforcing an already unhealthy dependency, cultural as well as economic. The PIP counters that Commonwealth has demonstrated the disastrous results of dependency in every sphere of life, from traffic accidents to prostitution: statehood, as "annexation" against the supposed will of the Puerto Rican people, can only increase the alleged economic and social evils of dependence.

Statehood, like independence, can be presented as demanding, in an uncertain future, material sacrifices for the sake of "dignity" that many Puerto Ricans are unwilling to face; hence both are confronted with the task of negotiating a form of statehood or a grant of independence that, somehow or other, embodies the best of all possible worlds for Puerto Rico by retaining, *at least for a negotiated transition period*, the privileges that derive from a status stigmatized as "colonial." In the case of statehood, these negotiations will test the imagination of congressmen and the flexibility of the federal Constitution.

The United States has repeatedly declared it will respect the wishes of the Puerto Ricans. The trouble is that these wishes are not always clear to congressmen when they visit the island, listen to conflicting testimony in committees, and scrutinize the results of island elections. Since, in the foreseeable future, independence will not muster enough votes to impress Congress, nor will Congress ever be moved to grant independence as the result of the international pressures orchestrated by the independence parties in the United Nations, the immediate choice must be between statehood and Commonwealth. If recent elections are any indication of the wishes of the Puerto Rican people, they are equally divided between the two options. Clearly if there was, as some statehooders advocate, a plebiscite between the two "classic options" of statehood and independence, statehood would win sufficient votes to impress Congress. But such a plebiscite is not politically feasible.

Can the United States do anything to break the impasse? It could, I think, at least present the Puerto Rican people with a clear picture of what its own intentions are, so that Puerto Ricans can vote in a plebiscite for solutions that Congress, as the other partner in any settlement, will accept. Congress, though it has never done this before, could set out the conditions on which it would accept Puerto Rico as a state and the improvements it would grant to "culminate" Commonwealth.

For good measure Congress should set out the transitional arrangements it would be prepared to grant an independent Puerto Rico in order to soften the shocks of severance. Without some such declaration of intent, Puerto Ricans will be asked to vote on a series of hypothetical options. Indecision in the United States feeds on the inconsistencies of the Puerto Ricans themselves and, above all, their ambiguities. Apart from the *independentistas*, the local political establishment displays a mixture of truculence and obeisance to the political establishment of Washington. With one hand they tug their forelocks, with the other they make threatening gestures.

Statehood appears clear-cut, the most logical of the two forms of permanent association with the United States that Puerto Ricans support at the polls. But while Congress has shown flexibility in accommodating the special problems of prospective states, the admission of Puerto Rico will pose difficulties. There will be objections that admitting a fifty-first state with half the per capita income of Mississippi will inflict intolerable burdens on federal resources, even though these burdens would constitute an insignificant proportion of the national budget. The transitional arrangements necessary to soften the economic shocks of statehood and the existence, even in a multicultural polity, of a Spanish-speaking state will allow reluctant congressmen to argue that Puerto Rico is willing to become a state only on privileged terms that will create a constitutional oddity.

While most Puerto Ricans would either welcome statehood as conferring the dignity of "first-class citizenship" or, if it were supported by the majority of the Puerto Rican people in a plebiscite, accept it, there is a minority of *independentistas* for whom no plebiscite, however scrupulously administered and supervised, could legitimize "annexation" without the magic "transfer of powers." For *independentistas*, the plebiscitary process must continue until it endorses independence as the only true expression of the general will. Of that minority who could not accept statehood as slamming the door on independence forever — since once done, statehood cannot be undone — some would resort to violence to express their opposition. This possibility would be no justification for refusing statehood should Puerto Ricans vote for it; it is merely a caution that Puerto Rico would be a troubled state where a minority of malcontents would reject the legitimacy of the Constitution as such. They would fall back on the old Spanish habit of the *retraimiento* and boycott a democratic system that failed to produce the desired result.

A decisive vote for statehood would force Congress to act. Supposing that Governor Romero and the statehooders had won both the 1980 election and subsequent plebiscite, and supposing that Congress had refused to admit Puerto Rico as a state, say on the grounds that the majority was small or, as the statehooders' opponents would certainly argue, the results of the plebiscite had been rigged by the party in power (an objection that makes it essential for the United States to allow international supervision of any future plebiscite), then it would be the statehooders who would be the discontented citizens, some turning to independence as the last defense of dignity. After behaving as loyal American citizens and democrats, their discontent would be justified.

As in the case of statehood, a decisive democratic vote in Puerto Rico for "culminated Commonwealth" would present difficulties to constitutional purists in Congress. Yet, however lacking in legal precision, Commonwealth enjoys two *political* advantages: it is in situ and functioning, however its performance may be criticized; and its very ambiguities become a merit when they avoid the polarization of opinion that would come with statehood or independence. It is in the interests of the

United States to recognize that, *as it stands*, Commonwealth satisfies no one except the aging conservatives of the PPD.

It may be that the New Thesis demands too much freedom too soon, but the United States has observed the erosion, by federal legislation, of the autonomy granted in 1952, and has done nothing to reverse the process and to restore to Commonwealth some of the vigor of the early years. It is a statehooder, Mayor Hernán Padilla, who complains that "the policies of the United States towards Puerto Rico have been ambiguous, inconsistent and at times unsympathetic."[1] The charge could be made with even more justification by the supporters of Commonwealth.

A lack of sympathy has at times distinguished American policies toward Puerto Rico. It reflects a failure to recognize that, in spite of their American citizenship, many Puerto Ricans feel they lack full rights of citizens in an age when de Tocqueville's equality of conditions is seen as an irreversible process. It represents a reluctance on the part of the United States to make a fundamental decision on Puerto Rico.

It must be made abundantly clear that the United States is not, as its enemies in the United Nations insist, exercising a colonialist-imperialist domination over a cowed and subject people. "Colonialism by consent" may seem a political monstrosity to Latin America and the Third World, but it is an inescapable fact that 90 percent of Puerto Ricans wish to remain a part of the United States. But they remain in a relationship that, as Governor Romero insists, retains "vestiges of colonialism." This puts a "special responsibility on Congress to see that the island's fate is not dealt with lightly." This is the verdict of Steven S. Rosenfeld of the *Washington Post*, one of the few journalists with a special concern for Puerto Rico. One thing is clear. America, first by conquering Puerto Rico and then, enthusiastically aided by the Puerto Ricans themselves, by absorbing it into the mainland economy, has acquired a special obligation.

Congress has to recognize that the island's economy cannot survive alone — however ineptly Puerto Ricans have squandered the $50 billion of American funds in transfer payments and capital investment that Puerto Rico has received since the 1940s — and that Puerto Rico has and will retain a separate cultural identity, however provincial that identity appears to the outside world.

To combine these two conditions demands not only understanding and respect for self-determination by the United States; it demands leadership in Puerto Rico by a political class that has found no substitute for Muñoz Marín's charisma to close the gap between the leaders and the led.

There are, a historian must conclude, problems whose intractability may appear to render them insoluble. But to refuse to confront those problems because they seem to present no immediate and pressing danger can only, in the long run, exacerbate them. Successive British governments after World War I treated what appeared to them as the obsessive concern of a small and divided community in Northern Ireland as a peripheral matter, easily forgotten beside great issues of the day. The problem did not go away. It festered. The opportunities for constructive statesmanship are now submerged in violence. For generations, the Canadian political establishment gave little attention to the plight of the French Canadians; their grievances and their party now pose an acute constitutional problem, even threatening the continued existence of the Canadian Confederation. This is not to maintain that Puerto Rico will become the scene of bitter and bloody sectarian violence of West Belfast or that Puerto Rican nationalism can create a Quebec within the American system. It is that the issue of Puerto Rico's relationship with the United States remains unresolved. "Status politics," as Muñoz Marín insisted in his political testament, "have always impeded the realization of the ideals of life and civilization." They still do.

NOTES

Chapter 1

1. General George W. Davis, military governor of Puerto Rico, 1899–1900, in his "Report on the Civil Affairs of Puerto Rico 1899" in *Annual Report of the War Department for the Fiscal Year ended June 30, 1899,* p. 535.

2. The view that the Charter of Autonomy of 1897 was granted to satisfy Cuban opinion has been consistently attacked by Puerto Rican nationalists. According to Andrés Sánchez Tarniella in *Nuevo enfoque sobre el desarrollo político de Puerto Rico* (Madrid: Afrodisio Aguada S.A., 1971), pp. 63–64, to argue that the charter was a "gratuitous" emergency concession of Spain is to deny that Puerto Rican history has any serious content. Yet the preamble stated that its purpose was "the pacification of Cuba" and that it was based on the program of the Cuban Autonomist party.

3. Quoted in Lidio Cruz Monclova, *Historia de Puerto Rico del siglo XIX,* vol. 1 (Río Piedras: Editorial Universitaria, 1952), p. 180.

4. *El Mundo,* February 10, 1946. An error, as he did not fail to point out, that had been rectified in the case of Cuba and the Philippines but that remained to be rectified in the case of Puerto Rico.

5. His hesitant policy is described in Ernest R. May, *Imperial Democracy: The Emergence of America as a Great Power* (New York: Harper and Row, 1961).

6. Wilfred Scawen Blunt, *My Diaries,* vol. 1 (London, 1919; reprint ed., New York: Octagon Books, 1980), p. 358.

7. See, for instance, María Dolores Luque de Sánchez, *La ocupación norteamericana y la ley Foraker* (Río Piedras: Editorial Universitaria, 1980), p. 27.

8. *Cincinnati Enquirer,* May 22, 1898. Quoted in E. Walters, *Joseph Benton Foraker* (Columbus, Ohio, 1948), p. 152.

9. Cf. José A. Cabranes, "Evolution of the American Empire" in *Congressional Record,* 93rd Cong., 1st sess., 119, no. 58, April 12, 1973. "The parallels between the South East Asian imbroglio and the colonial experience of the turn of the century have awakened an interest in the study of that imperial venture and its impact on American society."

10. For the state of the sugar industry see Andrés Ramos Mattei, *La hacienda azucarera: Su crecimiento y crisis en Puerto Rico (Siglo XIX)* (San Juan: CEREP, 1981). Puerto Rico produced about 70,000 tons, Cuba 3.5 million tons.

11. Andrés Ramos Mattei, "Las inversiones norteamericanas en Puerto Rico y la ley Foraker 1898–1900," *Caribbean Studies* 14, no. 3, pp. 53 ff.

12. *Selections from the Correspondence of Theodore Roosevelt and Henry Cabot Lodge*, vol. 1 (New York), p. 267 and passim.

13. Quoted in Julius W. Pratt, "American Business and the Spanish American War," *Hispanic American Historical Review* 14 (May 1934).

14. G.T. Davis, *A Navy Second to None* (Westport, Conn., 1971), p. 121.

15. For John Wesley Gaines's attack on imperialism see *Congressional Record*, 56th Cong., 1st sess., 1900, pt. 8, pp. 75–77.

16. Neville Maxwell, *India's China War* (London: Jonathan Cape, 1970), pp. 19–64. Great powers dislike anarchy in their spheres of influence. This has always been a determinant of U.S. policy in the Caribbean. Britain acquired Darjeeling from Sikkim in 1835 to create "an island of well governed British territory in the prevailing sea of Sikkim misrule." The United States has always feared a sea of misrule in the Caribbean.

17. See Carmelo Rosario Natal, *Puerto Rico: La crisis de la guerra hispanoamericana* (Hato Rey: Ramallo Bros., 1975), pp. 208–9.

18. Cf. the description of Stephen Crane in *The War Dispatches of Stephen Crane*, ed. R.W. Stallman and E.R. Hagemann (New York: New York University Press, 1964), pp. 193 ff.

19. For the Nationalist view of the Grito, see J.A. Corretjer, *La lucha para la independencia de Puerto Rico* (n.d.). The background is reexamined in Laird W. Bergad, "Hacia el Grito de Lares: café, estratificación social y conflictos de clase 1828–1869" in *Inmigración y clases sociales en el Puerto Rico del siglo XIX*, ed. Francisco A. Scarano (Río Piedras: Ediciones Huracán, 1981), pp. 147–87.

20. Pilar Barbosa de Rosario, *De Baldorioty a Barbosa. Historia del Autonomismo Puertorriqueño (1887–1896)* (San Juan, 1957), pp. 298 ff.

21. Henry K. Carroll, *Report on the Island of Porto Rico* (Washington, D.C., 1899; reprint ed., Salem, N.H.: Arno Press, 1975), p. 234.

22. A.C. Coolidge, *The United States and World Power* (New York, 1908; reprinted., Saint Clair Shores, Minn.: Scholarly Press, 1981), p. 134.

23. This claim was made by de Diego in 1913 in the presence of a delegation of American congressmen in order to rebut the accusation that Puerto Rico had been incapable of fighting for its freedom as had Cuba. See Ricardo Alegría, "Muñoz Rivera y de Diego ante la invasión norteamericana" in *Revista del Instituto de Cultura Puertorriqueña*, Año XV, no. 54 (1972): 19–22.

24. Elihu Root in *The Military and Colonial Policy of the United States*, R. Bacon and J. Brown Scott eds. (Cambridge, Mass., 1916; reprint ed., New York: Ams Press), p. 161.

25. For an account of the actions of the military governors, see J. Trías Monge,

Historia constitucional de Puerto Rico, vol. 1 (Río Piedras: University of Puerto Rico Press, 1980), pp. 165–85. It is a curious reflection that the military governors acted on an instruction drafted for Cuba which it was assumed would apply to Puerto Rico. Ibid., p. 159.

26. U.S. Congress, House Committee on Insular Affairs, *Committee Reports and Hearings, and Acts Relating Thereto*, 56th Cong., 1st and 2d sess., 1900–01, p. 116.

27. U.S. Congress, Senate Committee on the Pacific Islands and Puerto Rico, 56th Cong., 1st sess., 1900, S. Rept. 249.

28. Carroll, *Report on the Island of Porto Rico*, p. 58.

29. Davis was not illiberal. He was deeply distressed by Puerto Rican poverty and did what he could to relieve it. He was an advocate of greater self-government once Puerto Ricans merited it and American institutions had taken root – above all through education. See E.J. Berbusse, *The United States in Puerto Rico 1898–1900* (Chapel Hill: University of North Carolina Press, 1966), p. 101. General Davis's views and those of his officers and advisers are set out in the U.S. War Department's *Annual Report of the War Department for the Fiscal Year ended June 30, 1899,* and ibid. ending June 30, 1900. These are essential reading.

30. The "Philippines effect" is carefully argued in José A. Cabranes, *Citizenship and the American Empire* (New Haven: Yale University Press, 1979).

31. *Congressional Record*, 56th Cong., 1st sess., 1900, p. 2162.

32. Ibid., p. 3616.

33. Ibid., p. 2473.

34. The relevant cases were *Downes v. Bidwell* and *De Lima v. Bidwell*, both in 1901. The status of unincorporated territory was reaffirmed even after the grant of citizenship in 1917 in *Balzac v. Puerto Rico* (1922).

35. *Congressional Record*, 56th Cong., 1st sess., April 5, 1900, p. 4954.

36. Luis Muñoz Rivera, *Campañas Políticas*, vol. II (San Juan, 1925), p. 252. See Luque de Sánchez, *La ocupación norteamericana y la ley Foraker*, pp. 157–58. By 1903, even the Republicans were prepared to criticize: though the lower house was elected by Puerto Ricans, the legislature was a mere "decoration," entirely subject to the wishes of the appointed Executive Council.

37. See Edward J. Berbusse, *The United States in Puerto Rico 1898–1900* (Chapel Hill: University of North Carolina Press, 1966), p. 470.

38. Cf. J.H. Hollander, "The Finances of Puerto Rico," *Political Science Quarterly* 16 (December 1901), pp. 553–81.

39. *San Juan News*, June 29, 1901.

40. *Congressional Record*, 56th Cong., 1st sess., 1899–1900, p. 2266.

41. See Lyman J. Gould, *La Ley Foraker: raíces de la política colonial de los Estados Unidos* (Río Piedras: University of Puerto Rico Press, 1969), esp. pp. 181–209. The election of 1900 was not a popular endorsement of imperialism but a vote against Bryan. See T.H. Bailey, "Was the Presidential Election of 1900 a Mandate on Imperialism?" *Mississippi Valley Review* 24 (January 1937): 43–52.

42. Theodore Roosevelt, Jr., *Colonial Policies of the United States* (Garden City, N.Y., 1937), p. 99.
43. Quoted in Charles T. Goodsell, *Administration of a Revolution: Executive Reform in Puerto Rico under Governor Tugwell, 1941–1946* (Cambridge: Harvard University Press, 1965), note 14, p. 216.
44. Frank Otto Gatell, "Independence Rejected: Puerto Rico and the Tydings Bill of 1936," *Hispanic American Historical Review* 38 (1958), p. 28.
45. Quoted in R. Truman Clark, *Puerto Rico and the United States 1917–23* (Pittsburgh, Pa.: University of Pittsburgh Press, 1975), p. 10.
46. Alleyne Ireland, *Tropical Colonization* (New York: Macmillan, 1899), p. 219.
47. For a moderately optimistic view, see G. Milton Fowles, *Down in Porto Rico* (1906; reprint ed., New York: Gordon Press, 1976). For a total rejection of the legitimacy of colonial rule as exercised by the United States, see W.S. Sumner, "The Conquest of the United States by Spain," *Yale Law Journal* 8 (1890), pp. 176 ff.
48. K.H. Porter, ed., *National Party Platforms* (Urbana: University of Illinois Press, 1966), p. 138.
49. *Third Annual Report* [Governor Hunt] (Washington, D.C., 1903), p. 13.
50. Fowles, *Down in Porto Rico*, p. 146.
51. J.J. Young, "Colonial Autonomy," *Annals of the American Academy of Political and Social Science* 19, no. 3 (May 1902), p. 66.
52. Ibid., p. 148.
53. Tomás Blanco, *Prontuario histórico de Puerto Rico* (Río Piedras: Ediciones Huracán, 1981), p. 98.
54. Fowles, *Down in Porto Rico*, p. 150.

Chapter 2

1. For Matienzo Cintrón's campaign to resist U.S. control of Puerto Rican agrarian resources, see Díaz Soler, *Rosendo Matienzo Cintrón, guardián de una cultura* (Río Piedras, 1960), i, pp. 352 ff.
2. "Puerto Rican Political Parties," *Annals of the American Academy of Political and Social Science* 19, no. 3 (May 1902), p. 26.
3. As Nemesio Canales, a fierce critic of Americanization and Puerto Rican political mores alike, pointed out, Puerto Rico demanded not *more* justice, but justice. For more information on Canales, a friend of Muñoz Rivera who admired his writings, see below.
4. Senator James Kimble Vardaman of Mississippi, *Congressional Record*, 64th Cong., 2d sess., January 30, 1917, p. 2250. See below.
5. Muñoz Rivera had opposed the imposition of collective citizenship without a plebiscite. *Congressional Record*, 64th Cong., 1st sess., May 5, 1916, p. 7472. It must be noted that "conservative" in Muñoz Rivera's strictures referred to an attempt to establish a property franchise.

6. Representative Miller of Minnesota, ibid., pp. 7473 ff.

7. Senator Vardaman, *Congressional Record*, 64th Cong., 2d sess., p. 7474.

8. A.S. Link, *Wilson: The Road to the White House* (Princeton: Princeton University Press, 1968), p. 28.

9. Barbosa's daughter points out that every Puerto Rican politician had, at some time or other, demanded American citizenship. Pilar Barbosa de Rosario, *La política en dos tiempos* (San Juan, 1978), pp. 50–76. Latter-day sympathizers with independence, such as José de Diego, demanded citizenship as late as 1910.

10. For an excellent account of "Gore's Hell" see Thomas Mathews, *Puerto Rican Politics and the New Deal* (Gainesville: University of Florida Press, 1960), pp. 56 ff., esp. pp. 85 and 93.

11. Luis Muñoz Marín, *Memorias 1898–1940* (Universidad Interamericana de Puerto Rico, 1982), pp. 105 ff.

12. Thomas Mathews, *Puerto Rican Politics and the New Deal* (Gainesville: University of Florida Press, 1960), p. 30.

13. Rexford Guy Tugwell, *The Stricken Land* (New York: Doubleday and Co., 1947), p. 4.

14. Cf. the verdict of W.T. Perkins in *Denial of Empire: The United States and Its Dependencies* (Leiden, Holland: A.W. Sythoff, 1962), p. 138. The PRRA (the New Deal agency established by Executive Order in 1935) was "a partial response to a program that was itself a partial solution."

15. Mathews, *Puerto Rican Politics and the New Deal*, p. 250.

16. Quoted in Frank Otto Gatell, "Independence Rejected: Puerto Rico and the Tydings Bill of 1936," *Hispanic American Historical Review* 38 (1958), p. 33.

17. See Muñoz Marín's letter to Secretary of the Interior Ickes, January 5, 1937, printed in Surendra Bhana, *The United States and the Development of the Puerto Rican Status Question 1936–1968* (Wichita: University of Kansas Press, 1975), pp. 217–26.

18. Mathews, *Puerto Rican Politics and the New Deal*, p. 222.

19. Muñoz Marín, *Memorias 1898–1940*, p. 147.

20. W. Brown, *Dynamite on Our Doorstep: Puerto Rican Paradox* (New York: Greenberg, 1945), esp. p. 97. An extremely prejudiced and alarmist book, it is nevertheless based on firsthand information.

21. Quoted in Mathews, *Puerto Rican Politics and the New Deal*, preface.

22. For the rise of the PPD see below.

23. All quotations from Charles T. Goodsell, *Administration of a Revolution: Executive Reform in Puerto Rico under Governor Tugwell, 1941 – 1946* (Cambridge: Harvard University Press, 1965).

24. Bhana, *The United States and the Development of the Puerto Rican Status Question* (Wichita: University of Kansas Press, 1975), pp. 60 ff. Senator Tydings supported "complete, absolute and unconditional independence" as the only solution given the cultural cleavage (ibid., p. 68).

25. The liberals were bitterly divided by Muñoz Marín's quarrel with Barceló and won 252,407 votes. The Republican Union with 152,739 votes and the Socialists

with 144,249, combined in the Coalition, won the election. See Bolivar Pagán, *Historia de los partidos políticos puertorriqueños*, vol. 2 (San Juan: Librería Campos, 1956), pp. 69–116.

26. Tugwell, *The Stricken Land*, p. 37.

Chapter 3

1. For an account of the dramatic session in the House, see Antonio Fernós Isern, *Estado Libre Asociado de Puerto Rico: Antecedentes, creación y desarrollo hasta la época presente* (Río Piedras: Editorial Universitaria de Puerto Rico, 1974), pp. 77–79. The Elective Governor Act still held that the key finance officer, the auditor, and the judges of the Puerto Rican Supreme Court would continue to be appointed by the president of the United States.

2. See Henry Wells, "Administrative Reorganization in Puerto Rico," *Western Political Quarterly* 9 (1956): 470–90 and his *The Modernization of Puerto Rico: A Political Study of Changing Values and Institutions* (Cambridge: Harvard University Press, 1969), pp. 198–201. However, Charles T. Goodsell, *Administration of a Revolution: Executive Reform in Puerto Rico under Governor Tugwell, 1941–1946* (Cambridge: Harvard University Press, 1965), pp. 200 ff., argues that these reforms diminished the opportunities for innovation that existed under the looser structure of "administrative pluralism."

3. Muñoz Marín quoted in Carl J. Friedrich, *Puerto Rico: Middle Road to Freedom* (New York: Rinehart and Co., 1959), p. 29.

4. Muñoz Marín's testimony to the Senate, quoted in Fernós Isern, *Estado Libre Asociado de Puerto Rico*, pp. 155–62.

5. U.S. Congress, H.R. 2275, 81st Cong., 2d sess., 1951.

6. For a detailed discussion of the governor's powers see Carmen Ramos de Santiago, *El Gobierno de Puerto Rico*, 2nd ed. (Río Piedras: Editorial Universitaria de Puerto Rico, 1970), esp. pp. 596 ff. Muñoz Marín summoned, on occasion, the "Great Cabinet," which included officials of the Fomento.

7. See Surendra Bhana, *The United States and the Development of the Puerto Rican Status Question 1936–1968* (Wichita: University of Kansas Press, 1975), esp. pp. 160–61.

8. For a full discussion of Puerto Rico in the United Nations, see chapter 14.

9. The only new power granted was that the auditor and the judges of the Supreme Court of Puerto Rico would be appointed, not by the president of the United States, but by the governor of Puerto Rico. This swept away one of the more obvious, if minor, residuary traces of colonialism, but it was, in itself, a far less significant change than the Elective Governor Act of 1947, as Muñoz Marín himself confessed.

10. *San Juan Star*, December 7, 1962.

11. These became apparent when Muñoz Marín was negotiating for the presentation

in 1953 of the United States case in the United Nations that Puerto Rico had ceased
to be a "dependent territory," that is, a colony. The Department of the Interior
questioned Muñoz Marín's draft, which held that Puerto Rico had "ceased to be a
territory of the United States" and that insular laws could not be repealed by
"external authority." Muñoz Marín insisted that Congress could not repeal insular
laws and that only the courts could judge their constitutionality. He eventually
agreed to a draft that stated that the power of the Puerto Rican legislature "essentially parallels that of the state governments." The Department of the Interior
rejected Fernós Isern's interpretation of the phrase "in the nature of a compact" as
foreign to U.S. law; it was dropped from the final draft submitted to the United
Nations, although the U.S. delegates employed the term — the State Department
was willing to override the caution of the Department of the Interior.

12. C.J. Friedrich, *Puerto Rico: Middle Road to Freedom* (New York: Rinehart and
Co., Inc., 1959), p. 36.

13. According to R.J. Hunter, "Historical Survey of the Puerto Rican Status
Question," *U.S. - Puerto Rican Commission on the Status of Puerto Rico, Background
Papers* (Washington, D.C.: Government Printing Office, 1966), p. 125, a sense of
urgency had been created by the *independentistas*' renewed attack on Commonwealth
in the United Nations, triggered by President Eisenhower's pledge, in 1953, to
support the status that the Puerto Ricans desired.

14. Cf. Muñoz Marín's Delphic reply to journalists in *San Juan Star*, December 8,
1959.

15. *San Juan Star*, December 7 and 13, 1962 and January 17, 1963.

16. Interview by R.C. with Sánchez Vilella, January 1982.

17. Fernós Isern, *Estado Libre Asociado de Puerto Rico*, p. 558.

18. The Status Commission consisted of thirteen members. The secretary was Ben
Stephansky.

19. *Congressional Record*, 88th Cong., 1st sess., 1963. vol. 109, pt. 15, p. 20124.

20. "Vanguardia repudia resolución del PPD," *El Mundo*, February 28, 1967.

21. *Report of the United States – Puerto Rico Commission on the Status of Puerto Rico* (San
Juan, 1966), p. 25.

22. For these arguments see R. Garzaro, *Puerto Rico colonia de Estados Unidos* (Madrid:
Editorial Tecnos, 1980), p. 23.

23. In his testimony in House Subcommittee on Territorial and Insular Affairs,
Hearings on H.R. 11200 and H.R. 11201, 96th Cong., 2d sess., pp. 182 ff.

24. *San Juan Star*, January 30, 1970.

25. Both Muñoz Marín and Rafael Hernández Colón (the PPD leader and president
of the Senate) objected to the nomination of statehooders to the ad hoc committee.
Hernández Colón also objected to President Nixon's appointment of Dan Seymour,
president of J. Walter Thompson Advertising Agency (as it was possible that the
firm might have business in Puerto Rico and might be seeking government contracts), as the publicity agent of the ad hoc committee. *San Juan Star*, January 30,
1970.

26. For the rise of the younger generation in the PPD, see below.
27. See the arguments of Juan M. García Passalacqua in *La alternativa liberal* (Colección UPREX, Editorial Universitaria, 1974), pp. 84–85.
28. *Hearings on H.R. 11200* and H.R. *11201,* p. 32.
29. Ibid., pp. 22 ff.
30. Ibid., pp. 228 ff.
31. Jaime Benítez, then resident commissioner, believed that unforeseen congressional delays allowed a hostile campaign to be mounted against the "wishes of the majority of the Puerto Rican people"—a campaign that received acceptance because people were ill-informed. Cf. his interviews in *El Mundo,* May and July 1976.
32. *San Juan Star,* July 31, 1975.
33. When Governor Romero Barceló sought to justify his desertion of the traditional statehooders' support of the Republican party, he argued "the Democrats are more in tune (*estan más al tono*) with the social philosophy of the PNP than the Republicans." Speech of October 14, 1980.
34. Juan M. García Passalacqua, "The Issue of Self-Determination," *San Juan Star,* June 19, 20, and 23, 1981.
35. The PPD had wavered about participation in primaries because it would appear a step toward statehood and also because Republicans would be able to vote in Democratic primaries. Cf. *El Nuevo Día,* October 15, 1979.
36. Cf. Juan M. García Passalacqua. By commissioning an interagency study group to examine the economic effects of the status option in 1977, "the White House had at last, after eighty-two years, taken an active interest in Puerto Rico."
37. For a detailed examination of the position of Puerto Rico under the various federal programs, see *Economic Study of Puerto Rico* (Washington, D.C.: U.S. Department of Commerce, 1979), i, pp. 151–329.
38. A convenient summary of decisions is contained in *Experiences of Past Territories Can Assist Puerto Rican Status Deliberations* (Washington, D.C.: General Accounting Office, 1980), app. 4, pp. 75–88.
39. *Consentino v. International Longshoremen's Association* (1954).
40. *El Mundo,* May 21, 1974. The case in question was *Calero-Toledo v. Pearson Yacht Leasing Company.*
41. *San Juan Star,* January 7, 1982. For a detailed study of the legal issues in 1970, see D.M. Helfeld, "How much of the Federal Constitution is likely to be held applicable in the Commonwealth of Puerto Rico?" *Revista Jurídica Universidad de Puerto Rico* 39, no. 2 (1970): 169–206. Helfeld argues that the Supreme Court of the United States will base its decision, not on the territorial clause, but on the equal civil rights of U.S. citizens. The court has yet "to define with precision how and to what extent Puerto Rico fits within or is related to the American constitutional system."
42. Quoted in Bhana, *The United States and the Development of the Puerto Rican Status Question,* p. 143.
43. Court of Appeal to the First Circuit, *Figueroa v. the People of Puerto Rico* (232 F.2d

615 1956), quoted in Bhana, *The United States and the Development of the Puerto Rican Status Question*.

44. Mary Proudfoot, *Britain and the United States in the Caribbean* (London: Faber and Faber, 1954), p. 2.

Chapter 4

1. This flexibility and frequent changes of position on the status issue were products of the need to keep within one party the advocates of differing views on Puerto Rico's status. This was particularly the case with Muñoz Rivera's Unionists and, later, with Antonio R. Barceló's Liberals. It also accounts for Muñoz Marín's sometimes Delphic utterances on status during the PPD's early years. Cf. R.W. Anderson, *Party Politics in Puerto Rico* (Palo Alto: Stanford University Press, 1965), chap. II. Ideology on status has hardened since Anderson wrote in the early 1960s, even if the ideological debate on status remains a monopoly of the political class.

2. Cf. J.M. García Passalacqua, "The Power of the Mayors," in *San Juan Star*, March 31, 1980. "The new power brokers in Puerto Rican politics are the municipal mayors and they know it." The proof advanced for this proposition is that the two gubernatorial candidates ran behind the mayors in the 1980 election. Nevertheless, the mayors, without a local tax base, are dependent on the government and the legislature for funds.

3. The payment of party expenses by government grants was adopted in 1957 during the virtual monopoly of the PPD. Muñoz Marín wished to encourage opposition parties and to end the practice by which the PPD imposed compulsory party contributions on government servants.

Chapter 5

1. For a brief account of the early projects for a Free Associated State, see Surendra Bhana, *The United States and the Development of the Puerto Rican Status Question 1936–1968* (Wichita: University of Kansas Press, 1975), chap. 7. The concept of a free associated state had been set out in detail by the Republican Tous Sotó. For more on Sotó, see J.B. Sotó, *Puerto Rico ante el derecho de gentes* (San Juan, 1928).

2. The range of Muñoz Rivera's literary interests is evident in his essay "Puerto Rico: el ideal de una Patria," reprinted in *Antología del pensamiento puertorriqueño*, ed. E. Fernandez Méndez (Río Piedras: Editorial Universitaria, 1975), pp. 66–70.

3. His opponents regarded his reading of a message from President Roosevelt over the radio (December 22, 1934) as a trick, to make "a political hero" of a politician who was, at that time, a young man making his way in Barceló's Liberal party.

4. E.P. Hanson, the eulogist of Operation Bootstrap, maintained that Muñoz and Ernest Gruening, the Roosevelt-appointed director of the Division of Territories

and Insular Possessions, fell out because Muñoz would not condemn Riggs's assassins. Gruening, twenty-seven years later, recalled Muñoz stating that, having taken on the sugar interests, he would not take on the Nationalists. He reported a conversation that Muñoz later could not recall, in which Muñoz told him that "many lives had been lost in the liberation of Puerto Rico. I take the long-range view in contemplating the destiny of my country." To which Gruening replied, "I am afraid you are now just considering the destiny of Muñoz Marín." See F.O. Gatell, "Independence Rejected: Puerto Rico and the Tydings Bill of 1936," *Hispanic American Historical Review*, XXXVIII (February 1958), pp. 30. See also Thomas Mathews, *Puerto Rican Politics and the New Deal* (Gainesville: University of Florida Press, 1960), pp. 254 ff. Muñoz protested against the trials of *independentistas* at a time when Congress was considering independence in the hearings of the Tydings Bill (ibid., p. 272).

5. The phrase was used by Jaime Benítez, interview with R.C., July 1980.

6. This was made clear in a speech of July 17, 1951.

7. "The Economy of Puerto Rico" (U.S. Tariff Commission, 1946). Dorfman is said to have opened Muñoz's eyes to the implications of the most-favored-nation clause.

8. Teodoro Moscoso in *El Nuevo Día*, Sunday edition, April 25, 1982.

9. *El Mundo*, July 29, 1946.

10. U.S. Congress, Senate, *Hearings on S. 1407*, 78th Cong., 1st sess., 1943, pp. 491 ff.

11. Vicente Géigel Polanco, *La farsa del Estado Libre Asociado* (San Juan, 1972).

12. This was the case with political science professor Carmen Gautier and with many other university professors who were members of the PPD. Professor Gautier published a book defending the *independentista* position in the United Nations: *Puerto Rico y la ONU* (Río Piedras: Editorial Edil, 1978).

13. These were Sol Descartes, the Treasury secretary, who appeared on television in 1980 supporting the PNP; Jaime Benítez, chancellor and later president of the University of Puerto Rico; Rafael Picó, head of the Planning Board; and Teodoro Moscoso, the guiding spirit of Fomento.

14. Jaime Benítez according to Roberto Sánchez Vilella (interview with R.C., September 9, 1980).

15. J.M. García Passalacqua, *La alternativa liberal* (Coleccón UPREX, Editorial Universitaria, 1974), pp. 11, 16.

16. Negrón Lopez's adviser and ally on the university issue was Jaime Benítez. See Ismaro Velázquez, *Muñoz y Sánchez Vilella* (Río Piedras: UPREX, Editorial Universitaria, 1974), pp. 100 ff. Muñoz's support of the opposition was known. When asked for his view on a legislative proposal he replied "Ask Negrón" (interview of R.C. with Sánchez Vilella, January 1982).

17. Trying to unravel the conflicting testimony on the relationship between Sánchez Vilella and Muñoz, I was reminded of the Japanese film *Rashomon* — a murder seen through different eyes. There is complete conflict of evidence over the 1967 plebiscite: Sánchez Vilella and his supporters insist that Sánchez had *opposed* the plebiscite

on the grounds that the 1960 election results made its success doubtful; Muñoz's supporters maintain that Sánchez pressed for a plebiscite.

18. In order to secure registration for his party he bought a small party that was already registered. It should be noted that Sánchez's party did not abandon the stage management from above, considered by his supporters as the characteristic vice of the PPD.

19. Luis Ferré to the House Ways and Means Subcommittee on the Caribbean Basin Initiative. *San Juan Star*, March 25, 1982.

20. *San Juan Star*, March 22, 1982.

21. It was largely the work of Frederico Hernández Denton, Secretary of Consumer Affairs under Hernández Colón; Hernández Denton was formerly a member of the PIP.

22. The U.S. trade representative, Ambassador William Brock, calls the power to set tariffs demanded by the New Thesis "draconian measures [that] do not warrant serious consideration." *San Juan Star*, July 31, 1982.

23. *"Que pasa en el PPD," El Nuevo Día*, April 25, 1981. The "progressive autonomists" can count on the sympathy of Sánchez Vilella, for whom the "New Federalism" has forced a "reconsideration" of Commonwealth. As the linchpin of a "progressive autonomist" Popular Front that accepts free association and independence as legitimate, Sánchez has become the favorite politician of the PSP.

24. *San Juan Star*, October 5, 1982.

25. *El Nuevo Día*, September 29, 1982.

26. E.g., over the primaries. There are those who support permanent participation, those who supported participation in 1984 *only* because it was thought that Kennedy —expected to support the New Thesis—would run, and those who reject participation altogether.

27. The personalist interpretation of Puerto Rican politics has been challenged by a group of young Marxist historians, who seek to relate the life and death political parties to the structure of production, the dramatic changes in that structure wrought by the American invasion, and the subsequent domination of Puerto Rico by "imperialist capitalism." They work in the Center for the Study of Puerto Rican Reality (CEREP), supported by a grant from the Ford Foundation. The most perceptive of these young historians is Angel Quintero Rivera. Though I do not share his acceptance of the Marxist-Leninist model of capitalist imperialism, I find Quintero's analysis stimulating. A simplified version of that analysis is given in his *Conflictos de clase y política en Puerto Rico* (Río Piedras: Ediciones Huracán, 1977). A more detailed analysis is in his "La base social de la transformación ideológica del Partido Popular en la década del 40" in *Cambio y desarrollo en Puerto Rico*, ed. G. Navas Dávila (Río Piedras: Editorial Universitaria, 1980), pp. 35–103.

28. This was the verdict of Robert W. Anderson in the mid-1960s, though Anderson insists on the influence of the U.S. political system as favoring a two-party system in Puerto Rico. See his *Party Politics in Puerto Rico* (Stanford, Calif.: Stanford University Press, 1965), chap. 11.

29. The decline of the PPD among urban voters was already apparent in 1960. Cf. Marcia Quintero, *Elecciones de 1968 Puerto Rico* (San Juan: mimeo, 1972), p. 23. Mayagüez was the only large municipality where the PPD remained a predominant force in 1968.
30. According to the statehooder Luis Dávila Colón. Interview with R.C., August 26, 1982.
31. See Rafael L. Ramírez, *El arrabal y la política* (Río Piedras: Editorial Universitaria, 1976) for Ferré's campaign in the slum of Catano. For his local leaders' programs, see pp. 101–102.
32. The PPD had concentrated on the status issue in 1968, but only 4.2 percent of the lumpenproletariat considered the status position of the party it voted for; over 40 percent voted on the basis of local issues, driven by the assumption that direct, personal benefits would derive from the party they supported.
33. Oscar Lewis, *La Vida* (London: Secker and Warburg, 1967), p. 322.
34. Speech of June 6, 1982.
35. Harold J. Lidin in the *San Juan Star*, June 20, 1982.

Chapter 6

1. For the conditions of statehood, see "Experiences of Past Territories Can Assist Puerto Rico Status Deliberations," *Report of the Comptroller General to the Congress of the United States* (1980).
2. See, for example, "The American Statehood Process and Its Relevance to Puerto Rico's Colonial Reality: A Historical and Constitutional Perspective," San Juan Grupo de Investigadores Puertorriqueños, Inc. (mimeograph, 1980).
3. Celestino Iriarte, the Republican leader, in *El Mundo*, September 6, 1945.
4. See the writings of a young and enthusiastic statehooder, Luis Dávila Colón, published by the Grupo de Investigadores Puertorriqueños, Inc.
5. A view apparently shared by Governor Romero, *San Juan Star*, November 27, 1982.
6. Luis Dávila Colón (interview with R.C., July 1981). This seems a conventional figure. In December 1966 García Méndez, leader of the statehood PER, insisted on "at least 60 percent of the votes" as constituting triumph. R.B. Bothwell González, *Puerto Rico: cien años de lucha política* (Río Piedras: Editorial Universitaria, 1979), IV, p. 414.
7. In 1932, the old Republican party became the Unión Republicana Puertorriqueña and, under Rafael Martínez Nadal, the *Partido Estadista Republicano*. The struggle for leadership after 1941 resulted in twin leadership in 1952.
8. García Méndez, a future leader of the *estadistas*, denounced his leader as "a dictator in a delirium" and left the party. Cf., Bolivar Pagán, *Historia de los partidos políticos puertorriqueños 1898–1956* (San Juan: Librería Campos, 1959), ii, p. 149.
9. The most important of these were presented by the Socialist Bolivar Pagán when

he was resident commissioner. See *Congressional Record*, 1940–41, pt. 19, p. 769; and 1941–42, pt. 15, p. 914.

10. Congressman Marcantonio was originally an advocate of statehood. See F. Ojeda Reyes, *Vito Marcantonio y Puerto Rico* (Río Piedras: Ediciones Huracán, 1978), pp. 17 ff.

11. R.W. Anderson, *Party Politics in Puerto Rico* (Stanford, Calif.: Stanford University Press, 1965), pp. 109–110.

12. *El Mundo*, January 20, 1956.

13. *San Juan Star*, November 20, 1982.

14. Ibid., July 13, 1959.

15. Ibid., July 5, 1982.

16. For Ruth Benedict, "culture" is a complex of customs and beliefs embracing *all* aspects of a given society and which make life comprehensible to its members and governs relationships between them.

17. *San Juan Star*, December 6, 1959.

18. Cf. Rafael Ramírez, *El arrabal y la política* (Río Piedras: Editorial Universitaria, 1977), pp. 41–42.

19. *San Juan Star*, July 28, 1962.

20. Senator Nogueras, interview with R.C., September 15, 1980.

21. Puerto Rico is excluded from Supplementary Security Income and subject to ceilings under Medicaid, Aid to Families with Dependent Children, and Title XX of the Social Security Act. "As a result of these inequities," argues Governor Romero, "we have been obliged to provide ever increasing amounts of local funds to meet the basic needs of our economically disadvantaged citizens." See Barry B. Levine, "Cashing Out Food Stamps," in *The Journal* published by the Institute for Socioeconomic Studies, Winter 1982, pp. 50–51.

22. Much of the article (*Foreign Affairs*, April 1981) was directed against Professor Alfred Stepan's argument that independence might be in the long-term interests of the United States, since its denial fueled anti-Americanism in Latin America.

23. Luis R. Dávila Colón, "Equal Citizenship, Self-Determination and the U.S. Statehood Process: A Constitutional and Historical Analysis," *Journal of International Law* 13, no. 2 (1982), p. 374.

24. *Congressional Record*, Senate, August 2, 1979, S. 11374.

25. *El Nuevo Día*, April 30, 1978. Cf. the governor's statement on the admission of Hawaii and Nebraska, ibid., November 27, 1982.

26. Disillusioned statehooders had opted for independence in 1912. Romero was resurrecting the 1932 program of the Puerto Rican Republican party: "We will try to obtain as soon as possible from the United States the admission of Puerto Rico as a state of the United States of America and in case this demand is denied, or if Congress acts in such a way as to make it unattainable, then the Republican party will work to obtain full internal and external sovereignty."

27. Speech of July 4, 1982.

28. For information on Iglesias' early relations with Barbosa, see Gonzalo F. Cor-

dova, *Santiago Iglesias: Creador del Movimiento Obrero de Puerto Rico* (Río Piedras: Editorial Universitaria, 1980), chap. 2. Like Barbosa, Iglesias was a doctrinaire Republican and disciple of the Spanish Republican Pi y Margall; like Barbosa, he rejected Muñoz Rivera's alliance with Spanish monarchist politicians.

29. Gonzalo F. Cordova, *Santiago Iglesias: Creador del Movimiento Obrero de Puerto Rico* (Río Piedras: Editorial Universitaria, 1980), p. 50.

30. Santiago Iglesias Pantin, *Luchas emancipadoras*, ii (San Juan: Imprenta Venezuela, 1908), passim.

31. See Miles Galvin, *The Organized Labor Movement in Puerto Rico* (Madison, N.J.: Fairleigh Dickinson University Press, 1979), pp. 63–65.

32. Quoted in Blanca Silvestrini de Pacheco, *Los trabajadores puertorriqueños y el Partido Socialista 1932–40* (Río Piedras: Editorial Universitaria, 1979), p. 98. The manifesto of *Afirmación Socialista* is printed in Antonio G. Quintero Rivera, *Lucha obrera: Antología de grandes documentos en la historia obrero puertorriqueño* (San Juan: CEREP, 1971), pp. 108–117.

33. Cf. the verdict of Manuel Maldonado Denis in *Puerto Rico Mito y Realidad* (1979 ed.), p. 54. That the Socialists were "annexationists" and subordinated to the colonialist AFL was therefore disastrous for "the development of a revolutionary consciousness in Puerto Rico." "The masses went one way, the *independentistas* in the opposite direction."

34. This was expressed in the title of César Andreu Iglesias's first book, *Independence and Socialism* (San Juan: Librería Estrella Roja, 1951). He was, for a time, a member of the Communist party and always remained a Marxist.

Chapter 7

1. Prologue, by Margot Arce de Vázquez, to Antulio Parrilla, *Puerto Rico Supervivencia y Liberación* (Río Piedras: Ediciones Librería Internacional, 1971).

2. See Juan Antonio Corretjer, *La lucha por la independencia de Puerto Rico* (San Juan, 1950).

3. Manuel Maldonado Denis, *La conciencia nacional puertorriqueña* (Mexico City: Siglo Ventiuno Editores, 1972), p. 9. Albizu Campos's writings and speeches have been edited, with an introduction by J. Benjamin Torres, in *Pedro Albizu Campos Obras Escogodas*, 3 vols. (San Juan: Editorial Jelofe, 1975).

4. Betances advocated a Federation of the Antilles as early as 1867. For his views, see the selection of his works edited by Carlos M. Rama, *Las Antillas para los Antillanos* (San Juan: Instituto de Cultura Puertorriqueña, 1957).

5. *El Mundo*, June 28, 1933.

6. There is still doubt about who fired the first shot. For a brief account of these episodes see R.A. Johnson, *Puerto Rico: Commonwealth or Colony?* (New York: Praeger, 1980), pp. 24, 36–38.

7. For information on Albizu Campos's response to the sugar strikers (who were

striking against their own union as much as against their employers) see Antonio G. Quintero Rivera, *Lucha obrera: Antología de grandes documentos en la historia obrero puertorriqueño* (San Juan: CEREP, 1971), pp. 98–103.

8. The Nationalists' attempt to found their own trade union was a dismal failure. See Juan A. Corretjer, *El líder de la desperación* (San Juan, 1972), p. 44.

9. Albizu was particularly grieved by the cooperation of the Spanish colony with American business: this tarnished the image of Spain, the mother country.

10. American governors frequently insisted that some form of population control was the only way to remedy Puerto Rico's poverty. Governor Beverly stated this openly, and Albizu led a protest movement against what he presented as an attempt to destroy the nation: "the density of the population is the power of nationhood" (*"la densidad de la población es el poder de la nacionalidad definida"*). *El Mundo*, March 31, 1932.

11. PIP votes as a percentage of total votes: 1948, 10.9 percent; 1952, 19.1 percent; 1960, 3.0 percent; 1964, 2.8 percent; 1968, 3.4 percent; 1972, 4.5 percent; 1976, 6.4 percent.

12. The number of those arrested, according to Concepción de García's testimony to the Civil Liberties Commission of 1958, was between 700 and 1,000. Hard evidence suggests about 200. Cf. D. Helfeld, "Discrimination for Political Beliefs and Association" (submitted to the Puerto Rican Civil Liberties Commission, December 29, 1958), pp. 36 ff. For a further treatment of repression and denial of civil rights, see below.

13. See Manuel Maldonado Denis, "El futuro del movimiento independentista puertorriqueño," *Revista de Ciencias Sociales* 9, no. 3 (September 1965).

14. This has been the case especially if the party in power threatened an irreversible step toward statehood, which would permanently close the door to independence. Hence, in order to defeat Ferré at all costs in 1972, many *pipiolos* (and even more PSP militants) voted PPD; this pattern was repeated in 1980 to ward off a move toward statehood by Governor Romero Barceló.

15. In *Avance*, November 29, 1972.

16. Interview with R.C., January 1982.

17. The latter stages of this crisis are treated in Norma Tapia, *La crisis del PIP* (Editorial Edil, 1980). Norma Tapia is a prejudiced and bitter critic of Berríos.

18. Speech of January 12, 1953, quoted in R.W. Anderson, *Gobierno y partidos políticos en Puerto Rico* (Madrid: Editorial Tecnos, 1970), p. 129.

19. *El Mundo*, November 3, 1950.

20. See below.

21. *El Mundo*, August 4, 1973.

22. See G.H. Fromm, *César Andreu Iglesias* (Río Piedras: Ediciones Huracán, 1977).

23. Quoted in Tapia, *La crisis del PIP*, p. 130.

24. In César Andreu Iglesias's paper *La Hora*, which had become an open forum for *independentista* views and which was dependent on the PIP for distribution, etc., he sided with Colón and the Socialist wing: "The concept of a providential messianic

leadership is irreconcilable with Socialist principles. Nevertheless this seems to be how Rubén Berríos conceives his role." *La Hora*, February 16, 1973, quoted in G.H. Fromm, op. cit., p. 71. The PIP withdrew its support from *La Hora* and the paper closed.

25. Interview with R.C., January 1982.

26. See the *Programa PIP 1980* and *Para hacer lo que hay que hacer: Rubén Berríos Gobernador*.

27. Interview with R.C., January 1982. Berríos maintains that he warned the Cuban ambassador to the United Nations that the PSP was feeding him with "false information about the position in Puerto Rico" and that the ambassador alleged that Cuba could not push independence too strongly in the United Nations for fear of provoking a U.S. invasion.

28. *Independentistas* put great emphasis on Puerto Rican control of the petroleum, gas, and copper resources of Puerto Rico and insist on the potential bonanza they will provide if properly exploited—i.e., by Puerto Rico as an independent sovereign state, not through concessions granted by a subservient colonial government to American-dominated international consortia. *Independentista* "experts" are criticized as a "vociferous" but ignorant group, bent on exaggerating the probability of vast reserves of petroleum whose existence is viewed with skepticism by "knowledgeable, technical people." Whereas *independentistas* regard the colonial government as "unequal" in its struggle with the prospective exploiters of Puerto Rican mineral resources, their opponents claim that no government is "unequal" in relation to great companies like Western. See the controversy between Dr. Meyerhof and Dr. Morales Cardona in *Caribbean Monthly Bulletin*, Supplement, July–August 1977.

29. The Lomé Convention between the EEC and the former colonies of EEC countries is sometimes held as providing a model for the economic relations between a colonial power and its former dependencies. The convention gives *limited* privileged access to EEC markets to newly independent African and Caribbean nations.

30. For these arguments, see Rubén Berríos Martínez, "Puerto Rico and the Caribbean in the 1980s" (speech given to the Wilson Center's Latin American Program, Washington, D.C.).

31. Luis Araquistain, *La agonia antillana: El imperialismo Yanqui en el mar Caribe* (Madrid: Espasa Calpe, 1928), chap. 8.

32. For instance, a delegation of the student organization, the University Federation for Independence (FUPI), dominated by the PSP, attended a conference in Yemen, where motions were passed in support of the Puerto Rican students' strike. *Claridad*, January 1–7, 1982.

33. Cf. Fromm, *César Andreu Iglesias*, p. 47.

34. Mari Bras, "Violencia y Conciencia," *Claridad*, June 18, 1975.

35. J. Mari Bras, "Un acto de guerra," *Claridad*, March 15, 1970, and Iglesias' reply in *La Escalera* (June 1970). G. Fromm, author of the best study of Iglesias, participated in the controversy. See his *César Andreu Iglesias* (Río Piedras: Ediciones

Huracán, 1977), pp. 60−61. César Andreu left the MPI to join the PIP, where the quasi-Marxist *terceristas* were struggling against the leadership (see above). This radical mood within the PIP gave hope for the creation of a multi-class, democratic Popular Front for independence. When the "ultra leftists" were driven out of the PIP, César Andreu went with them.

36. Juan Angel Silén, *Apuntes para la historia del movimiento obrero puertorriqueño* (Río Piedras: Editorial Cultural, 1978), pp. 151 ff.

37. "El programa minimo socialista," *Pensamiento Crítico* (May−June 1980).

38. Interview by R.C. with Rubén Berríos, January 1982.

39. For example, the naming of a stadium after the governor's grandfather instead of after the local athletic hero; the mayor's indifference to the local flooding in Toa Baja. More typical is the championing of the local inhabitants' objections to mining operations in Utuado—that is, to the presence of "American imperialism."

40. *Programa socialista* (San Juan, 1978), p. 75.

41. Cf. José Luis González's observations on the PSP's reactions to the Polish crisis in *El Nuevo Día*, September 24, 1981. Cf. *Claridad*, January 1−7, 1982.

42. *San Juan Star*, January 31, 1981.

43. *Pensamiento Crítico* (October−November 1980), p. 2.

44. See the long interview with Mari Bras in *Pensamiento Crítico* (June−July 1981).

45. As in the Basque country and in Northern Ireland, what makes terrorism an intractable problem is not the number of the terrorists but the support they can mobilize from the general population. The durability and efficacy of Basque terrorism is inexplicable unless we realize that large sectors of the population are willing to protect the Basque nationalist terrorists of the ETA in trouble with the police.

46. Cf. *San Juan Star*, January 14, 1980.

Chapter 8

1. Cf. R.A. Packenham, *Liberal America and the Third World* (Princeton: Princeton University Press, 1973), pp. 3 ff.

2. Elihu Root in R. Bacon and J.B. Scott, eds., *The Military and Colonial Policies of the United States* (Cambridge, Mass., 1916; reprint ed., New York: AMS Press), pp. 70 ff.

3. The average annual wage of a family of five was $349. "Health and Socio-Economic Conditions on a Sugar Cane Plantation," *Puerto Rican Journal of Public Health and Tropical Medicine* 12, no. 4 (1937), pp. 405−90.

4. Quoted in Thomas Mathews, *Puerto Rican Politics and the New Deal* (Gainesville: University of Florida Press, 1960), p. 215.

5. See p. 205 ff.

6. By 1938, almost $60 million had been pumped into the island by the PRRA— 53 percent on labor or personnel services.

7. Percent Distribution of General Government Expenditures for Fiscal Year 1981: Education 30%; Health/Welfare 22%; Industrial/Agricultural/Commercial Development 8%; Public Safety and Protection 12%; Transportation/Communication 2%; Other 26%.

The effect of this expenditure can be seen in primary and secondary school enrollment, which rose between 1950 and 1981 from 431,000 to 713,000, and enrollment in the University of Puerto Rico from 11,000 to 53,000; and in the decline of the death rate over the same period from 10.5 per thousand to 6.3 per thousand.

On the receipt side, income tax now brings in $968m, excise taxes $533m, other revenues $276m, federal excise/customs refunds $316m, and federal grants-in-aid $605m. The most striking increase is in federal grants-in-aid, which in 1950 stood at $7m.

8. Cf. the verdict of D.D. Bourne and J.R. Bourne in *Thirty Years of Change in Puerto Rico* (New York: Praeger, 1966): "Planned change characterizes present-day Puerto Rico," p. 25.

9. Quoted in H. Springer, *Reflections on the Failure of the First West Indian Federation*, Occasional Papers of the Harvard Center for International Affairs, no. 4 (1962), p. 31. Industrialization by invitation had, it must be noted, failed to eliminate unemployment in Trinidad.

10. For a detailed and technical examination see M. Escobar, *The 936 Market: An Introduction* (San Juan, 1980). For a brief history of Article 936, see "Origins of the 936 Species—and How to Defend It," by Fomento Administrator José R. Madera, in the *San Juan Star*, August 15, 1982.

11. For the fate of CORCO, see below.

12. The statistics on the distribution of employment in 1968–79 show the decline of the old labor-intensive industries and the rise of industries that, relatively speaking, employed fewer hands.

Industry Group	1968	1973	1979	Absolute Change 1968–79	% Change 1968–79
	(in thousands)				
Tobacco products	7.0	5.6	2.2	− 4,800	− 69
Textile mill products	8.2	7.6	4.3	− 3,900	− 48
Leather and leather products	11.4	6.7	6.0	− 5,400	− 47
Apparel	40.2	40.7	35.4	− 4,800	− 12
Chemicals	4.5	11.0	16.3	11,800	262
Pharmaceuticals	1.4	5.0	10.0	8,600	614
Petroleum refining, rubber products, plastics	6.2	6.5	7.1	900	15
Machinery (except electrical, transportation equipment)	2.0	1.9	6.6	4,600	230
Electrical and electronic equipment	9.1	14.8	17.3	8,200	90
Scientific instruments	3.8	9.1	13.6	9,800	258

13. Direct dependence on the United States for exports and imports has declined. Financial dependence has not.

14. "Weak" states expand less in the upturn and suffer more in downturn than do strong states (G.H. Bard, "Regional Cycles of Manufacturing Employment in the United States," *Journal of American Statistical Association*, March 1960). Puerto Rico did not suffer from the earlier recessions of the 1950s because the economy was robust and sustained by infrastructural investment, and after 1970 the movements of the Puerto Rican economy did not correspond completely to those of the mainland.

15. Professor James Tobin calculated that investment in physical capital was sometimes as low as 20 percent of total investment.

16. Since 1976, Article 936 has allowed companies operating in Puerto Rico to repatriate their profits without paying federal tax. However, they must pay a tollgate tax on repatriated profits to Puerto Rico of 7 – 10 percent; the lower rates would apply to companies that invested 25 percent of these profits in Puerto Rico for a period of eight years. Romero's 1978 tax law granted new firms 90 percent exemption from Puerto Rican corporate income and property taxes for five years, 75 percent for the next five years and, for plants located in zones increasingly distant from San Juan and with high unemployment, exemptions at a minimum of 50 percent for twenty-five years. These concessions are extended to service industries, a recognition that Puerto Rico is seeking to move beyond exclusive reliance on manufacturing.

17. Ruth Gruber in the *New York Times Magazine*, May 21, 1972.

18. *Economic Study of Puerto Rico* (Washington, D.C.: Department of Commerce, 1979), I, p. 5. In the future, cited as Kreps Report.

19. Food stamps, as such, have been discontinued and payment is made directly to those who qualify by check.

20. K. Holbik and P.L. Swan, *Industrialization and Employment in Puerto Rico 1950 – 72* (Austin: University of Texas Business Research, 1975), pp. 50 ff. See also R.S. Burton, *The Effect of Minimum Wage Laws in the Economic Growth of Puerto Rico* (Cambridge, Harvard Center for International Affairs), p. 41.

21. 94th Congress, 2d sess., Hearings before the Subcommittee on Territorial and Insular Affairs on H.R. 11200 and H.R. 11201, p. 250.

22. Governor Romero and the PNP support the equal application of federal laws as a matter of principle, nor were they indifferent to the electoral appeal of support for higher wages, which enabled them to cast the PPD as the allies of the industrial oligarchs and enemies of the wage earners.

23. For union pressure for mainland wages, see Miles E. Galvin, *The Organized Labor Movement in Puerto Rico* (Madison, N.J.: Fairleigh Dickinson University Press, 1979), pp. 131 ff. As Galvin points out, what Puerto Rican experience proves is that the pressure of an unlimited supply of labor among the agrarian unemployed cannot permanently hold down wages in a developing economy.

24. See Kreps Report, I, p. 216.

25. Estimates of the loss to Puerto Rico of the administration's proposals varied between $600 million and $1.5 billion.

26. But see below.

27. The mayor of Dorado used CETA funds to subsidize public works that the municipality would otherwise have been unable to afford. *New York Times*, July 25, 1982.

28. Governor Romero succumbed to the charms of Professor Laffer. "Art Laffer suggested a 15 percent cut at one time but I had to tell him that I had a budget to balance." *San Juan Star*, November 13, 1980. Cf. *Washington Post*, May 3, 1981.

29. Speech of July 2, 1981.

30. According to the Kreps Report (I, p. 160), there has been a fifteenfold increase in net transfer payments between 1970 and 1977. Over the years during which these payments have come to the island, unemployment has roughly doubled.

31. *Puerto Rican Business Review*, Special Supplement (July–August 1981), p. 12.

32. *Caribbean Business*, April 18, 1981.

33. Diana Christopoulos, "Puerto Rico in the Twentieth Century," in *Puerto Rico and the Puerto Ricans*, ed. Adalberto López and James Petras (New York: John Wiley and Sons, 1974), p. 121.

34. The *independentistas*' submission to the Status Commission. Status of Puerto Rico, hearings before the United States-Puerto Rico Commission on the Status of Puerto Rico (eWashington, D.C.) vol. 1, p. 57.

35. Both, it must be noted, are manufactured on the island as well as on the mainland.

36. Cf. Fernando Picó, *Amargo Café* (Río Piedras: Ediciones Huracán, 1981) and *Libertad y servidumbre en el Puerto Rico del siglo XIX* (Río Piedras: Ediciones Huracán, 1979).

37. For the problems of the sugar industry see Andrés Ramos Mattei, *La hacienda azucarera: Su crecimiento y crisis en Puerto Rico (Siglo XIX)* (San Juan: CEREP, 1981).

38. See Truman R. Clark, *Puerto Rico and the United States 1917–23* (Pittsburgh: University of Pittsburgh Press, 1975), pp. 516 ff.

39. A typical criticism is put forward by José J. Villamil in "El modelo puertorriqueño: Los limites del crecimiento independiente," *Revista puertorriqueña de investigaciones sociales* 1, no. 1 (July–December 1976).

40. For this thesis, see *Labor Migration under Capitalism: The Puerto Rican Experience*, ed. History Task Force, Centro de Estudios Puertorriqueños (1979).

41. Manuel Maldonado Denis, *Puerto Rico: a Socio-Historic Interpretation* (New York: Vintage Press, 1972), p. 302. His detailed treatment is in *En las entrañas: Un análisis sociohistórico de la emigración puertorriqueña* (Havana, Cuba: Casa de las Americas, 1976).

42. One of the more alarming features of recent migratory trends has been the "brain drain" to the mainland of professionals who find salaries in Puerto Rico to be low and taxes high. It has been estimated that some 5,000 professionals have left the island including, in one year, half the graduates of the Engineering School of Mayagüez.

43. Kreps Report estimates, I, p. 21.

44. Werner Baer, "An Evaluation of a Successful Development Program," *Quarterly Journal of Economics* 73 (1959), p. 662. Dependence on the U.S. market has declined from 90 percent of exports to and imports from the United States in the 1960s to 80 percent of exports to and 60 percent of imports from the United States in 1980. While the Fomento seeks to attract foreign investors (e.g., from Spain), its main efforts are still directed toward the United States.
45. José R. Madera and Roberto Reixach Benítez, "The Strategy of Development" (San Juan, 1982).
46. Angel Quintero Alfaro (secretary for education, 1964–68) in *Educación y cambio social* (1974), p. 22.
47. Bertram Finn, former economic adviser to Governor Romero, argues that the props have encouraged "gross inefficiencies" that have become "impediments to our future growth." *San Juan Star*, January 19, 1982.
48. Henry Wells, *The Modernization of Puerto Rico: A Political Study of Changing Values and Institutions* (Cambridge: Harvard University Press, 1969).
49. "The Sad Case of Puerto Rico," *American Mercury* 16 (1929), p. 137.

Chapter 9

1. *Etiología de la violencia en Puerto Rico* (San Juan: Technical Services of Puerto Rico), p. 109.
2. R. Weisskoff, "Income Distribution and Economic Growth in Puerto Rico, Argentina and Mexico," *Income Distribution in Latin America*, ed. A. Foxley (Cambridge: Cambridge University Press, 1976), p. 28.
3. To Antonio Pedreira, writing in the 1930s as a defender of Puerto Rican values, *jíbaro* culture was the "quarry" from which Puerto Rico derived its particular forms of self-expression. Yet Pedreira recognized that the *jíbaro* was a vanishing species in an increasingly urbanized society and was driven to invent the figure of the "city *jíbaro*." See his "La actualidad del Jíbaro" in *Boletín de la Universidad de Puerto Rico*, Series VI, no. 1 (1935).
4. For an early but perceptive discussion of "deference" values as opposed to "welfare" values, see Henry Wells, *The Modernization of Puerto Rico: A Political Study of Changing Values and Institutions* (Cambridge: Harvard University Press, 1969), pp. 21–36.
5. M. Tumin and A. Feldman, *Social Class and Change in Puerto Rico* (Princeton: Princeton University Press, 1961). The data refer to the late 1950s.
6. Ibid., pp. 129, 196.
7. *Etiología de la violencia*, p. 99.
8. See Luis Nieves Falcón, "La opinión pública y las aspiraciones de los Puerto Riqueños" (mimeograph, 1970).
9. *Etiología de la violencia*, p. 108.

10. When Caguas, a PPD town, had no member in the House of Representatives, it received no funds from a PNP government (*San Juan Star*, January 8, 1982). Individual members present a large number of bills for benefits to their own districts. The representative of Caguas, when elected, proceeded to present a bill for funds to improve the market, provide hospital equipment, and finance a road widening and a bridge. Again this is an exaggeration of what would be regarded as normal practice in the United States if we regard the Puerto Rican legislature as corresponding to that of a state.

11. Nieves Falcón, "La opinion pública," p. 129.

12. Eduardo Seda Bonilla, *La cultura política de Puerto Rico* (Río Piedras: Ediciones Amauta, 1976), p. 129. For the position in 1963, see his *Actitud, conocimiento y apercepción de los derechos civiles en el público puertorriqueño* (San Juan, 1964). He found the general level of tolerance "very low" and the level of political intolerance high.

13. Letter to Edgar Hoover, June 29, 1966, from the Puerto Rican Civil Rights Commission. Hoover's reply was that the FBI would continue to do its duty.

14. For instance, the writer Maldonado Denis, who wished to attend a conference in Havana, was unable to do so because his passport was revoked. See Milton Pabón, *La cultura política puertorriqueña* (Río Piedras: Editorial Xaguey, 1972), p. 120.

15. For cases, see *Pensamiento Crítico* 4, no. 26 (October/November 1981), pp. 15–18. There is a lively internal debate on whether militants should or should not testify to grand juries.

16. Ibid., p. 3.

17. He was met at the airport by a bevy of photographers. For his comments, see the press of August 14, 1982.

18. Again, in certain cases where sensitive jobs are involved, positive vetting demands such enquiries.

19. Cf. the claim of Fernando Picó: "There is on this island a systematic, unrelenting petty and irrational persecution of socialists." *San Juan Star*, July 28, 1982.

20. Ibid., November 19, 1959.

21. The U.S. Justice Department has recently claimed that there is evidence of "broad and significant police corruption" in Puerto Rico. A senior police officer is alleged to have masterminded the kidnapping of a San Juan jeweler in September 1982. Opposition politicians and *independentistas* have publicized the "Jessica" case — that of a 19-year-old girl, allegedly killed in police custody in May 1980. See the *New York Times*, January 11, 1983.

22. For the development of electoral law see R. Schmidt Monge, "Notas sobre derecho electoral puertorriqueño," *Revista jurídica* 13 (1978), pp. 51–68.

23. In 1980, Jaime Benítez was so deeply disturbed by the violence of the election campaign of 1980 that he was impressed by an essay of the Spanish intellectual Julian Marías on the origins of the Spanish Civil War (interview with R.C., July 1980).

24. Quoted in A. López and J. Petras, eds., *Puerto Rico and the Puerto Ricans* (New York: John Wiley and Sons, 1974), p. 242.
25. Interview of R.C. with Ramón Arbona, formerly a member of the PSP and an editor of *Claridad*, August 20, 1980.

Chapter 10

1. Maria T. Babin, *Panorama de la cultura puertorriqueña* (New York: Biblioteca Puertorriqueña, 1958) cites thirteen classifications of skin color.
2. *La Cultura política de Puerto Rico* (Río Piedras: Ediciones Amauta, 1976), pp. 196, 179, 199. Similar views on racial discrimination have been expressed by the novelist Isabel Zenon Cruz.
3. David Lowenthal, *West Indian Societies* (London: Oxford University Press, 1972), pp. 3, 130.
4. "Las relaciones raciales en Puerto Rico," *Revista de Ciencias Sociales* 9, no. 4 (1965), p. 373. The leading case under the 1943 law concerned discrimination in a night-club.
5. F. Ferracuti et al., *Delinquents and Non-Delinquents in Puerto Rican Slum Culture* (Cambridge: Harvard University Press, 1975), p. 126.
6. F. Faust, "Delinquency and Labelling," *Crime and Delinquency* 19, no. 1 (January 1973), p. 41.
7. R.L. Scheele, "The Prominent Families of Puerto Rico," in *The People of Puerto Rico*, ed. J.H. Steward (Urbana: University of Illinois Press, 1956), pp. 418 ff. Out of two hundred upper-class women examined, sixteen showed signs of Negro blood.
8. H. Hoetink, *The Two Variants in Caribbean Race Relations* (London: Institute of Race Relations, Oxford University Press, 1967), p. 179.
9. A survey made during the 1980 election campaign reveals that 52 percent believed crime to be the most important issue; only 10.4 percent opted for status — just 4 percent above drug addiction. *Quarterly Economic Review, Second Quarter* 1980.
10. Oddly enough, drug addiction was noted as early as 1892. Blanca Silvestrini de Pacheco, "La Violencia en Puerto Rico de 1898 a 1940," in *Revista Interamericana* 7, no. 4 (1978) and 8, no. 1 (1978), esp. p. 76.
11. For example, serious crime in London has risen by 9 percent during 1982; 50 percent of all crimes are committed by youths under 21. The majority, as in Puerto Rico, are "opportunistic" crimes like car stealing.
12. See above for the voting patterns of the *caseríos* and *arrabales* in 1968.
13. See above.
14. This break corresponded with the struggle between the AFL and the more militant Congress of Industrial Organizations (CIO), now merged with the American Federation of Labor in the AFL-CIO. As so often, Puerto Rico was swept into the mainland currents; it was the CIO that organized the great dock strike of 1938.

For an excellent account of these developments see Gordon K. Lewis, *Puerto Rico: Freedom and Power in the Caribbean* (New York: M.R. Press, 1963), pp. 222–36.
15. For a brief sketch of these developments, see R.J. Alexander, *Communism in Latin America* (New Brunswick: Rutgers University Press, 1957).
16. Cooperate "*en el desarrollo del país.*" See his *Función del movimiento obrero en la democracia puertorriqueña* (San Juan, n.d.).
17. For the work of the government conciliation and arbitration services, see J. Machuca, "Sintesis historica del negociado de concilación y arbitraje," *Revista de Trabajo* 7, no. 29. The present service, which dates from 1952, is noted for its long meetings of up to twenty hours.
18. Often a company setting up a factory in Puerto Rico would negotiate wage levels with the mainland AFL union concerned: the Puerto Rican workers automatically became members of that union. According to Miles Galvin, *The Organized Labor Movement in Puerto Rico*, (Madison, N.J.: Fairleigh Dickinson University Press, 1979), p. 156, Keith Terpe of the Seafarers Union did more in a week than the old PPD organizer had done in a lifetime.
19. The independent light and power union, UTIER, is a legal trade union in the public sector and the most powerful in the island. The status of white-collar civil servants is less clear; their brotherhoods and professional associations do mount strikes (for instance, the strike by university employees in 1973 and 1976). The law, which is riddled with ambiguities, attempts to distinguish between government agencies that act like private concerns (e.g., the light and power company), where unions are legitimate, and government departments in the strict sense, where unions are technically illegal. See *Las huelgas en el sector público* (San Juan: Oficina del Gobernador, 1978). Strikes in the public sector increased as strikes in the private sector decreased: in 1964, the total number of employees involved in strikes was 19,894, of which 4,922 were in the public sector and 4,972 were in the private sector. In 1974, the total number of employees involved in strikes was 39,841, of which 31,448 were in the public sector and 8,393 were in the private sector (ibid., pp. 29–41).
20. Cf. *San Juan Star*, June 13, 1981.
21. Interview with R.C., December 1982. Quiñones Rodríquez is president of the brotherhood (i.e., union) of nonteaching university employees. Like many *independentistas* and old-style British Labor leaders, he is a man of strong religious convictions; he is a lay preacher of the Baptist Church. For his views, see his *Sindicalismo y política en Puerto Rico* (Río Piedras: Editorial Edil, Inc., 1977).
22. UTIER rank and file are said to resent the political involvement of some of their leaders in the PSP. Lausell, the UTIER president, ran for office in the 1980 elections; his union passed a resolution that no member who ran for political office could hold a union post. Cf. *Claridad*, November 20–26, 1981. Cf. the judgement of a radical: "To Puerto Rican workers the PSP remains an organization alien to their traditions and common-day life. It is seen as just another petty bourgeois party trying to use them for purposes they do not feel are theirs." Adalberto López and

James Petras, eds., *Puerto Rico and the Puerto Ricans* (New York: John Wiley and Sons, 1974), p. 250.

23. For an excellent short account see *San Juan Star*, September 30, 1981. The seafarers union, for example, recruited the television technicians.

24. *Pensamiento Crítico* 4, no. 24 (January – July 1981).

25. The AFL has consistently fought against the creation of a low-wage economy in Puerto Rico that will injure the interests of its mainland members.

26. *Claridad*, May 14 – 20, 1981.

27. Thus, the poor support the Catholic schools, which serve the rich. Luis Nieves Falcón, *La opinión pública y las aspiraciones de los puertorriqueños* (Río Piedras: mimeograph, 1940), pp. 114 ff. The inhabitants of public housing projects regard a car as a necessity (ibid., p. 76) and their ambition is to escape from the *caseríos* to a house in a middle-class "urbanization." Conversation with working-class shoppers soon reveals an obsession with brand names made familiar on the radio and in newspapers like *El Nuevo Día*.

28. For the position in the 1920s, see T. Benner, *Five Years of Founding the University of Puerto Rico 1924 – 29* (Río Piedras: University of Puerto Rico, 1965), p. 67.

29. See José Maravall, *Dictatorship and Political Dissent* (London: Tavistock Publications, 1978), pp. 98 – 165. In Cuba, before the domestication of university life under Castro, students played an important role. See J. Suchlicki, *University Students and Revolution in Cuba 1920 – 1968* (Coral Gables, Fla.: University of Miami Press, 1969).

30. Early student activists were the sons of the *hacendados* and were responsible for the student violence of the 1930s. See Isabel Picó de Hernández, "La protesta estudiantil en la década del '30. Del nacionalismo cultural al nacionalismo político," *Cuadernos* of CEREP, no. 3

31. Cf. the statement of the president of the Council of Higher Education: "The members of that organization should reflect the way of thinking (*la manera de pensar*) of the party in power." (*El Mundo*, May 14, 1970.)

32. Thus, a Spanish lecturer claimed he was dismissed for writing an attack on Governor Romero and the PNP in *El Nuevo Día*. The Middle States Association, to which UPR belongs, reported that "excessive politicization... has produced an unwieldy bureaucracy." This bureaucracy is alleged to be subservient to the government in power. Cf. the complaints of a PNP politician at resistance to his party's influence in UPR "but as soon as the elections are over we will force Almodovar [the Chancellor] to follow our recommendations or we will have his neck." *San Juan Star*, February 2, 1981.

33. For an account of the riots, written from an *independentista* viewpoint, see Luis Nieves Falcón et al., *Puerto Rico Grito y Mordaza* (Puerto Rico: Ediciones Librería Internacional, Inc., 1971). For the 1973 troubles, see J.A. Silén, *De la guerrilla cívica a la nación dividida* (1973).

34. The subsequent exploitation of the riots by the opposition is particularly illustrative of their propaganda techniques. The writers of *Puerto Rico Grito y Mordaza*,

Luis Nieves Falcón, ed. (Río Piedras: Ediciones Librería Internacional Inc., 1971) made no attempt to interview the police or the ROTC cadets as they maintained that the official police version was already covered in the press. Some students were beaten up by a crowd outside the police station: the crowd, it is asserted, *looked* like Cubans (pp. 152-53). Cubans are regarded as arch-reactionaries and 100 percent pro-American. For the controversy as to whether the riots were organized or not — a bone of contention among militants, some of whom take credit for organizing the riot, others of whom criticize its lack of organization — see *Pensamiento Crítico* 3, no. 21 (October-November 1980).

35. Cf. P. García Kuenzli in *Attitudinal Patterns of Contemporary Puerto Rican Society* (1980), who argues that "more people are turning to religion as a substitute for the political void" (p. 48).

36. *Pensamiento Crítico* 3, no. 19 (May 1980).

37. "Our university does not function as a university . . . . It costs money to run a university. Our university is broke." Professor Maximo Cerame of Mayagüez, February 5, 1981.

38. The daily press reported the strike in detail: see especially the issues September 23, 27, and 30; October 14, 20, and 21; November 2 and 30: and December 20, 1981.

39. S.S. Gotay, *El Pensamiento cristiano revolucionario en America Latina y el Caribe* (1982).

40. Senator Aponte Pérez of the PPD in *San Juan Star,* October 7, 1982.

41. For more on Muñoz Rivera, see A. Morales Carrión, *The Loneliness of Muñoz Rivera* (Washington, D.C.: Office of the Commonwealth of Puerto Rico, 1979).

42. T.C. Cochran, *The Puerto Rican Business Man* (Philadelphia: University of Pennsylvania Press, 1959), pp. 118, 132, 151.

43. In "Europe: Some Are More Equal," *The Listener,* October 14, 1976, p. 460. The effect of persistent conservative values in retarding industrial development has been repeatedly noted in the case of developing economies; in India "intangible resistances built into perhaps the world's most conservative culture" defeat planners. See Martin J. Wiener, *English Culture and the Decline of the Industrial Spirit 1950-1980* (Cambridge: Cambridge University Press, 1981), p.41. Cultural values hostile to "material" progress can lame even developed economies. Wiener argues that the persistence of "rural" and "gentry" cultural values has retarded, and still retards, a dynamic economy in Britain, setting "lasting social and psychological limits" on industrial progress after the 1850s.

44. *Grito y Mordaza,* p. 230.

45. For a list, see Eduardo Seda Bonilla, *Requiem para una cultura* (Río Piedras: Ediciones Bayoan, 1974), p. 66.

46. For the Lima case, see Milton Pabón, *La Cultura Politica Puertorriqueña* (Río Piedras: Editorial Xaquey, 1972).

47. For some insights into the Manichean world view of Puerto Rican conservatives, see Carlos Buitrago Ortiz, *Ideología y conservadurismo en el Puerto Rico de hoy* (San Juan, 1972). Conservatives, he argues, are particularly incensed by independent

thought in the University of Puerto Rico (p. 41). They support the presence of the ROTC.
48. Ronald Walker, "Romero Revisited," *San Juan Star,* October 8, 1982.
49. René Marqués, "El puertorriqueño docil," reprinted in *El Puertorriqueño docil y otros ensayos 1953 – 1971* (Editorial Antillana, 1977), pp. 151 – 217.

Chapter 11

1. Speech of January 13, 1963.
2. L. Nieves Falcón and P. Cintrón de Crespo, *Los maestros de instrucción pública de Puerto Rico* (Río Piedras: Editorial Universitaria, 1973), pp. 99 – 141.
3. Ricardo Alegría's *Cristóbal Colón y el Tesoro de los Indios Tainos de la Española* (San Juan: Instituto de Cultura Puertorriqueña, 1980) is an attempt to show the pre-conquest richness of Taino culture in Hispaniola. Alegría is an *independentista.*
4. *Isla y Pueblo: libros para el pueblo,* no. 22 (San Juan, 1966).
5. David Lowenthal, *West Indian Societies* (London: Oxford University Press, 1972), p. 37. In the British West Indies, whites constitute between 1 percent and 5 percent of the population.
6. See his *El país de cuatro pisos* (Río Piedras: Ediciones Huracán, 1980). González argues that the blacks were the basic and original ingredient in Puerto Rico, later "whitened" by immigration in the nineteenth century.
7. *"Somos — y lo seremos por mucho tiempo — un pueblo en formación,"* quoted in Eugenio Fernández Méndez, *Historia cultural de Puerto Rico* (San Juan: Ediciones "El Cemi," 1970).
8. Tomás Blanco, *Prontuario histórico de Puerto Rico* (Río Piedras: Ediciones Huracán, 1981), was first published in Madrid in 1935.
9. See Arcadio Díaz Quiñones, "La isla afortunada: sueños liberadores y utópicos de Luis Llorens Torres," *Sin Nombre* 6, no. 2 (December 1975), pp. 6 ff. Llorrens was a modernist influenced by Rubén Darío.
10. For *Indice,* see Candido Maldonado Ortiz, *Antonio S. Pedreira: Vida y obra* (University of Puerto Rico Press, 1974).
11. Antonio S. Pedreira, *Insularismo, Ensayos de interpretación puertorriqueña* (Madrid: Tipografia Artistica, 1934), p. 55.
12. René Marqués, *La vispera del hombre,* 2d ed. (Río Piedras: Editorial Cultural, 1970), p. 266.
13. Ibid., p. 33
14. For a bitter attack on de Diego, from a Marxist standpoint, see R. Campos and J. Flores, "Migración y cultura nacional puertorriqueñas: perspectivas proletarias," *Puerto Rico; identidad nacional y clases sociales,* ed. Angel G. Quintero Rivera (Río Piedras: Ediciones Huracán, 1981), pp. 81 ff.
15. Ricardo Alegría, *El Instituto de Cultura Puertorriqueña 1955 – 1973,* p. 7.
16. See *Claridad* for September 12 – 18, 1980; "La destrucción del Instituto de

Cultura," *El Nuevo Día,* September 16, 1980. For the demonstration against the new arts center, see *El Mundo* and *San Juan Star,* April 10, 1980. The PNP government withdrew funds from the magazine *Sin Nombre;* it also attempted to bring Arturo Morales Carrión's Puerto Rico Humanities Foundation, supported by federal funds, under the government. (*San Juan Star,* December 29, 1981.) Morales Carrión is a well-known PPD intellectual.

17. Campos and Flores, "Migración y cultura nacional puertorriqueñas," p. 129.

18. René Marqués, *El Puertorriqueño docil y otros ensayos 1953 – 1971* (Editorial Antillana, 1977), pp. 19 ff.

19. Ibid., p. 42.

Chapter 12

1. Quoted in Truman R. Clark, "The Imperial Perspective: Mainland Administration View of the Puerto Rican Economy 1898 – 1941," p. 509.

2. Cf. Theodore Roosevelt, Jr., *Colonial Policy of the United States* (New York: Doubleday, Doran & Co., 1937), pp. 100 – 115.

3. A. López, ed., *The Puerto Ricans: Their History and Culture* (New York: John Wiley and Sons, 1980), p. 314.

4. Diana Christopoulos, "Puerto Rico in the Twentieth Century," in *Puerto Rico and the Puerto Ricans,* ed. A. López and J. Petras (New York: John Wiley and Sons, 1974), p. 121.

5. Cf. Governor Pezuela in 1848: "Education brought the loss of America and since this is a matter that must be handled with greatest tact, those who desire to study should go to Spain" (quoted in E.J. Berbusse, *The United States in Puerto Rico, 1898 – 1900*, pp. 29 – 30).

6. Quoted in Ramón A. Mellado, *Culture and Education in Puerto Rico* (San Juan: Bureau of Publications, Puerto Rico Teachers Association, 1948), p. 8. See generally Aida Negrón de Montilla, *Americanization in Puerto Rico and the Public School System, 1900 – 1935* (Editorial Universitaria, Universidad de Puerto Rico, 1975). In 1915, Spanish was restored as the language of instruction in the first grades of primary schools.

7. See the short story of Abelardo Díaz Alfonso "Peyo Monce enseña inglés" and René Marqués's novel *La vispera del hombre* (1958). Both describe the tortures of English as the language of instruction. Cf. José Padín, *The Problem of English Teaching* (1916), pp. 12 ff.

8. Commissioner Huyke, *Consejo a la Juventud* (1921). Huyke was an early supporter of mainland emigration. "Your island is small and your future can develop here or in the nation of which you are a citizen" (pp. 17, 30).

9. Quoted in Aida Negrón de Montilla, *Americanization in Puerto Rico and the Public School System, 1900 – 1935*, p. 39.

10. *Report of the United States – Puerto Rico Commission on the Status of Puerto Rico* (U.S. Government Printing Office: Washington, D.C., 1966), p. 145.

11. Quoted in Surendra Bhana, *The United States and the Development of the Puerto Rican Status Question 1936 - 1968* (Wichita: University of Kansas Press, 1975), p. 29.

12. *El Defensor Cristiano* (1906), quoted in E. Pantogas García, "La iglesia protestante y la americanización de Puerto Rico," in *Revista de Ciencias Sociales* 18, nos. 3 – 4 (1934), p. 110.

13. For the gradual emergence of autonomous churches, see D.T. Moore, *Puerto Rico para Cristo* (Cuernavaca, Mexico: mimeograph, 1969). The idea of self-support began in the 1920s but did not acquire any strength in the "historic" churches until the 1950s.

14. Both Elihu Root and the military governors were against the wholesale implantation of English common law. See P.C. Jessup, *Elihu Root* (New York: Dodd, Mead & Co., 1938), vol. 2, pp. 375 – 376.

15. See José Trías Monge, "El Derecho en Puerto Rico," *Revista Jurídica*, Interamerican University 12, no. 1 (September–December 1977), and J.R. Velez Torres, "La presencia de las sistemas de derecho civil y de derecho anglo-sajon en la jurisprudencia puertorriqueña," ibid., 12, no. 3, esp. pp. 808 ff.

16. *La correspondencia de Puerto Rico*, January 18, 1902, quoted in Carmelo Delgado Cintrón, "Derecho y colonialismo," *RJIAU* 13, no. 3, p. 456. See also A.L. García Martínez, "Idiomas y derecho," *Revista del colegio de abogados de Puerto Rico* 20, no. 3, pp. 183 – 211.

17. See Sergio Peña Clos, "Anacronismo judicial," *El Nuevo Día*, March 18, 1981.

18. J.R. Velez Torres, "La presencia de las sistemas de derecho civil y de derecho anglo-sajon en la jurisprudencia puertorriqueña," p. 808.

19. *Report of the United States – Puerto Rico Commission on the Status of Puerto Rico*, p. 146.

20. Charles J. Beirne, *El problema de la americanización en escuelas católicas en Puerto Rico* (Editorial Universitaria, 1976), pp. 53, 55.

21. Leila Sussmann insists that while school attendance is up to the standards of developed nations, the quality of education received in public schools is at the level of less-developed nations. Poor quality is particularly noticeable in the state secondary schools, which, since the 1920s, have declined as a training ground for university students as this function has increasingly been taken over by the private sector. Leila Sussmann, "Democratization and Class Segregation in Puerto Rican Schooling: the U.S. Model Transplanted," in *Sociology of Education* 41 (1968), p. 322.

22. *Antología de Nemesio R. Canales* (Colección UPREX, 1974), vol. 2, pp. 33 – 35, 120.

23. The work of Stycos on population, of Perloff on economic development, and of Tumin on social change is dismissed by Rafael Ramírez as "making viable the continuation of colonialism," in *Caribbean Studies* 10, no. 14, pp. 5 – 17.

24. See the studies on Steward in *Review of the Inter-American University* 8, no. 1 (1978). The fieldwork was done in the late 1940s; the book was published in 1956.

25. Again, the contradictions surface. The Center for the Study of Puerto Rican Reality (CEREP) is actively engaged in a radical reinterpretation of Puerto Rican history and society, which is by implication an attack on American colonialism and the "distortions" inflicted by the conquest of 1898; it was supported by funds from the Ford Foundation.

26. See Germán de Granda, *Transculturación e interferencia lingüística en el Puerto Rico contemporánea 1898 - 1968* (Río Piedras: Editorial Edil, 1972), for a savage attack by a Spaniard of *independentista* sympathies on the adulteration ("interference" is a key word to *independentistas*) of the language spoken in Puerto Rico by imported Americanisms.

27. René Marqués, *El Puertorriqueño dócil*, p. 61. Boorstin's article "Self-Discovery in Puerto Rico" is in *The Yale Review* 45, no. 2 (December 1955): 229 – 45.

28. E. Fernández Méndez, *Historia cultural de Puerto Rico,* (San Juan: Ediciones el Cemi, 1970), p. 204.

29. "Most of the Indian historians had either participated in the national movement for independence or were influenced by it. Their contention was that the Golden Age in India had existed prior to the coming of the British and that the ancient past of India was a particularly glorious period of her history. This view was a natural and inevitable adjunct to the national aspirations of the Indian people in the early twentieth century." Romila Thapar, *A History of India* (London: Pelican Books, 1966), i, p. 17.

30. Cf. E. Seda Bonilla, *Social Change and Personality in a Puerto Rican Agrarian Reform Community* (Evanston: Northwestern University Press, 1973), pp. 166 – 67. Seda Bonilla is a prime exponent of the psychological stresses created by the loss of the old, cohesive, comforting world of "traditional" society. He argued that the revival of spiritism represents a desire to recapture its values.

31. *Status of Puerto Rico: Background Papers,* p. 340.

32. The U.S. Census defines a Puerto Rican as either a person born in Puerto Rico or a person with one parent so defined. Hence, third-generation Puerto Ricans born on the mainland would not be counted as Puerto Rican.

33. In 1940, there were approximately 70,000 Puerto Ricans on the mainland. In the 1940s 18,700 came each year; 41,200 in the 1950s, falling off to 14,000 in the 1960s. The peak year was 1953, with 69,000.

34. For example, in 1970, Puerto Ricans had an 80 percent school dropout rate compared with 49 percent for the total population of New York; Puerto Ricans' earnings were 47 percent of the national average; 74 percent of Puerto Rican families headed by females were below the poverty level compared with 36.2 percent of the total U.S. population. Of youths 16 – 19 years old, 29 percent of Puerto Ricans were unemployed as compared to 15.7 percent of whites; 35.8 percent of blacks; 19 percent of non-Puerto Rican Hispanics. For a summary see *The Next Step toward Equality* (National Puerto Rican Forum, 1978) and U.S. Department of Commerce,

Bureau of Census, *Persons of Spanish Origin in the United States* (No. 347, March 1979), p. 20.

35. *Empire State Report*, March 23, 1981.

36. Although Puerto Rican studies have lost their early momentum, valuable work on linguistics and social conditions is done by the Centro de Estudios Puertorriqueños of the City University of New York, available in the Centro's working papers.

37. A. López, "The Puerto Rican Diaspora," in *The Puerto Ricans: Their History and Culture*, p. 335.

38. Manuel Maldonado Denis, *En las entrañas: Un análisis sociohistórico de la emigración puertorriqueña*, p. 63.

39. L. Nieves Falcón, *El emigrante puertorriqueño* (1978). The work was financed by the John Hay Whitney Foundation. Luis Nieves Falcón dedicates his book to the immigrant workers: "This work is an attempt to reveal yet one more aspect of the oppressed Patria."

40. According to Manuel Maldonado Denis, a prominent *independentista* intellectual. For information on sterilization, see José Vazquez Calzada, "La esterilización femenina en Puerto Rico," *Revista de Ciencias Sociales* 17, no. 3 (1973), pp. 283–300. He calculates that by 1965, a third of Puerto Rican women between the ages of 29 and 49 had been sterilized — probably the highest rate in the world. Sterilization has steadily diminished with knowledge of modern methods of birth control; it was always more common among working-class women, who had neither the money for nor the knowledge of effective methods of contraception. It is of some interest that there seems no relationship between (formal) Catholicism and the practice of contraception and sterilization, in spite of the campaign of the church against both practices. The Catholic party of the 1960s was organized largely to combat the PPD government's support of family planning.

41. See the evidence of a detailed survey in the *New York Times*, May 1980. Their attitudes display some similarity to the children of West Indian immigrants in Britain, who call themselves Jamaicans or Trinidadians, refusing to call themselves British.

42. *Etiología de la violencia*, p. 84.

43. José Cabranes, *Congressional Report*, Sen. 119, no. 58, April 12, 1973.

Chapter 13

1. James A. Michener in *Playboy* (September 1981).

2. Cf. Dexter Perkins, *A History of the Monroe Doctrine* (Boston: Little, Brown, 1960), esp. pp. 267–69, and 334 ff.

3. Thomas Enders, Assistant Secretary for Inter-American Affairs, testimony to the Western Hemisphere Subcommittee of the Senate Foreign Relations Committee, Washington, D.C., December 14, 1981.

4. Interview with R.C., January 1982.

5. *San Juan Star*, March 16, 1981. For an *independentista* treatment of U.S. strategic interests in Puerto Rico, see M. Meyn and J. Rodríguez Beruf, *El aparato militar norteamericano en Puerto Rico* (San Juan: mimeograph, 1979).

6. Commander Gottshalk, United States Navy, interview with R.C., December 1982.

7. The Naval Ammunition Depot on Vieques was deactivated in 1948. It was reactivated as a direct response to the missile crisis. Quotation from speech of General Stilwell to Reserve Officers Association, June 27, 1982.

8. *Draft Environmental Impact Report* (DEIR), Department of the Navy (1979), app. B.5.

9. Chief of Staff, Roosevelt Roads, interview with R.C., August 1980.

10. See, for example, J.A. Corretjer, *Vieques y la lucha por la independencia* (San Juan, 1980).

11. See *Pensamiento Crítico*, March – April 1980 and May – June 1980. The local organization in Vieques is the "Crusade" run by Ismael González of the PSP; it has quarreled with the organization on the "large island," the National Committee for the Defense of Vieques.

12. Quotation from a protest of the mayor of Vieques against the Navy's proposal to acquire land. The proposal was dropped.

13. *El Mundo*, November 12, 1979.

14. Speech of February 1, 1982.

15. Interview with R.C., December 1981.

16. *Wall Street Journal*, February 11, 1980.

17. For the comments of Werner Baer on Puerto Rico as a model in the 1950s see his "Puerto Rico: An Evaluation of a Successful Development Program," *Quarterly Journal of Economics* 73 (1959), pp. 663 ff.

18. See below.

19. A very early instance of the bridge theory is the statement of the first commissioner for education that Puerto Ricans who could speak English would be "pioneers in extending our trade to South America." E.J. Berbusse, *The United States and Puerto Rico* (Chapel Hill: University of North Carolina Press, 1966), p. 214. The idea of using bilingual Puerto Ricans as agents for American companies in Latin America persists.

20. Arthur Schlesinger, Jr., *A Thousand Days* (London: André Deutsch, 1963), pp. 764 – 65.

21. According to Arthur Schlesinger, Jr.; see his *Robert Kennedy and His Times* (Boston: Houghton Mifflin, 1978), p. 578.

22. See below.

23. Arthur C. Borg, *The Problem of Puerto Rico's Status*, Senior Seminar in Foreign Policy, Seventeenth Session, Department of State 1974 – 75; and Alfred Stepan, "The United States and Latin America: Vital Interests and the Instruments of Power," *Foreign Affairs* 58, no. 3 (1980): 672 – 78.

24. According to the *San Juan Star*, April 5, 1982.

25. Interview with R.C., Department of State, December 1981.

26. Interview with R.C., January 14, 1982.

27. Theodore C. Sorensen, *Kennedy* (London: Hodder and Stoughton, 1965), p. 700.

28. Interview by R.C. with Harry Macpherson, December 1981.

29. Interview with R.C., January 1982.

30. Richard Neale, interview with R.C., December 1982.

31. Cf. *San Juan Star*, January 22, 1982, for Romero's qualms about the effect of the New Federalism on poor states.

32. *San Juan Star*, January 24, 1982.

33. Stuart Eizenstat, President Carter's domestic policy adviser. *San Juan Star*, December 31, 1981.

34. S. Bhana, *The United States and the Development of the Puerto Rican Status Question* (Wichita: University of Kansas Press, 1975), p. 70.

35. Information obtained during an interview by R.C. with Harry Macpherson, December 1981.

36. Truman R. Clark, *Puerto Rico and the United States* (Pittsburgh: University of Pittsburgh Press, 1975), p. 43.

37. For the Chardon plan see chap. 2.

38. Cf. Gary Martin and Alan Udall, "Structural Change in Puerto Rican Industry," *Puerto Rican Business Review*, August 1979: "Taken as a whole the changes in relative wages during the period probably tended to favor industries which are relatively skill-intensive in Puerto Rico while retarding the growth of industries dependent on mainly unskilled labor;" that is, the "traditional" industries.

39. Such jobs became "bottom jobs in the status hierarchy." Michael J. Piore, "Youth Unemployment and Economic Development Strategy in Puerto Rico" quoted in A.D. Little Inc., *Studies on the Impact of Sophisticated Manufacturing Industries on the Economic Development of Puerto Rico* (1981), p. 14.

40. Interviews by R.C., December 16, 1981 with officials of the Department of Commerce and the Senate Committee on Energy and Natural Resources. The first official quoted had a specialized knowledge of the island's economy and was unique among the officials I met in that he was familiar with the work of Puerto Rican economists written in Spanish.

41. Quoted in E.J. Berbusse, *The United States and Puerto Rico*, p. 171.

42. Quoted in T. Clark, *Puerto Rico and the United States*, pp. 13–14.

43. George Milton Fowles, *Down in Porto Rico* (New York: Eaton and Mains, 1906). Subsequent quotations are from this work. Their interest lies in the fact that Fowles was friendly to Puerto Rico and critical of the American government. He believed that Puerto Rico could become a "sister state." This makes his attitude all the more interesting.

44. General George W. Davis, "Report on the Civil Affairs of Puerto Rico 1899," p. 114.

45. Bailey W. Diffie and Justine W. Diffie, *Porto Rico: A Broken Pledge* (New York: Vanguard Press, 1931).
46. At the Conference on the Caribbean held at Warwick University, U.K., 29 May 1982.
47. Earl Parker Hanson, *Transformation: The Story of Modern Puerto Rico* (New York: Simon and Schuster, 1955).
48. *Puerto Ricans in the Continental United States: An Uncertain Future* (Washington, D.C.: Commission on Civil Rights, October 1976).
49. Cf. *Claridad*, January 1–7, 1982.
50. H. Hill, "Guardians of the Sweatshop," in *Puerto Rico and the Puerto Ricans*, ed. López and Petras, pp. 384 ff.
51. Oscar Lewis, *La Vida* (New York: Random House, 1966). In a small survey in Boston University, I found that it was the *only* book concerning Puerto Rico that my students had read.
52. In 1979, 59 percent of Americans interviewed by a Gallup poll were willing to accept Puerto Rico as a state; 67 percent were prepared to accept independence — this latter, a ten-point increase over 1962.
53. George Ball in the 1981 Cyril Foster Lecture at Oxford.

Chapter 14

1. The special Committee of Twenty-Four, known as the Decolonization Committee, is officially called the Special Committee on the Situation with Regard to the Implementation of the Decolonization on the Granting of Independence to Colonial Peoples and Countries. It was set up in 1960 to replace the older Committee on Information from Non–Self-Governing Territories.
2. In 1979, for example, the committee received thirty-one statements, the majority from organizations hostile to the United States. Especially noticeable are the radical Christian organizations, the Freemasons, and the representatives of the Puerto Rican legal community.
3. See especially the 1980 testimony of the chairman of the Comité unitario contra la represión y por la defensa de los presos políticos (UN A/AC 109/PV 1175), p. 37.
4. For more on Cerro Maravilla, see above. For Vieques see UN A/AC 109/PV 1175, pp. 2–7.
5. A/AC 109 PV1198, p. 26.
6. A/AC 109 PV196, pp. 62–68.
7. Senator Moynihan, C. R. Sen. August 2, 1979, S 11372, 10677.
8. For the text, see *Year of the United Nations 1953*, Department of Public Information, United Nations, New York, p. 539. For the refusal of a hearing, ibid., pp. 535 ff.
9. *El Mundo*, December 7, 1953.

10. Of the twenty-six favorable votes, sixteen came from Latin America. Argentina and Venezuela abstained; only Mexico, Honduras, and Guatemala voted against the resolution.

11. "Memorandum of the Puerto Rican Independence Party to the United Nations" (San Juan, mimeograph, 1953), p. 23. It was drawn up by Vicente Géigel Polanco.

12. The case against the resolution was submitted in "Supplementary Memorandum of the Puerto Rican Independence Party holding that the territory of Puerto Rico has not yet attained a complete measure of self-government" (New York, mimeograph, October 26, 1953).

13. It passed with twenty-six in favor, sixteen against, and eighteen abstentions. Those in favor included Batista's Cuba and Chiang Kai-shek's China. Nicaragua, Argentina, and Venezuela abstained.

14. Godkin Lecture (San Juan, mimeograph, 1959).

15. When Resolution 748(VIII) was passed, there were fifty-one countries in the United Nations; by the time Resolution 1514(XV) was passed, there were eighty-nine — nearly all the additional members were former colonies.

16. Gabriel Vicente Maura, "Puerto Rico ante la ONU," in *Claridad*, July 16 – 22, 1982.

17. For a useful summary see UN A/AC109/L1191, August 2, 1977.

18. See *Claridad*, September 3, 1972.

19. Mari Bras, Submissions of 1977 (in UN A/AC109/L1191).

20. Ibid., p. 24.

21. Letter of May 16, 1977 to the rapporteur of the U.N. Special Committee. A/AC 109 L1191, August 2, 1977, p. 42.

22. Cf. letter of June 28, 1974 to the rapporteur of the Special Committee. A/AC 10a/L76, p. 50.

23. *El Mundo*, September 7, 1982.

24. Letter of Hernández Colón to the rapporteur of the Committee of Twenty-Four, July 11, 1977.

25. Cf. the comments of José A. Cabranes, "Puerto Rico out of the Colonial Closet," *Foreign Policy* 33 (Winter 1978 – 79), p. 89.

26. *New York Times*, January 15, 1982.

27. Quotations from an interview by R.C. with Professor Luis Agrait, December 30, 1981.

28. For the details of these negotiations, see the articles by Juan Mari Bras in *El Mundo*, April 5 – 11, 1981. For a criticism of the operation, see the articles of Luis Mechani Agrait in *El Nuevo Día*, April 14 and 19, 1981.

29. The PPD argued that a democratic expression of the will of the Puerto Rican people did not demand, as the independence movement insisted, a *previous* transfer of powers. See Luis E. Agrait, *Traspaso de poderes: Práctica y teoría* (mimeographed, n.d.). The practices of decolonization had varied, and provided that the United Nations was satisfied that the inhabitants of a dependent territory had made a free and democratic choice, it had not insisted on the prior withdrawal of the colonial

power. The decolonization of a people, Professor Agrait, one of the most prominent PPD intellectuals, was to argue in 1980, is not something that takes place once and for all at one precise point in time; "decolonization must be understood and conceived of as a dynamic process which develops, manifests itself, and progresses through time." See UN A/AC 109/PV 1175, August 18, 1980, p.8. This was theoretical formulation of the policy of the PPD: that Commonwealth should be "culminated" by a significant extension of the powers of self-government.

30. Resolution A/AC 109/574.

31. The alliance of Mari Bras and the "progressive autonomists" of the PPD threatened the older (implied) alliance of the extremes of statehooders and *independentistas* to crush the autonomist middle. Cf. *San Juan Star*, August 30, 1978. Did Berríos Martínez hope that, if the "alternative futures" policy materialized, the statehooders would defeat the PPD and that then statehood would be refused by Congress leaving the true *independentistas* to pick up the pieces?

32. Testimony of Rubén Berríos in A/AC 109/L1334. Add. 1, p. 11.

33. This statement was made in 1982, when Governor Romero was perturbed by the appointment of his political rival, Mayor Hernán Padilla, as alternate delegate to the United Nations, where he was to present Puerto Rico's case (see the controversy in the Puerto Rican press during late September 1982).

34. Testimony of PNP in 1980, A/AC 109/L1334. Add. 1, pp. 2–4.

35. Press release of the U.S. Mission to the United Nations, 68(79), August 15, 1979.

36. Eric Swendsen in *Open Forum*, no. 20 (Spring/Summer 1979), pp. 21–27.

37. Speech of Governor Romero, August 24, 1981.

38. *Washington Post*, August 21, 1981.

39. Speech of April 8, 1982, in Barbados.

Chapter 15

1. *El Nuevo Día*, December 19, 1981.

2. See especially *San Juan Star*, January 29 and February 1, 1981.

3. Andrades's testimony (October 17) is suspect; he was a malcontent and allegedly floated his "revelations" to allow him to present a pending criminal prosecution as political persecution. Suárez and Stella's minute dissection, in the *San Juan Star*, of the statements of Villanueva, in charge of the *second* investigation by the Justice Department, seems to me convincing proof that Villanueva was willing to question vital witnesses whose evidence had been brushed aside at the *first* investigation *if* the PPD won; he is alleged to have pulled back when Romero won.

4. *El Nuevo Día*, October 15, 1980. Hernández Colón claimed that Romero "had a determined degree of participation," that the undercover agent had acted on his orders, and that he had played a part in the cover-up. According to Mari Bras, Romero had seen U.S. Attorney General Civiletti and persuaded him to close the

Cerro case in return for Romero's support for Carter's presidential candidacy. *Claridad*, September 19 – 26, 1980. The PSP asserted that the PNP was attempting to buy off Andrades.

5. Hernández Colón claimed that Romero knew of the transfer as far back as April (*El Nuevo Día*, October 2, 1980). The refugee crisis was precipitated by a leak in the *Chicago Tribune*.

6. The PSP were the main sinners. Cf. *Claridad*, September and October, esp. October 3 – 9, 1980. It organized a working-class protest based on the supposed threat of the refugees to the employment prospects of Puerto Ricans.

7. Cf. the reasoned article of a Cuban refugee in *El Nuevo Día*, October 10, 1980.

8. *El Nuevo Día* and *El Mundo*, November 1, 1980.

9. See *Claridad*, September 15 – 22, 1980 and *El Nuevo Día*, October 13, 1980.

10. *El Mundo*, August 8, 1980.

11. Cf. the complaints after the election that the PIP could not recruit enough poll watchers, etc. A mere examination of the professions of the PIP candidates is an indication of the nature of its social support.

12. Mari Bras (*Claridad*, September 19 – 25, 1980) declared his support for Hernández Colón's efforts to "enlarge" Commonwealth. "*La época que vivimos en el mundo apunta hacia la búsqueda de consensus*"; the main enemy was "*la claque más fascista del PNP.*" The PSP line that it was the *only* "*real*" (*verdadera*) opposition was in conflict with the suggestion that, in fact, the PPD was the only party that could defeat Romero.

13. *San Juan Star*, December 10, 1980.

14. *El Nuevo Día*, October 14, 1980.

15. *San Juan Star*, October 1, 1980.

16. A. Viglucci, editor of the *San Juan Star*, January 4, 1981. An editorial deploring the loss of faith in democratic institutions and hinting at civil war appeared in *El Mundo* on December 30, 1980. Cf. a similar editorial in *El Nuevo Día*, December 19, 1980.

17. *San Juan Star*, December 19, 1980.

18. *El Nuevo Día*, December 27, 1980.

19. *San Juan Star*, January 24, 1981.

20. Cf. the attempt of Representative José Granados Navedo to prove Hernández Colón had exercised undue pressure on Supreme Court judges over electoral decisions by telephoning them. Hernández Colón claimed the calls were routine calls about dates of hearings, etc., made by PPD officials. The point is, how did Granados get hold of the list of calls? The whole affair looks like petty persecution.

21. In the Tonos case the Federal District Court in Puerto Rico decided in favor of the PNP: the judge was the wife of a political adviser of Governor Romero. The verdict was reversed by the First District Court of Appeals for the First Circuit in Boston. If there had been a new election in District 31 — the town of Caguas — the PNP would have lost, but Romero's aim was to delay the seating of the PPD replacement as long as possible and in the meanwhile the PNP Speaker of the House

refused to give the replacement pay or an office until ordered to do so. See *El Mundo*, August 15, 1981.

22. *El Mundo*, March 22, 1982.

23. Ibid., December 21, 1981; *Claridad*, December 18–23, 1981.

24. See *El Reportero*, November 3, 1981, and *El Nuevo Día*, December 21, 1981.

25. *El Nuevo Día*, January 7, 1981.

26. *El Mundo*, December 30, 1980.

27. January 30, 1982.

28. Speech of April 16, 1981.

29. For a vivid portrayal of the frustrations of the younger generation of state-hooders see Luis R. Dávila Colón, *Los "hijos" de Muñoz: de la esperanza a la frustración* (San Juan: Grupo de investigadores puertorriqueños, Inc., 1982).

30. *San Juan Star*, March 15 and April 10, 1981.

31. F. Delano López, "The Severo Affair," *San Juan Star*, May 1, 1981.

32. The PPD claimed Romero was rigging the budget figures to show a deficit. Romero said that the PPD legislators were "uncooperative." See *El Reportero* January 21 and February 15, 1982 and *El Nuevo Día* February 21 and April 4, 1982.

33. Corrada himself had a brush with Representative Dellums. See *San Juan Star*, July 23, 1982. For a critical running commentary on what she calls the "clowns" and "buffoons" of the legislature, see Maggie Bobs's reports in the *San Juan Star* from January 1981 to August 1982 and William Dorvillier, "School for Bad Manners," *San Juan Star*, June 30, 1982.

34. The phrase used by Mari Bras, March 6, 1981. One of the advocates of a Third Party is Mrs. Padilla, wife of Romero's rival, Hernán Padilla.

35. Deputy Secretary of State Walter Stoessel, testimony to Senate Foreign Relations Committee, March 25, 1982, quoted in J. Sanford, *Caribbean Basin Initiative*, Issue Brief no. 1138 2074, Library of Congress Research Service. For a general discussion of the CBI and its weaknesses, see Robert Pastor, "Sinking in the Caribbean Basin," *Foreign Affairs* 60, no. 5 (Summer 1982): 1038–58.

36. Bertram Finn, *San Juan Star*, January 24, 1982.

37. *El Nuevo Día*, March 12, June 12, and July 18, 1981.

38. *San Juan Star*, January 25, 1981. The end of CETA threatened Mayor Padilla of San Juan with the loss of 4,800 jobs.

39. Interview with R.C., January 1982.

40. Editorial, *San Juan Star*, May 29, 1981.

41. All statements in R.C.'s interviews from members of the task force, the Department of the Interior, and the Senate Commission on Energy, in December–January 1981–1982.

42. *El Nuevo Día*, April 18, 1982.

43. Speech of April 18, 1982.

44. Hernández Colón, *San Juan Star*, August 1, 1982. See also *El Nuevo Día*, March 5, 1982.

45. Senator Nogueras, *San Juan Star*, March 22, 1982.

46. Statements of Luis Ferré and PNP representative Viera Martínez.
47. *San Juan Star*, July 3, 1982.
48. *San Juan Star*, July 7, 1982.
49. A confidential report of a group in the Department of Commerce connected with the Kreps Report, available in the Puerto Rican press in March 1982.
50. *San Juan Star*, December 29, 1981.

Conclusion

1. *San Juan Star*, November 21, 1981.

SELECT READING LIST

All select reading lists inevitably reflect their author's preferences. This bibliography also reflects the intellectual universe of Puerto Rico. It is the protesters who get into print and the *independentistas* have recently been more prolific than those who support Commonwealth, once the initial enthusiasms waned, or the statehooders. I have omitted articles that are mentioned in the text.

The Press and Official Sources

The Puerto Rican press, polemical as it often is, is invaluable. For reasons of convenience for English readers, I have usually quoted from the *San Juan Star,* but *El Nuevo Día* and *El Mundo* and *El Reportero* repeat the same news in Spanish and give useful commentaries and editorials. *Claridad,* published weekly, is the paper of the Puerto Rican Socialist Party (PSP). Both the *New York Times* and the *Washington Post* have occasional articles in moments of crisis.

Congressional debates and committee hearings provide insights into American policies and attitudes, especially in 1900, 1916 – 17, 1951 – 52, and 1959. The most significant official sources are listed in Berbusse, Bhana, Truman Clark, and Johnson (see below, "General Reading"). Two committee hearings contain important testimonies. The first is that of the Status Commission of 1964 – 66. For the hearings, see U.S. Congress, *Status of Puerto Rico, Hearings before the United States – Puerto Rico Commission on the Status of Puerto Rico,* 89th Cong., 2d sess., Document no. 108, vol. 1, *Legal-Constitutional Factors in Relation to the Status of Puerto Rico;* vol. 2, *Social-Cultural*

Factors in Relation to the Status of Puerto Rico; and vol. 3, *Economic Factors in Relation to the Status of Puerto Rico.* The background papers of the commission contain much valuable information. *Status of Puerto Rico Selected Background Papers* (Washington, D.C.: U.S. Government Printing Office, 1966).

The ad hoc committee hearings are contained in U.S. Congress, House Committee on Interior and Insular Affairs, *Compact of Permanent Union between Puerto Rico and the United States, Hearings before the Subcommittee on Territorial and Insular Affairs on H.R. 11200 and H.R. 11201,* Serial no. 94–44, pt. 1 and Serial no. 94–44, pt. 2, 94th Cong., 2d sess. (Washington, D.C.: U.S. Government Printing Office, 1976).

General Reading

My interest in Puerto Rico was first kindled by Gordon K. Lewis's remarkable *Puerto Rico: Freedom and Power in the Caribbean* (New York: Monthly Review Press, 1963). Though dated, it remains a penetrating study; the author's later, more radical views are presented in his *Notes on the Puerto Rican Revolution* (New York: Monthly Review Press, 1974). A useful study, which is a helpful guide in identifying official sources, is T. Whitney Perkins, *Denial of Empire: The United States and Its Dependencies* (Leiden, Holland: A.W. Sythoff, 1962), pp. 110–65. Two recent books, both critical of U.S. policies, are Roberta Ann Johnson, *Puerto Rico: Commonwealth or Colony?* (New York: Praeger Special Studies, 1980), with a useful bibliography, and Sakari Sariola, *The Puerto Rican Dilemma* (Port Washington, N.Y.: National University Publications, Kennikat Press, 1979), with perceptive studies of individual politicians and very useful footnote references to a wide range of works. The radical viewpoint is represented in Manuel Maldonado Denis, *Puerto Rico: A Socio-Historic Interpretation* (New York: Vintage Press, 1972), and Adalberto López and James Petras, eds., *Puerto Rico and the Puerto Ricans* (New York: John Wiley and Sons, 1974). Bailey W. Diffie and Justine Diffie's *Porto Rico: A Broken Pledge* (New York: Vanguard, 1931) has remained a progressive's bible.

History

The standard history is Lidio Cruz Monclava, *Historia de Puerto Rico* (Río Piedras: Editorial Universitaria, 1957 – 62), 3 vols. The war of 1898 and Puerto Rican reactions to the Americans are described in Carmelo Rosario Natal, *Puerto Rico: La crisis de la guerra hispanoamericano 1895–98* (Hato Rey: Ramallo Bros., 1975); it has a useful bibliography. There are abundant studies on American imperialism; the best guide is J.A. Field, Jr., "American Imperialism: The Worst Chapter in Almost

Any Book," *American Historical Review* 83, no. 3 (June 1978): 644 – 83. The early years of the American occupation and the coming of the Foraker Act are the themes of Edward J. Berbusse, *The United States and Puerto Rico 1898 – 1900* (Chapel Hill: University of North Carolina Press, 1966) — especially good on the Catholic Church; María Dolores de Sánchez, *La ocupación norteamericana y la Ley Foraker* (Río Piedras: Editorial Universitaria, 1980); Lyman J. Gould, *La Ley Foraker: Raíces de la política colonial de los Estados Unidos* (Colección UPREX, Universidad de Puerto Rico, 1969). The most illuminating study is that of José A. Cabranes, *Citizenship and the American Empire* (New Haven: Yale University Press, 1979). The legal issues are examined in José Trías Monge, *Historia constitucional de Puerto Rico*, vol. 1 (Río Piedras: Editorial Universitaria, 1980). The author is the president of the Puerto Rican Supreme Court.

The development of the status issue is well described in Surendra Bhana, *The United States and the Development of the Puerto Rican Status Question 1936 – 1968* (Wichita: University of Kansas Press, 1975), and Truman B. Clark, *Puerto Rico and the United States 1917 – 23* (Pittsburgh: University of Pittsburgh Press, 1975). Luis Muñoz Marín's recently published *Memorias 1898 – 1940* (Universidad Interamericana de Puerto Rico, 1982) is essential to the understanding of his attitudes. His early life is the subject of Carmelo Rosario Natal's *La juventud de Luis Muñoz Marín* (San Juan, 1976).

The politics of the period 1941 – 46 are described in two good studies, Charles T. Goodsell, *Administration of a Revolution: Executive Reform in Puerto Rico under Governor Tugwell, 1941 – 1946* (Cambridge: Harvard University Press, 1965), and Thomas Mathews, *Puerto Rican Politics and the New Deal* (Gainesville: University of Florida Press, 1960), the latter with a useful bibliography. Rexford Guy Tugwell, *The Stricken Land* (New York: Doubleday and Co., 1947), is one of the most revealing, if highly personal, studies of Puerto Rican politics by the last American governor.

The coming of Commonwealth is fully described by one of its architects, Antonio Fernós Isern, *Estado Libre Asociado de Puerto Rico: Antecedentes, creación y desarrollo hasta la época presente* (Río Piedras: Editorial Universitaria de Puerto Rico, 1974). The virtues of Commonwealth as a political invention and a plea for its further development are in Carl J. Friedrich's *Puerto Rico: Middle Road to Freedom* (New York: Rinehart and Co. Inc., 1959); a biting attack is in Vicente Géigel Polanco's collection of essays in *La farsa del Estado Libre Asociado* (Río Piedras: Editorial Edil Inc., 1972).

Puerto Rican Politics and Parties

A useful introduction to the Puerto Rican government structure is provided by Carmen Ramos de Santiago in *El Gobierno de Puerto Rico* (Río Piedras: Editorial Universitaria de Puerto Rico, 1979).

Two fine studies by American scholars are Henry Wells, *The Modernization of Puerto Rico: A Political Study of Changing Values and Institutions* (Cambridge: Harvard University Press, 1969), and Robert W. Anderson, *Party Politics in Puerto Rico*

(Stanford: Stanford University Press, 1965). Both treat the political system before the defeat of the Popular Democratic Party (PPD) in 1968.

The standard — and somewhat dry — history of Puerto Rican political parties is in Bolivar Pagán's *Historia de los partidos políticos puertorriqueños* (San Juan: Librería Campos, 1956). A very useful collection of manifestos, speeches, etc., is contained in Reece B. Bothwell González, *Puerto Rico: Cien años de lucha política,* 4 vols. (Río Piedras: Editorial Universitaria, 1979). For the Socialist party, see Clarence Senior, *Santiago Iglesias, Labor Crusader* (Hato Rey: Inter-American University Press, 1972), and Gonzalo F. Cordova, *Santiago Iglesias: Creador del movimiento obrero en Puerto Rico* (Río Piedras: Editorial Universitaria, 1980); both are favorable to Iglesias. By far the most intelligent treatment of the politics of the Marxist left in Puerto Rico is Georg H. Fromm, *César Andreu Iglesias* (Río Piedras: Ediciones Huracán, 1977). For the Nationalists, there is a short collection of the speeches of Albizu Campos, edited with a preface by Manuel Maldonado Denis, *La conciencia nacional puertorriqueña* (Mexico City: Siglo Ventiuno Editores, 1972). The Nationalist vision of Puerto Rican history is revealed in Juan Antonio Corretjer, *La lucha por la independencia de Puerto Rico* (San Juan, 1950).

For those who wish to taste the flavor of island politics, Norma Tapia's *La crisis del PIP* (Editorial Edil, 1980) is a bitter polemic against the leadership of Berríos Martínez; Ismaro Velázquez's *Muñoz y Sánchez Vilella* (Colección UPREX, Editorial Universitaria de Puerto Rico, 1974) is a defense of Sánchez and hostile to Muñoz; Juan M. García Passalacqua, *La alternativa liberal* (Colección UPREX, Editorial Universitaria, Universidad de Puerto Rico, 1974), is a provocative collection of essays. García Passalacqua is a frequent contributor of political commentaries in the *San Juan Star.*

Two studies highly critical of the Puerto Rican political system are Eduardo Seda Bonilla, *La cultura política de Puerto Rico* (Río Piedras: Ediciones Amauta, 1976), and Milton Pabón, *La cultura política puertorriqueña* (Río Piedras: Editorial Xaguey, 1972). There is an interesting study of the political life of the slums: Rafael L. Ramírez, *El arrabal y la política* (Editorial Universitaria, Universidad de Puerto Rico, 1977). Rosa Estrades, *Patterns of Political Participation of Puerto Ricans in New York* (Editorial Universitaria, Universidad de Puerto Rico, 1978), is a useful study of the political activities of the Puerto Rican community in New York in the 1960s and 1970s. There are some details for an earlier period in Felix Ojeda Reyes, *Vito Marcantonio y Puerto Rico* (Río Piedras: Ediciones Huracán, 1978).

Economics and Society

There is no satisfactory general economic history of Puerto Rico. For the economy before the American conquest of 1898, there are the penetrating studies of Fernando Picó, *Amargo café* (Río Piedras: Ediciones Huracán, 1981), for coffee, and Andrés Ramos Mattei, *La hacienda azucarera: su crecimiento y crisis en Puerto Rico (siglo XIX)* (San Juan: CEREP, 1981), for the sugar industry.

There have been many studies of the economy since 1952. Two useful reports are

James Tobin, *Report to the Governor. The Committee to Study Puerto Rico's Finances* (San Juan, 1975), and what is known as the "Kreps Report," that is, *Economic Study of Puerto Rico* (Washington, D.C.: Department of Commerce, 1979). There is an annual report to the governor by the Planning Board, and the *Business Review* published monthly by the Government Development Bank for Puerto Rico; both give current statistical information.

The issue of emigration has given rise to a Marxist critique. The thesis is contained in *Labor Migration under Capitalism* (New York and London: Monthly Review Press, 1979) and a violent attack on recent Commonwealth migration policies in Manuel Maldonado Denis, *En las entrañas: Un análisis sociohistórico de la emigración puertorriqueña* (Havana, Cuba: Casa de las Americas, 1976).

There is no study of present-day Puerto Rico to match in methodological sophistication the study of Puerto Rican society in the late 1950s by Melvin M. Tumin and Arnold S. Feldman, *Social Class and Social Change in Puerto Rico* (Princeton: Princeton University Press, 1961), or the massive study edited by Julian Steward, *The People of Puerto Rico* (Urbana: University of Illinois Press, 1956). *Puerto Rico: identidad nacional y clases sociales* (Río Piedras: Ediciones Huracán, 1981) contains challenging essays by Angel G. Rivera and José Luis González. The studies of the development of Puerto Rican society by Angel G. Quintero Rivera are acute and intelligent Marxist analyses; for a short presentation of his views, see his *Conflictos de clase y política en Puerto Rico* (Río Piedras: Ediciones Huracán, 1977), of which an English version is contained in Adalberto López and James Petras, eds., *Puerto Rico and the Puerto Ricans* (New York: John Wiley and Sons, 1974), pp. 195–213. Eduardo Seda Bonilla's *Social Change and Personality in a Puerto Rican Agrarian Reform Community* (Evanston: Northwestern University Press, 1973) studies the rural backwaters, and Oscar Lewis's *La Vida* (New York: Random House, 1966) is a series of interviews with the slum dwellers of La Perla in San Juan.

Labor movements have only recently been seriously studied. Their early history is the subject of a collection of documents edited by Antonio G. Quintero Rivera, *Lucha obrera: Antología de grandes documentos en la historia obrera puertorriqueña* (San Juan: CEREP, 1971). See also Juan Angel Silén, *Apuntes para la historia del movimiento obrero puertorriqueño* (Río Piedras: Editorial Cultural, 1978), and Blanca Silvestrini de Pacheco, *Los trabajadores puertorriqueños y el Partido Socialista (1932–40)* (Río Piedras: Editorial Universitaria, 1979). A very useful study of the trade union movement is Miles Galvin, *The Organized Labor Movement in Puerto Rico* (Madison: Fairleigh Dickinson University Press, 1979). A study of a single profession — schoolteachers — is *Los maestros de instrucción pública de Puerto Rico* (Editorial Universitaria, Universidad de Puerto Rico, 1975).

Culture and Americanization

A general history that emphasizes the nineteenth century is Eugenio Fernández Méndez, *Historia cultural de Puerto Rico* (San Juan: Ediciones el Cemi, 1970). Antonio Pedreira's *Insularismo, Ensayos de interpretación puertorriqueña* (Madrid: Tipografia Artistica, 1934) and Tomás Blanco's *Prontuario histórico de Puerto Rico* (Río Piedras: Ediciones Huracán, 1981) are products of the Puerto Rican cultural revival of the 1930s. For the present day, the essays of José Luis González and René Marqués — both novelists and short story writers — are superb studies on the borderlands of sociology, politics, and literature. The most important essays of René Marqués are collected in *El puertorriqueño docil y otros ensayos* (Editorial Antillana, 1977). A few of González's essays are collected in his *El país de cuatro pisos* (Río Piedras; Ediciones Huracán, 1980); see also a series of interviews with González, *Conversación con José Luis González,* ed., Arcadio Díaz Quiñones (Río Piedras: Ediciones Huracán, 1977). A series of essays lamenting American influence and the loss of a "Puerto Rican" culture are contained in Eduardo Seda Bonilla's *Requiem para una cultura* (Río Piedras: Ediciones Bayoan, 1974).

The linguistic controversy is polemically treated in Germán de Granda, *Transculturación e interferencia lingüística en el Puerto Rico contemporáneo* (Río Piedras: Ediciones Edil, 1972). Americanization in the school system has been the subject of two studies: Aida Negrón de Montilla, *Americanization in Puerto Rico and the Public School System* (Editorial Universitaria, 1975), and Charles J. Beirne, *El problema de la americanización en escuelas católicas en Puerto Rico* (Editorial Universitaria, 1976). For a treatment of the Protestant Church as an instrument of Americanization, see E. Pantogas García, "La iglesia protestante y la americanización de Puerto Rico," in *Revista de Ciencias Sociales* 18, nos. 3 – 4 (September – December 1974): 100 ff.

Finally, novels and short stories reveal rare insights into social and cultural life. Pedro Juan Soto's *Usmail* (Editorial Cultural, 1959) studies racial tensions in the 1930s; his *Spiks* (Editorial Cultural, 1956) shows life in the Puerto Rican community in New York, as does José Luis González, *En Nueva York y otras desgracias* (Ediciones Huracán, 1981). Soto's *Ardiente suelo, fria estación,* 2d ed. (Ediciones Huracán, 1978) describes the plight of a New York Puerto Rican seeking his roots on the island. César Andreu Iglesias's *Los derrotados* (Río Piedras: Ediciones Puerto, 1973) gives an insight into the minds of Puerto Rican Nationalist supporters of the armed struggle. To understand Puerto Rico's present cultural and social problems and tensions, an attempt should be made to read Luis Rafael Sánchez's difficult novel *La guaracha del Macho Camacho* (Buenos Aires: Ediciones de la Flor, 1976). Of René Marqués' works, the most illustrative is perhaps *La vispera del hombre,* 2d ed. (Río Piedras: Editorial Cultural, 1970).

INDEX

DATE DUE